Vital Records of Sandwich New Hampshire 1887-2007

Richard P. Roberts

HERITAGE BOOKS
2009

HERITAGE BOOKS
AN IMPRINT OF HERITAGE BOOKS, INC.

Books, CDs, and more—Worldwide

For our listing of thousands of titles see our website
at
www.HeritageBooks.com

Published 2009 by
HERITAGE BOOKS, INC.
Publishing Division
100 Railroad Ave. #104
Westminster, Maryland 21157

International Standard Book Numbers
Paperbound: 978-0-7884-5026-6
Clothbound: 978-0-7884-8252-6

Table of Contents

INTRODUCTION

Early vital records of many New Hampshire towns can be located either through the State's Vital Records Department or on microfilms made available through LDS Family History Centers. Some, however, have been lost or are inaccessible for various reasons. A valuable, but labor intensive, source of information for events occurring in 1887 and thereafter is the vital statistics which are provided in a section of the Annual Town Reports of many New Hampshire towns. Many of these town reports have been collected at the New Hampshire State Library in Concord, as well as more local repositories.

The amount of information published in these Annual Town Reports varies tremendously over time. Early records are far more detailed and comprehensive. Recent records are rather cursory, but issues of confidentiality amd sensitivity to the privacy of those residents still living offsets the lack of information of genealogical value.

While the information provided is often very helpful, one must keep in mind that it is not fool-proof or universally accurate, nor is it the primary source or the actual vital record itself. The fact that much of the data is self-reported suggests that it is reliable. However, errors in transcription, spelling (particularly with respect to French-Canadian and European families), and printing are often obvious. In addition, there may be, for example, two children listed as the third child of a particular couple, or the mother's maiden name, age or place of birth differs or is inconsistent from one entry to another. It is also important to note that a birth, marriage or death may have been reported in another town although the subject resided in Sandwich, or the entry may not have been made in the first place.

Despite these shortcomings, the information contained in the Annual Town Reports can be a valuable tool for the genealogist. Marriage and death records from the late 1800's often identify parents who were married nearly a century before. Finally, those families that have remained in Sandwich or adjacent towns for several generations can be traced and connected to the present.

Births – To the extent that the information is available, the entries in the list of births are given as follows: child's name; date of birth; place of birth (where provided); the number of children in the family; father's name, place of birth, age and occupation; and the mother's maiden name, age and place of birth. As noted above, the amount of information in earlier records is substantially greater than in more recent years.

At times, the given names of many children are missing from the early records. In this case, the sex of the child is given and they are listed chronologically at the beginning of the surname heading. On occasion, the child's name can be determined from marriage or death records, as well as secondary sources.

Marriages – To the extent that the information is available, the entries in the list of marriages follow this format: groom's name; groom's residence; bride's name; bride's residence; date of marriage; place of marriage (where provided); H, signifying husband's information and W, signifying wife's information, each in the following order – age, occupation, number of the marriage (if other than the first), father's name, father's place of birth, father's occupation, mother's name, mother's place of birth, and mother's occupation. The name of the official conducting the marriage has been omitted but is generally provided in the original document. A separate listing of brides in alphabetical order follows this section in order to allow for cross-referencing.

Deaths – To the extent available, the entries in the list of deaths contain the following information: name of decedent; date of death; place of death; age at death; cause of death; marital status; birthplace; father's name; father's place of birth; mother's name; and mother's place of birth.

BIRTHS

ABBOTT,
son, b. 1/17/1888; tenth; Reuben F. Abbott (farmer, Tamworth) and Abbie A. ----- (Sandwich)
daughter, b. 12/18/1906; second; Herbert E. Abbott (farmer, Sandwich) and Alice M. Gilman (Tamworth)
child, b. 11/5/1908; first; Everett H. Abbott (farmer, Sandwich) and Lizzie E. Gilman (Tamworth)
daughter, b. 4/30/1909; third; Herbert E. Abbott (farmer, Sandwich) and Alice M. Gilman (Tamworth)
Edna Louise, b. 1/6/1917; fifth; Herbert E. Abbott (farmer, Sandwich) and Alice M. Gilman (Tamworth)
Percy L., b. 3/21/1903; first; Herbert E. Abbott (farmer, Sandwich) and Lillian H. Smith (Sandwich)

ADAMS,
Louisa, b. 1/29/1921; second; John R. Adams (auto mechanic, Boston, MA) and Seville H. Martyn (Lynn, MA)
Marjorie, b. 6/9/1895; first; Isaac C. Adams (Sandwich) and Helen E. Hastings (Cambridge, MA)

ADRIANCE,
Cody Ward, b. 3/3/1995 in Russia; H. Benson Adriance II and Alexandra Jane Lyde (1996)
Tristan Benson, b. 5/15/1993 in Concord; Henry Benson Adriance II and Alexandra Jane Lyde

ALCOCK,
Carolyn Fleurette, b. 6/27/1947 in Wolfeboro; first; George A. Alcock, Jr. (carpenter, Boston, MA) and Carolyn E. Reed (Athens, NY)
Daphne Reed, b. 10/15/1950 in Laconia; second; George Albert Alcock, Jr. (carpenter, MA) and Carolyn Elizabeth Reed (NY)

ALLEN,
child, b. 5/11/1910; first; Melvin C. Allen (engineer, Laconia) and Mildred S. Angier (Weymouth, MA)
Melvin Lawson, b. 8/2/1914; second; Melvin C. Allen (stage driver, Laconia) and Mildred S. Angier (Weymouth, MA)

ALOSA,
Grayson Autumn, b. 9/6/2002 in Concord; Zachary Alosa and Rebecca Alosa

AMBROSE,
daughter, b. 2/28/1892; first; L. C. Ambrose (farmer, Sandwich) and Hattie E. Tilton (Sandwich)
son, b. 3/11/1893; second; Langdon Ambrose (farmer, Sandwich) and Hattie E. Tilton (Sandwich)
Agnes Harriet, b. 11/1/1916; first; Jesse L. Ambrose (farmer, Sandwich) and Mabel E. Williams (Knoxville, TN)
Eugenia May, b. 1/25/1938; first; Langdon J. Ambrose (student, N. Sandwich) and Ada M. Collins (Canaan, VT)
Jesse Langdon, II, b. 7/15/1981 in Sandwich; Langdon J. Ambrose II and Christine Worthen
Joshua McLaren, b. 2/20/1984 in Sandwich; Langdon Jesse Ambrose II and Christine Worthen
Langdon Jesse, b. 6/22/1919; second; Jesse L. Ambrose (farmer, Sandwich) and Mabel Williams (Knoxville, TN)
Langdon Jesse, Jr., b. 9/5/1956 in Wolfeboro; first; Langdon J. Ambrose (welder, NH) and Gladys R. Anthony (NH)

AMES,
stillborn son, b. 5/6/1925; first; Harold B. Ames (laborer, Brockton, MA) and Charlotte Hoag (Sandwich); residence – Moultonboro
Nathan Matthew, b. 4/22/1985 in North Conway; Robert John Ames and Doon Maura Mustapha

ANDERSON,
Charles Francis M., b. 2/22/2001 in Concord; Brent Anderson and Kimberly Anderson

ANGIER,
Sylbert Una, b. 8/15/1922; first; Ryvers F. Ainger (teamster, Sandwich) and Grace E. Wallace (Sandwich)

ARLEN,
Barry Oliver, b. 6/1/1950 in Laconia; fifth; George Percy Arlen (lumberman, NH) and Eugenia B. Whitney (NH)

ATWOOD,
daughter, b. 5/5/1887; third; O. Will Atwood (farmer, Sandwich) and Maggie E. ----- (NS)
son, b. 9/21/1889; fourth; O. W. Atwood (farmer, Sandwich) and M. E. Bulge (Richmond, NS)
daughter, b. 5/13/1891; first; Harry A. Atwood (farmer, Sandwich) and Stella E. Burrough (Sandwich)
son, b. 11/25/1906; second; Frank L. Atwood (farmer, Sandwich) and Florence Brown (Sandwich)
child, b. 11/24/1910; first; Alta J. Atwood (Sandwich)
stillborn daughter, b. 3/11/1954 in Laconia; second; Herbert Loring Atwood (truck driver, NH) and Priscilla Stacy (NH)
Dorothy B., b. 1/8/1902; first; Frank L. Atwood (farmer, Sandwich) and Florence M. Brown (Sandwich)
Gerald Alan, b. 9/1/1937; third; Gerald W. Atwood (laborer, Sandwich) and Virginia A. Moody (Madison)
Herbert Loring, b. 4/12/1934; second; Gerald W. Atwood (laborer, Sandwich) and Virginia Moody (Madison)
Richard Allan, b. 7/21/1956 in Laconia; third; Hubert L. Atwood (truck driver, NH) and Priscilla N. Stacy (NH)

AVERY,
son, b. 1/12/1925; first; Guy Avery (trucking, Rumney) and Viola Mudgett (Sandwich)
Arthur Jesse, b. 12/8/1927; third; Guy L. Avery (laborer, Campton) and Viola E. Mudgett (Sandwich)
Delbert C., b. 10/21/1911; first; Harry C. Avery (farmer, Rumney) and Flora E. Hodgson (Sandwich)
Lauretta Ruth, b. 10/31/1919; second; Arthur W. Avery (lumber, Rumney) and Jennie Manning (Halifax, NS)
Willis Kennith, b. 3/13/1918; first; Arthur W. Avery (farmer, Rumney) and Jennie B. Manning (Halifax, NS)

BAGLEY,
daughter, b. 4/10/1889; fifth; Martha A. Bagley (Sandwich) and ------- (Meredith)
daughter, b. 7/5/1899; Erastus M. Bagley (laborer, Sandwich) and Alice M. Webster (Laconia)
daughter, b. 1/27/1904; second; Erastus M. Bagley (laborer, Campton) and Alice M. Webster (Laconia)
son, b. 5/2/1905; third; Erastus M. Bagley (laborer, Campton) and Alice M. Webster (Laconia)
child, b. 6/26/1908; fourth; Erastus M. Bagley (farmer, Thornton) and Alice M. Webster (Laconia)

BALL,
Cynthia Remick, b. 10/3/1951 in Laconia; third; Littleton Ball (salesman, VA) and Patricia Remick (MA)
Littleton Read, Jr., b. 5/31/1949 in Winchester, MA; second; Littleton Read Ball (salesman, Portsmouth) and Patricia Remick (Winchester, MA)

BARNES,
Eleanor May, 2/10/1938; third; Fred E. Barnes (laborer, Tamworth) and Florence M. Whiting (S. Tamworth)

Ruth Lena, b. 2/10/1938; second; Fred E. Barnes (laborer, Tamworth) and Florence M. Whiting (S. Tamworth)

BATCHELDER,
Christine Lynn, b. 4/11/1983 in Sandwich; Stephen Bently Batchelder and Bonnie Lee Vintinner
Daniel Stephen, b. 12/24/1984 in Sandwich; Stephen Bentley Batchelder and Bonnie Lee Vintinner
Gerald Timothy, b. 1/27/1952 in Laconia; first; Lewis H. Batchelder, Jr. (laborer, NH) and Judith Mary Wallace (NH)
Louis H., b. 10/30/1904; first; Joseph Batchelder (farmer, Holderness) and Fannie E. Smith (Sandwich)
Nancy Joyce, b. 8/5/1953 in Laconia; second; Lewis H. Batchelder, Jr. (carpenter, NH) and Judith Mary Wallace (NH)

BEACH,
Barbara, b. 6/2/1925; first; Watson E. Beach (gardener, Manchester) and Florence Hudson (New Ipswich)
Joan, b. 4/10/1931; third; Watson E. Beach (farmer, Manchester) and Florence Hudson (New Ipswich)
John Titus, b. 8/21/1929; second; Watson E. Beach (farmer, Manchester) and Florence Hudson (New Ipswich)

BEDARD,
Frank W., b. 10/9/1923; first; Ferdinand Bedard (laborer, St. Johnsbury, VT) and Frances G. Webster (Sandwich)

BEEDE,
Blanch, b. 3/16/1888; first; Daniel Q. Beede (teamster, Gilmanton) and Bertha B. ----- (Moultonborough); residence – Worcester, MA

BEMIS,
son, b. 8/28/1892; second; Irven G. Bemis (machinist, Whitefield) and Rose B. Willey (Sandwich); residence – Boston

BENNETT,
stillborn daughter, b. 4/21/1904; first; Edward W. Bennett (carpenter, Sandwich) and Mamie E. Davis (Tamworth)
daughter, b. 12/16/1917; third; Edward Bennett (carpenter, Sandwich) and Mary Davis (Tamworth)
son, b. 12/16/1921; fourth; Edward W. Bennett (carpenter, Sandwich) and Mary E. Davis (Tamworth)
Charles James, b. 1/6/1989 in North Conway; Kenneth James Bennett and Lisa Marie Walker
Christopher W., b. 11/4/1990 in North Conway; Kenneth J. Bennett and Lisamarie Walker
Kayla Ann, b. 5/2/1985 in Laconia; Kenneth James Bennett and Karen Joy Stokes
Lawrence E., b. 12/13/1912; second; E. W. Bennett (farmer, Sandwich) and Mamie Davis (Tamworth)

BERG,
Asa Nichols, b. 2/24/1990 in North Conway; Gunnar Berg and Martha Nichols
Eliza J., b. 5/3/1991 in North Conway; Gunnar Berg and Martha Nichols

BERRY,
Arthur Scott, b. 1/26/1946 in Laconia; fourth; Francis S. Berry (mechanic, Wolfeboro) and Fannie E. Roberts (Buckfield, ME)
Judith Lee, b. 1/5/1943 in Plymouth; fifth; Robert M. Berry (carpenter, Farmington) and Marian J. Nickles (Candia)

BICKFORD,

daughter, b. 8/8/1887; second; John T. Bickford (farmer, Rochester) and Addie Bennett (Sandwich)

daughter, b. 5/1/1890; third; John T. Bickford (farmer, Rochester) and Addie Bennett (Sandwich)

daughter, b. 5/24/1892; fourth; John Bickford (farmer, Sandwich) and Addie Bennett (Sandwich)

daughter, b. 9/3/1892; first; Silas H. Bickford (farmer, Sandwich) and Nellie E. Brown (Sandwich)

daughter, b. 8/16/1893; first; James Bickford (farmer, Sandwich) and Eva A. Bickford (Tamworth)

daughter, b. 8/21/1896; second; James B. Bickford (farmer, Sandwich) and Eva C. ----- (Tamworth)

daughter, b. 9/17/1901; third; Silas H. Bickford (laborer, Sandwich) and Nellie E. Brown (Sandwich)

daughter, b. 11/10/1922; first; Fred A. Bickford (farmer, E. Haverhill) and Stella Crawford (N. Holderness)

daughter, b. 2/20/1937; first; Carl O. Bickford (laborer, Meredith) and Elva Floyd (S. Tamworth)

Alexander Lee, b. 5/20/1985 in Hanover; Randall Mark Bickford and Mary Barbara Lee

Andrew Lee, b. 5/20/1985 in Hanover; Randall Mark Bickford and Mary Barbara Lee

Arlene Pearl, b. 6/14/1922; first; Karl H. Bickford (laborer, Moultonboro) and Helen L. Denney (Meredith)

Betty Louise, b. 9/13/1926; fourth; Karl H. Bickford (clerk, Sandwich) and Helen L. Denney (Meredith)

Carl H., b. 2/20/1901; first; George O. Bickford (laborer, Moultonboro) and Margaret B. Hudson (NS)

Charles Elliott, b. 8/2/1970 in Laconia; Charles R. Bickford, Jr. (NH) and Jill S. Chase (NH)

Charles Roy, Jr., b. 1/31/1943 in Laconia; first; Charles R. Bickford (laborer, Meredith) and Edna A. Burrows (Sandwich)

Fred Eric, b. 5/30/1950 in Laconia; first; Fred Marsena Bickford (poultryman, NH) and Ingrid Emma Ingles (MA)
Frederick T., b. 6/30/1990 in Concord; Fred E. Bickford and Joanne Comer
Harold, b. 1/25/1904; first; John F. Bickford (laborer, Tamworth) and M. Carrie Fifield (Sandwich)
Janet Louise, b. 6/28/1952 in Laconia; second; Fred M. Bickford (lumberman, NH) and Ingrid Emma Bickford (MA)
Jennifer Lynn, b. 5/25/1959 in Wolfeboro; fourth; Fred M. Bickford (lumbering, NH) and Ingrid E. Ingles (MA)
Joanna Karen, b. 6/20/1969 in Laconia; Fred M. Bickford and Ingrid E. Ingles
Karl H., b. 11/3/1923; second; Karl H. Bickford (laborer, Moultonboro) and Helen L. Denney (Meredith)
Margretta Joyce, b. 6/19/1932; third; Fred A. Bickford (farmer, E. Haverhill) and Stella M. Crawford (N. Holderness)
Ralph Brian, b. 4/11/1962 in Laconia; fifth; Fred M. Bickford (lumbering, NH) and Ingrid Ingles (MA)
Randall Mark, b. 3/12/1955 in Laconia; third; Fred Marsena Bickford (lumbering, NH) and Ingrid Emma Ingles (MA)
Shannon, b. 3/22/1965 in Laconia; first; Charles Roy Bickford (Bartlett Tree, NH) and Jill Chase (NH)
Stella, b. 6/3/1895; second; Silas Bickford (Sandwich) and Nellie Brown (Sandwich)
Thelma Rosalie, b. 11/2/1924; third; Karl H. Bickford (laborer, Moultonboro) and Helen L. Denney (Meredith)

BIGELOW,
daughter, b. 7/5/1906; first; Walter R. Bigelow (laborer, Sandwich) and Lilla F. Mudgett (Sandwich)
Beverly Betty, b. 2/1/1947 in Laconia; first; William E. Bigelow (teacher, Holland, VT) and Reta M. Ordway (New Hampton)

BLACKEY,
son, b. 1/31/1890; first; Elijah S. Blackey (farmer, Sandwich) and Lizzie A. Wade (Ctr. Harbor)
son, b. 9/23/1891; second; Elijah S. Blackey (farmer, Sandwich) and Lizzie A. Wade (Centre Harbor)
son, b. 1/29/1893; third; Elijah S. Blackey (farmer, Sandwich) and Lizzie Wade (Center Harbor)
daughter, b. 10/3/1895; fourth; Elijah S. Blackey (Sandwich) and Lizzie A. Wade (Center Harbor)
stillborn son, b. 8/14/1917; third; Harry H. Blackey (chauffeur, Sandwich) and Katherine J. Edwards (Boston, MA)
Philip Raye, b. 3/15/1919; fourth; Harry H. Blackey (engineer, Sandwich) and Katherine Edwards (Boston, MA)

BLANCHARD,
daughter, b. 9/2/1888; first; Walter E. Blanchard (farmer, Sandwich) and Clara F. (Seabrook)
daughter, b. 2/24/1893; first; George A. Blanchard (farmer, Sandwich) and Adele H. Jaclard (Moultonboro)
son, b. 1/13/1897; second; George A. Blanchard (farmer, Sandwich) and Adele H. Jacklard (Moultonboro)

BLODGETT,
Gloria Glea, b. 9/6/1934; second; August L. Blodgett (carpenter, Dedham, MA) and Helen C. Burrows (Sandwich)
Loraine M., b. 5/14/1932; first; August L. Blodgett (carpenter, Dedham, MA) and Helen Burrows (Sandwich)

BLUMBERG,
Lawrence J., b. 5/6/1911; first; Simon Blumberg (clerk, Liverpool, England) and Stella E. Clay (Sandwich)
Lewis Clay, b. 10/27/1939; fourth; Lawrence Blumberg (forestry, Sandwich) and Louise Carter (Sandwich)

BOARDMAN,
Maxine Sandra, b. 10/9/1943 in Laconia; first; Carlos W. Boardman (lumberman, Windsor, VT) and Margaret H. Burrows (Sandwich)

BODGE,
child, b. 6/3/1911; fifth; Harry E. Bodge (farmer, Moultonboro) and Annie M. Glidden (Tamworth)
daughter, b. 11/10/1912; sixth; Harry E. Bodge (laborer, Moultonboro) and Annie M. Glidden (Tamworth)
Edgar, b. 11/29/1904; third; Harry E. Bodge (laborer, Moultonboro) and Annie M. Glidden (Tamworth); residence - Moultonboro
Gladys E., b. 8/2/1908; fourth; Henry E. Bodge (laborer, Moultonboro) and Anna M. Glidden (Tamworth)
Stanley Everett, b. 9/16/1945 in Wolfeboro; first; Lillian M. Bodge (Moultonboro)

BONNEY,
Elisabeth Ashley, b. 2/2/1980 in Laconia; Joseph L. Bonney III and Barbara L. Steckbeck

BOOTY,
daughter, b. 9/15/1984 in Laconia; Geoffrey Rollen Booty and Helen Todd Platt
Hannah, b. 9/3/1985 in North Conway; Peter Thomas Booty and Diane H. Decker
Robin, b. 3/20/1989 in Concord; Peter Thomas Booty and Diane H. Decker

BORTMAN,
Miles Richmond, b. 4/7/1993 in Laconia; David Carl Bortman and Dena Rae Rosenthal
Seve Julian, b. 10/8/1995 in Laconia; David C. Bortman and Dena Rae Rosenthal

BREWER,

Terry Elizabeth, b. 9/18/1958 in Laconia; second; Robert W. Brewer (salesman, MA) and Jane A. Pinney (CT)

BROWN,

daughter, b. 3/11/1887; Moses Brown (laborer)

son, b. 4/22/1897; second; Daniel O. Brown (laborer, Sandwich) and Lizzie B. Fogg (Sandwich)

son, b. 12/18/1899; Charles F. Brown (farmer, Sandwich) and Nellie M. Snow (Sandwich)

daughter, b. 3/9/1901; second; Charles F. Brown (farmer, Sandwich) and Nellie M. Snow (Sandwich)

daughter, b. 4/28/1902; third; Charles F. Brown (farmer, Sandwich) and Nellie Snow (Sandwich)

son, b. 2/18/1904; fourth; Charles F. Brown (farmer, Sandwich) and Nellie M. Snow (Sandwich)

son, b. 2/19/1904; first; Frank W. Brown (laborer, Sandwich) and Alice G. Elliott (Sandwich)

son, b. 6/28/1906; first; George E. Brown (farmer, Sandwich) and Myrtle G. Grant (Sandwich)

child, b. 3/16/1908; second; Frank W. Brown (laborer, Sandwich) and Alice G. Elliott (Sandwich)

Bertha Natalie, b. 5/15/1921; second; Clarence R. Brown (fire watchman, Sandwich) and M. Louise Follett (Ashland)

Calvin Daniel, b. 1/4/1916; third; Earl S. Brown (teamster, Campton) and Eliza J. Elliott (Rumney)

Deborah Ann, b. 10/20/1956 in Laconia; third; Frank G. Brown (mechanic, NH) and Jean F. Leach (NH)

E., son, b. 5/8/1899; seventh; Moses G. Brown (laborer, Errol) and Chestina A. Robin (NS)

Edith B., d. 2/17/1890; sixth; Moses G. Brown (farmer, Errol) and Chestina A. Robin (PQI, NS)

Frank Granville, b. 6/6/1926; first; Clarence M. Brown (chauffeur, Sandwich) and Elizabeth Meader (Ryegate, VT)

James Frank, b. 5/10/1951 in Laconia; first; Frank Granville Brown (woodsman, NH) and Jean Frances Leach (NH)
Janet, b. 5/4/1936; second; Clarence M. Brown (laborer, Sandwich) and Elizabeth Meader (Ryegate, VT)
Jason Andrew, b. 2/23/1984 in Laconia; Randolph Brown and Anne Susan Tilton
Jed Adam, b. 12/1/1988 in Laconia; Randolph Brown and Anne Susan Tilton
Jeffrey Allan, b. 7/27/1986 in Laconia; Randolph Brown and Anne Susan Tilton
Justin Adley, b. 9/27/1990 in Laconia; Randolph Brown and Anne Susan Tilton
Katherine Jean, b. 10/20/1953 in Laconia; second; Frank Granville Brown (mechanic, NH) and Jean Frances Leach (NH)
Katherine Michelle, b. 3/17/1980 in Laconia; Randolph Brown and Anne S. Tilton
Lena May, b. 3/20/1894; first; Daniel O. Brown (laborer, Sandwich) and May E. Fogg (Sandwich)
Mary Louise, b. 10/29/1919; first; Clarence Brown (fire watchman, Sandwich) and M. Louise Follett (Ashland)

BRYANT,
son, b. 6/8/1900; first; Walter C. Bryant (farmer, Moultonboro) and Lizzie Severance (Sandwich)
son, b. 9/30/1901; second; Walter C. Bryant (farmer, Moultonboro) and Mary L. Severance (Sandwich)
daughter, b. 9/6/1905; fourth; Walter C. Bryant (farmer, Moultonboro) and Lizzie M. Severance (Sandwich)
Diane Barbara, b. 5/2/1952 in Laconia; first; Milton Robinson Bryant (farmer, NH) and Barbara May Hunt (MA)
Edith M., b. 9/26/1887; first; Walter C. Bryant (laborer, Moultonboro) and Jennie M. Bickford (Moultonboro)
Elaine Lynn, b. 1/29/1958 in Laconia; third; Milton R. Bryant (maintenance, NH) and Barbara M. Hunt (MA)

Elizabeth Jane, b. 2/16/1985 in Hanover; Milton Robinson Bryant, Jr. and Louisa Wells Brewer
Frances Adelaide, b. 7/20/1934; third; William Asa Bryant (carpenter, Sandwich) and Sylvia L. Avery (Rumney)
Geraldine Louise, b. 11/19/1924; first; John W. Bryant (laborer, Sandwich) and Madeline M. Robinson (Cambridge, MA)
Jacqueline, b. 9/27/1928; first; William Asa Bryant (carpenter, Sandwich) and Sylvia Avery (Rumney)
James Roger, b. 7/15/1948 in Laconia; second; John W. Bryant, Jr. (farmer, Cambridge, MA) and Laura Mae Wilkins (Springfield, MA)
John W., b. 9/4/1903; third; Walter C. Bryant (farmer, Moultonboro) and Lizzie M. Severance (Sandwich)
Leon F., Jr., b. 9/1/1926; second; Leon F. Bryant (farmer, Camden, ME) and Beryl C. Baker (Philadelphia, PA)
Linda Ann, b. 11/19/1940; first; Loren R. Bryant (laborer, Holland, VT) and Beulah Merryfield (Sandwich)
Mary Lorraine, b. 8/20/1929; third; W. S. Bryant (carpenter, Sandwich) and Dorothy Atwood (Sandwich)
Milton Robinson, b. 4/18/1932; fourth; John W. Bryant (farmer, Sandwich) and Madeline Robinson (Cambridge, MA)
Milton Robinson, Jr., b. 12/3/1954 in Laconia; second; Milton Robinson Bryant (carpenter, NH) and Barbara May Hunt (MA)
Milton Robinson, III, b. 10/10/1981 in Concord; Milton R. Bryant, Jr. and Louisa W. Brewer
Phyllis Marian, b. 4/22/1927; third; John W. Bryant (farmer, Sandwich) and Madeline Robinson (Cambridge, MA)
Rita, b. 3/6/1933; second; William A. Bryant (farmer, Sandwich) and Sylvia L. Avery (Rumney)
Shirley Colleen, b. 11/11/1927; second; Winfield S. Bryant (carpenter, Sandwich) and Dorothy B. Atwood (Sandwich)
Stewart Reed, b. 10/30/1924; first; Winfield S. Bryant (laborer, Sandwich) and Dorothy B. Atwood (Sandwich)

Walter L., b. 3/11/1925; first; Leon Bryant (farmer, Camden, ME) and Beryl Bacon (Philadelphia, PA)

BRYAR,

Bonnie Ellen, b. 5/19/1947 in Wolfeboro; first; Keith F. Bryar (minister, Laconia) and Marion C. Goodwin (Wells, ME)

Gregory Goodwin, b. 10/7/1948 in Laconia; second; Keith F. Bryar (minister, Laconia) and Marion E. Goodwin (Wells, ME)

BRYER,

Charles A., b. 1/18/1888; first; Frank A. Bryer (farmer, Sandwich) and Annie Bryer (Boston, MA)

BUKER,

Benjamin James, b. 9/12/1979 in Hanover; Kim B. Buker (NH) and Rita M. Horn (MO)

Casey Elyse, b. 11/29/1987 in Dover; Kim Bradford Buker and Rira M. Horn

Mary, b. 6/12/1895; third; F. M. Buker (Lewiston, ME) and Ellen F. Wilder (Waitsfield, VT)

Sibyl, b. 3/11/1894; second; Fred M. Buker (clergyman, Lewiston, ME) and Ellen F. Wilder (Waitsfield, VT)

BULLARD,

daughter, b. 8/3/1906; eighth; Henry W. Bullard (bank treasurer, Cambridge, MA) and Mary A. Palmer (Stoneham, MA); residence - Arlington, MA

Ashley Larcom, b. 11/11/1974 in Laconia; Howard B. Bullard (OK) and Betty V. Webster (NY)

Lucy Webster, b. 7/22/1979 in Sandwich; H. Benjamin Bullard III (OK) and Betty Y. Webster (NY)

Travis Benjamin, b. 12/10/1975 in Sandwich; Howard B. Bullard (OK) and Betty V. Webster (NY)

BUNDY,
daughter, b. 4/6/1904; first; Oscar E. Bundy (painter, Newburyport, MA) and Sarah E. Skinner (Sandwich)
Margaret J., b. 6/9/1906; second; Oscar E. Bundy (painter, Newburyport, MA) and Sarah E. Skinner (Sandwich)

BURBANK,
Ashley R., b. 4/24/1901; second; James G. Burbank (laborer, Campton) and Rose A. Ganet (Bridgewater)

BURNHAM,
son, b. 4/5/1904; second; Charles S. Burnham (farmer, Sandwich) and Grace Chase (Bellfontain, OH)
Jewell, b. 4/9/1902; first; Charles S. Burnham (laborer, Sandwich) and Grace Chase (Bellefontain, OH)
Sylvia Bell, b. 2/16/1906; third; Charles S. Burnham (stage driver, Sandwich) and Grace Chase (OH)

BURROWS,
daughter, b. 3/17/1898; first; John G. Burrows (farmer, Sandwich) and Hattie F. Smith (Sandwich)
son, b. 7/4/1900; first; Newel J. Burrows (farmer, Sandwich) and Nellie F. Hodge (Sandwich)
daughter, b. 7/30/1900; first; Charles H. Burrows (farmer, Sandwich) and Amy M. Gilman (Sandwich)
daughter, b. 9/26/1901; second; Charles H. Burrows (farmer, Sandwich) and Amy M. Gilman (Sandwich)
son, b. 3/30/1904; third; Charles H. Burrows (farmer, Sandwich) and Amy M. Gilman (Sandwich)
son, b. 10/2/1904; first; Harry L. Burrows (farmer, Sandwich) and Adelaide S. Hull (Ashland)
daughter, b. 11/2/1905; second; John G. Burrows (farmer, Sandwich) and Hattie F. Smith (Sandwich)
child, b. 6/28/1908; second; Fred M. Burrows (farmer, Sandwich) and Grace E. Skinner (Moultonboro)

stillborn child, b. 1/5/1910; fourth; Charles H. Burrows (farmer, Sandwich) and Amy M. Gilman (Sandwich)

Alicia Mae, b. 7/15/1982 in Laconia; Jere G. Burrows and Suzanne M. Buckley

Amy Louise, b. 3/29/1971 in Laconia; Bruce J. Burrows (NH) and Jill S. Downs (NH)

Barbara Jane, b. 4/3/1947 in Laconia; third; Austin G. Burrows (clerk, Sandwich) and M. Thelma Dumas (Woburn, MA)

Bruce Jessie, b. 6/12/1940; seventh; Nathaniel H. Burrows (laborer, Sandwich) and Edrie H. Gordon (New York, NY)

Chester J., b. 11/6/1913; second; Newell J. Burrows (farmer, Sandwich) and Nellie F. Hodge (Sandwich)

Chester J., Jr., b. 1/2/1944 in Laconia; first; Chester J. Burrows (woodsman, 40, Sandwich) and Beatrice V. Plume (28, Groton)

Clayton Frank, b. 12/23/1925; third; Frank N. Burrows (laborer, Sandwich) and Hilda Macdonald (Wolfeboro)

Donna Rae, b. 3/3/1950 in Laconia; second; Donald Henry Burrows (laborer, NH) and Ramona B. Willoughby (NH)

Edith S., b. 2/4/1903; first; Fred N. Burrows (farmer, Sandwich) and Grace E. Skinner (Moultonboro)

Edna Alice, b. 10/11/1909; third; Harry L. Burrows (farmer, Sandwich) and Addie S. Hull (Ashland)

Florence G., b. 1/24/1904; second; Fred N. Burrows (farmer, Sandwich) and Grace E. Skinner (Moultonboro)

Geoffrey Alan, b. 3/3/1950 in Laconia; first; Charles Gordon Burrows (post office clerk, NH) and Anna Louise Geers (NH)

James Maurice, b. 7/5/1924; second; Frank N. Burrows (laborer, Sandwich) and Hilda B. McDonald (Wolfeboro)

Jere Gordon, b. 1/29/1953 in Laconia; third; Charles Gordon Burrows (PO clerk, NH) and Anna Louise Geers (NH)

Jessica Anne, b. 7/24/1980 in Laconia; Jere G. Burrows and Suzanne M. Buckley

Jon Lester, b. 7/13/1950 in Laconia; second; Lester D. Burrows, Jr. (truck driver, NH) and Marjorie Nelson (NH)

Lanette Elizabeth, b. 2/9/1976 in Laconia; Peter Burrows (NH) and Enid Loretta Reeder (CA)

Leslie Howard, b. 8/19/1936; sixth; Nathaniel H. Burrows (laborer, Sandwich) and Edrie Gordon (New York, NY)

Lester D., Jr., b. 7/28/1923; first; Lester D. Burrows (farmer, Sandwich) and Beatrice Doughty (Bailey's Isl., ME)

Luther J., b. 9/18/1907; second; Harry L. Burrows (farmer, Sandwich) and Addie S. Hull (Ashland)

Margaret Helen, b. 5/7/1927; fourth; Frank Burrows (laborer, Sandwich) and Hilda Macdonald (Wolfeboro)

Mary Lou, b. 3/4/1942 in Laconia; second; Austin G. Burrows (clerk, 32, Sandwich) and Mary T. Dumas (25, Woburn, MA)

Nancy Jane, b. 5/12/1944 in Laconia; second; Fred W. Burrows (mail carrier, 36, Sandwich) and Nora E. Davis (31, Tamworth)

Peggy Ann, b. 12/26/1945 in Sandwich; second; Chester J. Burrows (lumberman, Sandwich) and Beatrice V. Plume (Groton)

Peter, b. 4/2/1940; first; Fred W. Burrows (mail carrier, Sandwich) and Nora E. Davis (Tamworth)

Phillip Taylor, b. 12/31/1933; second; Frank Burrows (laborer, Sandwich) and Eldora Taylor (Sandwich)

Richard Austin, b. 1/25/1938; first; Austin G. Burrows (salesman, C. Sandwich) and Thelma M. Dumas (Woburn, MA)

Robert N., b. 7/18/1933; fifth; Nathaniel H. Burrows (laborer, Sandwich) and Edsie H. Gordon (New York, NY)

Robin Charles, b. 2/7/1951 in Laconia; second; Charles Gordon Burrows (PO clerk, NH) and Anna Louise Geers (NH)

Robin Neecka, b. 3/28/1974 in Wolfeboro; Peter Burrows (NH) and Enid L. Reeder (CA)

Roger Newell, b. 11/1/1930; first; Frank N. Burrows (laborer, Sandwich) and Eldora F. Taylor (Sandwich)

Roxy Maude, b. 2/1/1917; third; Newell J. Burrows (farmer, Sandwich) and Nellie F. Hodge (Sandwich)
Sandra Jean, b. 4/4/1966 in Laconia; third; Roger N. Burrows (construction, Sandwich) and Blanche Patrick (Goffstown)
Scott Henry, b. 11/6/1980 in Laconia; Thomas F. Burrows and Donna M. Grisco
Steven Nelson, b. 3/30/1947 in Laconia; first; Lester D. Burrows, Jr. (marker, Ctr. Sandwich) and Marjorie L. Nelson (Moultonboro)
Thomas Frank, b. 9/8/12959 in Wolfeboro; first; Roger N. Burrows (truck driver, NH) and Blanche E. Patrick (NH)
Vida Victoria, b. 6/12/1922; first; Frank N. Burrows (laborer, Sandwich) and Hilda B. McDonald (Wolfeboro)
William Allen, b. 12/24/1954 in Laconia; fourth; Austin Gilman Burrows (clerk, NH) and Thelma Mary Dumas (MA)

BUTCHER-NESBITT,
Robert A., b. 3/4/1993 in Plymouth; Robert Arthur Butcher, Jr. and Caroline Hathaway Nesbitt

BUZZELL,
Kenneth Lloyd, b. 8/22/1952 in Plymouth; first; Lloyd Merrill Buzzell (laborer, NH) and Beryle Ann Boynton (NH)

BYRNE,
Joseph Thomas, III, b. 7/15/1983 in Wolfeboro; Joseph Thomas Byrne, Jr. and Vickie Lynne Holroyd

CAMPBELL,
daughter, b. 7/13/1892; seventh; John N. Campbell (farmer, Bedford) and Benne'ta Bancroft (Londonderry)
child, b. 8/11/1911; first; John Campbell (farmer, Sandwich) and Grace Elliott (Sandwich)
son, b. 11/26/1913; second; John W. Campbell (laborer, Sandwich) and Grace C. Elliott (Sandwich)

Delphine, b. 4/26/1922; third; John N. Campbell (laborer, Sandwich) and Grace E. Elliott (Sandwich)
Jeanne, b. 11/3/1925; fourth; John Campbell (laborer, Sandwich) and Grace Elliott (Sandwich)
Paul Douglas, b. 4/30/1943 in Wolfeboro; third; Everett Campbell (laborer, Sandwich) and Pauline E. Bragg (Laconia)

CANFIELD,
Benjamin Thomas, b. 8/18/2005 in Laconia; Thomas Canfield and Amy Canfield
Christopher Joseph, b. 4/2/1976 in Laconia; John R. Canfield (NJ) and Frances Betka (NJ)
Elizabeth Theresa, b. 7/9/1981 in Laconia; John R. Canfield and Frances Betka
Joseph Thomas, b. 7/22/1978 in Laconia; John R. Canfield (NJ) and Frances Betka (NJ)
Joshua Andrew, b. 6/7/2007 in Laconia; Thomas Canfield and Amy Canfield
Matthew Joseph, b. 3/4/1974 in Wolfeboro; John R. Canfield (NJ) and Frances Betka (NJ)
Michael Andrew, b. 2/3/1980 in Laconia; John R. Canfield and Frances Betka
Thomas Matthew, b. 4/27/1977 in Laconia; John R. Canfield (NJ) and Frances Betka (NJ)

CAREY,
Kyle Anne, b. 11/2/1984 in Laconia; Richard Adams Carey and Lois Anne Kuglin

CARNEY,
Martin Aidan, b. 4/29/2001 in Laconia; Martin Carney and Lora Carney
Owen Patrick, b. 12/8/2003 in Laconia; Martin Carney and Lora Carney

CARTER,

daughter, b. 2/8/1899; first; Alonzo F. Carter (farmer, Bartlett) and Bertha L. Atwood (Sandwich)

son, b. 11/12/1899; Almon E. Carter (merchant, Sandwich) and Addie L. Webster (Sandwich)

stillborn son, b. 2/8/1900; second; Alonzo F. Carter (farmer, Bartlett) and Bertha L. Atwood (Sandwich)

son, b. 9/7/1901; third; Almon E. Carter (merchant, Sandwich) and Addie L. Webster (Sandwich)

daughter, b. 11/30/1904; fifth; Almon E. Carter (merchant, Sandwich) and Addie L. Webster (Sandwich)

daughter, b. 7/5/1906; sixth; Almon E. Carter (farmer, Sandwich) and Addie L. Webster (Sandwich)

child, b. 2/12/1908; seventh; Almon E. Carter (farmer, Sandwich) and Addie L. Webster (Sandwich)

son, b. 10/19/1909; eighth; Almon E. Carter (chauffeur, Sandwich) and Addie L. Webster (Sandwich)

daughter, b. 10/23/1912; first; Andrew Carter (farmer, Cochituate, MA) and Ethel M. Chandler (Lynn, MA)

son, b. 7/22/1916; tenth; Almon E. Carter (chauffeur, Sandwich) and Addie L. Webster (Sandwich)

Anita Marie, b. 11/28/1962 in Laconia; third; James W. Carter (truck driver, NH) and Ethel M. Wallace (NH)

David Franklin, b. 5/17/1947 in Laconia; second; Almon E. Carter, Jr. (truck driver, Sandwich) and Frances E. Martin (Sandwich)

Florence E., b. 11/29/1903; fourth; Almon E. Carter (merchant, Sandwich) and Addie L. Webster (Sandwich)

Gordon Winslow, b. 8/9/1956 in Laconia; second; James W. Carter (lumberman, NH) and Ethel M. Wallace (NH)

James Winslow, b. 5/13/1937; first; Almon E. Carter, Jr. (laborer, Sandwich) and Frances E. Martin (Sandwich)

Kevin James, b. 7/28/1955 in Laconia; first; James Winslow Carter (mill worker, NH) and Ethel Marie Wallace (NH)

CARTLAND,
daughter, b. 11/25/1887; first; Joseph J. Cartland (farmer, Parsonsfield, ME) and Dora ----- (Parsonsfield, ME)
daughter, b. 11/25/1887; second; Joseph J. Cartland (farmer, Parsonsfield, ME) and Dora ----- (Parsonsfield, ME)
daughter, b. 11/14/1900; first; Joseph Cartland (farmer, Parsonsfield, ME) and Harriet MacLean (Lynn, MA)

CATALANO,
Abigail Kathryn, b. 2/13/1994 in Sandwich; Bart Anthony Catalano and Kathryn Ann Swan
Caleb Salvatore, b. 2/12/1996 in Ctr. Sandwich; Bart Anthony Catalano and Kathryn Ann Swan
Joshua Richard, b. 12/5/1998 in Sandwich; Bart A. Catalano and Kathryn Anne Swan

CEDERBERG,
Neil Eric, b. 7/16/1997 in Plymouth; Eric R. Cederberg and Tavia D. Street

CHENEY,
Bruce Herbert, b. 7/28/1941; second; Albert M. Cheney (teamster, Moultonboro) and Elinor L. Ladd (Limerick, ME)

CHICK,
stillborn son, b. 8/9/1900; first; Frank O. Chick (farmer, Sandwich) and Eva M. Sargent (Ashland)

CHILSON,
daughter, b. 8/6/1890; first; Herbert A. Chilson (lumberman, Cumberland, RI) and Angie P. Follett (Stratton, VT)

CLARK,
son, b. 3/8/1887; first; Emily Clark (Sandwich)

daughter, b. 6/18/1887; first; Herman Clark (farmer, Holderness) and Nellie Smith (Sandwich)
son, b. 8/18/1889; second; Charles S. Clark (farmer, Sandwich) and Nellie L. (Exeter)
stillborn daughter, b. 8/16/1900; third; Charles S. Clark (farmer, Sandwich) and Nellie Brown (Exeter)
Kenneth Hazen William, b. 10/28/1987 in sox; Kenneth William Clark and Carol Ann Publicover
Langdon S., b. 4/20/1925; first; Sumner B. Clark (foreman, Sandwich) and Gladys Munroe (Worcester, MA)

CLAY,
daughter, b. 7/21/1888; second; Henry N. Clay (painter) and Almena Pettingill (Sandwich); residence – Campton

CLINE,
Allison Elizabeth, b. 5/17/1989 in North Conway; James Allison Cline and Audrey Karen King

COCHRAN,
Elwin James, b. 7/15/1950 in Laconia; first; James Allen Cochran (lumberman, NH) and Myrtle Edna Barnes (NH)
Sheila Jean, b. 10/10/1952 in Laconia; second; James Alan Cochran (lumberman, NH) and Myrtle Edna Barnes (NH)

COLBY,
Phyllis, b. 11/21/1925; second; William Colby (laborer, Bow) and Frances Gilman (Sandwich)
Susan Victoria, b. 1/3/1924; first; William W. Colby (laborer, Bow) and Frances D. Gilman (Sandwich)

COLLINS,
Lee Wendell, Jr., b. 1/27/1977 in Laconia; Lee W. Collins (NH) and Sandra M. Peaslee (NH)

Michelle Marie, b. 8/24/1973 in Laconia; Lee W. Collins (NH) and Sandra M. Peaslee (NH)

COLSON,
Gladys Margaret, b. 9/26/1952 in Plymouth; second; Leon LeRoy Colson (unemployed, ME) and Priscilla Mae Murray (ME)
Leon LeRoy, Jr., b. 8/28/1951 in Plymouth; second; Leon LeRoy Colson (laborer, ME) and Priscilla Mae Murray (ME)

CONELLY,
Raphael Emerson, b. 3/13/1969 in Plymouth; William A. Conelly and Pamela A. Emerson

CONNOLLY,
Isabella Rose, b. 6/12/1998 in Concord; Paul C. Connolly and Brenda L. Goershel

CONRAD,
Lane, b. 12/10/1956 in Wolfeboro; fourth; Harold Conrad (doctor, PA) and Helena Davis (MA)
Marcia, b. 11/6/1959 in Wolfeboro; fifth; Harold Conrad, Jr. (physician, PA) and Helena Davis (MA)

COOK,
daughter, b. 12/20/1900; first; George O. Cook (farmer, Rock Creek, IL) and Mary R. Brown (Conway)
daughter, b. 7/24/1903; third; George O. Cook (farmer, Rock Creek, IL) and Mary R. Brown (N. Conway)
stillborn son, b. 7/15/1905; fourth; George O. Cook (farmer, Rock Creek, IL) and Mary R. Brown (N. Conway)
Alan Wayne, b. 9/13/1953 in Laconia; second; John Otis Cook (laborer, NH) and Patricia Forristall (MA)
Celia May, b. 2/20/1921; first; Lena M. Cook (Sandwich) and "she says E. E. Brown"

Cynthia, b. 6/21/1934; third; Wilbur A. Cook (laborer, Sandwich) and Edna R. Adams (Athol, MA)

Edith Frances, b. 3/28/1918; fifth; George O. Cook (farmer, Rock Creek, IL) and Mary R. Brown (N. Conway)

Heidi Lynn, b. 3/21/1957 in Laconia; first; Wilbur A. Cook (farmer, Sandwich) and Joan N. Berry (Plymouth)

Holly Berry, b. 8/10/1955 in Laconia; first; Wilbur Asa Cook, Jr. (farmer, NH) and Joan Nickles Berry (NH)

Joanne Marie, b. 10/20/1932; first; Lawrence Cook (laborer, Sandwich) and Dorothy E. Tivey (Boston, MA)

John Otis, b. 7/31/1902; second; George O. Cook (farmer, Rockcreek, IL) and Mary R. Brown (N. Conway)

Lawrence M., b. 2/3/1911; first; Merle C. Cook (farmer, Moultonboro) and Lucy McCormick (NS)

Lorraine Elizabeth, b. 5/21/1928; third; Merle Cook (caretaker, Moultonboro) and Lucy McCormick (Canada)

Marjorie, b. 4/12/1942 in Laconia; Wilbur A. Cook (laborer, 31, Sandwich) and Edna R. Adams (34, Athol, MA)

Nancy Adams, b. 12/15/1939; fourth; Wilbur Cook (laborer, Sandwich) and Edna Adams (Athol, MA)

Robert Wilbur, b. 8/2/1958 in Laconia; third; Wilbur A. Cook, Jr. (farmer, NH) and Joan N. Berry (NH)

Wilbur Asa, b. 4/21/1911; fourth; George C. Cook (farmer, Rock Creek, IL) and Mary R. Brown (N. Conway)

Wilbur Asa, Jr., b. 6/24/1930; first; Wilbur A. Cook (farmer, Sandwich) and Edna R. Adams (Athol, MA)

COOKE,

Angus Robert, b. 7/10/1962 in Newton, MA; second; Ian McL. Cooke (teacher, HI) and Janet R. Appleton (Australia)

COOLIDGE,

Brian Patrick, b. 2/6/1985 in Laconia; Peter B. Coolidge and Susan J. Hutchinson

COOMBS,
Jackson Burley, b. 8/4/1988 in Exeter; Jeffery Teal Coombs and Sheri-Jean Bentley
Theodore Carter, b. 5/26/1987 in Exeter; Jeffery Teal Coombs and Sheri Jean Bentley

CORLISS,
Janet Mae, b. 10/26/1934; first; Louis F. Corliss (farmer, W. Dennis, MA) and Marjorie Thornton (Springfield, MA)

COVEY,
Uradel Philetus, III, b. 12/6/1968 in Laconia; Uradel P. Covey, Jr. and Charlotte M. Brown

CRAM,
daughter, b. 12/2/1909; first; Charles S. Cram (carpenter, Canada) and Emma M. Grant (Moultonboro)
son, b. 2/3/1913; second; Charles S. Cram (carpenter, Cavatcool, Canada) and Emma M. Grant (Moultonboro)

CROCKETT,
son, b. 1/18/1905; fourth; Charles H. Crockett (farmer, Meredith) and Rose A. Gault (Bridgewater); residence – Ashland

CROCKFORD,
Claire Anne, b. 9/12/2005 in Manchester; Richard Crockford and Laura Galonski
Conor M., b. 4/21/1992 in Laconia; Richard E. Crockford, Jr. and Catherine S. Graham

CUNNINGHAM,
Isabel A., b. 9/19/1997 in Laconia; Daniel J. Cunningham and Sarah B. Johnston
Lenore Ann, b. 1/12/1974 in Laconia; Howard N. Cunningham (NH) and Constance M. Nicolosi (MA)

Lucy, b. 5/3/1999 in Laconia; Daniel Cunningham and Sarah Cunningham

CURRIER,
son, b. 8/7/1899; Leon Currier (farmer) and Emily Hodgdon
son, b. 9/7/1903; second; Leon H. Currier (farmer, Sandwich) and Emily V. Hodgdon (Sandwich)
Stephen Webster, b. 3/12/1942 in Laconia; first; Lewis H. Currier (carpenter, 38, Sandwich) and Theodore L. Post (36, Keyport, NJ)

D'AGOSTINO,
Joseph Anthony, Jr., b. 2/26/1987 in Laconia; Joseph Anthony D'Agostino and Elizabeth Ione Gunther

DAIGNEAU,
Carol Lee, b. 12/22/1946 in Laconia; sixth; Ernest J. Daigneau (carpenter, Franklin) and Louise A. Roucher (Lowell, MA)
Darlene Ann, b. 10/14/1948 in Laconia; seventh; Ernest J. Daigneau (carpenter, Franklin) and Louise Anne Roucher (Lowell, MA)

DAIL,
Patrick McClenney, b. 7/26/1985 in Laconia; Richard Alvin Dail and Susan Leigh Stonefifer

DANIELOVICH,
Alexander Bennett, b. 2/7/1994 in Laconia; Steven James Danielovich and Linda Fraser
Fraser A., b. 1/27/1991 in Concord; Steven J. Danielovich and Linda Fraser

DANIELS,
daughter, b. 11/28/1895; first; Uriah M. Daniels (Albany) and Nellie Nichols (Moultonboro)

DARLING,

son, b. 8/7/1893; first; Henry M. Darling (farmer, NB) and Nellie J. Dow (Tamworth)

daughter, b. 10/22/1894; first; William D. Darling (farmer, Campton) and Nellie P. Knowles (Haverhill)

daughter, b. 5/2/1896; second; W. D. Darling (farmer, Campton) and Nellie P. Knowles (Haverhill, MA)

daughter, b. 12/3/1897; third; Will S. Darling (farmer, Campton) and Nellie P. Knowles (Haverhill, MA)

daughter, b. 2/22/1899; fourth; William D. Darling (farmer, Campton) and Nellie P. Knowles (Haverhill, MA)

DAVEY,

son, b. 1/2/1897; second; George H. Davey (laborer, NB) and Jennie Vittum (Sandwich)

Everett E., b. 4/27/1918; first; Guy E. Smith (chauffeur, Moultonboro) and Hazel A. Davey (Sandwich)

DAVIE,

daughter, b. 6/12/1895; first; George H. Davie (NB) and Jennie Vittum (Sandwich)

daughter, b. 4/27/1909; ninth; George H. Davie (laborer, St. John, NB) and Jennie Vittum (Sandwich)

DAVIS,

daughter, b. 4/5/1899; third; Henry G. Davis (laborer, NB) and Jennie Vittum (Sandwich)

son, b. 1/24/1907; eighth; George H. Davis (laborer, PEI) and Jennie Vittum (Sandwich)

son, b. 12/3/1917; eighth; Charles J. Davis (laborer, Newmarket) and Katherine Holland (Newmarket)

stillborn son, b. 1/20/1919; ninth; Charles J. Davis (farmer, Newmarket) and Katherine Holland (Newmarket)

son, b. 6/18/1931; third; Forest E. Davis (carpenter, Wakefield) and Charlotte Hoag (Sandwich)
Bernard, b. 3/14/1905; seventh; George Henry Davis (laborer, PEI) and Jennie Vittum (Sandwich)
Bertha, b. 3/14/1905; sixth; George Henry Davis (laborer, PEI) and Jennie Vittum (Sandwich)
Bette Ann, b. 6/29/1938; fifth; Forrest E. Davis (carpenter, Wakefield) and Charlotte Hoag (Sandwich)
Doris A., b. 5/18/1901; fourth; George H. Davis (laborer, NB) and Jennie Vittum (Sandwich)
Ellsworth, b. 6/7/1941; seventh; Forrest E. Davis (carpenter, Wakefield) and Charlotte Hoag (Sandwich)
Forrest Ellsworth, b. 4/19/1929; first; Forrest E. Davis (carpenter, Wakefield) and Charlotte Hoag (Sandwich)
Lilia, b. 10/30/1933; third; Forest E. Davis (carpenter, Wakefield) and Charlotte Hoag (Sandwich)
Ronald, b. 12/19/1939; fifth; Forest Davis (carpenter, Wakefield) and Charlotte Hoag (Sandwich)

DAY,
Jane Lois, b. 9/4/1949 in Laconia; fourth; Norbert A. Day (mechanic, NH) and Celia M. Cook (NH)
Janet Ann, b. 6/7/1945 in Laconia; second; Norbert A. Day (mechanic, Moultonboro) and Celia M. Cook (Sandwich)
Janice Ann, b. 6/7/1945 in Laconia; third; Norbert A. Day (mechanic, Moultonboro) and Celia M. Cook (Sandwich)
Joan Lois, b. 9/4/1949 in Laconia; fifth; Norbert A. Day (mechanic, NH) and Celia M. Cook (NH)
Kathleen Lena, b. 10/18/1943 in Laconia; first; Norbert A. Day (mechanic, Moultonboro) and Celia M. Cook (Sandwich)
Perley Clayton, Jr., b. 7/9/1945 in North Conway; first; Perley C. Day (laborer, Porter, ME) and Alice E. Anthony (E. Hiram, ME)

DEARBORN,
son, b. 2/14/1934; first; Kenneth A. Dearborn (clerk, Bristol, VT) and Sarah B. Davis (Ossipee)
Earline Jeannette, b. 3/30/1925; seventh; Earl J. Dearborn (merchant, Lincoln, VT) and Helen Guyer (St. Johnsbury, VT)
Jean Ethelyn, b. 8/18/1926; eighth; Earl J. Dearborn (merchant, Lincoln, VT) and Helen Guyer (St. Johnsbury, VT)

DECATO,
daughter, b. 10/1/1889; fifth; Henry N. Decato (millwright, E. Canaan) and Ellen Sawyer (E. Canaan)

DEMING,
Beth An, b. 6/12/1962 in Laconia; second; Roger Deming (caretaker, NH) and Martha G. White (MA)
Roberta, b. 3/21/1953 in Laconia; first; Roger Deming (self-employed, NH) and Martha Gerry White (MA)

DENNEY,
Dolores Edith, b. 12/17/1944 in Laconia; fourth; Harold C. Denney (lumber worker, 30, Boston, MA) and Alice E. Hillard (28, Laconia)
Norman Jean, b. 12/9/1939; second; Harold Denney (laborer, Boston, MA) and Alice Hilliard (Laconia)

DENNY,
son, b. 6/5/1903; first; Harry A. Denny (weaver, Center Harbor) and Edith M. Clark (Sandwich); residence - Meredith

DIMICK,
Constance L., b. 3/19/1929; third; William E. Demick (laborer, Fryeburg, ME) and Edna M. Lozier (Chicopee, MA)
John Philip, b. 10/27/1934; fourth; William E. Dimick (laborer, Fryeburg, ME) and Edna Marie Lozier (Chicopee, MA)

Sherman W., b. 7/18/1920; first; William E. Demick (laborer, Fryeburg, ME) and Dorothy Wing (Lynn, MA)
Virginia Marie, b. 1/6/1925; first; William E. Demick (mechanic, Fryeburg, ME) and Edna Lozier (Chicopee, MA)
William Edward, Jr., b. 7/11/1926; second; William E. Dimick (carpenter, Fryeburg, ME) and Edna Lozier (Chicopee, MA)

DODGE,
daughter, b. 2/25/1887; Charles W. Dodge (farmer, Wenham, MA) and Sarah E. (Sandwich)
son, b. 8/21/1898; fourth; E. L. Dodge (furrier, Woodcastle, ME) and Charlotte Webster (Boston, MA); residence – Somerville

DOLAN,
Robert Edward, b. 11/18/1994 in North Conway; Robert Owen Dolan and Julie Eleanor Richardson

DOLLEY,
child, b. 7/20/1888; first; Fred M. Dolley (printer, Gorham) and Emma A. Cook (Stoneham, MA)

DONEAU,
Dorothy Helen, b. 8/31/1914; first; Felix J. Doneau (shoe cutter, Haverhill, MA) and Alice R. Smith (Hampton)

DORR,
son, b. 3/3/1896; fifth; Orrin J. Dorr (farmer, Sandwich) and Marjorie McSorley (WI)

DORREY,
Margaret May, b. 12/25/1906; second; William H. Dorrey (laborer, Boston, MA) and Margaret Allen (ME)

DORSEY,
Ethel Louise, b. 3/13/1909; third; William H. Dorsey (painter, Boston, MA) and M. A. Allen (Bowdoin, ME)

DOWNS,
daughter, b. 2/10/1892; third; Edward F. Downs (laborer, Tamworth) and Annie M. Spooner (Haverhill)
Denita Ann, b. 9/1/1962 in Wolfeboro; first; Clifford F. Downs, Jr. (gas del., NH) and Bonita M. Swan (NH)
Eldora M., b. 1/4/1894; fourth; Edward F. Downs (laborer, Tamworth) and Annie M. Spooner (Haverhill)

DREW,
Philip William, b. 3/9/1920; first; William P. Drew (lumber, Dover) and Lena M. Tappan (Sandwich)
Selden Edison, b. 5/23/1921; second; William P. Drew (laborer, Dover) and Lena M. Tappan (Sandwich)
Wilbur John, b. 10/20/1922; first; William P. Drew (laborer, Dover) and Lena M. Tappan (Sandwich)

DRUAR,
Katherine R., b. 3/7/1991 in Concord; Michael J. Druar and Deborah J. Fagan

DUMAS,
Noelle Elizabeth, b. 12/12/1967 in Laconia; first; Raymond J. Dumas (student, Salem, MA) and Carol L. Galley (Harrisburg, PA)

DUNLAP,
Robert Arthur, Jr., b. 11/29/1972 in Laconia; Robert A. Dunlap (MA) and Judith A. Gibson (MA)

DUNTLEY,
son, b. 2/1/1/902; second; Arthur S. Duntley (farmer, Manchester) and Maude V. Gilman (Denmark, ME)
R., son, b. 12/10/1899; Arthur S. Duntley (farmer, VT) and Maud V. Gilman (Denmark, ME)

EATON,
Eleanor Anna, b. 5/29/1998 in Laconia; Brian Scott Eaton and Lydia Eleanor Koenig
Elizabeth Martha, b. 11/27/2000 in Laconia; Brian Eaton and Lydia Eaton
Lindsey Gerli, b. 3/12/1983 in Concord; Toby Vining Eaton and Madeleine Marie Gerli
William Tyler, b. 8/11/1984 in Sandwich; Toby Vining Eaton and Madeleine Marie Gerli

ELDRIDGE,
Carrie Ann, b. 9/24/1982 in Laconia; Chester C. Eldridge and June E. Bogatkowski
Laura Jean, b. 2/7/1981 in Laconia; Chester C. Eldridge and June E. Bogatkowski
Matthew Allen, b. 9/24/1982 in Laconia; Chester C. Eldridge and June E. Bogatkowski

ELLIOTT,
daughter, b. 7/28/1890; seventh; John G. Elliot (farmer, Meredith) and Ida E. Rowe (Sandwich)
daughter, b. 9/11/1892; eighth; John G. Elliott (farmer, Center Harbor) and Ida E. Rowe (Sandwich)
daughter, b. 7/26/1899; Elmer Elliott (farmer, Tuftonboro) and Maud L. Mitchell (Sandwich)
son, b. 7/20/1900; second; Elmer Elliott (farmer, Tuftonboro) and Maud Mitchell (Sandwich)
daughter, b. 4/6/1902; first; Cora Elliott (Sandwich)

daughter, b. 9/18/1902; third; Elmer Elliott (farmer, Tuftonboro) and Maud Mitchell (Sandwich)
son, b. 3/21/1905; fourth; Elmer Elliott (farmer, Tuftonboro) and Maud Mitchell (Sandwich)
daughter, b. 10/29/1905; first; Lewis Elliott (laborer, Sandwich) and Sarah Pierce (RI)
son, b. 7/16/1906; fifth; Elmer Elliott (farmer, Tuftonboro) and Maud Mitchell (Sandwich)
child, b. 8/20/1911; sixth; Elmer Elliott (farmer, Tuftonboro) and Maud Mitchell (Sandwich)
son, b. 4/13/1914; second; Lewis C. Elliott (farmer, Sandwich) and Sarah A. Pierce (Cranston, RI)
stillborn son, b. 8/5/1917; third; Elmer Elliott (farmer, Tuftonboro) and Maude L. Mitchell (Sandwich)
Barry Preston, b. 7/16/1959 in Wolfeboro; fourth; Preston B. Elliott (salesman, RI) and Patricia A. Steves (NH)
Bryan Edwin, b. 7/16/1959 in Wolfeboro; third; Preston B. Elliott (salesman, RI) and Patricia A. Steves (NH)
Cheryl Penelope, b. 5/12/1946 in Wolfeboro; first; Phillip Elliott (lumber worker, Sandwich) and Virginia Forestall (Framingham, MA)
Darlene Marion, b. 1/24/1958 in North Conway; second; Preston Elliott (salesman, NH) and Patricia A. Steves (NH)
Edward Harold, b. 12/8/1929; third; Harold Elliott (laborer, Sandwich) and Evelyn Roebarge (Tuftonboro)
Faith Ann, b. 8/8/1948 in Wolfeboro; second; Phillip Elliott (woodsman, Sandwich) and Virginia Forristall (Framingham, MA)
Forrest K., b. 9/18/1992 in Lebanon; Barry P. Elliott and Jennifer Kondrotas
Kimberly Faith, b. 4/19/1970 in Wolfeboro; Raymond B. Elliott (MA) and Pamela R. Ball (NH)
Lynda Lee, b. 2/26/1952 in Wolfeboro; third; Phillip Elliott (woodsman, NH) and Virginia Forristall (MA)

Pauline Sarah, b. 10/15/1922; third; Lewis C. Elliott (farmer, Sandwich) and Sarah A. Pierce (Evanston, RI)
Phillip, b. 4/7/1921; first; Susie M. Elliott (Sandwich)
Raymond Douglas, b. 1/9/1939; second; Dennis Elliott (wood chopper, Sandwich) and Leona Batchelder (Meredith)
Richard H., b. 8/8/1925; first; Harold Elliott (laborer, Sandwich) and Evelyn Roebarge (Tuftonboro)
Shirley Hope, b. 8/14/1923; first; Josiah R. Elliott (student, Plymouth) and Helen E. Bryant (Sandwich); residence – Plymouth

EMERSON,
Gail Denley, b. 12/10/1939; first; Denley Emerson (insurance, Brookline, MA) and Harriet Rothbun (Canton, MA)
Jill Beverly, b. 7/5/1942 in Laconia; second; Denley W. Emerson (machinist, 24, Boston, MA) and Harriet A. Rathbun (26, Canton, MA)
Pamela Arnold, b. 6/10/1943 in Laconia; third; Denley W. Emerson (machinist, Boston, MA) and Harriet A. Rathbun (Canton, MA)

ENGLE,
Alan Edward, b. 8/18/1968 in Wolfeboro; Robert C. Engle and Janice D. Stein

ENRIGHT,
Ariel S., b. 4/25/1991 in Sandwich; John E. Enright and Linda S. Jacobs
Margaret Julia, b. 1/12/1989 in N. Sandwich; John Edward Enright and Linda Susan Jacobs

EVERETT,
Chloe E., b. 3/11/1990 in Sandwich; William D. Everett and Kimberly L. Fairley

Samuel Alexander, b. 8/4/1993 in Sandwich; William Dickenson Evertt and Kimberly Lynn Farley

FACCIOLO,
Anastasiya May, b. 1/7/1992 in Moscow, Russia; Louisa Norris Facciolo (1995)
Donka Luisa, b. 11/11/1986 in Sofia, Bulgaria; Luisa Facciolo (1993)

FACCIOLO-MOORE,
Karina Luisa, b. 7/26/1987 in nvx; Nancy Marlow Moore

FARMER,
Rosie May, b. 5/10/1914; first; Fred Farmer (farmer, Plymouth) and Mabel Burrows (Sandwich)

FISK,
Melanie Jane, b. 6/14/1950 in Laconia; third; Harrison Sears Fisk (visual education dealer, MA) and Irma LaV. Underwood (SC)

FLECK,
Emelia Jane, b. 5/29/1978 in Laconia; Robert W. Fleck (MA) and Lynda Norton (MA)

FLEISCHMANN,
Jeffrey Dean, b. 12/3/1985 in Laconia; Andrew Hall Fleischmann and Christina Anne Villadolid
Opal Lourdes Lee, b. 8/2/1988 in Laconia; Andrew Hall Fleischmann and Christina Anne Villadolid
Sophia Rose, b. 1/24/2007 in North Conway; Thomas Fleischmann and Kathleen Greene

FLETCHER,

Riley Balance, b. 9/22/2001 in North Conway; Nathan Fletcher and Julie Ann Ballance

FLOYD,

Alyssa Joanne, b. 3/20/2001 in Laconia; Gary Floyd and Diane Floyd

Ethan Robert, b. 1/23/1998 in Laconia; Gary Perley Floyd and Diane Frances Muzzi

FOGG,

son, b. 1/29/1890; first; Elias H. Fogg (farmer, Sandwich) and Elmira A. Beede (Sandwich)

son, b. 5/2/1899; third; Harrison W. Fogg (laborer, Sandwich) and Cora A. Abbott (Sandwich)

son, b. 1/6/1902; first; Herbert C. Fogg (blacksmith) and Bessie A. Nutter (Sandwich); residence - Ashland

daughter, b. 2/3/1914; second; John W. Fogg (farmer, Sandwich) and Annie Kelley (NS)

Alice Estella, b. 6/30/1946 in Laconia; first; Joseph A. Fogg (lumber worker, Gilmanton) and Dorritt Brown (Sandwich)

Alston T., b. 10/31/1903; first; Eugene W. Fogg (laborer, Sandwich) and Minnie L. Osgood (Conway)

Jason Arthur, b. 11/4/1978 in Laconia; Joseph E. Fogg (NH) and Deborah A. Miksch (NJ)

Joseph Errol, b. 4/21/1948 in Laconia; second; Joseph A. Fogg (woodsman, Gilmanton) and Dorritt Brown (Sandwich)

Joshua Ethan, b. 9/30/1982 in Laconia; Joseph E. Fogg and Deborah A. Mikach

Ruth W., b. 12/11/1912; first; John W. Fogg (farmer, Sandwich) and Annie I. Kelley (NS)

FORBES,
Keith Lear, b. 7/22/1946 in Laconia; first; Walter A. Forbes, Jr. (laborer, Winchendon, MA) and Sylberts U. Angier (Sandwich)

FORD,
daughter, b. 10/27/1913; first; Edmund M. Ford (laborer, Cabot, VT) and Grace L. Smith (Westburk, VT)
Alice Logan, b. 7/13/1984 in Concord; Gordon Merrill Ford and Elli Marie Hayes
Meredith Elizabeth, b. 5/18/1982 in Concord; Gordon M. Ford and Elli M. Hayes

FORRISTALL,
William Hindaugh, b. 12/17/1945 in Laconia; first; William H. Forristall, Jr. (mechanic, Brookline, MA) and Helen Peaslee (Sandwich)

FOSS,
son, b. 2/24/1887; first; Charles H. Foss (farmer, Sandwich) and Hattie F. Duelley (MA)
son, b. 6/3/1893; first; Charles L. Foss (farmer, Tamworth) and Nellie Batchelder (Sandwich)
stilborn son, b. 11/20/1920; first; Millard R. Foss (carpenter, Moultonboro) and Doris A. Davis (Sandwich)

FRANCIS,
Caitlin Heather, b. 2/21/1984 in Laconia; Joseph Craig Francis and Nanci Lee Eldridge

FRANK,
Lindsey Alyson, b. 9/7/1995 in Laconia; Douglas R. Frank and Lisa Ann Cook
Michael D., b. 7/8/1990 in Laconia; Douglas R. Frank and Lisa Cook

FRASE,
Melissa K., b. 11/28/1992 in Laconia; Kim K. Frase and Lauren A. Ulitz

FRENCH,
Raymond, b. 4/6/1897; third; Freeman E. French (farmer, Sandwich) and Sally F. Beede (Sandwich)

FROST,
Maxine Rosamond, b. 10/19/1934; eighth; Herbert Frost (lumber, Conway) and Eurtie Harmon (Standish)

FRY,
Shirley Louise, b. 5/24/1937; first; Clarence H. Fry (laborer, Sandwich) and Louise E. Adams (Sandwich); residence – Moultonboro

FRYE,
son, b. 8/3/1905; third; Orrin C. Frye (manufacturer, Sandwich) and Nellie A. Wood (Lebanon); residence - Lowell, MA
daughter, b. 11/9/1907; second; Lewis N. Frye (laborer, Moultonboro) and Jennie F. Hoyt (Tuftonboro)
Herbert, b. 3/24/1917; third; Lewis W. Frye (laborer, Moultonboro) and Jane F. Hoyt (Tuftonboro)

GABRIEL,
Stacey Linnae, b. 1/2/1985 in Hanover; Robert Todd Gabriel, Jr. and Junemarie Barbara Meehan

GAGNE,
Juanita Marie, b. 9/25/1944 in Wolfeboro; fourth; William Joseph Gagne (lumberman, ME) and Pearl Ella Rollins (NH)

GALE,

son, b. 11/13/1888; first; Amos Gale (farmer, Dover) and Jennie Wade (Moultonborough)

GARLAND,

daughter, b. 9/5/1898; fifth; Seth D. Garland (blacksmith, Tuftonboro) and Estella H. Hanson (Sandwich)
daughter, b. 9/29/1902; sixth; Seth D. Garland (blacksmith, Tuftonboro) and Estella Hanson (Sandwich)
stillborn son, b. 1/29/1918; second; Lewis D. Garland (laborer, Sandwich) and Ebba O. Sisberg (Cambridge, MA)
Beverly May, b. 4/7/1935; second; Lawrence E. Garland (asst. foreman, Moultonboro) and Catherine M. Cote (Ashland)
Emily Eleanor, b. 12/25/1920; third; Lewis D. Garland (stage driver, Sandwich) and Ebba O. Sioberg (Cambridge, MA)
Evelyn Mae, b. 10/5/1915; first; Lewis D. Garland (stage driver, Sandwich) and Ebba O. Sioberg (Cambridge, MA)
Louis D., b. 9/5/1896; fourth; Seth D. Garland (blacksmith, Tuftonboro) and Estella H. Hanson (Sandwich)

GAULT,

stillborn daughter, b. 5/19/1902; first; George F. Gault (farmer, Salmon Falls) and Eva M. Bagley (Sandwich)
daughter, b. 12/26/1903; second; George F. Gault (farmer, Salmon Falls) and Eva M. Bagley (Sandwich)
stillborn son, b. 5/2/1907; third; George F. Gault (laborer, Salmon Falls) and Eva M. Bagley (Sandwich)
son, b. 1/17/1913; fifth; George F. Gault (laborer, Salmon Falls) and Eva M. Bagley (Sandwich)
stillborn daughter, b. 11/7/1915; sixth; George F. Gault (laborer, Salmon Falls) and Eva M. Bagley (Sandwich)
Ethel P., b. 11/4/1910; fourth; George F. Gault (laborer, Salmon Falls) and Eva M. Bagley (Sandwich)

GILE,
Harry Elbredge, b. 5/11/1928; seventh; Leroy Gile (chauffeur, Rochester) and Ella Gautier (Hampton Falls)

GILMAN,
son, b. 6/9/1889; second; John F. Gilman (mechanic, Denmark, ME) and Laura E. Bennett (Sandwich)
daughter, b. 12/23/1906; third; Maud V. Gilman (Denmark, ME)
daughter, b. 6/20/1907; first; E. S. Gilman (painter, Winchester) and Victoria Wallace (Sandwich)
son, b. 6/5/1913; Warren S. Gilman (blacksmith, Sandwich) and Alta J. Atwood (Sandwich)
son, b. 9/12/1914; second; Warren S. Gilman (blacksmith, Sandwich) and Alta J. Atwood (Sandwich)
Carrie, b. 11/20/1916; third; Warren S. Gilman (blacksmith, Sandwich) and Alta J. Atwood (Sandwich)
Clarence William, b. 12/16/1926; third; Wilbur J. Gilman (laborer, Fryeburg, ME) and Lena M. Brown (Sandwich)
David William, b. 10/15/1951 in Laconia; second; Clarence William Gilman (truck driver, NH) and Doris Mildred Davis (MA)
Dennis Wilbur, b. 12/27/1922; first; Wilbur J. Gilman (laborer, Fryeburg, ME) and Lena M. Brown (Sandwich)
Lillian E., b. 7/11/1925; second; Wilbur Gilman (laborer, Fryeburg, ME) and Lena Brown (Sandwich)
Sherry Marie, b. 8/17/1949 in Inagua, Bahamas; second; Dennis W. Gilman (carpenter, NH) and Corinne M. Plummer (NH)

GLINES,
son, b. 5/19/1896; second; David E. Glines (farmer, Sandwich) and Abby L. Brown (Conway)
daughter, b. 10/8/1900; third; David E. Glines (teamster, Sandwich) and Addie F. Brown (N. Conway)

GLOVER,
daughter, b. 12/16/1888; first; Charles E. Glover (farmer, Nashua) and Nellie Fifield (Sandwich)

GOEWEY,
Emily Grace, b. 6/28/2000 in Concord; Reed Goewey and Julie Goewey
Kelli Carynne, b. 11/10/2004 iun Concord; Reed Goewey and Julie Goewey

GOODWIN,
Sydney Clifton, b. 2/4/1921; first; Clifton J. Goodwin (farmer, Haverhill, MA) and Myrtle M. Vittum (Sandwich)

GOTS[C]HALL,
Abbott, Jr., b. 3/3/1940; first; Abbott Gotshall (storekeeper, Hyde Park, MA) and Bertha Woodworth (Digby, NS)
Diana Faith, b. 10/8/1941; second; Abbott Gotschall (store keeper, Hyde Park, MA) and Bertha L. Woodworth (Digby, NS)
Mary Anne, b. 8/25/1943 in Laconia; third; Abbott Gotshall (store owner, Hyde Park, MA) and Bertha L. Woodworth (Digby, NS)

GRANT,
daughter, b. 6/28/1890; first; Arlistus U. Grant (farmer, Sandwich) and Lizzie A. Bennett (Sandwich)
daughter, b. 4/2/1892; third; George A. M. Grant (millman, Sandwich) and Clara A. Heddle (Sandwich)
Lyle, b. 2/15/1913; first; Alliston Grant (laborer, Sandwich) and Sylvia Evans (Tamworth)

GRAVES,
son, b. 9/17/1907; first; Ross M. Graves (farmer, Sandwich) and Annie M. Bemis (Stow, ME)

child, b. 4/20/1911; second; Ross M. Graves (farmer, Sandwich) and Annie M. Bemis (Stowe, ME)
son, b. 6/21/1913; first; C. E. Graves (farmer, Sandwich) and Nellie E. Whiting (Tamworth)
Dorothy A., b. 2/27/1916; second; Clarence E. Graves (farmer, Sandwich) and Nellie E. Whiting (Tamworth)

GRAY,
son, b. 4/22/1896; second; Irving Gray (laborer, Plymouth, MA) and Etta M. Corliss (Sandwich)
son, b. 8/24/1900; third; Irvin Gray (farmer, Plymouth) and Etta Corliss (Sandwich)
daughter, b. 10/31/1901; fourth; Lysander B. Gray (blacksmith, Madison) and Annie E. Twombly (Madison)
daughter, b. 5/1/1906; fourth; Irving Gray (farmer, Plymouth) and Mary E. Corliss (Sandwich)
daughter, b. 3/23/1933; fourth; Richard Gray (farmer, Sandwich) and Sylvia B. Burnham (Sandwich)
Alice, b. 7/31/1923; first; Richard Gray (laborer, Sandwich) and Sylvia B. Burnham (Sandwich)
Danielle Marie, b. 7/24/1981 in Portsmouth; Mark D. Gray and Marianne Jewett
Edith, b. 7/22/1934; fifth; Richard Gray (farmer, Sandwich) and Sylvia B. Burnham (Sandwich)
Elizabeth, b. 10/29/1925; second; Richard Gray (laborer, Sandwich) and Sylvia Burnham (Sandwich)
Gracie M., b. 2/28/1895; first; Irving Gray (Plymouth) and Mary E. Corliss (Sandwich)
Helen, b. 5/23/1933; fourth; Richard Gray (laborer, Sandwich) and Sylvia B. Burnham (Sandwich)(1934)
Julia G., b. 4/22/1913; fourth; Irving H. Gray (clergyman, Strafford) and Gladys C. Pease (Gilmanton)
Marilyn, b. 9/26/1936; sixth; Richard Gray (laborer, Sandwich) and Sylvia Burnham (Sandwich)

Mary Etta, b. 5/3/1942 in Laconia; seventh; Richard Gray (laborer, 41, Sandwich) and Sylvia B. Burnham (36, Sandwich)
Richard, b. 12/4/1929; third; Richard Gray (laborer, Sandwich) and Sylvia Burnham (Sandwich)
Shawn Stephanie, b. 11/18/19563 in Laconia; second; Robert Edward Gray (saw mill manager, NH) and Elizabeth B. Micklon (NH)
William Irving, b. 6/15/1944 in Laconia; eighth; Richard Gray (carpenter, 43, Sandwich) and Sylvia B. Burnham (38, Sandwich)

GREEN,
daughter, b. 7/11/1897; fifth; Ralph E. Green (farmer, Moultonboro) and Ella L. Burrows (Sandwich)
stillborn daughter, b. 4/3/1933; fourth; Wilber J. Green (laborer, Moultonboro) and Mina E. Towle (Center Harbor); residence – Moultonboro

GREENE,
Brianna Hambrook, b. 5/2/1985 in Laconia; William Marston Greene and Susan Jean Hambrook
Carroll Cleveland, b. 11/9/1922; first; Joseph F. Greene (farmer, Newbury, VT) and Ethel M. Abbott (Sandwich)
Erin Reeves, b. 4/17/1983 in Laconia; William Marston Greene and Susan Jean Hambrook
Eveleth Whiting, b. 10/16/1978 in Laconia; William M. Greene (MA) and Susan J. Hambrook (NH)
Herbert Marston, b. 6/26/1980 in Laconia; William M. Greene and Susan J. Hambrook
Jamie Elijah, b. 6/14/1990 in North Conway; Christopher W. Greene and D. Catherine Arsenault
Lily Jayne Catherine, b. 9/7/1995 in Laconia; Eric S. Greene and Susan Marie Walsh

Ralph Leslie, b. 7/20/1927; second; Wilbur J. Greene (farmer, Sandwich) and Mina E. Towle (Center Harbor)
Trevor Travis, b. 3/23/1989 in Laconia; William Marston Greene and Susan H. Hambrook

GRINNELL,
Liam Hunter, b. 3/9/1995 in North Conway; William L. Grinnell, Jr. and Karen Jean Elliott

GUY,
son, b. 9/2/1894; first; Will Guy (brakeman, Bethlehem) and Millie M. Tibbetts (Haverhill)

HADLEY,
Elena Mae, b. 8/25/1989 in Portland, ME; Thomas L. Hadley and Michelle E. Gregoire
Leon Albert, b. 4/1/1986 in Laconia; Thomas Leland Hadley and Michelle Elaine Gregoire

HAIGHT,
Alison Mary, b. 4/26/2000 in Laconia; Randall Haight and Joanne Haight

HALEY,
daughter, b. 10/5/1890; first; Harry O. Haley (laborer, Tuftonboro) and Flora B. Tilton (Sandwich)

HALL,
daughter, b. 8/26/1948 in Laconia; seventh; Ernest Hall (laborer, Revere, MA) and Dorothy M. Foss (Lynn, MA)
Dorothy Adaline, b. 8/17/1943 in Sandwich; fourth; Ernest F. Hall (chauf.-mech., Revere, MA) and Dorothy M. Foss (Lynn, MA)
Lillian Joan, b. 8/13/1947 in Laconia; sixth; Ernest F. Hall (laborer, Revere, MA) and Dorothy M. Foss (Lynn, MA)

HAMBROOK,

Abigail F., b. 3/4/1966 in Laconia; eighth; Francis Hambrook (forester-surveyor, Albany, NY) and Mary F. Reeves (Tokyo, Japan)

James Matthew, b. 2/8/1961 in Laconia; seventh; Francis G. Hambrook (forester, NH) and Mary F. Reeves (Japan)

Kate Elizabeth, b. 4/29/1998 in Laconia; James M. Hambrook and Cynthia Jane Graham

Mary Ann, b. 5/21/1953 in Laconia; second; Francis Gerald Hambrook (forester consultant, NY) and Mary Frances Reeves (Japan)

Michael Harry, b. 4/6/1959 in Laconia; sixth; Francis G. Hambrook (forester, NY) and Mary F. Reeves (Japan)

Patricia Louise, b. 6/14/1956 in Laconia; fourth; Francis G. Hambrook (consultant, NY) and Mary F. Reeves (Japan)

Ryan James, b. 7/14/1996 in Laconia; James Matthew Hambrook and Cynthia Jane Graham

Sheila Bridget, b. 3/7/1958 in Laconia; fifth; Francis G. Hambrook (forestry consultant, NY) and Mary Frances Reeves (Japan)

HAMILTON,

Edward George, b. 1/14/1945 in Laconia; first; Edward G. Hamilton (US Navy, Laconia) and Ruth M. Evins (Leominster, MA)

Rachel Rebecca, b. 1/5/1979 in Laconia; David P. Hamilton (NJ) and Ellen L. Long (MD)

HANSEN,

stillborn daughter, b. 2/6/1912; first; Charles G. Hansen (painter, Sandwich) and Susan H. Foss (Holyoke, MA)

HANSON,
son, b. 10/23/1892; second; Frank L. Hanson (laborer, Sandwich) and Ida M. Priest (Nariganset Pier)
daughter, b. 3/17/1893; first; William H. Hanson (laborer, Sandwich) and Minnie Whedon (Sangate, VT)
son, b. 1/11/1896; third; Frank L. Hanson (vet. surgeon, Sandwich) and Ida M. Priest (Peacedale, RI)
daughter, b. 1/13/1899; fourth; Frank L. Hanson (v. surgeon, Sandwich) and Ida M. Priest (Peacedale, RI)
son, b. 10/21/1901; fifth; Frank L. Hanson (laborer, Sandwich) and Ida M. Priest (Peacedale, RI)
son, b. 12/22/1905; sixth; Frank L. Hanson (laborer, Sandwich) and Ida M. Priest (Peace Dale, RI)
Charles, b. 8/23/1891; first; Frank L. Hanson (vet. dentist, Sandwich) and Ida M. Priest (RI)
Charles Lee, b. 9/14/1914; first; Charles G. Hanson (laborer, Sandwich) and Hazel S. Foss (Holyoke, MA)

HARDING,
Joshua, b. 10/25/1979 in Worcester, MA; Edward Harding (CT) and Laura J. Larkin (MA)

HARRIMAN,
daughter, b. 11/30/1898; first; Hiram Harriman (farmer, Albany) and Charlotte Conn (NB)

HART,
Burleigh S., b. 10/22/1905; first; Elmer B. Hart (insurance agt., Sandwich) and Ethel A. Burleigh (Sandwich)
Carry Anna, b. 1/30/1974 in Wolfeboro; Peter D. Hart (NH) and Elizabeth O. Compton (MO)
Harrison A., b. 4/5/1894; first; Elmer B. Hart (clerk, Sandwich) and Nellie A. Atwood (Sandwich)
Isaiah Peter, b. 4/12/1977 in Sandwich; Peter D. Hart (NH) and Elizabeth O. Compton (MO)

Mary, b. 8/8/1889; Harrison N. Hart (physician, Sandwich) and L S. Severance (Boston, MA)

HATCH,
son, b. 2/3/1893; third; Eugene R. Hatch (shoemaker) and Nellie M. Hatch (Antrim)

HAWES,
Ada Frances, b. 10/25/1915; second; Casper C. Hawes (laborer, Springfield, MA) and Ada B. Vittum (Sandwich)
Dora, b. 11/10/1913; first; Caspar S. Hawes (farmer, Springfield, MA) and Ada B. Vittum (Sandwich)
Virginia Vittum, b. 8/24/1918; third; Casper M. Hawes (farmer, Springfield, MA) and Ada B. Vittum (Sandwich)

HAYNES,
Norbert W., b. 6/22/1923; first; George W. Haynes (laborer, Alexandria) and Pernie Whitehouse (Moultonboro); residence – Bristol

HEARD,
Emily J., b. 1/20/1914; second; William Heard (merchant, Sandwich) and Lillian P. Thompson (Worcester, MA)
Gordon, b. 5/16/1908; first; Howard B. Heard (farmer, Sandwich) and Georgia Tasker (Bartlett)
Pauline Page, b. 9/30/1937; first; Stuart W. Heard (postmaster, Malden, MA) and Lillian L. Dow (Laconia)
Rowan Gabriel, b. 1/23/1998 in Laconia; Paul A. Israelson and Patricia Dorothy Heard
Wendy Thompson, b. 11/12/1940; second; Stuart W. Heard (postmaster, Medford, MA) and Lilliam Dow (Laconia)
William A., 2nd, b. 9/2/1896; first; William Heard (farmer, Sandwich) and Mary A. Kellough (Halifax, NS)

HEATH,
son, b. 27/1887; tenth; Benjamin H. Heath (laborer, Sandwich) and Lydia A. Moulton (Holderness)
daughter, b. 8/9/1892; first; Albert Heath (laborer, Sandwich) and Eda Lucas (Montpelier, VT)
Fred J., b. 1/2/1895; second; Thomas E. Heath (Sandwich) and Edith A. Lucks (Montpelier, VT)

HENLE,
Frederick Valentine, b. 8/28/1970 in Laconia; James M. Henle (Philippines) and Portia Casambre (Washington, DC)

HEWITT,
Carroll Tilton, b. 12/20/1923; second; Arthur Hewitt (carpenter, Jamaica Plain, MA) and Edith M. Haley (Sandwich)
Linwood Arthur, b. 7/5/1922; first; Arthur Hewitt (carpenter, Jamaica Plain) and Edith M. Haley (Sandwich)

HILL,
daughter, b. 12/1/1901; first; Walter F. Hill (laborer, N. Brookfield, MA) and Florence E. Peck (Merimac, WI)
child, b. 9/10/1908; second; Walter F. Hill (farmer, N. Brookfield) and Florence E. Peck (Merrimack, WI)
Sandra Fay, b. 3/5/1945 in Laconia; fourth; Guy L. Avery (logging, Groton) and Susie M. Elliott (Whiteface)

HIRD,
Aislinn Sophia, b. 6/27/2003 in Laconia; Stephen Hird and Julia Hird
Ronan Stephen, b. 10/13/2005 in Laconia; Stephen Hird and Julia Hird

HOAG,
son, b. 11/3/1901; second; Albert B. Hoag (physician, Sandwich) and Abbie F. Peaslee (Sandwich)

daughter, b. 10/7/1905; third; Albert B. Hoag (physician, Sandwich) and Abbie F. Peaslee (Sandwich)
Erin Elizabeth, b. 7/30/1983 in Laconia; Peter Coffin Hoag and Gloria Jean Eldridge
Isabella Grace, b. 2/23/2000 in North Conway; Jonathan Billings and Johanna Hoag
Johanna, b. 8/20/1975 in Laconia; Roland B. Hoag, Jr. (MA) and Susan A. Chappell (NH)
Peter Coffin, b. 12/2/1954 in Laconia; third; Roland Boyden Hoag (lawyer, MA) and Barbara Simonds (MA)
Peter Coffin, Jr., b. 11/29/1979 in Laconia; Peter C. Hoag (NH) and Gloria J. Eldridge (NH)
Phoebe Adele, b. 4/7/2002 in North Conway; Roland Hoag and Heather Phelps
Roland Boyden, b. 5/20/2005 in North Conway; Roland Hoag III and Heather Phelps

HOAG-BILLINGS,
Fiona Fern, b. 12/2/2002 in North Conway; Jonathan Billings and Johanna Hoag

HODGDON,
son, b. 9/14/1889; eighth; Cyrus Hodgdon (farmer, Yorkshire, England) and Annie E. Snow (Thornton)

HODGE,
daughter, b. 8/8/1901; first; Norman F. Hodge (carpenter, Sandwich) and Effie M. Abbott (Holderness)
son, b. 11/5/1902; second; Norman F. Hodge (laborer, Sandwich) and Effie M. Abbott (Sandwich)

HOPE,
Charity Blanchard, b. 2/15/1970 in Plymouth; Dr. Peter P. Hope (England) and Janet Starr Best (NY)

Mary Starr, b. 8/21/1976 in Laconia; Peter B. Hope (NY) and Janet Starr Best (England)
Stephen Albert, b. 11/21/1971 in Laconia; Peter B. Hope (NY) and Janet S. Best (England)

HOUSTON,
Everett M., Jr., b. 3/29/1943 in Wolfeboro; second; Everett M. Houston (laborer, Barre, VT) and Elizabeth H. Doe (Wolfeboro)
James Jay, b. 5/2/1949 in Wolfeboro; fourth; Everett M. Houston (painter, Barre, VT) and Elizabeth H. Doe (Wolfeboro)
Jane, b. 12/14/1946 in Wolfeboro; third; Everett M. Houston (woodcraft, Barre, VT) and Elizabeth H. Doe (Wolfeboro)

HOWARD,
Susan, b. 7/7/1942 in Plymouth; first; Judson D. Howard (minister, 26, Kansas City, MO) and Esther Currier (25, Colebrook)

HOYT,
daughter, b. 5/1/1889; third; George S. Hoyt (farmer, Sandwich) and Lydia C. Wentworth (Sandwich)

HULL,
daughter, b. 9/30/1897; first; Charles E. Hull (laborer, E. Boston, MA) and Florence N. Green (Belmont)

HURD,
William Aaron, b. 11/10/1924; first; William A. Hurd (laborer, Freedom) and Hazel A. Davey (Sandwich)
William Aaron, V, b. 10/22/1944 in Laconia; first; William A. Hurd IV (US Army, 19, Sandwich) and Phyllis L. Johnson (18, Perryman, MD)

HUTCHINS,

stillborn daughter, b. 7/8/1917; first; Earl U. Hutchins (laborer, Thornton) and Florence M. Wallace (Lakeport)

Daniel Edward, b. 8/1/1984 in Laconia; Oris Edward Hutchins and Holly Joanne Blackstone

Deanna Lynn, b. 4/17/1967 in Concord; second; Edward C. Hutchins, Sr. (body man, Tamworth) and Shirley L. Lawrence (Laconia)

Donald Preston, b. 9/17/1923; fourth; Walter S. Hutchins (laborer, Tamworth) and Grace E. Roebarge (Tuftonboro)

Edward C., b. 11/5/1965 in Concord; Edward C. Hutchins (bodyman, NH) and Shirley Lawrence (NH)

Marion Kimberly, b. 7/3/1969 in Concord; Edward C. Hutchins and Shirley L. Lawrence

Nicole Lynn, b. 11/12/1970 in Concord; Edward C. Hutchins (NH) and Shirley L. Lawrence (NH)

Oris Edward, b. 9/18/1951 in Laconia; first; Edward Clarence Hutchins (lumberman, NH) and Mary Louise Boone (MA)

INGARI,

Aaron Joseph, b. 5/11/1993 in Plymouth; Joseph Charles Ingari and Rosemarie Carol de Mars

Joyce Andrea, b. 11/29/1995 in Plymouth; Joseph C. Ingari and Rosemarie C. De Mars

IRVING,

daughter, b. 4/28/1892; first; George L. Irving (farming, Sandwich) and Ludia Tibbetts (Wolfeboro)

son, b. 7/27/1894; fourth; George L. Irving (laborer, Sandwich) and Lydia Tebbetts (Wolfeboro)

daughter, b. 2/15/1897; fifth; George L. Irving (farmer, Sandwich) and L. E. Tibbetts (Rochester)

daughter, b. 5/10/1903; fourth; George L. Irving (farmer, Sandwich) and Lydia Tibbetts (Rochester)

JACKSON,

Christopher Prince, b. 12/7/1957 in Wolfeboro; first; Howard S. Jackson, Jr. (civil engineer, Boston, MA) and Frances V. Berry (Plymouth)

Donald Wilson, b. 3/8/1934; sixth; Roland Jackson (caretaker, Greenville, ME) and Euphemia MacDonald (NS)

Reiahn L., b. 6/20/1992 in North Conway; Willie L. Jackson and Sherreita R. Ashby

JENNINGS,

Samara Paula, b. 1/4/1982 in Sandwich; Paul B. Jennings and Cynthia M. Boewe

JEWETT,

Richard Garland, b. 12/25/1914; first; George M. Jewett, Jr. (shipping clerk, Wilmot) and Grace E. Garland (Center Harbor); residence – Franklin

JOHNSON,

daughter, b. 5/30/1915; second; Edwin E. Johnson (farmer, NY) and Sylvia R. Elliott (Sandwich); residence – Tamworth

Hunter Tell, b. 3/5/1997 in North Conway; Russell S. Johnson and Leslie J. Hughes

Jacob Spencer, b. 3/8/1993 in North Conway; Russell Spencer Johnston and Leslie Hughes

Jeremiah H., b. 5/2/1991 in North Conway; Russel S. Johnson and Leslie Hughes

Katherine Louise, b. 1/27/1949 in Laconia; first; Albert Leighton Johnson (lineman, ME) and Hazel E. Taylor (Sandwich)

Zachary James, b. 3/8/1993 in North Conway; Russell Spencer Johnston and Leslie Hughes

JOHNSTON,

Charles C., b. 4/6/1964 in Laconia; fourth; Richard B. Johnston (forester, NJ) and Janet I. Burnham (CT)

Charly E., b. 7/27/1991 in North Conway; Charles C. Johnston and Grace E. McLendon

Elijah Stuart, b. 10/28/2005 in North Conway; Richard Johnston and Mariann Johnston

Heather Loring, b. 3/19/1969 in Laconia; Richard B. Johnston and Janet I. Burnham

Melissa Butler, b. 9/5/1960 in Laconia; second; Richard B. Johnston (forestry consultant, NJ) and Janet I. Burnham (CT)

Richard Baker, b. 3/7/1962 in Laconia; third; Richard B. Johnston (forester, NH) and Janet I. Burnham (CT)

Sarah Burnham, b. 4/21/1958 in Laconia; first; Richard B. Johnston (forester, NJ) and Janet I. Burnham (CT)

Shirley Orissa, b. 8/11/1958 in Wolfeboro; second; Lloyd J. Johnston (gardening, Canada) and Lorraine O. McWilliams (ME)

William Ryder, b. 5/3/1995 in North Conway; Charles C. Johnston and Grace E. McLendon

JONES,

Senica J., b. 12/11/1905; first; Arthur J. Jones (carpenter, Moultonboro) and Minnie K. Tappan (Sandwich); residence – Moultonboro

JORDAN,

Victoria Rose, b. 10/24/2002 in Laconia; Peter Jordan and Billy Jean Jordan

KEITH,

Lisa Peabody, b. 3/1/1957 in Laconia; third; Rowland D. H. Keith (engineer, New Haven, CT) and Margaret P. Cannon (New Haven, CT)

KENNEY,
Derek Edgar, b. 4/19/1982 in Laconia; Charles W. Kenney and Denise M. Thibault

KEYSER,
Landan Dillman, b. 7/21/2002 in Sandwich; Todd Keyser and Laura Heald-Keyser

KNOWLES,
stillborn son, b. 5/27/1903; first; Annie J. Knowles (Meredith); residence – Plymouth

KNOX,
Darrell Charles, b. 10/18/1947 in North Conway; first; Charles E. Knox (mechanic, Ossipee) and Emily E. Nickerson (Fryeburg, ME)

KOCH,
Samuel Doyle, b. 8/30/1984 in Sandwich; Eugene Barnes Koch and Deborah Lynn Chappell

KONDRATO,
stillborn son, b. 4/14/1949 in Laconia; first; Charles Kondrato (painter, Woburn, MA) and Ruby Wilson (Winchester, MA)

KYLE,
Jacob Andrew, b. 8/1/1984 in Sandwich; Michael Raymond Kyle and Lucy Sedgwick Freeman

LALLY,
Megan Katherine, b. 9/22/1989 in Laconia; Edward James Lally and Charlene Elaine Bosley
Ryan M., b. 12/5/1991 in Plymouth; Edward J. Lally and Charlene E. Bosley

LAMB,
Jasmine Opal, b. 6/29/1976 in Sandwich; Albert B. Lamb (MA) and Janina Popenoe (DC)
Roland Oliver, b. 8/31/1978 in Sandwich; Albert Lamb (MA) and Janina Popenoc (DC)
Rosamond Jane, b. 7/22/1973 in Sandwich; Albert B. Lamb (MA) and Janet Popence (DC)

LAMPREY,
Mark Edward, II, b. 5/17/1979 in Plymouth; Mark E. Lamprey (ID) and Holly J. Follansbee (NH)

LARRABEE,
Wendy Ann, b. 11/1/1963 in Laconia; second; Richard M. Larrabee (sales representative, NJ) and Carmela R. Cardinale (NY)

LAWN,
Roger Colby, b. 12/5/1947 in Laconia; first; Evan Lawn (teacher, Philadelphia, PA) and Elisabeth Caverly (York, PA)

LEACH,
son, b. 11/10/1893; first; Alice Leach (Moultonboro)
daughter, b. 9/19/1933; sixth; William A. Leach (farmer, Moultonboro) and Dorothy E. Weld (Manchester)
Alice Louise, b. 9/11/1940; eighth; William A. Leach (farmer, Concord) and Dorothy Weld (Manchester)
Arthur Tappan, b. 5/12/1925; first; William A. Leach (farmer, Concord) and Dorothy Weld (Manchester)
Bertha Mae, b. 9/19/1933; sixth; William A. Leach (farmer, Moultonboro) and Dorothy E. Weld (1934)
David Chester, b. 4/3/1939; eighth; William Leach (farmer, Concord) and Dorothy Weld (Manchester)
Earle Stanley, b. 6/28/1931; fourth; William A. Leach (farmer, Concord) and Dorothy E. Weld (Manchester)

Ernest William, b. 6/28/1931; fifth; William A. Leach (farmer, Concord) and Dorothy E. Weld (Manchester)
Jean Frances, b. 2/28/1927; second; William A. Leach (farmer, Concord) and Dorothy E. Weld (Manchester)
John Sheldon, b. 9/3/1951 in Laconia; first; Arthur Tappan Leach (woodsman, NH) and Caroline Forristall (MA)
Julia Marion, b. 8/6/1944 in Sandwich; eleventh; William A. Leach (farmer, 44, Concord) and Dorothy E. Weld (35, Manchester)
Mary Anne, b. 10/19/1942 in Sandwich; tenth; William A. Leach (farmer, 42, Concord) and Dorothy Weld (33, Manchester)
Raymond Chester, b. 7/31/1936; seventh; William Leach (laborer, Concord) and Dorothy Weld (Manchester)
Ruth Ethel, b. 8/9/1929; third; William Leach (farmer, Concord) and Dorothy Weld (Manchester)
Sally Jean, b. 4/9/1953 in Laconia; second; Arthur Tappen Leach (forestry service, NH) and Caroline Forristall (MA)
Wendy Elaine, b. 4/2/1962 in Laconia; second; David C. Leach (laborer, NH) and Nancy A. Freeto (NH)

LEAR,
Andrea Susan, b. 7/21/1957 in Wolfeboro; second; Peter C. S. Lear (teacher, Berkeley, CA) and Shirley J. Brown (Batavia, NY)
Benjamin Hastings, b. 2/11/1968 in Plymouth; Peter C. Lear and Shirley J. Brown
Christina Louise, b. 4/22/1962 in Plymouth; third; Peter C. Lear (silversmith, CA) and Shirley J. Brown (NY)
Rebecca Amy, b. 5/22/1954 in Laconia; first; Peter Conrad Lear (metal smith, CA) and Shirley Jean Brown (NY)

LEE,
stillborn daughter, b. 11/15/1889; first; Bert Lee (laborer) and Mabel Eaton

LEHMANN,
Anna Mary Sanborn, b. 12/10/1981 in Sandwich; William H. C. Lehmann and Carol A. Anderson
Elizabeth Lawrence, b. 8/23/1989 in Laconia; William Hugh Campbell Lehmann and Linda Kunhardt
Thomas W., b. 8/11/1991 in Plymouth; William Lehmann, Jr. and Linda L. Kunhardt

LEIGHTON,
Theresa Ann, b. 7/10/1968 in Laconia; Charles L. Leighton and Sally A. Covey

LESTER,
Karl Maxwell, b. 6/23/1946 in Laconia; second; Eugene M. Lester (student, Springfield, ME) and Suzanne Rowell (Algiers, Algeria)

LEVESQUE,
Michelle Denise, b. 9/13/1971 in North Conway; Glenn L. Levesque (MA) and Suzanne C. Parkhill (NY)

LEWIS,
Mary Alice, b. 7/2/1924; third; Arthur H. Lewis (roofer, Stoneham, MA) and Philomene LeBlanc (E. Pepperell, MA)

LITTLE,
Jay Alton, b. 10/8/1959 in Laconia; third; Clayton A. Little (driver salesman, NH) and Joan Beach (NH)
Suzanne, b. 3/21/1964 in Laconia; fourth; Clayton A. Little (R.H. Smith Corp., NH) and Joan Beach (NH)

LITTLEFIELD,
Melvin Orace, b. 10/29/1938; first; Orace R. Littlefield (laborer, Brownfield, ME) and Beatrice M. Johnson (Tamworth)

Paul Alton, Jr., b. 9/3/1959 in Wolfeboro; second; Paul A. Littlefield (laborer, ME) and Marjorie Cook (NH)

LIVEY,

Malcomb Keith, b. 5/15/1930; third; Edward F. Livey (laborer, Everett, MA) and Lilla M. Mudgett (Sandwich)

MACCORMACK,

Frances Irene, b. 8/31/1945 in Laconia; stillborn; second; George C. MacCormack (laborer, Campton) and Frances M. Wallace (Sandwich)

Isabelle Mae, b. 10/14/1943 in Laconia; first; George C. MacCormack (laborer, Campton) and Frances M. Wallace (Sandwich)

MACDONALD,

Alfred Wayne Morris, b. 2/13/1940; sixth; Ernest E. MacDonald (laborer, Union) and Ethel B. Diack (Quincy, MA)

Clyde Malcolm, b. 5/22/1944 in Laconia; eighth; Ernest E. MacDonald (US Army, 37, Union) and Ethel B. Diack (36, Quincy, MA)

Donald Mark, b. 12/30/1955 in Plymouth; seventh; Alan Perley MacDonald (marine mechanic, NH) and Arline Esther Kimball (ME)

Janet Carrol, b. 2/16/1938; fifth; Ernest E. MacDonald (laborer, Union) and Ethel B. Diack (Quincy, MA)

Patricia Jean, b. 4/26/1935; third; Ernest E. MacDonald (laborer, Union) and Ethel B. Diack (Quincy, MA)

Rose Marie, b. 1/19/1942 in Laconia; seventh; Ernest E. MacDonald (laborer, 34, Union) and Ethel B. Diack (34, Quincy, MA)

Yvonne Ann, b. 1/17/1937; fourth; Ernest MacDonald (laborer, Union) and Ethel Diack (Quincy, MA)

MACK,

stillborn daughter, b. 7/5/1889; first; Herbert G. Mack (farmer, Sandwich) and Clara N. Hines (Sandwich)

son, b. 2/5/1890; first; Fred M. Mack (laborer, Tamworth) and Nellie E. Abbott (Ashland)

son, b. 1/22/1891; second; Herbert G. Mack (laborer, Tamworth) and Clara W. Hinds (Sandwich)

son, b. 2/1/1899; third; Fred M. Mack (farmer, Tamworth) and Nellie E. Abbott (Ashland)

Frank P., Jr., b. 1/22/1888; second; Frank P. Mack (farmer, Sandwich) and Lydia E. Tibbetts (Rochester)

Lester Manville, b. 7/15/1918; first; Ernest M. Mack (laborer, Sandwich) and Beryl M. Kell (Pittsfield)

MACKENZIE,

Roena Catharine, b. 8/8/1922; second; Neil A. MacKenzie (laborer, Medford, MA) and Ada R. Drew (Dover)

MAGUIRE,

Debra Raye, b. 8/4/1957 in Wolfeboro; second; Edward J. Maguire (carpenter, Meredith) and Rita M. Young (Pittsfield, VT)

MAILAND,

Ronald Dillon, b. 4/2/1996 in Lebanon; Ronald John Mailand and Mary Sells Robinson

Samuel Forrest, b. 6/8/1994 in Lebanon; Ronald John Mailand and Mary Sells Robinson

MARCHAND-CORREIA,

Gavin Graham, b. 2/11/2007 in North Conway; George Correia and Valerie Ann Marchand

MARDEN,
Francis A., b. 9/14/1908; second; James F. Marden (farmer, Melrose, MA) and Alice M. Tappan (Sandwich)

MARGESON,
Jennifer, b. 3/14/1973 in Wolfeboro; Richard C. Margeson (PA) and Lois A. Broderick (NJ)

MARSHALL,
Alexander Samson, b. 12/2/2004 in Sandwich; Crofton Marshall and Andrea Marshall
Augustus Freedom, b. 9/18/2007 in Sandwich; Crofton Marshall and Andrea Marshall
Crofton Sankey, b. 7/5/1972 in Laconia; Derek C. Marshall (England) and Linda M. Whitworth (CT)

MARSTON,
daughter. b. 2/11/1890; first; James L. Marston (mechanic, Sandwich) and Grace Stanton (Lewiston, ME)
Ellen L., b. 11/26/1903; second; James L. Marston (farmer, Sandwich) and Grace Stanton (Lewiston, ME)
John S., b. 6/9/1907; third; James L. Marston (basket mfr., Sandwich) and Grace Stanton (Lewistin, ME)
Margaret, b. 6/16/1901; first; Charles S. Marston (farmer, Sandwich) and Hannah Knowlton (Tamworth)

MARTEL[L][E],
Donald, b. 3/26/1938; fourth; Elziar J. Martelle (farmer, St. Monique, Canada) and Beatrice M. Palmer (Sandwich)
Forest E., b. 6/1/1916; first; Elziar Martell (laborer, Canada) and Beatrice M. Palmer (Sandwich)
Haven Clyde, b. 3/1/1941; fifth; Elzear J. Martel (farmer, St. Monique, Canada) and Beatrice M. Palmer (Sandwich)
James R., b. 10/26/1964 in Laconia; first; Raymond J. Martel (poultry business, NH) and Arline G. Pelchat (NH)

Linda Lee, b. 11/21/1963 in Laconia; second; Haven C. Martel (carpenter, NH) and Jo-Ann V. Daigneau (NH)
Menta Maureen, b. 12/11/1949 in Laconia; first; Forest E. Martel (poultry farm proprietor, NH) and Alberta E. Robinson (NH)
Morton C., b. 7/21/1928; third; Edgar J. Martell (farmer, Canada) and Beatrice J. Palmer (Sandwich)
Randall Scott, b. 1/14/1962 in Laconia; first; Haven C. Martel (carpenter, NH) and Jo-Ann V. Martel (NH)
Raymond, b. 10/4/1922; second; Elzear Martell (laborer, Quebec) and Beatrice M. Palmer (Sandwich)
Richard, b. 5/17/1965 in Laconia; third; Haven C. Martel (carpenter, NH) and Jo-Ann Daigneau (NH)

MARTIN,
son, b. 8/10/1892; first; "S. Davis, she says" (Moultonboro) and Bessie J. Martin (Sandwich)
son, b. 8/25/1941; second; Wilbur E. Martin (laborer, Sandwich) and Dora E. Peaslee (Sandwich)
stillborn daughter, b. 1/7/1943 in Laconia; third; Wilbur E. Martin (farmer, Sandwich) and Dora E. Peaslee (Sandwich)
Esther Louise, b. 12/21/1918; second; Eugene F. Martin (farmer, Sandwich) and Sarah H. Bundy (Sandwich)
Hunter Hawkins, b. 4/7/2000 in Laconia; John Martin and Michelle Martin
John, b. 4/8/1914; fifth; James F. Martin (farmer, Melrose, MA) and Mary A. Tappan (Sandwich)
John Ethan, b. 4/7/2003 in Laconia; John Martin and Michelle Martin
Julia, b. 3/14/1912; fourth; James F. Martin (farmer, Melrose, MA) and Alice M. Tappan (Sandwich)
Julia G., b. 11/4/1910; third; James F. Martin (farmer, Melrose, MA) and Alice M. Tappan (Sandwich)
Mary, b. 12/13/1915; sixth; James F. Martin (farmer, Melrose, MA) and Mary A. Tappan (Sandwich)

Rita Ann, b. 12/14/1938; first; Wilbur E. Martin (laborer, Sandwich) and Dora E. Peaslee (Sandwich)
Wilbur E., b. 6/6/1913; first; Eugene F. Martin (farmer, Sandwich) and Sadie E. Skinner (Moultonboro)

MASON,
Barbara Marie, b. 6/20/1919; first; Arthur H. Mason (laborer, Tamworth) and Blanche M. Ames (Tamworth)
Coleman Avery, b. 6/5/1999 in Laconia; Philip Mason and Amy Mason
Molly Madeline, b. 10/21/2002 in Laconia; Philip Mason and Amy Mason

MATTHEWS,
Genevieve Ellen, b. 5/27/1938; fifth; Clifford R. Matthews (woodworker, Craftsbury, VT) and Marjorie T. Bartley (S. Reading, VT)

MAUCH,
Joshua Jonathan, b. 9/1/1985 in Sandwich; Daniel John Mauch and Janina Popenoe
Matthew E., b. 6/13/1965 in Laconia; fourth; Raymond H. Mauch (self-employed, NH) and Frances Traum (NJ)

McCORMACK,
stillborn son, b. 5/18/1951 in Laconia; third; George C. McCormack (laborer, NH) and Frances Marion Wallace (NH)
George Edwin, b. 10/7/1935; first; George C. McCormack (laborer, Campton) and Frances Wallace (Sandwich)
Gregory Alan, b. 8/5/1964 in Laconia; first; George E. McCormack (carpenter, NH) and Linda Taylor (NH)
Marion Violet, b. 1/14/1955 in Laconia; third; George C. McCormack (lumberman, NH) and Frances Mary Wallace (NH)

Tina Mae, b. 4/5/1966 in Laconia; second; George E. McCormack (carpenter, Sandwich) and Linda Taylor (Laconia)

McCRILLIS,
daughter, b. 9/30/1887; first; Alonzo McCrillis (farmer, Sandwich) and Lulu Clark (Sandwich)
daughter, b. 5/6/1889; second; Alonzo McCrillis (farmer, Sandwich) and Lulie M. Clark (Sandwich)
son, b. 10/28/1890; third; Alonzo McCrillis (farmer, Sandwich) and Lulie M. Clark (Sandwich)
daughter, b. 12/8/1900; fourth; Alonzo McCrillis (farmer, Sandwich) and Lulu M. Clark (Sandwich)
daughter, b. 9/12/1918; first; Neal McCrillis (farmer, Sandwich) and Marion Bullard (Arlington, MA)

McDONALD,
Ernest Ellsworth, Jr., b. 9/6/1933; second; Ernest Ellsworth McDonald (laborer, Union) and Ethel Diack (Quincy, MA)

McFADDEN,
Branten W., b. 10/27/1997 in Claremont; Corey B. McFadden and Karen S. Riemer

McKENNA,
Michael James, b. 12/17/1986 in Laconia; James Thomas McKenna and Virginia Marie Daigle

McNAMARA,
Mackenzie S., b. 4/17/1991 in Plymouth; Stephen J. McNamara and Emily J. Dorais

MELLOTT,
Eliana Adelle, b. 6/14/1999 in Laconia; Harold Mellott and Amy Mellott

MERRIFIELD,

Beulah Pearl, b. 4/8/1922; first; Norman Merrifield (chauffeur, Porterfield, ME) and Doris L. Gault (Sandwich)

MERRIMAN,

Ashley Elizabeth, b. 10/5/1976 in Laconia; Roger B. Merriman III (MA) and Ediberth Farrington (OH)
Hannah Smith, b. 12/11/1979 in Concord; Thomas E. Merriman (NH) and Pamela J. Power (MA)
Jacob Owen, b. 11/5/1983 in Concord; Thomas Edward Merriman and Pamela Jane Power
Slader Randles, b. 10/5/1976 in Laconia; Roger B. Merriman III (MA) and Ediberth Farrington (OH)

METCALF,

Anne, b. 5/22/1950 in Laconia; first; Winslow Harris Metcalf (restaurant operator, RI) and Nancy Lovrien Lear (CA)
William Harris, b. 2/12/1953 in Laconia; second; Winslow Harris Metcalf (garage mech., RI) and Nancy L. Lear (CA)

MICHAEL,

Alex Townsend, b. 3/27/1962 in Laconia; fifth; Monroe Michael (clerk, NY) and Bernice R. Adams (NH)
Anthony Adams, b. 3/31/1949 in Laconia; second; Monroe Michael (express businessman, NY) and Bernice R. Adams (NH)
Kevin, b. 12/12/1953 in Laconia; fourth; Monroe Michael (express business, NY) and Bernice R. Adams (NH)
Robert d'Este, b. 11/21/1955 in Laconia; second; Phillip Michael (teacher, NY) and Mary d'Este (NJ)
Sandra, b. 3/9/1951 in Laconia; first; Philip Michael (student, NY) and Mary Locke d'Este (NJ)
Timothy, b. 8/11/1951 in Laconia; third; Monroe Michael (express trucker, NY) and Bernice Rachel Adams (NH)

MICHALSKI,
Angela Rose, b. 8/8/1993 in Laconia; Paul Vincent Michalski and Susan Marion Welch

MIKELINICH,
Sophia Annabelle, b. 11/9/2005 in Portsmouth; Kenneth Mikelinich and Lina Mikelinich

MILBURY,
Trevor Cook, b. 8/28/1989 in Laconia; William Forest Milbury and Holly Berry Cook

MINER,
Timothy Alan, b. 2/11/1952 in Laconia; fourth; Robert Francis Miner (craftsman, PA) and Louisa Post Sutton (NJ)

MINICHIELLO,
Marie T., b. 10/29/1966 in Laconia; first; Ralph J. Minichiello (teacher, Salem, MA) and Patricia A. Vlasuk (Peabody, MA)
Michele Ann, b. 12/29/1968 in Laconia; Ralph J. Minichiello and Patricia A. Vlasuk

MISAVAGE,
Eben, b. 9/1/2004 in North Conway; Christopher Misavage and Nancy Fredrickson
Elijah, b. 10/25/2001 in North Conway; Christopher Misavage and Nancy Fredrickson

MITCHELL,
Rebecca Margaret, b. 5/25/1974 in Wolfeboro; John C. Mitchell (ME) and Patricia A. Ruel (NH)

MOHAN,

Patrick Joseph, b. 6/5/2002 in Laconia; Patrick Mohan and Kimberlie Mohan

MOODY,

Raymond Elmer, b. 5/5/1922; first; Elmer P. Moody (laborer, Albany) and Margaret R. McBride (Boston, MA)

MOORE,

Abigail Winchester, b. 4/29/1985 in Hanover; Courtenay Wadsworth Moore and Ann Marie Winchester

MOORHOUSE,

Lewis Alfred, b. 10/17/1943 in Temple, TX; first; Alfred B. Moorhouse (Capt., USA, Brookline, MA) and Kathryn E. Pollok (Temple, TX)

MORSE,

child, b. 12/1/1910; fourth; Mearl V. Morse (laborer, Auburn) and Susie Barry (Barrington)

Elizabeth Grace, b. 2/6/2000 in Concord; Eric Morse and Amy Morse

William Archer, b. 5/26/2003 in Concord; Eric Morse and Amy Morse

MORTON,

Tammy Lee, b. 9/11/1973 in Wolfeboro; Daniel J. Morton (MA) and Carol A. Butler (MA)

Thomas Ansel, b. 1/31/1974 in Wolfeboro; Lee Sherwood Morton (CT) and Jane W. Givens (TX)

MOULTON,

daughter, b. 1/16/1888; first; Hebert E. Moulton (farmer, Albany) and Julia A. Tilton (Sandwich)

son, b. 10/6/1888; second; Cyrus A. Moulton (carpenter, Moultonborough) and Lizzie B. (Sandwich)
son, b. 5/26/1900; first; Edgar C. Moulton (farmer, Newark, VT) and Myrtie M. Brown (N. Conway)
Hiram M., b. 7/20/1915; second; Edgar C. Moulton (farmer, Newark, VT) and Myrtie M. Brown (N. Conway)
Irene Ruth, b. 10/8/1934; third; Joseph B. Moulton (farmer, Sandwich) and Ruth M. Hodge (Sandwich)
Norman Edgar, b. 12/5/1919; first; Joseph B. Moulton (laborer, Sandwich) and Ruth M. Hodge (Sandwich)
Pauline, b. 5/5/1907; first; Arthur P. Moulton (clerk, Sandwich) and Maude Smith (Sandwich)
Royce S., b. 12/9/1925; first; Charles W. Moulton (laborer, Moultonboro) and Leila Cram (Sandwich); residence – Moultonboro

MUDGETT,
son, b. 4/26/1887; first; Elisha Mudgett (farmer, Sandwich) and Luella Atkins (Sandwich)
daughter, b. 7/29/1887; Erastus W. Mudgett (laborer)
son, b. 11/23/1888; second; Elisha Mudgett (farmer, Sandwich) and Luella Atkins (Sandwich)
daughter, b. 12/29/1889; first; Fred N. Mudgett (farmer, Sandwich) and Ora A. Fogg (Sandwich)
daughter, b. 7/14/1894; second; Fred W. Mudgett (laborer, Sandwich) and Ora A. Fogg (Sandwich)
daughter, b. 7/30/1896; third; F. W. Mudgett (farmer, Sandwich) and Ora A. Fogg (Sandwich)
son, b. 8/4/1902; fourth; Fred W. Mudgett (farmer, Sandwich) and Ora A. Fogg (Sandwich)
son, b. 11/14/1905; second; Eugene C. Mudgett (farmer, Sandwich) and Eva M. Davis (Sandwich)
daughter, b. 9/15/1906; fifth; Fred W. Mudgett (farmer, Sandwich) and Ora A. Fogg (Sandwich)

son, b. 11/--/1909; sixth; Fred W. Mudgett (farmer, Sandwich) and Ora A. Fog (Sandwich)

child, b. 3/10/1911; fourth; Eugene E. Mudgett (farmer, Sandwich) and Eva Davis (Sandwich)

son, b. 2/16/1913; third; Jesse A. Mudgett (farmer, Sandwich) and Jennie E. Sturgis (Albany)

son, b. 6/13/1913; fifth; E. E. Mudgett (farmer, Sandwich) and Eva M. Davis (Sandwich)

daughter, b. 2/10/1916; sixth; Eugene E. Mudgett (farmer, Sandwich) and Eva M. Davis (Sandwich)

stillborn daughter, b. 7/2/1923; tenth; Jesse A. Mudgett (farmer, Sandwich) and Jennie E. Sturgis (Albany)

Adella J., b. 7/2/1923; ninth; Jesse A. Mudgett (farmer, Sandwich) and Jennie E. Sturgis (Albany)

Alan Jay, b. 6/15/1961 in Wolfeboro; sixth; James R. Mudgett (NE T&T Co., NH) and Carolyn M. Conner (NH)

Alice Annie, b. 11/27/1915; fourth; Jesse A. Mudgett (farmer, Sandwich) and Jennie E. Sturges (Albany)

Bessie E., b. 8/27/1920; seventh; Jesse Mudgett (farmer, Sandwich) and Jennie E. Sturgis (Albany)

Bruce Elliott, b.9/19/1938; fourth; Fred C. Mudgett (truckman, Sandwich) and Marion Elliott (Sandwich)

Charles D., b. 12/17/1917; fifth; Jesse A. Mudgett (farmer, Sandwich) and Jennie E. Sturgess (Albany)

David Arnold, b. 8/2/1935; first; Elisha W. Mudgett (laborer, Sandwich) and Myrtle Fennell (Lynn, MA)

Dennis James, b. 9/28/1936; second; Elisha W. Mudgett (laborer, Sandwich) and Myrtle Fennell (Lynn, MA)

Donald Merton, b. 10/27/1924; seventh; Eugene E. Mudgett (farmer, Sandwich) and Eva M. Davis (Sandwich)

Elisha W., b. 2/10/1911; second; Jesse A. Mudgett (farmer, Sandwich) and Jennie E. Sturgis (Albany)

Elmer R., b. 6/16/1895; second; Charles H. Mudgett (Sandwich) and Emma M. Fogg (Sandwich)

Elnora Louise, b. 3/15/1925; twelfth; Jesse Mudgett (farmer, Sandwich) and Jennie Sturgis (Albany)
Elwood Jesse, b. 12/27/1918; sixth; Jesse A. Mudgett (farmer, Sandwich) and Jennie E. Sturgis (Albany)
Ernest M., b. 6/2/1928; eighth; Eugene E. Mudgett (farmer, Sandwich) and Eva M. Davis (Sandwich)
Francis Coffering, b. 7/10/1944 in Wolfeboro; third; Francis C. Mudgett (laborer, 31, Sandwich) and Ruth A. Shaw (26, Moultonboro)
Frank, b. 8/14/1894; third; Elisha Mudgett (farmer, Sandwich) and Leuella Atkins (Sandwich)
Gail Evelyn, b. 4/8/1941; fifth; Elisha W. Mudgett (laborer, Sandwich) and Myrtle V. Fennell (Lynn, MA)
Garry Scott, b. 12/19/1954 in Wolfeboro; fourth; James Roger Mudgett (equip. instal'r, NH) and Carolyn Mae Conner (NH)
George Elwin, b. 5/21/1928; fourteenth; Jesse A. Mudgett (laborer, Sandwich) and Jennie Sturgis (Albany)
Gloria Ruth, b. 10/10/1941; second; Francis C. Mudgett (laborer, Sandwich) and Ruth A. Shaw (Moultonboro)
Hazel Marian, b. 3/31/1926; first; Fred C. Mudgett (mechanic, Sandwich) and Marian Elliott (Sandwich)
Helen Elizabeth, b. 5/19/1927; thirteenth; Jesse Mudgett (farmer, Sandwich) and Jennie Sturgis (Albany)
James Roger, b. 7/4/1925; second; Frank L. Mudgett (farmer, Sandwich) and Annie McInnis (Roxbury, MA)
James Roger, Jr., b. 7/10/1950 in Wolfeboro; first; James Roger Mudgett (factory worker, Sandwich) and Carolyn May Conner (Ossipee)
Jayne, b. 1/1/1959 in Wolfeboro; fifth; James R. Mudgett (telephone company, NH) and Carolyn M. Conner (NH)
Joel Raymond, b. 2/16/1952 in Wolfeboro; second; James Roger Mudgett (New England Tel. & Tel., NH) and Carolyn May Conner (NH)

Katherine Louise, b. 4/19/1947 in Laconia; fifth; Fred C. Mudgett (laborer, Ctr. Sandwich) and Marion L. Elliott (Whiteface)

Keith Albert, b. 10/22/1937; third; Elisha Mudgett (laborer, Sandwich) and Myrtle Fennell (Lynn, MA)

Lewis Fred, b. 4/14/1928; second; Fred C. Mudgett (laborer, Sandwich) and Marion L. Elliott (Sandwich)

Lilla M., b. 6/16/1908; third; Eugene E. Mudgett (farmer, Sandwich) and Eva M. Davis (Sandwich)

Linwood C., b. 9/16/1930; third; Fred C. Mudgett (truck driver, Sandwich) and Marion L. Elliott (Sandwich)

Marilyn Jean, b. 3/15/1934; first; Ronald E. Mudgett (farmer, Sandwich) and Thelma M. Waters (Dorchester, MA)

Marjorie Joy, b. 9/1/1953 in Laconia; fourth; Robert Eugene Mudgett (plumber, NH) and Thelma Mae Walters (MA)

Mark Haven, b. 10/10/1953 in Laconia; third; James Roger Mudgett (NE T&T, NH) and Carolyn Mae Conner (NH)

Patricia Florence, b. 7/3/1938; first; Francis C. Mudgett (laborer, Sandwich) and Ruth A. Shaw (Moultonboro)

Robert Henry, b. 4/15/1917; first; Frank L. Mudgett (farmer, Sandwich) and Annie McInnis (Boston, MA)

Stephen James, b. 4/29/1941; first; Roger Girard (laborer) and Adella J. Mudgett (Sandwich)

Sybil S., b. 5/5/1903; first; Eugene E. Mudgett (farmer, Sandwich) and Eva M. Davis (Sandwich)

Viola Edna, b. 1/9/1909; first; Jesse A. Mudgett (farmer, Sandwich) and Jenie E. Sturgess (Albany)

Wayne Marvin, b. 6/15/1939; fourth; Elisha Mudgett (laborer, Sandwich) and Myrtle Fennel (Lynn, MA)

William Ellis, b. 5/5/1922; eighth; Jesse A. Mudgett (farmer, Sandwich) and Jennie E. Sturgis (Albany)

NASON,

Amanda Lynn, b. 5/5/1986 in Laconia; Scott Farnsworth Nason and Heidi Lynn Cook

Benjamin Scott, b. 9/18/1987 in Laconia; Scott Farnsworth Nason and Heidi Lynn Cook

NEDEAU,

Alaina Josephine, b. 3/29/2004 in Laconia; David Nedeau and Birgit Johnson-Nedeau

Rebecca Sylvia, b. 4/15/2002 in Laconia; David Nedeau and Birgit Johnson-Nedeau

NELSON,

Carol Jeanne, b. 4/4/1949 in Laconia; first; Kenneth W. Nelson (lathe operator, Quincy, MA) and Frances A. Spalding (Concord)

Charles Henry, b. 7/17/1919; fifth; Thomas Nelson (laborer, Norway) and Henrietta Brown (Quincy, MA)

Charlotte Hope, b. 4/5/1927; sixth; Thomas Nelson (farmer, Norway) and Henrietta Brown (Quincy, MA)

Connor Wagner, b. 9/24/1999 in Laconia; Robert Nelson and Kathryn Nelson

Cynthia Marie, b. 3/2/1959 in Wolfeboro; fifth; Kenneth W. Nelson (janitor, NH) and Frances A. Spaulding (NH)

Kenton Warren, b. 8/1/1921; sixth; Thomas Nelson (laborer, Norway) and Henrietta Brown (Quincy, MA)

Marjorie Lee, b. 2/17/1957 in sox; fourth; Kenneth W. Nelson (janitor, Sandwich) and Frances A. Spaulding (Concord)

Mary Louise, b. 7/10/1950 in Laconia; second; Kenneth Warren Nelson (janitor, NH) and Frances Ann Spalding (NH)

Patricia Anne, b. 7/9/1952 in Laconia; third; Kenneth Warren Nelson (janitor, NH) and Frances Anne Spaulding (NH)

NICHOLS,

daughter, b. 6/7/1887; second; William E. Nichols (farmer, Moultonborough) and Minnie S. Fogg (Shrewsbury, MA)

son, b. 4/11/1889; third; Will E. Nichols (farmer) and Emma L. Fogg (Shrewsbury, MA)

son, b. 1/22/1891; fourth; William E. Nichols (farmer, Moultonboro) and Emma S. Fogg (Shrewsbury, MA)
daughter, b. 2/8/1893; fifth; William E. Nichols (farmer, Moultonboro) and Emma S. Fogg (Shrewsbury, MA)
daughter, b. 11/30/1897; seventh; William E. Nichols (farmer, Moultonboro) and Emma S. Fogg (Shrewsbury, MA)
stillborn daughter, b. 6/25/1901; first; Celia H. Nichols (Sandwich)
Marilyn P., b. 12/29/1924; second; Fred A. Nichols (mechanic, Boston, MA) and Lillian Bauld (Halifax, NS)
Raymond, b. 8/8/1895; sixth; William E. Nichols (Moultonboro) and Emma S. Fogg (Sandwich)

NICKERSON,
son, b. 11/2/1892; second; Jerome Nickerson (farmer, Sandwich) and Eltheria Wentzel (Sandwich)
Codie R., b. 1/24/1992 in Laconia; Murray E. Nickerson III and Rebecca J. Gray

NICOLAY,
Ariana Aurora Chloe Lirakis, b. 7/27/1986 in Ctr. Sandwich; Franz Carl Nicolay and Susan Alexander Lirakis
Sophia Solara Moon, b. 4/24/1982 in Sandwich; Franz C. Nicolay and Susan A. Lirakin

NICOLL,
Cathy Ann, b. 6/16/1971 in Laconia; Francis B. Nicoll (MA) and June A. Hodge (Canada)

NIXON,
Dean William, b. 9/22/1948 in Laconia; second; William D. Nixon (machine operator, Plymouth, MA) and Bertha L. Marshall (Boston, MA)
Edith Carline, b. 8/20/1953 in Laconia; fourth; William Door Nixon (lumberman, MA) and Bertha Laurie Marshall (MA)

Florence Evelyn, b. 9/27/1951 in Laconia; third; William Dorr Nixon (lumberman, MA) and Bertha Laurie Marshall (MA)
James Lyle, b. 6/21/1956 in Laconia; fifth; William D. Nixon (lumberman, MA) and Bertha L. Marshall (MA)
Marilyn Dorr, b. 2/1/1947 in Laconia; first; William D. Nixon (painter, Plymouth, MA) and B. Laurie Marshall (Boston, MA)

NOLAN,
Jack Irwin, Jr., b. 3/21/1947 in Laconia; first; Jack I. Nolan (US Marines, Akron, OH) and June L. Vittum (Oklahoma City, OK)

NUDD,
Caroline Tappan, b. 4/17/1918; second; Wallace Nudd (laborer, Sandwich) and Blanch LeClare (Northfield, VT)
Edna May, b. 12/12/1919; third; Wallace Nudd (laborer, Sandwich) and Blanche LeClair (Northfield, VT)
Elizabeth Delia, b. 9/24/1927; seventh; Wallace Nudd (truck dr., Sandwich) and Blanche LeClair (Penacook)
Elvira Delia, b. 7/16/1925; sixth; Wallace Nudd (laborer, Sandwich) and Blanche LeClair (Northfield, VT)
Evelina, b. 11/4/1932; tenth; Wallace Nudd (laborer, Sandwich) and Blanche LeClair (Northfield, VT)
Frederick Leroy, b. 10/15/1939; fifteenth; Wallace Nudd (painter, Sandwich) and Blanche Leclaire (Northfield, VT)
Geraldine Susie, b. 9/11/1936; eleventh; Wallace Nudd (painter, Sandwich) and Blanche LeClaire (Northfield, VT)
Josephine M., b. 11/11/1923; fifth; Wallace Nudd (laborer, Sandwich) and Blanche LeClair (Northfield, VT)
Linda Kay, b. 4/17/1949 in Wolfeboro; first; Elizabeth D. Nudd (NH)
Rachel Blanche, b. 3/10/1922; fourth; Wallace Nudd (farmer, Sandwich) and Blanche LeClair (Northfield, VT)

Ronald Eugene, b. 1/2/1931; tenth; Wallace Nudd (farmer, Sandwich) and Blanche LeClair (Northfield, VT)
Wallace, b. 6/29/1895; first; Walter E. Nudd (Canterbury) and Marjorie Wallace (Sandwich)
Wallace Raymond, b. 6/19/1929; eighth; Wallace Nudd (truck dr., Sandwich) and Blanche LeClair (Wakefield, VT)
Walter, b. 4/10/1916; first; Wallace Nudd (painter, Sandwich) and Blanche LeClaire (Northfield, VT)

NUNGESSER,
Caleb Andrew, b. 7/26/1995 in Laconia; William L. Nungesser and Colleen M. McDermott
Joshua William, b. 2/21/1994 in Laconia; William Lynn Nungesser and Colleen Mary McDermott
Samuel J., b. 9/6/1992 in Concord; William L. Nungesser and Colleen M. McDermott

NUTTER,
daughter, b. 6/30/1889; second; Benjamin M. Nutter (farmer, Sandwich) and Effie M. Abbott (Holderness)
son, b. 8/12/1891; third; Benjamin Nutter (carpenter, Sandwich) and Effie M. Abbott (Sandwich)

NYDEGGER,
Sophia Rose, b. 1/13/2006 in North Conway; Ashley Nydegger and Tammy Nydegger

NYE,
Marshall E., III, b. 7/23/1990 in Sandwich; Marshall E. Nye, Jr. and Diane C. Hanson
Victoria Marie, b. 12/14/1984 in Sandwich; Marshall Edson Nye, Jr. and Diane Catherine Hanson

O'BRIEN,

daughter, b. 7/10/1904; first; Frank J. O'Brien (weaver, Philadelphia) and Mabel A. Tappan (Sandwich); residence – Philadelphia

OLAFSEN,

Erin Lea, b. 5/28/1981 in Laconia; Steven A. Olafsen and Tracey D. Keown

Greta Mae, b. 6/14/1986 in Laconia; Steven Arthur Olafsen and Tracey Drew Keown

Tora Lynn, b. 4/13/1983 in Laconia; Steven Arthur Olafsen and Tracey Drew Keown

OXTON,

Jessica Calantha, b. 10/11/1985 in Laconia; Kenneth Alan Oxton and Cynthia Locke Sears

PALMER,

daughter, b. 10/27/1899; James O. Palmer (farmer, Sandwich) and Etta A. Vittum (Sandwich)

son, b. 2/19/1901; second; James O. Palmer (farmer, Sandwich) and Etta A. Vittum (Sandwich)

Abigail Renee, b. 4/27/1989 in Concord; Bruce Allan Palmer and Michelle Deidre Perry

Chester Archie, b. 10/27/1919; first; Archie H. Palmer (laborer, Sandwich) and F. L. Harriman (Sandwich)

Gordon, b. 11/4/1904; first; William F. Palmer (farmer, Sandwich) and Lulu B. Gordon (Charlestown, MA)

Perley E., b. 5/22/1900; first; Herbert A. Palmer (laborer, Sandwich) and Amy T. Tappan (Sandwich)

Vanessa L., b. 11/1/1990 in Laconia; Bruce A. Palmer and Michelle D. Perry

PAMPANIN,
Michael T., Jr., b. 5/28/1979 in Sandwich; Michael T. Pampanin (PA) and Carissa A. Hull (MA)

PARKER,
daughter, b. 12/19/1894; second; Warren F. Parker (laborer, Frankport, ME) and Addie F. Brown (Conway)

PEABODY,
Michael Lincoln, b. 9/20/1952 in Laconia; first; Arthur William Peabody (forester, NJ) and Nancy Jane Lincoln (NJ)

PEARSON,
Dagmar, b. 12/29/1969 in Laconia; Dana Pearson and Jean Obermeyer
Devon, 3/22/1992 in North Conway; Carl A. Pearson and Myriam R. Tambasco
Heather, b. 4/18/1963 in Plymouth; second; Dana H. Pearson (clerk, NH) and Jean Obermeyer (MA)
Jennifer, b. 9/30/1960 in Wolfeboro; first; Dana H. Pearson (TV repairman, NH) and Jean Obermeyer (MA)

PEASLEE,
son, b. 9/5/1888; first; John N. Peaslee (farmer, Sandwich) and Helen B. (Lawrence, MA)
daughter, b. 4/20/1897; first; David J. Peaslee (carpenter, Sandwich) and Dora E. Trask (Waltham, MA)
son, b. 6/26/1899; David T. Peaslee (carpenter, Sandwich) and Dora E. Trask (Waltham, MA)
son, b. 10/13/1901; third; David J. Peaslee (carpenter, Sandwich) and Dora E. Trask (Waltham, MA)
son, b. 3/14/1904; fourth; David J. Peaslee (carpenter, Sandwich) and Dora E. Trask (Waltham, MA)
child, b.5/23/1908; fifth; David J. Peaslee (carpenter, Sandwich) and Dora E. Trask (Sandwich)

child, b. 2/11/1910; sixth; David J. Peaslee (carpenter, Sandwich) and Dora E. Trask (Waltham, MA)

son, b. 1/2/1928; second; Ralph Q. Peaslee (laborer, Sandwich) and Elizabeth M. Moody (Tamworth)

Adam Charles, b. 10/15/1984 in Laconia; Daniel Charles Peaslee and Elaine Lynn Bryant

Amanda Jayne, b. 2/14/1986 in Laconia; Jonathan Robert Peaslee and Debrta Jayne Harris

Andrew Nelson, b. 11/18/1960 in Laconia; fourth; Robert N. Peaslee (contractor, NH) and Pauline E. Burrows (NH)

Brenda Joyce, b. 9/26/1957 in Wolfeboro; second; Earle C. Peaslee (trucking, Sandwich) and Margaretta J. Bickford (Sandwich)

Bryan Daniel, b. 6/27/1987 in Laconia; Daniel Charles Peaslee and Elaine Lynn Bryant

Burton Frye, b. 4/2/1920; first; David J. Peaslee (laborer, Sandwich) and Bernice Frye (Lowell, MA)

Charles Almon, b. 9/10/1951 in Laconia; third; Charles Hoyt Peaslee (woodsman, NH) and Charlotte Mae Avery (MA)

Charles Hoyt, b. 12/4/1925; first; Earle Peaslee (laborer, Sandwich) and Louise Carter (Sandwich)

Clare Jean, b. 7/13/1933; sixth; Ralph Q. Peaslee (trucking, Sandwich) and M. Elizabeth Moody (Tamworth)

Daniel Charles, b. 2/14/1954 in Laconia; second; Robert Nelson Peaslee (carpenter, NH) and Pauline Elizabeth Burrows (NH)

David William, b. 12/20/1928; second; Rosco D. Peaslee (carpenter, Sandwich) and Dorothy E. Robinson (Cambridge, MA)

Donald, b. 2/7/1932; fifth; Ralph Q. Peaslee (farmer, Sandwich) and Mary E. Moody (Tamworth)

Dora E., b. 10/24/1917; first; Ruth M. Peaslee and (she says) William A. Beane (machinist, Nashua)

Doris Marian, b. 9/9/1923; first; Roscoe D. Peaslee (carpenter, Sandwich) and Dorothy E. Robinson (Cambridge)

Earle C., b. 6/4/1930; second; Earle C. Peaslee (auto mechanic, Sandwich) and Louise H. Carter (Sandwich)
Garret Earle, b. 8/25/1954 in Laconia; first; Earle Charles Peaslee (truck driver, NH) and Margaretta J. Bickford (NH)
Hannah Marie, b. 3/21/1984 in Laconia; Jonathan Robert Peaslee and Debra Jayne Harris
Helen, b. 12/31/1928; third; Ralph Q. Peaslee (farmer, Sandwich) and Mary Elizabeth Moody (Tamworth)
Janice A., b. 8/10/1930; third; Roscoe D. Peaslee (carpenter, Sandwich) and Dorothy E. Robinson (Cambridge, MA)
Jonathan Robert, b. 3/16/1959 in Laconia; second; Robert N. Peaslee (carpenter, NH) and Pauline E. Burrows (NH)
Kerry David, b. 2/226/1954 in Laconia; second; David William Peaslee (laborer, NH) and Mary Vivian Noble (MA)
Louise Carolyn, b. 11/16/1931; third; Earle C. Peaslee (garage operator, Sandwich) and Louise H. Carter (Sandwich)
Mary Louise, b. 3/20/1926; first; Ralph Peaslee (truckster, Sandwich) and Mary E. Moody (Tamworth)
Nathaniel Andrew, b. 7/26/1985 in Wolfeboro; Andrew Nelson Peaslee and Cheryl Ann Baker
Ralph Quimby, b. 8/20/1930; fourth; Ralph Q. Peaslee (truckman, Sandwich) and Mary E. Moody (Tamworth)
Robert Nelson, b. 4/14/1921; second; David J. Peaslee (carpenter, Sandwich) and Bernice Frye (Lowell, MA)
Sandra Marie, b. 8/22/1951 in Laconia; first; David William Peaslee (US Army, NH) and Mary Vivian Noble (MA)
Susan Elizabeth, b. 1/11/1953 in Laconia; first; Robert Nelson Peaslee (builder, NH) and Pauline E. Burrows (NH)

PENDLETON,
Anabel Grace, b. 10/29/2007 in North Conway; Linwood Pendleton and Jessica Morton

PENNIMAN,
daughter, b. 10/11/1893; fifth; W. S. Penniman (farmer, Sandwich) and Addie Hatch (Colebrook)
son, b. 4/22/1897; sixth; W. S. Penniman (farmer, Sandwich) and Addie M. Hatch (Colebrook)
stillborn daughter, 12/28/1900; seventh; W. S. Penniman (farmer, Sandwich) and Addie M. Hatch (Colebrook)
Jennie L., b. 7/10/1887; fourth;W. S. Penniman (farmer, Sandwich) and Addie M. ----- (Colebrook)

PERKINS,
daughter, b. 5/1/1889; fourth; Forrest T. Perkins (farmer, Sandwich) and Nora ----- (Eaton)
son, b. 12/4/1889; first; Melvin E. Perkins (stage driver, N. Sandwich) and Georgiana Knight (Tamworth)
Ellen Winslow, b. 10/15/1978 in Sandwich; John E. Perkins (NC) and Anne Metcalf (NH)
Gladys G., b. 8/21/1894; eighth; Frank H. Perkins (clergyman, Manchester) and Fannie Sanborn (Orange)
Harold C., stillborn, b. 9/25/1895; first; A. W. Perkins (Jackson) and Ella M. Bryer (Sandwich)

PERRAULT,
Alfred L., b. 1/2/1913; fifth; Allie E. Perrault (farmer, Warwick, Canada) and Bessie M. Smith (Sandwich)

PERSONS,
Robert Corliss, b. 8/13/1959 in Laconia; first; Todd B. Persons (reporter, NJ) and Janet M. Corliss (NH)

PETTENGILL,
son, b. 12/25/1896; first; S. B. Pettengill (pro. cook, Sandwich) and Helen Delaney (NS)
Jan, b. 10/22/1964 in Laconia; fifth; Ramsey W. Pettengill (Prudential Life Ins. Co., NH) and Florence E. Hubley (MA)

Patricia A. M., b. 9/6/1927; first; L. W. Pettengill (hotel cook, Sandwich) and Helen A. Sloan (Centerville, MD)

PHILLIPS,
daughter, b. 6/17/1905; eighth; Michael Phillips (horse dealer, Burlington, VT) and Eliza Benway (Burlington, VT); residence - Burlington, VT

PICONE,
Matthew Stephen, b. 8/28/1974 in Wolfeboro; Stephen L. Picone (MA) and Donna L. Foisy (NH)

PIERCE,
child, b. 3/11/1908; first; James A. Pierce (carpenter, Cranston, RI) and Nettie G. Vittum (Sandwich)
son, b. 7/25/1914; third; James A. Pierce (carpenter, Providence, RI) and Nettie G. Vittum (Sandwich)
Dianne Elizabeth, b. 10/2/1942 in Laconia; first; Maurice A. Pierce (farm mgr., 33, Sandwich) and Alice R. Whiting (31, Tamworth)
Maurice, b. 6/29/1910; second; James A. Pierce (carpenter, Providence) and Nettie G. Vittum (Sandwich)

PLUME,
Donna Averena, b. 9/29/1938; first; Merton H. Plume (pile driver, Groton) and Eleanor A. Slack (Groton, VT)

PLUMER,
son, b. 10/21/1893; fourth; Wilfred Z. Plumer (farmer, Sandwich) and Lizzie E. Webster (Meredith)

PLUMMER,
daughter, b. 1/31/1890; third; W. L. Plummer (farmer, Sandwich) and Lizzie S. Webster (Meredith)
child, b. 9/15/1908; first; Hattie M. Plummer (Sandwich)

son, b. 9/22/1914; second; James H. Plummer (farmer, Sandwich) and Nettie E. Irving (Sandwich)
stillborn son, b. 4/16/1926; sixth; Clarence R. Plummer (farmer, Sandwich) and Luella M. Sturgis (Sandwich)
stillborn daughter, b. 1/12/1935; tenth; Clarence R. Plummer (laborer, Sandwich) and Luella M. Sturgis (Sandwich)
stillborn daughter, b. 12/25/1939; thirteenth; Clarence Plummer (farmer, Sandwich) and Luella Sturgis (Sandwich)
Alice Mae, b. 1/3/1934; ninth; Clarence R. Plummer (laborer, Sandwich) and Luella Mae Sturgis (Sandwich)
Charles Franklin, b. 7/6/1922; third; Clarence R. Plummer (farmer, Sandwich) and Luella M. Sturgis (Sandwich)
Clarence Rogers, b. 6/24/1921; second; Clarence R. Plummer (farmer, Sandwich) and Luella M. Sturgis (Sandwich)
Edna Louise, b. 10/8/1927; seventh; C. R. Plummer (carpenter, Sandwich) and Luella M. Sturgis (Sandwich)
Edward Jesse, b. 11/22/1923; fourth; Clarence R. Plummer (laborer, Sandwich) and Luella M. Sturgis (Sandwich)
Ellen Elizabeth, b. 6/28/1920; first; Clarence R. Plummer (millman, Sandwich) and Luella M. Sturgis (Sandwich)
James Harold, b. 2/26/1911; first; James H. Plummer (farmer, Sandwich) and Nettie Irving (Sandwich)
Janet Edna, b. 6/13/1936; first; James Plummer, Jr. (laborer, Sandwich) and Edna Nelson (Moultonboro)
Lorraine Anne, b. 4/27/1938; twelfth; Clarence R. Plummer (laborer, Sandwich) and Luella M. Sturgis (Sandwich)
Raymond Edward, b. 5/21/1925; fifth; Clarence R. Plummer (farmer, Sandwich) and Luella Sturgis (Sandwich)
Roy Jesse, b. 6/14/1930; eighth; Clarence R. Plummer (laborer, Sandwich) and Luella May Mudgett (Athol, MA)
Shirley Winona, b. 6/17/1936; eleventh; Clarence R. Plummer (farmer, Sandwich) and Luella M. Sturgis (Sandwich)

POHL,
Christine Marie, b. 8/4/1975 in Laconia; Peter W. Pohl (CT) and Suzanne W. Bourque (NH)
Peter William Longhlin, b. 11/8/1982 in Hanover; Peter W. Pohl and Suzanne M. Bourque

POPAM,
son, b. 7/11/1891; second; James A. Popam (carpenter, St. Andrews, NB) and Betsy Gilman (Denmark, ME)

PORTER,
Jason Edward, b. 10/19/1982 in Laconia; David E. Porter and Suzanne E. Colbert
Lisa Louise, b. 12/14/1984 in Laconia; Daniel R. Porter and Kathy Mae Smart

POWERS,
Finn Michael, b. 4/2/2003 in Laconia; Matthew Powers and Bethany Powers
Seamus Matlack, b. 9/28/2005 in Laconia; Matthew Powers and Bethany Powers

PRAY,
Ernest, b. 5/7/1900; fifth; Joseph Pray (blacksmith, Somersworth) and H. Lamountaine (NS)

PRESBY,
Retta, b. 12/23/1940; third; Harold F. Presby (teacher, Henniker) and Vera S. Thomas (Claremont)

QUIMBY,
daughter, b. 4/10/1887; second, Preston Quimby (farmer, Sandwich) and Dell A. ----- (Boston, MA)
son, b. 8/25/1888; first; Sherman Quimby (farmer, Sandwich) and Ursula A. Watson (Tamworth)

son, b. 11/27/1888; fifth; Stanley F. Quimby (farmer, Sandwich) and Etta ----- (Tamworth)
son, b. 7/4/1889; third; Preston Quimby (farmer, Sandwich) and Dell A. Banks (Boston, MA)
son, b. 6/3/1890; third; H. H. Quimby (farmer, Sandwich) and Amy M. Clark (Sandwich)
daughter, b. 2/14/1893; fourth; H. H. Quimby (farmer, Sandwich) and Amy M. Clark (Sandwich)
son, b. 9/17/1894; fifth; Herman Quimby (farmer, Sandwich) and Amy M. Clark (Sandwich)
stillborn daughter, b. 6/26/1907; first; W. S. Quimby (farmer, Sandwich) and Edith M. Durgin (Randolph, MA)
child, b. 7/2/1910; third; J. Page Quimby (farmer, Meredith) and Delia M. Burrows (Sandwich)
Rosalie, b. 8/23/1910; first; Wilbur E. Quimby (farm manager, Sandwich) and Ida N. Lindstrom (Sweden)

QUINN,
Alice Ashley, b. 2/23/2001 in North Conway; Andrew Quinn and Shannon Quinn
Maxwell Andrew Kerrie, b. 7/17/2003 in North Conway; Andrew Quinn and Shannon Quinn
William Charles, b. 7/14/1980 in Sandwich; William J. Quinn and Carol Ann Cloud

READ,
Allison Sorlien, b. 8/11/1982 in Sandwich; William G. Read and Patricia A. Sorlien
Christopher Todd, b. 8/31/1960 in Wolfeboro; fourth; Kirke P. Read (loom fixer, RI) and Patricia A. Ruel (NH)
Karen DeVous, b. 5/5/1959 in Laconia; third; Kirke P. Read (loom fixer, RI) and Patricia A. Ruel (NH)
Kelsey Wilson, b. 8/25/1986 in N. Sandwich; William Goodwin Read and Patricia Sorlien

Margaret Ann, b. 8/23/1939; second; Theodore O. Read (woodworker, Rehoboth, MA) and Deborah Packard (St. Anthony's, NF)
Mark Packard, b. 5/24/1957 in Laconia; second; Kirke P. Read (loom fixer, Providence, RI) and Patricia A. Ruel (Plymouth)
Ralph Kirke, b. 6/24/1955 in Laconia; first; Kirke Packard Read (technician, RI) and Patricia Anne Ruel (NH)
Theodore Otis, Jr., b. 7/5/1945 in Laconia; third; Theodore O. Read (road comm.., Rehoboth, MA) and Deborah G. Packard (St. Anthony's, NF)
Victoria, b. 5/20/1954 in Inagua, Bahamas; third; Barton Read (executive, MA) and Penelope Hutchinson (MA)

REICHERT,
Linda Ann, b. 8/17/1949 in Laconia; third; George Reichert (mechanic, NY) and Mildred A. Crucevich (NY)
Richard, b. 12/5/1947 in Laconia; second; George Reichert (mechanic, New York, NY) and Mildred A. Crucevich (New York, NY)

REIDY,
Diana C., b. 9/13/1997 in Laconia; Daniel E. Reidy and Janet M. Crawford
Ian Johnston, b. 3/11/2003 in Laconia; Daniel Reidy and Janet Reidy

REINELT,
Jane Elizabeth, b. 9/2/1936; first; Antone G. Reinelt (clergyman, Fall River, MA) and Evelyn Holt (New Bedford, MA)

RICHARDS,
stillborn son, b. 1/18/1921; second; Blair Richards (chauffeur, Framingham, MA) and Alice M. Brown (Braintree, MA); residence – Boston, MA

Blair, b. 1/18/1921; first; Blair Richards (chauffeur, Framingham, MA) and Alice M. Brown (Braintree, MA); residence – Boston, MA

RICHARDSON,
Svava Polly, b. 8/14/1995 in Laconia; Glen C. Richardson and Marcella R. Webster

RICHMOND,
Lecia Page, b. 6/4/1954 in Laconia; third; Gene William Richmond (salesman, IL) and Marcia Elaine Lounsbury (NH)

ROBERGE,
Ernest Leroy, III, b. 3/7/1972 in Laconia; Ernest L. Roberge, Jr. (NH) and Beverly C. DeWitt (NJ)

ROBIN,
Roxane Kimball, b. 3/20/1999 in Concord; Andrew Robin and Anna Robin

ROBINSON,
stillborn daughter, b. 5/6/1905; first; Charles Robinson (farmer, Sandwich) and Florence E Mason (Moultonboro); residence - Moultonboro
son, b. 11/18/1906; second; Charles Robinson (farmer, Sandwich) and Edith F. Mason (Moultonboro)
daughter, b. 4/13/1933; premature; sixth; Clarence E. Robinson (farmer, Bridgewater) and Harriet Comett (Concord, VT)
Elaine Gertrude, b. 4/25/1929; fourth; Clarence Robinson (teamster, Bridgewater) and Harriet Comette (Concord)
Raymond E., b. 6/16/1932; fifth; Clarence E. Robinson (laborer, Bridgewater) and Harriet Cormett (Concord, VT)
Richard Arnold, b. 11/5/1939; Thelma L. Robinson (Ashland)

RODGERS,
David Paul, b. 4/25/1960 in Wolfeboro; first; Morton L. Rodgers (carpenter, NH) and Eileen Taylor (NH)
John Lawrence, b. 2/14/1962 in Wolfeboro; second; Morton L. Rodgers (stone mason, NH) and Eileen Taylor (NH)

ROGERS,
son, b. 4/25/1892; second; Henry J. Rogers (smith, Sandwich) and Mary McDough (Ireland)
son, b. 4/16/1894; third; Henry Rogers (blacksmith, Sandwich) and Mary McDonough (Galway, Ireland)
stillborn son, b. 4/9/1917; second; James S. Rogers (forester, Newbury, MA) and Ida L. Rand (Somerville, MA)

ROLLINS,
Jan, b. 5/26/1950 in Laconia; fourth; Steven Weston Rollins (conservation officer, NH) and Virginia Barbara Davis (MA)

ROTH,
Matthew Scott, b. 5/11/1970 in Rochester; Melvin Dean Roth (NH) and Doris V. Mellett (KS)

ROUNER,
Jonathan Kerr, b. 5/21/1960 in Wolfeboro; third; Leroy S. Rouner (teacher, NH) and Rita Rainsford (NY)

ROWELL,
Amy Jessica, b. 3/11/1978 in Laconia; Frank D. Rowell (MA) and Patricia A. Harding (Canada)
Mathew Frank, b. 11/25/1980 in Laconia; Frank D. Rowell and Patricia A. Harding

RUSSELL,
Audrey Elizabeth, b. 11/14/1930; eighth; William W. Russell (postmaster, Sandwich) and Nellie E. Craig (Somerville, MA)
Beverly Nellie, b. 1/12/1924; fourth; William W. Russell (postmaster, Sandwich) and Nellie E. Craig (Somerville, MA)
Elise, b. 1/1/1932; ninth; William W. Russell (postmaster, Sandwich) and Nellie E. Craig (Somerville, MA)
Irma, b. 12/4/1916; first; William W. Russell (postmaster, Sandwich) and Nellie E. Craig (Somerville, MA)
Marlene Ann, b. 10/3/1933; tenth; William Wesley Russell (postmaster, Sandwich) and Nellie E. Craig (Somerville, MA)
Muriel, b. 12/1/1918; second; William Russell (postmaster, Sandwich) and Nellie E. Craig (Somerville, MA)
Murray Andrew, b. 12/24/1934; eleventh; William W. Russell (carpenter, Sandwich) and Nellie E. Craig (Somerville, MA)
Norma, b. 9/7/1928; seventh; William W. Russell (postmaster, Sandwich) and Nellie E. Craig (Somerville, MA)
Priscilla, b. 1/17/1927; sixth; William W. Russell (postmaster, Sandwich) and Nellie E. Craig (Somerville, MA)
Ruth Ethel, b. 12/18/1925; fifth; William W. Russell (postmaster, Sandwich) and Nellie Craig (Somerville, MA)
William Wesley, b. 1/15/1921; third; William W. Russell (postmaster, Sandwich) and Nellie E. Craig (Somerville, MA)

RYAN,
Patrick Scott, b. 11/20/1969 in Laconia; Daniel F. Ryan and Donna R. Burrows

ST. CYR,
Ella Madeline, b. 4/5/2002 in North Conway; Jeffrey St. Cyr and Michelle Greene

SADLER,

Henry Allen, Jr., b. 10/27/1946 in Laconia; third; Henry A. Sadler, Jr. (mechanic, Swampscott, MA) and Priscilla F. Ulman (Swampscott, MA)

SAGLIBENE,

Desha, b. 2/18/1963 in Laconia; second; Salvatore R. Saglibene (NY) and Lucille Longum (NY)

SANDERS,

Abigael Mary, b. 12/25/2002 in Lebanon; Steven Sanders and Karen Sanders

Hunter Mark, b. 11/28/2000 in Lebanon; Steven Sanders and Karen Sanders

SAPOWICZ,

Lindsay Anne, b. 5/22/1987 in Sandwich; Michael John Sapowicz and Tracey Ann Hodgdon

SAUJON,

Thomas Ray, b. 5/28/1984 in Sandwich; Royce Alton Saujon II and Frances Hannah Weinroth

SAUNDERS,

Shelly Ann, b. 11/14/1963 in Laconia; second; Warren T. Saunders, Jr. (mechanic, NY) and Judith L. Berry (NH)

SAWYER,

son, b. 10/9/1900; second; George S. Sawyer (laborer, Campton) and Emma G. Clark (PEI)

son, b. 5/30/1902; third; George S. Sawyer (farmer, Campton) and Emma G. Clark (PEI)

daughter, b. 4/3/1904; fourth; George S. Sawyer (farmer, Campton) and Emma G. Clark (PEI)

daughter, b. 3/10/1906; fifth; George S. Sawyer (farmer, Campton) and Emma G. Clark (PEI)
stillborn daughter, b. 12/25/1907; sixth; George Sawyer (farmer, Campton) and Emma G. Clark (PEI)

SCRIGGINS,
daughter, b. 12/29/1890; first; Arthur Scriggins (laborer, Sandwich) and Flora Blackey (Moultonborough)
daughter, b. 4/7/1897; second; Arthur C. Scriggins (laborer, Sandwich) and Flora L. Blackey (Meredith)
daughter, b. 7/8/1899; Frank Scriggins (farmer, Sandwich) and Carrie E. Blackey (Meredith)
stillborn son, b. 5/20/1901; Frank W. Scriggins (laborer, Sandwich) and Carrie E. Blackey (Meredith)

SEDLEWICZ,
Michael, b. 12/1/1953 in Laconia; second; Eugene Seglewicz (school teacher, NH) and Jacqueline T. Wheelock (NH)
Paul, b. 12/29/1954 in Laconia; third; Eugene Sedlewicz (teacher, NH) and Jacqueline T. Wheelock (NH)

SEELEY,
Melissa Fay, b. 11/4/1997 in Laconia; Allen K. Seeley and Holli H. Long
Nicole Hope, b. 8/19/1999 in Laconia; Allen Seeley and Holli Seeley
Sandra Patricia, b. 3/13/1942 in Wolfeboro; second; Pauline E. Bragg (21, Laconia)

SEVERANCE,
daughter, b. 9/29/1888; fifth; John W. Severance (farmer, Sandwich) and Ellen M. (Boscawen)
son, b. 12/28/1890; sixth; John W. Severance (farmer, Sandwich) and Helen M. Mills (Boscawen)

SEYMOUR,
Ralph Jason, b. 1/12/1971 in Laconia; Ralph B. Seymour (England) and Nancy Breed (MA)

SHAMBAUGH,
Benjamin Scott, b. 9/7/1985 in Laconia; Benjamin Dibble Shambaugh and Lisa Marie Scott
Jeremy Scott, b. 12/12/1981 in Laconia; Benjamin D. Shambaugh and Lisa M. Scott

SILCOX,
Judith, b. 1/25/1947 in Laconia; first; Frederick L. Silcox (discharged veteran, Lowell, MA) and Jeanne Campbell (N. Sandwich)
Julie, b. 9/15/1953 in Laconia; second; Frederick Lewis Silcox (cabinet maker, MA) and Jeanne Campbell (NH)

SIMPSON,
Beverly Velgora, b. 3/18/1924; first; Irving H. Simpson (restaurant keeper, Levant, ME) and Jennie E. Thomas (Oakland, ME); residence – Greenville, ME

SINGER,
Scarlet Salaambo, b. 8/10/1976 in Sandwich; Noel J. Singer (RI) and Ann Hughes (LA)

SKINNER,
son, b. 4/23/1891; fourth; Charles Skinner (farmer, Sandwich) and Jennie Torry (Porter, ME)
daughter, b. 1/22/1892; first; Lucian C. Skinner (farmer, Sandwich) and Hattie E. Horn (Sandwich)

SLOTHOWER-MINOR,
Thomas A., b. 10/4/1992; Timothy A. Minor and Patricia L. Slothower

SMART,

Aubrey May, b. 9/27/2001 in Laconia; Mark Smart and Tammy Smart

SMITH,

daughter, b. 1/16/1887; fifth; Hartwell Smith (farmer, Sandwich) and Alice ----- (Ossipee)

son, b. 6/12/1887; second; Charles L. Smith (farmer, Meredith) and M. J. ----- (Boston, MA)

daughter, b. 8/17/1887; first; Frank E. Smith (farmer, Sandwich) and Lizzie E. ----- (Amesbury, MA)

daughter, b. 2/5/1888; first; Lewis E. Smith (farmer, Sandwich) and Carrie E. Willey (Sandwich)

son, b. 8/20/1889; third; Charles L. Smith (farmer, Meredith) and M. L. Blatchford (Boston)

daughter, b. 8/19/1890; first; Samuel B. Smith (farmer, Sandwich) and Nellie Taylor (Sandwich)

son, b. 1/29/1891; first; Willis H. Smith (farmer, Sandwich) and Clara M. Mudgett (Franklin)

daughter, b. 4/2/1892; first; Charles O. Smith (tinman, Sandwich) and Mary E. Pierce (Sandwich)

son, b. 4/16/1894; second; Charles O. Smith (tinsmith, Sandwich) and Mary E. Pierce (Sandwich)

daughter, b. 1/4/1897; first; Willis Smith (farmer, Sandwich) and Bertha Felch (Sandwich)

son, b. 3/12/1898; second; Willis H. Smith (farmer, Sandwich) and Clara M. Mudgett (Franklin)

daughter, b. 8/22/1903; first; Harry H. Smith (farmer, Sandwich) and Bessie Blanchard (Sandwich)

son, b. 8/2/1905; third; Charles O. Smith (tinsmith, Sandwich) and Mary E. Pierce (Sandwich)

stillborn daughter, b. 3/18/1914; first; Leon A. Smith (farmer, Sandwich) and Maude L. Tilton (Sandwich)

daughter, b. 3/18/1914; second; Leon A. Smith (farmer, Sandwich) and Maude L. Tilton (Sandwich)

stillborn son, b. 10/13/1920; first; Julius H. Smith (farmer, Sandwich) and Isabel H. Smith (Holderness)

Charles H., b. 12/21/1904; first; Charles H. Smith (fur dealer, Ossipee) and Eva D. Tappan (Sandwich)

Clyde Roland, b. 11/14/1919; second; G. Roland Smith (farmer, Sandwich) and Alice P. Davey (Sandwich)

Dorothy, b. 12/24/1907; second; C. H. Smith (fur dealer, Ossipee) and Eva D. Tappan (Sandwich); residence – Moultonboro

Gail Eliza, b. 9/9/1945 in Laconia; fifth; Ellsworth M. Smith (US Army, Middleton, MA) and Olga L. Weeks (Warren)

George R., b. 6/23/1895; second; Samuel B. Smith (Sandwich) and Nellie E. Taylor (Sandwich)

Julia C., b. 1/9/1913; first; Frank M. Smith (merchant, Sandwich) and Julia M. Sherman (Buffalo, NY)

Kenneth Arven, b. 10/23/1920; second; Harry H. Smith (farmer, Sandwich) and Bessie Blanchard (Sandwich)

Kenneth Arven, b. 8/14/1939; first; Kenneth Smith (ice man, Sandwich) and Pearl Smith (Sandwich)

Lawrence Roland, b. 9/16/1945 in Laconia; first; Samuel M. Smith (truck driver, Sandwich) and Maevina A. Locke (Laconia)

Lloyd C., b. 8/12/1909; third; John A. Smith (laborer, Moultonboro) and Florence Dearborn (Sandwich); residence – Moultonboro

Pearl Elizabeth, b. 7/3/1921; third; G. Roland Smith (farmer, Sandwich) and Alice P. Davey (Sandwich)

Richard Edward, Jr., b. 11/7/1972 in Laconia; Richard E. Smith (NH) and Linda L. Covey (NH)

Samuel M., b. 8/27/1917; first; George Roland Smith (farmer, Sandwich) and Alice P. Davie (Sandwich)

SORRELL,

Alex D., Jr., b. 3/15/1965 in Laconia; first; Alex D. Sorrell (truck driver, NH) and Minnie Avery (NH)

Crystal Lee, b. 4/19/1968 in Laconia; Alex D. Sorell, Jr. and Minnie May Avery

SPAULDING,

daughter, b. 4/10/1905; first; Ralph H. Spaulding (farmer, Tamworth) and Essie I. Hanson (Winchester, MA)

STARKEY,

Leslie Earl, b. 10/26/1916; seventh; Fred E. Starkey (millman, Winchendon, MA) and Fannie Ames (E. Bridgewater, MA)

STARMER,

Elanor Schoell, b. 10/25/1978 in Boston, MA; John S. Starmer (NC) and Nancy G. Oeschle (NY)

STEELE,

Benjamin Belknap, b. 5/24/1952 in Littleton; second; Frederick Lincoln Steele (teacher, NH) and Mary Ramsen Lloyd (ME)

Edward Twitchell, b. 4/25/1957 in Littleton; third; Frederic L. Steele (teacher, Tamworth) and Mary R. Lloyd (York, ME)

Nathaniel Allen, b. 3/13/1950 in North Conway; seventh; Frederic Lincoln Steele (teacher, Tamworth) and Mary Ramsen Lloyd (York, ME)

STEEVES,

Deborah R., b. 5/16/1963 in Laconia; second; Seymour J. Steeves, Jr. (minister, MA) and Bette A. Doughty (MA)

James A., b. 6/28/1964 in Laconia; third; Seymour J. Steeves, Jr. (minister, MA) and Bette Ann Doughty (MA)

John Mark, b. 1/12/1960 in Laconia; first; Rev. Seymour Steeves (clergyman, MA) and Bette Ann Doughty (MA)

STEVENS,
Julia M., b. 11/24/1887; second; Frederick A. Stevens (farmer, Plymouth) and Emma D. ----- (Enfield)

STOKES,
Herbert, b. 3/7/1926; sixth; Arthur Stokes (laborer, Harrison, ME) and Harriet Hutchins (Tamworth)
Karen Joy, b. 3/15/1957 in Laconia; second; Reginald E. Stokes (lumberman, Tamworth) and Janice A. Peaslee (Sandwich)
Randy Scott, b. 5/25/1953 in Laconia; first; Reginald Edward Stokes (woodsman, NH) and Janice Aileen Peaslee (NH)

STONE,
Howard William, b. 3/21/1998 in Laconia; Ronnie Paul Stone and Jacqueline Lisa Oliver

STONESIFER,
Justin Q., b. 9/3/1991 in North Conway; David A. Stonesifer and Kimberly Z. Wixon

STRAYER-BENTON,
Jackson Lloyd, b. 3/18/1984 in Sandwich; Richard Lloyd Benton and Frances Drayton Strayer
Kathryn Mary, b. 11/13/1982 in Sandwich; Richard L. Benton and Frances D. Strayer

STREETER,
Jorja Lorraine, b. 4/23/2005 in Laconia; Bradley Streeter and Karen Streeter

STROTHER,
Raven Lucille, b. 10/2/2002 in North Conway; Philip Strother and Ashley Bullard

Willow Larcom, b. 1/27/2001 in North Conway; Philip Strother and Ashley Bullard

STURGEON,

Christopher J., b. 7/24/1960 in Laconia; first; Fred J. Sturgeon (NH State Highways, NH) and Donna J. Richardson (NH)

Debra Jean, b. 12/2/1956 in Laconia; first; Ronald W. Sturgeon (mach. operator, NH) and Beverly A. Clifford (NH)

Dorothy Mae, b. 7/15/1935; second; Wilfred J. Sturgeon (laborer, Van Buren, ME) and Erma V. Stokes (Harrison, ME)

Edward Rene, b. 10/2/1950 in Laconia; sixth; Wilfred Joseph Sturgeon (laborer, ME) and Irma Stokes (ME)

Fred Joseph, b. 4/15/1944 in Plymouth; fifth; Wilfred J. Sturgeon (laborer, 31, Van Buren, ME) and Erma V. Stokes (29, Harrison, ME)

Kenneth Edward, b. 1/3/1934; first; Wilfred J. Sturgeon (laborer, Vanburen, ME) and Irma Stokes (Harrison, ME)

Rita Mae, b. 1/10/1940; fourth; Wilfred J. Sturgeon (laborer, Van Buren, ME) and Erma Stokes (Harrison, ME)

Ronald Wilfred, b. 3/28/1938; third; Wilfred J. Sturgeon (laborer, Van Buren, ME) and Erma Stokes (Harrison, ME)

STURGESS,

daughter, b. 10/10/1902; first; Jennie Sturgess (Albany)

SWAN,

Allen Brady, b. 3/15/1954 in Laconia; second; Bernard Everett Swan (lumbering, ME) and Mary L. Bryant (NH)

Bernard Winfield, b. 10/23/1952 in Laconia; first; Bernard Everett Swan (lumbering, ME) and Mary Loraine Bryant (NH)

Bonita Marie, b. 4/24/1945 in Laconia; first; Dean E. Swan (US Army, Percy) and Phyllis M. Bryant (N. Sandwich)

Christopher H., b. 2/6/1964 in Laconia; fourth; Bernard E. Swan (carpenter, MO) and Mary L. Bryant (NH)

Colleen M., b. 3/11/1966 in Laconia; fifth; Bernard E. Swan (carpenter, Gilead, ME) and Mary L. Bryant (Sandwich)
Kimberly Bryant, b. 4/12/1959 in Laconia; second; Dean E. Swan (construction worker, NH) and Phyllis M. Bryant (NH)
Regina Lynn, b. 7/7/1956 in Laconia; third; Bernard E. Swan (lumberman, ME) and Mary L. Bryant (NH)

SZYMUJKO,
Hilary Loring, b. 12/28/1984 in Laconia; Jeffery Alexander Szymujko and Sara Burnham Johnston
Jeffery Alexander, II, b. 10/15/1982 in Laconia; Jeffery A. Szymujko and Sarah B. Johnston

TALBOT,
Lois Elizabeth, b. 2/7/1929; second; Cecil A. Talbor (laborer, Boxh'e, IA) and Lena M. Cook (Sandwich)

TAPPAN,
daughter, b. 3/24/1891; first; Frank H. Tappan (farmer, Sandwich) and Hattie Knowles (Moultonboro)
son, b. 10/1/1891; second; Samuel A. Tappan (sawyer, Sandwich) and Emma Smith (Woodstock)
daughter, b. 12/26/1891; second; Alfred M. Tappan (laborer, Sandwich) and Eliza J. Smith (Sandwich)
daughter, b. 8/1/1892; first; George H. Tappan (farmer, Sandwich) and Inez A. Page (Belgrade, ME)
son, b. 2/22/1901; second; Fred Tappan (farmer, Sandwich) and Abbie E. Wakefield (Canada)
son, b. 10/15/1906; third; Fred Tappan (farmer, Sandwich) and Abbie E. Wakefield (Melbourn, Canada)

TASKER,
son, b. 6/29/1899; Elmer H. Tasker (druggist, Strafford) and Evelyn Burleigh (Sandwich)

F. B., daughter, b. 2/20/1898; first; Elmer H. Tasker (druggist, Strafford) and Evelyn Burleigh (Sandwich)

TAYLOR,
daughter, b. 12/18/1887; fourth; Charles G. Taylor (smith, Sandwich) and Eliza Henderson (Sandwich)
son, b. 10/6/1909; first; William H. Taylor (farmer, Sandwich) and C. E. Skinner (Sandwich)
child, b. 6/25/1911; second; William Taylor (farmer, Sandwich) and Christina E. Skinner (Sandwich)
daughter, b. 9/2/1914; third; William H. Taylor (farmer, Sandwich) and Christine E. Skinner (Sandwich)
daughter, b. 7/26/1916; fourth; William H. Taylor (farmer, Sandwich) and Christine E. Skinner (Sandwich)
Carrie, b. 9/3/1942 in Laconia; fourth; Paul Taylor (laborer, 31, Sandwich) and Marion Gray (28, Sanbornton)
Doris, b. 9/3/1938; third; Paul A. Taylor (laborer, Sandwich) and Marion Gray (Sanbornton)
Eileen, b. 10/5/1937; second; Paul Taylor (laborer, Sandwich) and Marion Gray (Sanbornton)
Elva Elaine, b. 6/30/1935; first; Charles E. Taylor (plumber, Lynn, MA) and Berenice E. Dodge (Laconia)
Gerald Alan, b. 9/1/1937; first; Sumner E. Taylor (truck driver, Parsonsfield, ME) and Alice A. Mudgett (Sandwich); residence – Rochester
Harold Edwin, b. 10/22/1923; third; Walter L. Taylor (farmer, Sandwich) and Agnes M. Wallace (Tamworth)
Hazel Elizabeth, b. 9/30/1928; fifth; Walter L. Taylor (caretaker, farmer, Lynn, MA) and Agnes Wallace (Tamworth)
Linda, b. 4/18/1947 in Laconia; sixth; Paul A. Taylor (farmer, Sandwich) and Marion E. Gray (Sanbornton)
Pamela Joyce, b. 6/17/1945 in Laconia; second; Charles E. Taylor (farmer, Lynn, MA) and Bernice E. Dodge (Laconia)
Pauline, b. 2/27/1936; first; Paul A. Taylor (laborer, Sandwich) and Marion Gray (Sanbornton)

Robert Emerson, b. 9/13/1925; fourth; Walter Taylor (caretaker, Sandwich) and Agnes Wallace (Tamworth)
William H., II, b. 5/6/1966 in Laconia; second; William H. Taylor (laborer, Sandwich) and Jean M. Rogers (Tamworth)
William Henry, b. 3/6/1946 in Laconia; fifth; Paul A. Taylor (farmer, Sandwich) and Marion E. Gray (Sanbornton)

TEWKSBURY,
daughter, b. 5/27/1888; third; J. H. Tewksbury (farmer, Sandwich) and Sarah L. (Salem, MA)
son, b. 1/12/1902; first; Wesley Tewksbury (farmer, Sandwich) and Nettie Barnes (Tamworth)

THERIAULT,
Victor Joseph, b. 1/18/1945 in Laconia; first; Camile Theriault (pulp cutter, Paquetville, NB) and Anna M. B. Durand (St. Jean de Matha, PQ)

THOMPSON,
stillborn son, b. 3/7/1887; first; Elmer Thompson (laborer, Sandwich) and Eva Smith (Sandwich)
daughter, b. 8/14/1890; second; E. E. Thompson (farmer, Sandwich) and Eva Smith (Sandwich)
son, b. 1/1/1892; first; James R. Thompson (painter, Sandwich) and Florence Wentzell (Sandwich)
son, b. 6/16/1892; third; Elmer Thompson (farmer, Sandwich) and Eva A. Smith (Sandwich)
son, b. 11/5/1907; fifth; E. S. Thompson (farmer, Sandwich) and Eva A. Smith (Sandwich)
Arlene L., b. 10/30/1917; first; Arthur G. Thompson (farmer, Sandwich) and Lulu B. Sanborn (Campton)
Betty Jane, b. 7/2/1942 in Plymouth; second; Hugh W. Thompson (fishman, 37, Madison) and Roxie Burrows (25, Sandwich)

THORNDIKE,
Shane William, b. 6/30/1986 in Laconia; Townsend Davis Thorndike and Melissa Jane Yeager
Townsend Eric, b. 3/22/1985 in Laconia; Townsend Davis Thorndike and Melissa Jane Yeager

TIBBETTS,
daughter, b. 5/10/1887; first; Edwin Tibbetts (mill man, Haverhill) and Kate J. ----- (Dalton)
child, b. 8/29/1910; second; Henry T. Tibbetts (laborer, Benton) and Blanche I. Scriggins (Sandwich)
Constance, b. 10/6/1939; first; Elmer Haven Tibbetts (carpenter, Sandwich) and Maude Whitehouse (Moultonboro)
Deborah, b. 10/2/1926; first; Willard R. Tibbetts (electrician, Sandwich) and Gwendoline A. Handley (Newton, MA)
Nancy, b. 8/22/1940; first; Paul W. Tibbetts (electrical eng., Sandwich) and Antonia A. Mazzola (Quincy, MA)
Paul W., b. 4/16/1907; first; H. T. Tibbetts (farmer, Benton) and Iona B. Scriggins (Sandwich)

TILTON,
son, b. 9/24/1898; first; Frank E. Tilton (farmer, Sandwich) and Clara B. Tappan (Sandwich)
son, b. 3/24/1904; first; John F. Tilton (carpenter, Sandwich) and Sadie M. Dow (Sandwich)
child, b. 1/12/1908; second; John F. Tilton (laborer, Sandwich) and Sadie M. Dow (Sandwich)
child, b. 2/24/1911; third; John Tilton (farmer, Sandwich) and Sadie Dow (Sandwich)
stillborn son, b. 1/18/1923; fifth; John F. Tilton (farmer, Sandwich) and Sadie M. Dow (Sandwich)
son, b. 11/18/1933; third; Herbert Tilton (farmer, Sandwich) and Eleanor Davis (Moultonboro)
Alice E., b. 3/16/1919; fourth; John F. Tilton (farmer, Sandwich) and Sadie M. Dow (Sandwich)

Anne Susan, b. 9/7/1948 in Laconia; first; Howard F. Tilton (carpenter, Ctr. Sandwich) and Ferne Gladys Tilton (Campbellton, PA)
Herbert John, Jr., b. 7/17/1931; first; Herbert J. Tilton (farmer, Sandwich) and Eleanor F. Davis (Moultonboro)
Howard, b. 11/10/1923; first; Herman F. Tilton (farmer, Sandwich) and Gertrude A. Martin (Brockton, MA)
Howard Forest, Jr., b. 6/19/1951 in Laconia; second; Howard Forest Tilton (carpenter, NH) and Ferne Gladys Mountz (PA)
Lorraine Grace, b. 6/24/1927; second; Herman Tilton (mechanic, Sandwich) and Gertrude Martin (Brockton, MA)
Sandra Doane, b. 7/26/1936; fifth; Herbert J. Tilton (farmer, Sandwich) and Eleanore Davis (Moultonboro)
Veda May, b. 8/19/1932; second; Herbert Tilton (laborer, Sandwich) and Eleanor Davis (Moultonboro)

TIVEY,
Berton E., b. 3/16/1929; second; Edward F. Tivey (laborer, Everett, MA) and Lilla M. Mudgett (Sandwich)

TOBIN,
Gregory Hughes, Jr., b. 4/16/1987 in Laconia; Gregory Hughes Tobin, Sr. and Nelda Evelyn Kelly

TOURIGNY,
Normand Joseph, b. 7/14/1957 in Laconia; fourth; Normand J. Tourigny (tool maker, MA) and Charlotte M. Avery (Clinton, MA)

TRACY,
Keegan Doyle, b. 8/21/1997 in Laconia; Kim Tracy and Paula J. Doyle
Melanie, b. 10/23/1983 in Sandwich; Kim Tracy and Sally Anne Hindersinn

Samantha Rose, b. 4/19/1995 in Laconia; Kim Tracy and Paula Jayne Doyle

TURNER,

stillborn daughter, b. 8/31/1898; third; Cornelius Turner (farmer, Bangor, ME) and Bertha A. Canney (Sandwich)

daughter, b. 7/1/1912; sixth; Cornelius Turner (farmer, Bangor, ME) and Bertha M. Canney (Sandwich)

Carrie E., b. 10/21/1893; first; Cornelius Turner (farmer, Bangor, ME) and Bertha A. Canney (Sandwich)

Cornelius, b. 3/21/1907; fifth; Cornelius Turner (farmer, Sandwich) and Bertha A. Canney (Sandwich)

Elva, b. 9/22/1895; second; Cornelius Turner (Bangor, ME) and Bertha Kenney (Sandwich)

Ethel F., b. 9/28/1901; fourth; Cornelius Turner (farmer, Bangor, ME) and Bertha Canney (Sandwich)

ULMAN,

Virginia, b. 3/5/1910; second; Jacob Ulman (poultryman, Boston, MA) and Alice W. Newhall (Lynn, MA)

VAZZANO,

Stephanie Magnolia Wiley, b. 8/14/1986 in Laconia; Anthony Joseph Vazzano and Susan Elizabeth Wiley

VIERUS,

Theresa A., b. 12/9/1990 in Plymouth; David A. Vierus and Jennifer Pearson

VITTUM,

daughter, b. 10/20/1888; fifth; Jacob F. Vittum (farmer, Sandwich) and Mary O. (Sandwich)

daughter, b. 7/20/1894; first; Aubrey Vittum (laborer, Sandwich) and Emma Chandler (Lynn, MA)

son, b. 3/21/1897; second; Audrey M. Vittum (laborer, Sandwich) and Emmaline Chandler (Lynn, MA)
stillborn daughter, b. 6/2/1898; first; Otis Vittum (farmer, Sandwich) and Alberta Danforth (Lynn, MA)
daughter, b. 8/28/1899; Ottis Vittum (farmer, Lynn, MA) and Alberta Danforth (Sandwich)
daughter, b. 3/12/1907; first; M. W. Vittum (farmer, Sandwich) and Emma Campbell (Sandwich)
son, b. 8/3/1913; first; Ernest Vittum (laborer, Sandwich) and Agnes M. Ames (Tamworth)
George W., b. 9/15/1916; first; George W. Vittum (farmer, McPherson, KS) and Ethel G. Strong (Charlestown, MA)
Katherine Simpson, b. 5/20/1975 in Laconia; Lewis M. Vittum (NH) and Sharon R. Oxner (Canada)
Pauline, b. 7/7/1919; third; George W. Vittum (farmer, McPhercon, KS) and Ethel G. Strong (Charlestown, MA)
Richard Carl, b. 5/24/1949 in Laconia; first; Carl S. Vittum (carpenter, OK) and Carolyn L. Peaslee (NH)
Steven Kenneth, b. 4/13/1954 in Laconia; first, Kenneth David Vittum (farmer, OK) and Eleanor May Aldrich (NH)
Susan Louise, b. 11/25/1950 in Laconia; second; Carl Strong Vittum (contractor, OK) and Carolyn Louise Peaslee (NH)
Virginia, b. 1/3/1918; second; George W. Vittum (farmer, McPherson, KS) and Ethel G. Strong (Charlestown, MA)

WADE,
stillborn son, b. 3/8/1893; first; Edwin D. Wade (laborer, Moultonboro) and Ida M. Martin
child, b. 2/18/1908; second; Frank H. Wade (engineer, Moultonboro) and Mary L. Clough (Tamworth)

WAKEFIELD,
son, b. 10/29/1906; fourth; William H. Wakefield (farmer, Melbourn, Canada) and Bessie E. Cumming (Moncton, NB)

stillborn child, b. 5/26/1910; fifth; William H. Wakefield (farmer, Canada) and Bessie E. Conning (Moncton, NB)
daughter, b. 3/3/1915; sixth; William H. Wakefield (farmer, Canada) and Bessie E. Conning (Moncton, NB)
son, b. 1/27/1916; second; Clarence H. Wakefield (farmer, Moultonboro) and Clara M. Messer
Frank W., b. 3/18/1908; first; Ralph Wakefield (laborer, Moultonboro) and Mary E. Webster (Sandwich)
Thelma Georgette, b. 7/3/1918; fifth; Ralph Wakefield (laborer, Moultonboro) and Mary E. Webster (Sandwich)
Wilfred C., b. 6/15/1913; first; C. H. Wakefield (farmer, Moultonboro) and Clara M. Messer (Moultonboro)

WALKER,
daughter, b. 8/16/1904; second; Walter C. Walker (stage driver, Holliston, MA) and Hattie B. Bickford (Tamworth); residence – Tamworth

WALLACE,
son, b. 7/24/1890; second; Eugene P. Wallace (farmer, Ctr. Harbor) and May Estes (Sandwich)
stillborn daughter, b. 2/3/1895; first; Harry Wallace (Sandwich) and Effie M. Hatch (Groveton)
daughter, b. 2/2/1903; third; Marcellus Wallace (farmer, Sandwich) and Harriett L. Smith (New Hampton)
son, b. 11/10/1904; fourth; Marcellus Wallace (farmer, Thornton) and Harriet L. Smith (New Hampton)
son, b. 2/5/1907; fifth; M. C. Wallace (farmer, Thornton) and Harriet L. Smith (New Hampton)
child, b. 10/13/1911; third; Harry J. Wallace (barber, Sandwich) and Mabel Prescott (Sandwich)
son, b. 3/17/1914; eighth; Marcellus C. Wallace (farmer, Thornton) and Harriet L. Smith (New Hampton)
son, b. 8/13/1929; seventh; Bradley Wallace (fireman, Concord) and Gladys Locke (Hooksett)

Albert Marcellus, b. 4/16/1926; fourth; Bradley L. Wallace (laborer, Lakeport) and Gladys M. Locke (Hooksett)
Carl Elwin, b. 7/12/1897; Harry Wallace (farmer, Sandwich) and Effie M. Hatch (Groveton)
Clyde Elwin, b. 4/14/1920; second; Harry Wallace (farmer, Sandwich) and Hattie M. Plummer (Sandwich)
Effie, b. 3/15/1965 in Plymouth; third; Bruce E. Wallace (teacher, MA) and Joyce L. Pfeifer (MA)
Ethel Marie, b. 10/5/1936; first; Asahel Wallace (laborer, Sandwich) and Roxy Burrows (Sandwich)
Frances M., b. 4/25/1915; first; Harry Wallace (farmer, Sandwich) and Hattie Plummer (Sandwich)
Neoma Harriett, b. 8/17/1941; Asabel A. Wallace (laborer, Sandwich) and Ethelyn Davis (Warren)
Raymond Frank, b. 7/20/1928; sixth; Bradley E. Wallace (farmer, Concord) and Gladys Lock (Hooksett)

WALTERS,
Robert Earle, b. 10/11/1957 in Wolfeboro; fifth; Kenneth E. Walters (painter, Malden, MA) and Gloria R. Chapin (Springfield, MA)
Scott David, b. 6/28/1956 in Wolfeboro; fourth; Kenneth E. Walters (painter, MA) and Gloria R. Chapin (MA)

WALZ,
Allison Hathaway, b. 5/30/1987 in Laconia; Philip Liggett Walz and Laura Lynne Macomber

WARREN,
Tony Alvah, b. 6/24/1944 in Laconia; sixth; Herman C. Warren (teamster, 29, Denmark, ME) and Mary L. Sanborn (24, Bridgton, ME)

WATKINS,

Alfred Earl, b. 8/22/1918; first; Charles Watkins (clergyman, London, England) and Letitia C. Mitchell (Byron, ME)

WATSON,

daughter, b. 12/12/1889; first; Daniel S. Watson (farmer, Tamworth) and Fannie M. Pitman (Alexandria)

daughter, b. 12/12/1889; second; Daniel S. Watson (farmer, Tamworth) and Fannie M. Pitman (Alexandria)

son, b. 11/5/1893; third; Daniel S. Watson (farmer, Tamworth) and Mary M. Pitman (Alexandria)

daughter, b. 6/6/1897; fourth; Daniel S. Watson (farmer, Tamworth) and Fannie M. Pitman (Alexandria)

daughter, b. 8/1/1899; Daniel S. Watson (farmer, Tamworth) and Fannie Pitman (Alexandria)

child, b. 2/19/1911; sixth; Daniel Watson (farmer, Tamworth) and Fannie M. Pitman (Alexandria)

Ann Lee, b. 7/23/1940; first; Arthur J. Watson (carpenter, Sandwich) and Marion E. Robinson (Cambridge, MA)

Janet Mae, b. 11/12/1932; second; Elmer D. Watson (laborer, Sandwich) and Bernice A. Leach (Tamworth)

Richard Elmer, b. 6/9/1929; first; Elmer D. Watson (caretaker, Sandwich) and Bernice Leach (Tamworth)

WATT,

stillborn son, b. 7/23/1920; second; George G. Watt (bank clerk, W. Roxbury, MA) and Elizabeth Eddy (Auburn, NY)

WEBB,

Martha Ann, b. 11/24/1967 in Laconia; second; John L. Webb, Jr. (service station, Philadelphia, PA) and Eleanor Hall (Springfield, MA)

Mary E., b. 9/23/1964 in Laconia; first; John L. Webb, Jr. (accountant, PA) and Eleanor Hall (MA)

WEBSTER,
daughter, b. 10/1/1889; first; Frank H. Webster (farmer, Sandwich) and Lizzie G. Tappan (Sandwich)

WEED,
son, b. 9/5/1890; fourth; Larkin D. Weed (carpenter, Sandwich) and Elsie A. Peaslee (Sandwich)
son, b. 4/17/1906; first; John J. Weed (carpenter, Sandwich) and Lucy M. Smith (Sandwich)
daughter, b. 3/5/1909; first; Chester A. Weed (carpenter, Sandwich) and Ella C. Hoag (Tamworth)
daughter, b. 1/19/1912; second; Chester A. Weed (carpenter, Sandwich) and Ella C. Hoag (Tamworth)
Carl Larkin, b. 8/17/1941; first; Charles L. Weed (civil engineer, Sandwich) and Elinor L. Lord (Woburn, MA)
Charles Larkin, b. 2/8/1918; second; Cleveland Weed (carpenter, Sandwich) and Lottie M. Vittum (Galva, KS)
Helen, b. 10/18/1912; first; Cleveland Weed (carpenter, Sandwich) and Lottie M. Vittum (Galva, KS)
John Henry, b. 1/18/1949 in Laconia; second; Charles Larkin Weed (carpenter, Sandwich) and Esther M. Reeves (Woburn, MA)
Marjorie Esther, b. 12/23/1949 in Laconia; third; Charles L. Weed (contractor, NH) and Esther M. Reeves (MA)

WEEKS,
C. Colby, b. 11/18/1887; second; Calvin Weeks and Alida M. Hines (Sandwich)
Cheryl Lynn, b. 10/30/1969 in Wolfeboro; Peter K. Weeks and Kathi-Anne Lambert

WEIL-COOLEY,
Abram Baker, b. 6/7/2005 in Sandwich; John Cooley and Suzanne Weil

Maya Robie, b. 8/30/2001 in Sandwich; John Cooley and Suzanne Weil

WELCH,
Amy Nicole, b. 1/7/1988 in Plymouth; Michael William Welch and Lisa Marie Bixby
Marion R., b. 8/31/1965 in Laconia; third; John Welch (carpenter, NH) and Charlotte Moore (NH)
Susan Marion, b. 6/26/1961 in Laconia; second; John W. Welch (mill worker, NH) and Charlotte J. Moore (NH)

WELD,
Max J., b. 10/24/1905; first; Max L. Weld (farmer, W. Berkshire, VT) and Myra R. Tappan (Sandwich); residence – VT

WEND,
Dorothea, b. 1/4/1947 in Laconia; fourth; Milton Wend (author & craftsman, Albany, NY) and Florence Halpin (New York, NY)

WHEDON,
son, b. 11/23/1894; third; Oscar A. Whedon (laborer, Sangate, VT) and Anna B. Mudgett (Sandwich)
son, b. 3/24/1898; fourth; Oscar A. Whedon (laborer, Sandgate, VT) and Annie B. Mudgett (Sandwich)

WHITE,
son, b. 12/15/1894; first; Charles M. White (laborer, ME) and Hattie M. Bryant (Sandwich)
son, b. 12/17/1897; third; Fred A. White (carpenter, Hallowell, ME) and Sadie A. Marden (Freedom, ME)
son, b. 7/2/1901; third; Charles M. White (carpenter, Hallowell, ME) and Hattie M. Bryant (Sandwich)
Brandon Michael, b. 1/20/2000 in Laconia; Lindsay White and Patricia White

Emily Assunta, b. 10/5/1979 in Laconia; Douglas H. White (PA) and Patricia A. Gallo (NJ)
Emma L., b. 9/1/1901; first; Fred L. White (farmer, Sandwich) and Annie M. Tappan (Sandwich)
Keener S., 3rd, b. 8/6/1966 in Laconia; first; Keener S. White, Jr., (pilot, Beaver Falls, PA) and Dorothy Hoag (Boston, MA)
Laura Anne, b. 4/25/1983 in Concord; Douglas Hazard White and Patricia Anne Gallo
V. C., daughter, b. 5/31/1899; second; Charles M. White (farmer, Hallowell, ME) and Hattie M. Bryant (Sandwich)
Walter Clark, b. 7/12/1918; first; Walter L. White (farmer, Phillipston, MA) and Florence A. Clark (Sandwich)
William Allan, b. 9/1/1942 in Laconia; first; Walter C. White (laborer, 24, Sandwich) and Isabelle V. Young (22, Bath)

WHITEHOUSE,
daughter, b. 1/28/1889; G. L. Whitehouse (farmer, Tamworth) and Clara L. Tappan (Sandwich)

WHITING,
Bernard Charles, b. 6/23/1923; second; Victor Whiting (farmer, Tamworth) and Madalene Elliott (Sandwich)
Elisabeth Ann, b. 9/30/1942 in Laconia; first; Willard R. Whiting (farm mgr., 21, Meredith) and Ruth P. Young (22, Westford)
Harold R., b. 9/10/1925; fourth; Victor Whiting (laborer, Sandwich) and Madeline Elliott (Sandwich)
Lewis Raymond, b. 11/26/1956 in Laconia; first; Raymond V. Whiting (mach. operator, NH) and Geraldine S. Nudd (NH)

WHITWORTH,
son, b. 8/2/1899; R. H. Whitworth (dyer, England) and Addie E. Smith (Sandwich); residence – Methuen, MA

WICHLAND,
Kathleen Suzanne, b. 9/18/1988 in Peterborough; V. Robert Wichland, Jr. and Suzanne Elizabeth Daschbach

WIGGIN,
Earnest E., d. 3/12/1890; third; George O. Wiggin (minister, Pittsfield) and Lizzie M. Ward (Lowell, MA)

WILLIAMS,
Elaine Marie, b. 5/18/1956 in Laconia; first; Ward B. Williams (draftsman, ME) and Bette A. Davis (NH)

WILLOUGHBY,
Harriet Rose, b. 3/2/1949 in Plymouth; first; Kyle E. Willoughby (farmer, Rumney) and Minerva B. Wallace (Ctr. Sandwich)

WOOD,
Adelberta, b. 7/10/1915; second; Edgar J. Wood (photo eng., Milton, NY) and Edna Langville (Truro, NS)
Edgar J., b. 3/9/1917; third; Edgar J. Wood (engraver, Milton, NY) and Edna M. Langille (NS)

WOODAMAN,
Rebecca Ann, b. 6/14/1996 in North Conway; Michael Jacob Woodaman and Kristine Anne Heffner

WOODWARD,
Marilyn Jean, b. 12/26/1939; first; Robert Woodward (forestry, Laconia) and Priscilla Perkins (Ctr. Ossipee)

WRIGHT,
Peter, b. 10/29/1939; first; Jonathan Wright (salesman, Plymouth, CT) and Barbara Smith (Waterbury, CT)

YOUNG,
daughter, b. 5/29/1934; third; Claiborne Young (headmaster, Wilton) and Mary Tucker (OH)

ZIHERL,
Chelsea O., b. 5/31/1992 in Laconia; Edward J. Ziherl and Olga L. Krajeski

Marriages

ABBOTT,

Arthur F. of Sandwich m. Bertha M. **Felch** of Sandwich 11/17/1898 in Sandwich; H – 23, farmer, b. Ashland, s/o Reuben F. Abbott (Tamworth) and Abby A. Abbott (Sandwich); W – 16, b. Sandwich, d/o Herbert Felch (Sandwich) and Anna Felch (Sandwich)

Arthur F. of Moultonboro m. Diane B. **Bryant** of Sandwich 5/2/1971 in Sandwich; H – s/o Charles Abbott and Jeanette Harmon; W – d/o Milton Bryant and Barbara Hunt

Everett H. m. Lizzie E. **Gilman** 2/8/1907 in Sandwich; H – 19, farmer, b. Sandwich, s/o Reuben F. Abbott (Sandwich) and Abbie A. Tappan (Sandwich); W – 16, b. Tamworth, d/o James W. Gilman (Tamworth) and Hattie B. Davis (Tamworth)

Everett H. of Sandwich m. Mayme M. **Green** of Newbury, VT 2/14/1921 in Newbury; H – 33, millman, b. Sandwich, s/o Freeman Abbott (Sandwich) and Annie Tappan (Sandwich); W – 41, housekeeper, b. Newbury, VT, d/o Joseph P. Bailey (Ryegate, VT) and Lucy R. Martin (Ryegate, VT)

Herbert E. of Sandwich m. Lillian H. **Smith** of Sandwich 8/17/1902 in Sandwich; H – 20, farmer, b. Sandwich, s/o Reuben F. Abbott (Tamworth) and Abbie A. Tappan (Sandwich); W – 16, b. Sandwich, d/o I. Hartwell Smith (Sandwich) and Alice M. Nute (Ossipee)

Ralph H. of Sandwich m. Bernice I. **Blackey** of Moultonboro 1/28/1924 in Sandwich; H – 17, laborer, b. Tamworth, s/o Herbert E. Abbott (Sandwich) and Alice M. Gilman (Tamworth); W – 14, at home, b. S. Tamworth, d/o John L. Blackey (Moultonboro) and Katherine M. Whiting (S. Tamworth)

ADRIANCE,
Edwin L. of Sandwich m. Paula N. **Richmond** of Sandwich 8/7/1976 in Sandwich; H – s/o Vanderpoel Adriance, Jr. and Jane S. Locke; W – d/o Julian Richmond and Edna D. Apteker

ALCOCK,
Frederick Paul of Ashland, MA m. Jo-Anne **Wilbur** of Ashland, MA 10/10/1964; H – 23, laborer, s/o George A. Alcock and Isabelle Manning; W – 21, at home, d/o Benjamin F. Ross and Tanyia Anacki

ALLEN,
Herman A. of Sandwich m. Cora B. **Bagley** of Sandwich 11/24/1904 in Sandwich; H – 30, farmer, b. Moultonboro, s/o Charles A. Allen and Sylvia Nickerson (MA); W – 29, housekeeper, b. Sandwich, d/o Charles Bagley (W. Thornton) and Martha Mudgett (Sandwich)
Melvin C. m. Mildred S. **Angier** 4/24/1909 in Moultonboro; H – 25, laborer, b. Laconia, s/o Charles A. Allen and Sylvia A. Littlefield (Conway); W – 20, b. MA, d/o Frank E. Angier (Randolph, MA) and Addie A. French (Braintree, MA)

AMARAL,
Gregory Kevin of Sandwich m. Kathryn Anne **Fogg** of Sandwich 3/13/1993

AMBROSE,
David G. of Meredith m. Pauline **Vittum** of Sandwich 3/26/1942; H – 26, contractor, b. Moultonboro, s/o David E. Ambrose (Meredith) and Victorine J. Blanchard (Sandwich); W – 22, waitress, b. Sandwich, d/o George W. Vittum (McPherson, KS) and Ethel G. Strong (Charlestown, MA)
Jesse L. of Sandwich m. Mabel E. **Williams** of Sandwich 12/31/1915 in Sandwich; H – 22, farmer, b. Sandwich, s/o

Langdon Ambrose (Sandwich) and Hattie E. Tilton (Sandwich); W – 23, tel. operator, b. Knoxville, TN, d/o Fred W. Williams (Utica, NY) and Agnes Booker (Bloomingdale, TN)

Langdon J. of Sandwich m. Ada M. **Collins** of Colebrook 7/6/1937 in Colebrook; H – 18, student, b. Sandwich, s/o Jesse L. Ambrose (Sandwich) and Mabel E. Williams (Knoxville, TN); W – 23, teacher, b. Colebrook, d/o Guy Collins (Colebrook) and Evie ----- (Colebrook)

Langdon J. of Sandwich m. Gladys R. **Anthony** of Tamworth 6/18/1955; H – 35, welder, b. NH, s/o Jesse L. Ambrose (NH) and Mabel E. Williams (TN); W – 17, at home, b. NH, s/o Arnold G. Anthony (ME) and Ruth Frances Berry (NH)

AMES,

Carl Wilson of Tamworth m. Jean Abbie **Wheeler** of Sandwich 2/29/1952; H – 28, lumbering, b. NH, s/o Claude Palmer Ames (NH) and Blanche J. Jeffers (NH); W – 18, at home, b. NH, d/o Sidney Wheeler (NH) and Cora Bunnell (VT)

Charles E. of Tamworth m. Evalena L. **Nudd** of Sandwich 9/14/1951; H – 19, woodsman, b. NH, s/o Milton C. Ames (NH) and Emma G. Ames (NH); W – 18, at home, b. NH, d/o Wallace Nudd (NH) and Blanche LeClaire (NH)

Roy M., Jr. of Tamworth m. Sheila J. **Cochran** of Sandwich 5/23/1973 in Tamworth; H – s/o Roy M. Ames, Sr. and Lois Conner; W – d/o James Cochran and Myrtle Barnes

William H. of Moultonboro m. Jean P. **Vachon** of Sandwich 3/26/1965; H – 33, carpenter, s/o Harold B. Ames and Charlotte E. Wakefield; W – 29, bookkeeper, d/o Oliver J. Maheux and Virginia J. Jacques

ANAIR,

Roland W., Jr. of Meredith m. Mary **Leach** of Sandwich 4/30/1966; H – 24, tape weaving, s/o Roland W. Anair, Sr.

and Edna Messer; W – 23, lab tester, d/o William A. Leach and Dorothy Weld

ANDERSON,
Richard D. of Meredith m. Margaret H. **Parris** of Sandwich 2/14/1962; H – 31, laborer, s/o Frank Anderson and Lena Page; W – 34, gen. labor, d/o Frank Burrows and Hilda MacDonald
Wallace W. of Sandwich m. Arlene L. **Mitchel** of Sandwich 3/6/1977 in Ctr. Harbor; H – s/o Alfred W. Anderson and Edna Soule; W – d/o Stephen G. Lee and Laura Pierson
William A. of New York, NY m. Mary L. **Cavey** of New York, NY 9/10/1977 in Sandwich; H – s/o Albert O. Anderson and Agnes Ness; W – d/o James E. Cavey and Marie Sharp

ANGEVINE,
Alain Georges of Francin, France m. Christina Wells **O'Brien** of Francin, France 7/14/1996

ANGIER,
Ryvers F. of Laconia m. Grace E. **Wallace** 10/2/1908; H – 24, farmer, b. Sandwich, s/o E. C. Angier (MA) and Emma Hoddle (Sandwich); W – 21, housekeeper, b. Sandwich, d/o Eugene P. Wallace (Sandwich) and Mary Eaton (Sandwich)

ANTHONY,
David L. of Sandwich m. Elizabeth N. **Plummer** of Sandwich 6/23/1968; H – s/o Olney P. Anthony and Mabel H. Jacobs; W – d/o James H. Nixon and Edith Dorr

ASPINWALL,
William of Sandwich m. Ethel **Henderson** of Colebrook 9/23/1925 in Colebrook; H – 43, farmer, b. England, s/o George Aspinwall (England) and Phoebe Whittaker

(England); W – 19, at home, b. Tamworth, d/o Harry Henderson (Tamworth) and Teresa Kelly (Boston, MA)

ATWOOD,

Albert C. of Sandwich m. Emma L. **Bigelow** of Sandwich 6/4/1891 in Sandwich; H – 47, farmer, b. Sandwich, s/o Ira Atwood and Eliza Atwood; W – 45, b. Canada, d/o Stephen Place and Sarah Place

Albert C. of Sandwich m. Nellie G. **Brown** of Sandwich 6/2/1903 in Sandwich; H – 59, farmer, b. Sandwich, s/o Ira Atwood and Eliza A. Godfrey; W – 45, housekeeper, b. Dover, d/o T. Stackpole (Dover) and Elizabeth Heard (Sanford, ME)

Daniel D. of Sandwich m. Emily E. **Atwood** of Sandwich 6/21/1925 in Sandwich; H – 75, jeweler, b. Sandwich, s/o Harrison Atwood (Sandwich) and Sarepta Hatch (Tamworth); W – 54, housekeeper, b. Sandwich, d/o James Burrows (Lebanon, ME) and Sophia Wallace (Sandwich)

Frank L. of Sandwich m. Florence M. **Brown** of Sandwich 9/22/1900 in Sandwich; H – 38, farmer, b. Sandwich, s/o Harrison Atwood (Gray, ME) and Augusta Atwood (Sandwich); W – 22, housewife, b. Sandwich, d/o J. Page Brown and Augie Brown (Gray, ME)

Gerald A. of Sandwich m. Mary Lou **Burrows** of Sandwich 4/26/1963; H – 25, mechanic, s/o Gerald W. Atwood and Virginia Moody; W – 21, beautician, d/o Austin G. Burrows and Thelma M. Dumas

Gerald W. of Sandwich m. Virginia E. **Moody** of S. Tamworth 2/18/1929; H – 22, laborer, b. Sandwich, s/o Frank L. Atwood (Sandwich) and Florence Brown (Sandwich); W – 18, at home, b. Albany, d/o William Moody (Tuftonboro) and Mabel Moore (Tamworth)

Harry A. of Sandwich m. Estella J. **Burrows** of Sandwich 12/24/1889 in Laconia; H – 22, farmer, b. Sandwich, s/o

Albert C. Atwood and Nellie E. Atwood; W – 19, b. Sandwich, d/o James W. Burrows and Sophia Burrows

Hubert L. of Sandwich m. Carol J. **Libby** of Tuftonboro 9/3/1966; H – 32, truck driver, s/o Gerald W. Atwood and Virginia Moody; W – 25, machine operator, d/o Walter R. Smith and Doris H. Mack

Hubert Loring of Sandwich m. Lorraine Priscilla **Stacy** of Tamworth 5/26/1951; H – 17, truck driver, b. NH, s/o Gerald W. Atwood (NH) and Virginia Moody (NH); W – 18, student, b. NH, d/o Nathan John Stacy (NH) and Gladys Marion Ames (NH)

John G. of Sandwich m. Martha J. **Felch** of Sandwich 10/10/1904 in Sandwich; H – 65, blacksmith, b. Sandwich, s/o Ira Atwood (Sandwich) and Eliza Godfrey (Rye); W – 66, housekeeper, b. Moultonboro, d/o Winthrop Grant (Ossipee) and Lavinia Gates (Newington)

Richard A. of N. Sandwich m. Darlene A. **Davis** of N. Sandwich 7/4/1991

Walter G. of Sandwich m. Ethel E. **Cawthorne** of Leominster, MA 12/25/1903 in Leominster, MA; H – 28, farmer, b. Sandwich, s/o Charles H. Atwood (Sandwich) and Eliza Stevenson (Tamworth); W – 30, b. Marlboro, MA, d/o Edwin Cawthorne (Northwood, MA) and Georgianna Crosby (Billerica, MA)

AUGUSTINE,

Charles Whitney of Brookline, MA m. Debbi Lyn **Kerr** of Brookline, MA 8/6/1988

AVERY,

Guy L. of Sandwich m. Viola E. **Mudgett** of Sandwich 11/7/1924 in Moultonboro; H – 21, trucking, b. Rumney, s/o Arthur W. Avery (Campton) and Florence Clifford (Boston, MA); W – 16, at home, b. Sandwich, d/o Jesse Mudgett (Sandwich) and Jennie Sturgis (Albany)

AYERS,
Charles H. of Tuftonboro m. Josephine M. **Nudd** of Sandwich 9/4/1949; H – 21, laborer, b. NH, s/o Levi L. Ayers (NH) and Ruth E. Champaigne (NH); W – 25, housework, b. NH, d/o Wallace Nudd (NH) and Blanche LeClaire (VT)

BACK,
Philip J. of Medford, MA m. Mary A. **McManus** of Somerville, MA 7/27/1963; H – mechanic, s/o Frank J. Back and Viola Rugg; W – 23, at home, d/o Edgar J. Kinnie and Florence Gross

BAGLEY,
Erastus M. of Sandwich m. Alice M. **Webster** of Sandwich 4/21/1893 in Sandwich; H – 19, laborer, b. Campton, s/o Charles M. Bagley (Campton) and Martha Bagley (Sandwich); W – 18, b. Laconia, d/o Charles Webster (Sandwich) and M. M. Webster (Center Harbor)

BAJOWSKI,
John Michael of Anchorage, AK m. Mildred Loretta **Evamme** of Anchorage, AK 8/24/1989

BARGHOUT,
Alexander S. of Dorchester, MA m. Elaine L. **Katapodis** of Dorchester, MA 11/12/1954; H – 21, carpenter, b. MA, s/o Saba Barghout (Syria) and Rose Khoury (Syria); W – 20, office worker, b. MA, d/o Spiros Katapodis (Greece) and Elsie Whalan (Newfoundland)

BARNETT,
Stephen Vincent of Putney, VT m. Isabel Sanchez **de Bustamante** of Sandwich 6/14/1997

BARRIE,

James M. of Greenwich, CT m. Diana F. **Gotshall** of Sandwich 11/21/1964; H – 29, retail executive, s/o John W. Barrie and Sarah V. Macdonald; W – 23, secretary, d/o Abbott Gotshall, Sr. and Bertha L. Woodworth

BATCHELDER,

Lewis Hartwell of Sandwich m. Judith Mary **Wallace** of Sandwich 10/20/1951; H – 18, laborer, b. NH, s/o Lewis H. Batchelder (NH) and Esther Marion Dodge (NH); W – 18, at home, b. NH, d/o Scott E. Wallace (NH) and Mary Joan Falvey (RI)

BATES,

Frank Dudley of Sandwich m. Elizabeth **MacGregor** of Sandwich 3/14/1998

BAUM,

Carl M. of Rockport, ME m. Mary A. **Combe** of Sandwich 10/20/1979 in Sandwich; H – s/o William C. Baum and Miriam Walstead; W – d/o Louis J. Combe and Helen Batinovich

BEACH,

Watson E. of Sandwich m. Florence E. **Hudson** of New Ipswich 6/23/1923 in New Ipswich; H – 23, painter, b. Manchester, s/o John F. Beach (Salisbury, VT) and Edith M. Kelley (Sunderland, VT); W – 20, teacher, b. New Ipswich, d/o Delbert Hudson (Marlborough, MA) and Eva M. Keyes (New Ipswich)

BEAL,

Douglas Welch of Millis, MA m. Terri Lynn **Klippert** of Newton, MA 8/27/1988

BEAN,
Stephen W. of Sandwich m. Marjorie Lee **Nelson** of Sandwich 9/25/1988

BECKMAN,
Thomas H. of Milwaukee, WI m. Bonnie L. **Zuponcic** of Milwaukee, WI 7/14/1973 in Sandwich; H – s/o Harry Beckman and Jane Smith; W – d/o Frank Zuponcic and Josephine Debelar

BEEDE,
George E. of Sandwich m. Dolly C. **Wallace** of Sandwich 9/6/1893 in Sandwich; H – 27, farmer, b. Sandwich, s/o J. Edwin Beede (Sandwich) and Augusta Beede (Tilton); W – 24, dressmaker, b. Sandwich, d/o Asahel Wallace (Sandwich) and Caroline L. Wallace (Sandwich)
James H. of Sandwich m. Harriet **Burrows** of Sandwich 11/15/1920 in Manchester; H – 44, farmer, b. Sandwich, s/o J. Edwin Beede (Sandwich) and Augusta Sullivan (Sanbornton); W – 47, housekeeper, b. Sandwich, d/o Daniel Foss (Sandwich) and Mary Caverly

BELLEVILLE,
Travis Steven of Allenstown m. Julia Marie **Dennett** of Sandwich 10/1/1994

BENNETT,
Edward W. of Sandwich m. Mamie E. **Davis** of Tamworth 12/28/1902 in Chocorua; H – 23, carpenter, b. Sandwich, s/o Wyatt F. Bennett (Sandwich) and Mary A. Hancock (England); W – 17, housekeeper, b. Tamworth, d/o William Davis and Mary M. Money
Kenneth J. of Sandwich m. Karen J. **Stokes** of Sandwich 9/27/1981

Kenneth James of Sandwich m. Lisamarie **Walker** of Sandwich 10/14/1989

BENTON,
Perrin m. Mabel Tappan **O'Brien** 6/4/1907 in Sandwich; H – 63, carpenter, b. Colebrook, s/o Hiram H. Benton (Colebrook) and Annette Wallace (Londonderry); W – 23, housewife, b. Sandwich, d/o Jonathan Tappan (Sandwich) and Julia Nute (Sandwich)
Richard L., Jr. of Sandwich m. Frances D. **Strayer** of Sandwich 6/30/1979 in Moultonboro; H – s/o Richard L. Benton and Nancy Browne; W – d/o Paul J. Strayer and Sarah Kollock

BENVENUTO,
John F. of Somerville, MA m. Ellen L. **Fleischmann** of Somerville, MA 9/14/1985

BERG,
Gunnar of N. Sandwich m. Martha **Nichols** of Brighton, MA 9/24/1983

BERKING,
Charles R. of Moultonboro m. Susan J. **Peaslee** of Moultonboro 10/18/2003 in Sugar Hill

BERNT,
Harold of Center Harbor m. Madeleine Marie **Gerli** of Sandwich 3/26/1994

BERRY,
Fred W. of Moultonboro m. Grace L. **Dearborn** of Sandwich 5/19/1901 in Sandwich; H – 22, farmer, b. Moultonboro, s/o George T. Berry (Moultonboro) and Emma B. Berry (Meredith); W – 19, b. Sandwich, s/o John Dearborn (Effingham) and Dora Dearborn (Sandwich)

Nahum J. of Center Harbor m. Honora **Hayes** 9/6/1908; H – 41, housekeeper, b. MA, s/o Aaron Berry (ME) and Lydia Johnson (MA); W – 30, teacher, b. St. John, NB, d/o John Hayes and Mary Hayes

BIBBER,
Ross E. of Boston, MA m. Helen G. **Martin** of Sandwich 5/26/1928 in Laconia; H – 21, rest. manager, b. Halifax, NS, s/o Amos Webb and Lelilia Webb; W – 18, at home, b. Melrose, MA, d/o Levi Martin and Ella J. Martin

BIBBS,
Michael Derek of New York, NY m. Rachel Ann **McCarthy** of New York, NY 7/31/1993

BICKFORD,
Carl O. of Sandwich m. Elva L. **Floyd** of Tamworth 4/8/1937 in Plymouth; H – 27, farmer, b. Meredith, s/o Roy F. Bickford (Meredith) and M. Leonora Brown (Gilford); W – 25, teacher, b. Tamworth, d/o Perley E. Floyd (Tamworth) and Nettie Grant (Sandwich)
Charles R. of Sandwich m. Edna A. **Burrows** of Sandwich 8/16/1932; H – 24, farmer, b. Meredith, s/o Roy F. Bickford (Meredith) and M. Leonora Brown; W – 22, at home, b. Sandwich, d/o Harry L. Burrows (Sandwich) and Adelaide S. Hull (Ashland)
Charles R., Jr. of Sandwich m. Jill S. **Chase** of Sandwich 9/6/1964; H – 21, student, s/o Charles R. Bickford and Edna A. Burrows; W – 18, student, d/o Elliott W. Chase and Virginia S. Davis
Fred A. of Rumney m. Stella M. **Crawford** of Ashland 2/22/1920 in Sandwich; H – 26, lumber, b. E. Haverhill, s/o Nathan A. Bickford (Dorchester) and Viola Avery (Rumney); W – 24, housekeeper, b. N. Holderness, d/o Henry A. Crawford (Ashland) and Emma McDonald (NS)

Fred Eric of Sandwich m. Joanne **Comer** of Sandwich 2/18/1989
Fred M. of Sandwich m. Ingrid E. **Ingles** of Sandwich 6/18/1949; H – 23, farmer, b. NH, s/o Fred A. Bickford (NH) and Stella Crawford (NH); W – 22, student, b. MA, d/o Eric G. Ingles (Sweden) and Emma Helen Larsson (MA)
Fred M. of Sandwich m. Janet I. **Johnston** of Sandwich 8/13/1976 in Sandwich; H – s/o Fred A. Bickford and Stella Crawford; W – d/o Dwight E. Burnham and Bernice D. Snyder
Karl H. of Sandwich m. Helen Louise **Denney** of Sandwich 10/4/1921 in Meredith; H – 20, laborer, b. Moultonboro, s/o George O. Bickford (Sandwich) and Margaret Hudson (Amherst, NS); W – 16, spinner, b. Sandwich, d/o Harry A. Denney (Meredith) and Edith M. Clark (Sandwich)
Silas H. of Sandwich m. Nellie E. **Brown** of Sandwich 1/4/1892 in Sandwich; H – 25, farmer, b. Sandwich, s/o Noah W. Bickford (Rochester) and A. M. Bickford; W – 19, b. Sandwich, d/o Page Brown (Sandwich) and Angie Brown
Wyatt T. of Sandwich m. A. **Hall** of Ossipee 9/9/1906 in Moultonboro; H – 65, farmer, b. Sandwich, s/o Freeman Bickford; W – 78, housewife, b. Ossipee, d/o Robert -----

BICKNELL,
Brooks E. of Boulder, CO m. Melinda A. **Grinold** of Boulder, CO 6/6/1987

BIGELOW,
Walter R. m. Lillian F. **Mudgett** of Sandwich 12/25/1905 in Sandwich; H – 20, s/o William R. Bigelow (Canada) and Emma L. Bigelow (Canada); W – 19, b. Sandwich, d/o Erastus W. Mudgett (Sandwich) and Susan M. Mudgett (Haverhill)

BLACKEY,
Earl R. of Moultonboro m. Linda M. **Rowan** of Sandwich 7/2/1977 in Moultonboro; H – s/o Herbert F. Blackey and Beatrice Dalton; W – d/o Robert J. Rowan and Suzanne Robbins
Elijah S. of Sandwich m. Lizzie A. **Wade** of Sandwich 11/24/1887 in Sandwich; H – 39, farmer, b. Sandwich, s/o Ira Blackey (Sandwich) and Sarah Blackey (Thornton); W – 18, b. Center Harbor, d/o Lyman Wade (Moultonboro) and Martha Wade (Center Harbor)
Ralph A. of Sandwich m. Grace Chase **Burnham** of Sandwich 2/2/1921 in Sandwich; H – 29, farmer, b. Sandwich, s/o Elijah Blackey (Sandwich) and Lizzie Wade (Sandwich); W – 40, housekeeper, b. Belle Fontaine, OH, d/o Samuel Chase (Conway) and Betsy Carter (Conway)

BLANCHARD,
Charles of Sandwich m. Nancy M. **Fellows** of Sandwich 10/22/1901 in Sandwich; H – 65, merchant, b. Sandwich, s/o August Blanchard and Betsey Ambrose (Moultonboro); W – 67, housewife, b. Sandwich, d/o Nathan Mason (Sandwich) and Charlotte P. Quimby (Sandwich)
Charles E. of Sandwich m. M. Elisabeth **Sawyer** of Bartlett 11/2/1893 in Bartlett; H – 33, publisher, b. Sandwich, s/o Arven Blanchard (Hopkinton) and Nellie S. Blanchard (Sandwich); W – 27, compositor, b. Lovell, ME, d/o Barnet W. Sawyer (Lovell, ME) and Drucilla Sawyer (Lovell, ME)
Charles O. of Sandwich m. G. Ella **Smith** of Sandwich 6/1/1892 in Sandwich; H – 41, farmer, b. Eaton, s/o Thomas C. Blanchard (Sandwich) and Sarah Blanchard (Sandwich); W – 39, teacher, b. Sandwich, d/o James M. Smith (Sandwich) and Lydia F. Smith (Sandwich)
George A. of Sandwich m. Adele H. **Jaclard** of Moultonboro 3/18/1891 in Moultonboro; H – 27, farmer, b. Sandwich,

s/o Arven Blanchard and Nellie S. Blanchard; W – 27, b. Moultonboro, d/o A. P. Jaclard and Harriett S. Jaclard

Harry of Sandwich m. Mildred M. **Tibbetts** of Sandwich 9/11/1916 on the Summit of Mt. Washington; H – 36, real estate, b. Sandwich, s/o Owen Blanchard (Hopkinton) and Helen S. Creighton (Sandwich); W – 40, housekeeper, b. Benton, d/o William Tibbetts (England) and Katherine King (Canada)

BLEIER,

Barry B. of Milwaukee, WI m. Margot **Dunbar** of Cambridge, MA 7/5/1969; H – s/o Harold R. Bleier and Evelyn Barrett; W – d/o Roger M. Dunbar and Jessie Schermerhorn

BLUMBERG,

Lawrence J. of Sandwich m. Barbara H. **Forbes** of Holderness 12/29/1940; H – 29, woodworker, b. Sandwich, s/o Simon N. Blumberg (Liverpool, England) and Estella Clay (Sandwich); W – 20, hair-dresser, b. Somerville, MA, d/o Arthur W. Forbes (Kemp, NS) and Dorothy J. Haskell (Holderness)

Lawrence J. of Sandwich m. Maevina L. **Smith** of Sandwich 10/26/1961; H – 50, cabinet maker, s/o Simon N. Blumberg and Estella Clay; W – 26, dietician, d/o Jack Locke and Ethel Pryor

Simon N. of Sandwich m. Stella E. **Clay** of Sandwich --/8/1911; H – 25, clerk, b. Liverpool, England, s/o Levi Blumberg (Germany) and Mary Blumberg (Germany); W – 22, b. Sandwich, d/o Henry N. Clay (Leominster) and Almenia Pettingill (Sandwich)

BOARDMAN,

Carlos Weston of Hartford, VT m. Margaret Helen **Burrows** of Sandwich 11/24/1942; H – 36, laborer, b. Norwich, VT, s/o Weston C. Boardman (Hartford, VT) and Ethel Hodgdon

(Northampton, MA); W – 15, at home, b. Sandwich, d/o Frank N. Burrows (Sandwich) and Hilda B. MacDonald (Wolfeboro)

BORTMAN,
David C. of Sandwich m. Dena R. **Rosenthal** of Sandwich 8/21/1982
David C. of Ctr. Sandwich m. Cia R. **Khakaura** of Ctr. Sandwich 8/25/2000

BOURGHALEM,
Farid of Paris, France m. Rebecca A. **Cole** of Sandwich 1/20/2002 in Sandwich

BOUTWELL,
Henry W. of Manchester m. Mary **Stanton** of Sandwich 11/5/1895 in Sandwich; H – 47, physician, b. Lyndeboro, VT; W – 34, teacher, b. Sandwich, d/o Levi Stanton and Annie Stanton

BOWDEN,
David K. of Sandwich m. Babette Hall **Bennett** of Chappaqua, NY 8/20/1995

BOYD,
James S. of Tamworth m. Elmer R. **Hill** of Sandwich 7/21/1894 in Sandwich; H – 28, laborer, b. St. Johns, NB, s/o Hugh Boyd (St. John, NB) and Elizabeth Boyd (St. John, NB); W – 29, housewife, b. PA, d/o Benjamin Hill (Sandwich) and Elizabeth Hill (Sandwich)

BRADFIELD,
Robert John, III of Sandwich m. Tracy Jean **Banks** of Concord 12/26/1998

BREED,

Richard Allen of Tamworth m. Elizabeth Hoag **Weed** of Roslindale, MA 9/26/1942; H – 34, machinist foreman, b. Watertown, MA, s/o Edwin S. Breed (Lynn, MA) and Stella E. Murray (Pittsfield, MA); W – 30, med. sec., b. Sandwich, d/o Chester A. Weed (Sandwich) and Ella C. Hoag (Tamworth)

BRITTON,

Marry of Tuftonboro m. Carrie **Taylor** of Sandwich 5/23/1959; H – 21, mechanic, s/o Fred J. Britton and Ruth Simms; W – 16, at home, d/o Paul A. Taylor and Marion E. Gray

BRODERICK,

Roric S. of Sandwich m. Catherine E. **Hope** of Sandwich 9/25/1995

BROWN,

Arthur B. of Sandwich m. Alice K. **Simons** of Laconia 9/21/1968; H – s/o Andrew J. Brown and Ida Beaudine; W – d/o Charles D. Knowlton and Sarah P. Tilton

Carroll G. m. Eunice **Whiting** 6/11/1927; H – 20, laborer, b. Sandwich, s/o George E. Brown (Sandwich) and Myrtle J. Grant (Sandwich); W – 16, at home, b. Tamworth, d/o Fred Whiting (Tamworth) and Georgia Jeffers (Tamworth)

Charles F. of Sandwich m. Nellie M. **Snow** of Sandwich 12/9/1899 in Whiteface; H – 54, farmer, b. Sandwich, s/o Daniel Brown (Sandwich) and ----- Brown (Tamworth); W – 20, housekeeper, b. Sandwich, d/o James N. Snow (Strafford) and Lucy M. Snow (Sandwich)

Clarence M. of Sandwich m. Elizabeth **Meader** of Ryegate, VT 7/5/1925 in Sandwich; H – 21, laborer, b. Sandwich, s/o Frank W. Brown (Sandwich) and Alice G. Elliott (Sandwich); W – 21, teacher, b. Ryegate, VT, d/o Granville Meader (Ryegate, VT) and Rhenie Peach (Ryegate, VT)

Clarence R. of Sandwich m. M. Louise **Follett** of Lebanon 9/23/1918 in Sandwich; H – 21, watchman, b. Sandwich, s/o Daniel O. Brown (Sandwich) and Elizabeth Fogg (Sandwich); W – 18, teacher, b. Ashland, d/o Charles F. Follett (S. Tamworth) and S. Abbie Wallace (S. Tamworth)

Donald E. of Sandwich m. Jane T. **Kroeger** of Sandwich 4/18/1987

Edward I. of Meredith m. Nancy A. **Cook** of Sandwich 6/18/1957; H – 24, truck driver, b. NH, s/o Glenn I. Brown (NH) and Dorothy Ambrose (NH); W – 17, b. NH, d/o Wilbur A. Cook (NH) and Edna R. Cook (NH)

Edgar E. of Sandwich m. Evelyn B. **Battis** of Laconia 6/23/1928; H – 29, millman, b. Sandwich, s/o Moses Brown and Christine Robins (PEI); W – 20, at home, b. Laconia

Frank G. of Sandwich m. Jean F. **Leach** of Sandwich 9/27/1945; H – 19, farm work, b. Sandwich, s/o Clarence M. Brown (Sandwich) and Elizabeth Meader (Ryegate, VT); W – 18, housework, b. Sandwich, d/o William A. Leach (Concord) and Dorothy E. Weld (Manchester)

Frank W. of Sandwich m. Alice G. **Elliott** of Sandwich 4/9/1903 in Meredith; H – 34, laborer, b. Sandwich, s/o John P. Brown (Nottingham) and Angie Palmer (Bath, ME); W – 16, b. Sandwich, d/o John G. Elliott and Ida Rowe (Sandwich)

George E. of Sandwich m. Myrtie G. **Grant** of Sandwich 11/29/1900 in Sandwich; H – 19, farmer, b. Sandwich, s/o Charles F. Brown (Sandwich) and Harriet N. Brown (Sandwich); W – 19, housewife, b. Sandwich, d/o George A. M. Grant (Sandwich) and Clara H. Grant (Sandwich)

George E. of Sandwich m. Margaret **Mentiply** of Cambridge, MA 4/30/1932; H – 49, farmer, b. Sandwich, s/o Charles F. Brown (Sandwich) and Harriet Bennett (Sandwich); W – 49, cook, b. Scotland, d/o James Mentiply (Scotland) and Betsy Bell (Scotland)

George W. of Sandwich m. Josephine **Harrington** of Framingham, MA 11/9/1914 in N. Sandwich; H – 42, laborer, b. Cape Elizabeth, ME, s/o Royal P. Brown (Isle of Shoals, ME) and Christie H. Ward (Eaton); W – 36, housekeeper, b. Providence, RI, d/o Philip Harrington (Providence, RI) and Sarah J. Green (Providence, RI)

Joel N. of Melrose, MA m. Lizzie S. **Hart** of Sandwich 6/6/1895 in Sandwich; H – 53, b. Newbury, VT, s/o James E. Brown (Conway) and Mabel Brown; W – 35, b. Sandwich, d/o Sargent Severance (Sandwich) and Mary Severance

Lyle A. of Nashua m. Susan M. **Bullard** of Sandwich 7/11/1931; H – 34, manufacturer, b. Marion, IN, s/o Charles A. Brown (Chillecothe, OH) and Georgia LaBell (Chicago, IL); W – 27, at home, b. Arlington, MA, d/o Harry Bullard (Cambridge, MA) and Maybelle Palmer (Winchester, MA)

Orin Franklin of Moultonboro m. Helen Louise **Richardson** of Sandwich 6/20/1953; H – 42, laborer, b. MA, s/o Burtis Brown and Laura Lena Dorman; W – 33, at home, b. NH, d/o Jess Olden (NY) and Martha Ladd (NH)

Randolph of Derry m. Ann Susan **Tilton** of Derry 2/8/1975 in Sandwich; H – s/o Bernard W. Brown and Dorothea Cheney; W – d/o Howard F. Tilton, Sr. and Ferne Mountz

Warren J. of Sandwich m. Nellie G. **Chandler** of Lynn 10/25/1896 in Sandwich; H – 54, farmer, b. Sandwich, s/o R. S. Brown (Sandwich) and Lydia S. Brown (Sandwich); W – 38, housekeeper, b. Lynn, MA, d/o Timothy Stackpole (Dover)

BROWNLIE,

Albert C. m. Dorothy W. **Peaslee** 8/6/1927; H – 31, plumber, b. Everett, MA, s/o John Brownlie (London, England) and Caroline Dickinson (London, England); W – 26, at home, b. Lynn, MA, d/o Charles S. Wing (Fayette, ME) and Dora B. Preston (Manchester)

BROZOVICH,

Shawn Daniel of Farmington Hills, MI m. Carrie Lynne **Miller** of Canton, OH 8/26/1994

BRYANT,

Edward J. of Sandwich m. Eva M. **Smith** of Sandwich 2/5/1902 in Sandwich; H – 25, laborer, b. Sandwich, s/o Clarence E. Bryant (Sandwich) and Mary H. Martin (Tamworth); W – 21, teacher, b. Sandwich, d/o Charles H. Smith (Sandwich) and Margaret Hale (Bethlehem)

John E. G. of Sandwich m. Helen B. **Leete** of Lansdowne, PA 11/14/1958; H – 74, retired, s/o John E. Bryant (Canada) and Antoinette Reazin (Canada); W – 60, retired, d/o Edward Rufus Barnard (CT) and Stella F. Saunders (MA)

John W. of Sandwich m. Madeline M. **Robinson** of Sandwich 1/5/1923 in Sandwich; H – 19, laborer, b. Sandwich, s/o Walter C. Bryant (Moultonboro) and Elizabeth M. Severance (Sandwich); W – 16, at home, b. Cambridge, MA, d/o Wiliam J. Robinson (Portland, ME) and Nettie L. Quimby (Stewartstown)

John W., Jr. of Sandwich m. Laura M. **Wilkins** of Meredith 9/30/1945; H – 19, truck driver, b. Cambridge, MA, s/o John W. Bryant (Sandwich) and Madeline Robinson (Cambridge, MA); W – 18, at home, b. Springfield, MA, d/o Lawrence A. Wilkins (Haverhill) and Hazel H. Danforth (Springfield, MA)

Milton R. of Sandwich m. Barbara M. **Hunt** of Sandwich 9/4/1949; H – 17, farmer, b. NH, s/o John W. Bryant (NH) and Madelaine M. Robinson (MA); W – 17, at home, b. MA, d/o Kenneth L. Hunt (MA) and Doris E. Perkins (MA)

Milton R., Jr. of Sandwich m. Louisa W. **Brewer** of Sandwich 1/10/1976 in Ctr. Harbor; H – s/o Milton R. Bryant and Barbara M. Hunt; W – d/o Roberts W. Brewer and Jane A. Pinney

Stewart R. of Sandwich m. Helen F. **Nelson** of Moultonboro 6/11/1946; H – 21, carpenter, b. Sandwich, s/o Winfield S. Bryant (Sandwich) and Dorothy B. Atwood (Sandwich); W – 18, hairdresser, b. Moultonboro, d/o Jacob Nelson (Norway) and Lanora Wakefield (Moultonboro)

Walter C. of Sandwich m. Lizzie M. **Severance** of Sandwich 5/15/1899 in Sandwich; H – 32, farmer, b. Moultonboro, s/o William Bryant (Center Harbor) and Lucinda F. Bryant (Moultonboro); W – 19, b. Sandwich, d/o John Severance (Sandwich) and Helen M. Severance (Boscawen)

Walter C. of Sandwich m. Rose **Plummer** of Sandwich 2/20/1919 in Sandwich; H – 52, farmer, b. Moultonboro, s/o William Bryant (Moultonboro) and Lucinda Glines (Moultonboro); W – 42, housekeeper, b. Ireland, d/o John McBride (Ireland) and Ellen Devlin (Ireland)

William A. of Sandwich m. Sylvia L. **Avery** of Sandwich 2/10/1924 in Sandwich; H – 22, laborer, b. Sandwich, s/o Walter C. Bryant (Moultonboro) and Elizabeth M. Severance (Sandwich); W – 18, at home, b. Rumney, d/o Arthur W. Avery (Campton) and Florence Clifford (Boston, MA)

Winfield S. of Sandwich m. Dorothy B. **Atwood** of Sandwich 7/7/1919 in Sandwich; H – 18, painter, b. Sandwich, s/o Walter C. Bryant (Moultonboro) and Mary Severance (Sandwich); W – 17, at home, b. Sandwich, d/o Frank L. Atwood (Sandwich) and Florence Brown (Sandwich)

BRYAR,

Charles A. of Belmont, MA m. Katherine R. **Flett** 7/15/1908; H – 20, student, b. Sandwich, s/o Frank A. Bryar (Sandwich) and Annie Leary (Boston, MA); W – 20, merchant, b. Hyde Park, d/o George C. Flett (Belmont) and Marguerette Watson (Boston)

Fred E. of Sandwich m. Maud A. **Quimby** of Sandwich 6/13/1896 in Sandwich; H – 25, physician, b. Laconia, s/o

J. G. Bryar (Laconia) and Flora Bryar (Compton, PQ); W – 20, teacher, b. Sandwich, d/o S. F. Quimby (Sandwich) and Susan Quimby (Tamworth)

Fred E. of Sandwich m. Florence G. **Mooney** of Sandwich 11/25/1914 in Laconia; H – 43, physician, b. Laconia, s/o James G. Bryar (Laconia) and Flora Simonds (Compton, Canada); W – 22, nurse, b. Alexandria, Canada, d/o Harry Mooney and Sarah B. McDonald (Alexandria, Canada)

BUCHER,

R. Lawrence of Sandwich m. Page A. **Rozelle** of Sandwich 9/10/1983

BUCHMAN,

Thomas A., Jr. of Detroit, MI m. Loretta M. **Keese** of Sandwich 8/27/1965; H – 20, US Navy, s/o Thomas Buchman, Sr. and Ivell A. Schmitz; W – 18, at home, d/o John D. Keese, Jr. and Florence M. Waugh

BULLARD,

H. Benjamin, IV of N. Sandwich m. Betty V. **Webster** of N. Sandwich 7/11/1992

Howard B., IV of Guilford, CT m. Betty V. **Webster** of Sandwich 8/4/1973 in Sandwich; H – s/o Howard B. Bullard III and Patricia Gilpin; W – d/o John R. Webster and Louise VanVoorhees

BUNDY,

Oscar E. of Sandwich m. Sarah E. **Skinner** of Sandwich 5/6/1903 in Sandwich; H – 25, painter, b. Newburyport, s/o Edwin Bundy (Springfield, VT) and Elizabeth Buzzell (Moultonboro); W – 17, b. Sandwich, d/o Charles E. Skinner (Sandwich) and Jennie Torry (Patten, VT)

BURLEIGH,

Clarence B. of Augusta, ME m. Sarah P. **Quimby** of Sandwich 11/24/1887 in Sandwich; H – 23, journalism, b. Linneus, ME, s/o Edwin C. Burleigh and Mary J. Burleigh; W – 23, b. Sandwich, d/o Joseph H. Quimby (Sandwich) and Nancy J. Quimby (Sandwich)

Thomas E. of Sandwich m. Mary E. **Bigelow** of Sandwich 1/25/1893 in Sandwich; H – 24, laborer, b. Sandwich, s/o Frank E. Burleigh (Sandwich) and Emely Burleigh (Sandwich); W – 25, b. Lyndon, VT, d/o William R. Bigelow (Lyndon, VT) and Emma L. Atwood (Sandwich)

BURNHAM,

Charles S. of Sandwich m. Grace **Chase** of Sandwich 5/24/1901 in Sandwich; H – 19, clerk, b. Sandwich, s/o E. W. Burnham (Sandwich) and Susan Burnham (Sandwich); W – 22, dressmaker, b. Bellefontaine, OH, d/o Samuel Chase (Conway) and Betsey Chase (Albany)

Charles S. of Sandwich m. Jeantte T. **Clark** of Rockland, MA 1/7/1920 in Center Harbor; H – 37, US mail, b. Sandwich, s/o E. W. Burnham (Sandwich) and Susan M. Smith (Sandwich); W – 38, housekeeper, b. Hingham, MA, d/o Charles M. Clark (Portland, ME) and Elizabeth M. Tower (Hingham, MA)

BURNS,

David P. of Sandwich m. Regina A. **Nadeau** of New Hampton 9/9/2000

Michael Evans of Sandwich m. Jacqueline Ella **Heard** of Sandwich 8/7/1993

BURRITT,

Arthur Ware of Chocorua m. Joan Ellen **Guild** of Sandwich 5/7/1988

BURROWS,

Austin G. of Sandwich m. Thelma **Dumas** of Billerica, MA 4/19/1936 in Billerica, MA; H – 26, laborer, b. Sandwich, s/o Charles Burrows and Amy Gilman; W – 18, hairdresser, b. Woburn, MA, d/o Godfrey Dumas and Lumena LeBlanc

Bruce J. of Sandwich m. Jill S. **Downs** of Portsmouth 8/17/1968; H – s/o Nathaniel Burrows and Edrie Gordon; W – d/o Edward S. Downs and Jane Fielding

Charles G. of Sandwich m. Anna L. **Geers** of Northwood 7/29/1949; H – 25, post office clerk, b. NH, s/o Nathaniel H. Burrows (NH) and Edrie H. Gordon (NY); W – 24, home demons., b. NH, d/o Lawrence M. Geers (NH) and Ada Berg (Sweden)

Charles H. of Sandwich m. Amy M. **Gilman** of Sandwich 1/1/899 in Sandwich; H – 37, farmer, b. Sandwich, s/o Nathaniel Burrows (Lebanon, ME) and Sarah D. Burrows (Sandwich); W – 24, housekeeper, b. Sandwich, d/o John C. Gilman (Sandwich) and Maria E. Gilman (Sandwich)

Chester J. of Sandwich m. Beatrice **Plume** of Sandwich 2/26/1934; H – 20, laborer, b. Sandwich, s/o Newell J. Burrows (Sandwich) and Nellie Hodge (Sandwich); W – 18, housekeeper, b. Groton, d/o Percy Plume (Ft. Kent, ME) and Grace Pickering (Rumney)

Chester J., Jr. of Sandwich m. Patricia A. **Randlett** of Ashland 10/28/1967; H – 23, laborer, s/o Chester J. Burrows, Sr. and Beatrice V. Plume; W – 22, keypunch operator, d/o Warren E. Randlett and Gladys T. Clogston

Donald H. of Sandwich m. Beatrice **Willoughby** of Moultonboro 7/9/1948; H – 21, painter, b. Rumney, s/o Nathaniel Burrows (Sandwich) and Edrie Gordon (New York, NY); W – 17, at home, b. Moultonboro, d/o Carl Willoughby (Springfield, MA) and Mabel Larson (Laconia)

Frank N. of Sandwich m. Hilda B. **McDonald** of Sandwich 11/26/1921 in Sandwich; H – 21, laborer, b. Sandwich, s/o

Newell Burrows (Sandwich) and Nellie P. Hodge (Sandwich); W – 17, at home, b. Wolfeboro, d/o A. M. McDonald (N. Wakefield) and Helen Bickford (Wolfeboro)

Frank N. of Sandwich m. Eldora F. **Taylor** of Sandwich 3/8/1930; H – 29, laborer, b. Sandwich, s/o Newell J. Burrows (Sandwich) and Nellie Hodge (Sandwich); W – 15, at home, b. Sandwich, d/o William H. Taylor (Sandwich) and Christine Skinner (Sandwich)

Fred N. of Sandwich m. Grace E. **Skinner** of Sandwich 5/30/1902 in Sandwich; H – 25, farmer, b. Sandwich, s/o Nathaniel Burrows (Lebanon) and Sarah D. Thompson (Sandwich); W – 18, b. Moultonboro, d/o Charles E. Skinner (Sandwich) and Jennie Torrey (Patten, ME)

Fred Walter of Sandwich m. Nora E. **Davis** of Tamworth 12/31/1935; H – 26, mail carrier, b. Sandwich, s/o Fred N. Burrows (Sandwich) and Grace E. Skinner (Moultonboro); W – 21, at home, b. Tamworth, d/o Alva Davis (Ossipee) and Florence Wiggin (Ossipee)

Harry L. of Sandwich m. Adelaid S. **Hull** of Sandwich 5/21/1904 in Meredith; H – 21, farmer, b. Sandwich, s/o James W. Burrows (Milton) and Sophia E. Wallace (Sandwich); W – 20, b. Plymouth, d/o Luther B. Hull (Plymouth) and Emma E. DeMott (Boston)

James M. of Sandwich m. Rita D. **Morrison** of Ashland 11/26/1945; H – 21, laborer, b. Sandwich, s/o Frank N. Burrows (Sandwich) and Hilda B. MacDonald (Wolfeboro); W – 18, housework, b. Ashland, d/o Clifton W. Morrison (Laconia) and Doris A. Beaman (Ashland)

Jere Gordon of Sandwich m. Suzanne Mae **Buckley** of Sandwich 1/19/1980

John G. of Sandwich m. Hattie Foss **Smith** of Sandwich 10/3/1891 in Sandwich; H – 28, farmer, b. Sandwich, s/o James N. Burrows and L. E. Burrows; W – 19, b. Sandwich, d/o Daniel Foss and Mary E. Foss

Jon L. of Sandwich m. Wendy L. **Evans** of Tamworth 11/3/1973 in Tamworth; H – s/o Lester Burrows, Jr. and Marjorie Nelson; W – d/o Gordon Evans and Marilyn Larrabee

Jon Lester of Moultonboro m. Darlene Elliott **Racine** of Ctr. Sandwich 7/11/1992

Lester D. of Sandwich m. Beatrice **Doughty** of Bailey's Island, ME 2/12/1923 in Sandwich; H – 18, laborer, b. Sandwich, s/o Harry L. Burrows (Sandwich) and Adelaide S. Hull (Ashland); W – 22, teacher, b. Bailey's Island, ME, d/o Stephen Doughty (Chebeague, ME) and Mary C. Johnson (Bailey's Island, ME)

Lester D., Jr. of Sandwich m. Marjorie L. **Nelson** of Moultonboro 11/23/1945; H – 22, marker, b. Sandwich, s/o Lester D. Burrows (Sandwich) and Beatrice W. Doughty (Bailey's Island); W – 20, at home, b. Moultonboro, d/o Jacob Nelson (Norway) and Lanora Wakefield (Moultonboro)

Luther J. of Sandwich m. Rosealie E. **Quimby** of Sandwich 5/23/1931; H – 23, laborer, b. Sandwich, s/o Harry L. Burrows (Sandwich) and Adelaide S. Hull (Ashland); W – 20, teacher, b. Sandwich, d/o Wilbur E. Quimby (Sandwich) and Ida Lindstrom (Sweden)

Luther James of Sandwich m. Gladys Mae **Townsley** of Laconia 6/28/1953; H – 46, carpenter, b. NH, s/o Harry L. Burrows (NH) and Adelaide S. Hull (NH); W – 42, teacher, b. MA, d/o Willis M. Townsley (MA) and Mabel Newcomb (MA)

Nathaniel of Sandwich m. Edrie H. **Gordon** of Rumney 10/13/1923 in Sandwich; H – 19, laborer, b. Sandwich, s/o Charles H. Burrows (Sandwich) and Amy M. Gilman (Sandwich); W – 21, teacher, b. New York, NY, d/o Jesse H. Gordon (Landaff) and Martha E. Nourse (Derby Ctr., VT)

Newell J. of Sandwich m. Nellie F. **Hodge** of Sandwich 7/30/1896 in Sandwich; H – 23, farmer, b. Sandwich, s/o J. W. Burrows and Sophia Burrows (Sandwich); W – 17, b.

Sandwich, d/o John N. Hodge (Sandwich) and Etta Hodge (Holderness)

Phillip F. of Meredith m. Alice E. **Elliott** of Meredith 8/28/1971 in Meredith; H – s/o Frank Burrows and Eldora Taylor; W – d/o Harold Weeks and Ruth Davis

Phillip T. of Sandwich m. Patricia M. **Hodgdon** of Moultonboro 3/14/1959; H – 25, unemployed, s/o Frank N. Burrows and Eldora F. Taylor; W – 19, bobbin winder, d/o Samuel F. Hodgdon and Margery Harriman

Robert N. of Sandwich m. Beverly F. **Davis** of Laconia 4/20/1957; H – 23, US Air Force, b. NH, s/o Nathaniel Burrows (NH) and Edrie Gordon (NH); W – 17, student, b. NH, d/o Richard L. Davis (NH) and Melba M. Evans (TX)

Robert N. of Sandwich m. Dorothy **McCarthy** of Sandwich 12/19/1987

Roger N. of Sandwich m. Blanche E. **Patrick** of Center Harbor 12/13/1958; H – 28, truck driver, s/o Frank N. Burrows (NH) and Eldora F. Taylor (NH); W – 22, housework, d/o Elizabeth Patrick

Thomas F. of Sandwich m. Donna M. **Grisco** of Sandwich 6/28/1980

BURT,

Albert E. of Ashland m. Edith S. **Quimby** of Sandwich 7/6/1931; H – 42, life insurance, b. Sutton, PQ, s/o Almon Burt (Dunham, Canada) and Ida M. Beard (Iron Hill, Canada); W – 37, at home, b. Boston, MA, d/o Edward E. Quimby (Sandwich) and Grace M. Harris (Canning, NS)

BURTON,

Francis A. of Moultonboro m. Virginia B. **Emerson** of Sandwich 1/11/1969; H – s/o Earl Burton and Elizabeth Miller; W – d/o William J. Davis and Beatrice Lowell

CAHOON,
Dennis F. of Moultonboro m. Roberta A. **Deming** of Sandwich 8/4/1974 in Sandwich; H – s/o John Cahoon and Marie Hogan; W – d/o Roger Deming and Martha White

CAILEY,
Gloyd R. of Bristol m. Janet E. **Plummer** of Sandwich 1/20/1956; H – 24, laborer, b. NH, s/o Roger S. Cailey (NH) and Dora M. Reid (NH); W – 19, clerical work, b. NH, d/o James H. Plummer, Jr. (NH) and Edna B. Nelson (NH)

CAMPBELL,
Everett of Sandwich m. Pauline Eleanor **Seeley** of Sandwich 5/2/1942; H – 27, laborer, b. Sandwich, s/o John W. Campbell and Grace Elliott (Sandwich); W – 21, at home, b. Laconia, d/o Rupert D. Bragg (Center Harbor) and Blanche George (Plymouth)
John N. of Sandwich m. Mary A. **Fifield** of Sandwich 8/8/1900 in Sandwich; H – 52, farmer, b. Bedford, s/o Abner Campbell (Bedford) and Mary Campbell (Merrimac); W – 51, housewife, b. Ossipee, d/o Thomas Knox
John W. m. Grace **Elliott** 12/19/1910; H – 22, farmer, b. Sandwich, s/o John N. Campbell (Londonderry) and Bernice Bancroft (Meredith); W – 20, b. Sandwich, d/o John Elliott (Sandwich) and Ida E. Rowe (Canada)

CANFIELD,
Thomas Matthew of Sandwich m. Amy Elizabeth **MacMillan** of Meredith 8/7/2004 in Meredith

CAREY,
Richard A. of N. Sandwich m. Susan A. **Pelizza** of N. Sandwich 4/21/2000

CARINI,

Peter Augustus of S. Hadley, MA m. Johanna Beth **Knowles** of S. Hadley, MA 9/20/1997

CARLETON,

Dean W., Jr. of N. Sandwich m. Marybeth R. **Chase** of N. Sandwich 6/1/1991

CARLSON,

Walter R. of Sandwich m. Agnes J. **Garland** of W. Hartford, CT 6/1/1968; H – s/o Andrew J. Carlson and Irene M. Holmstrom; W – d/o David Watson and Margaret Forster

Walter R., Jr. of Sandwich m. Georgia A. **White** of Wolfeboro 9/7/1957; H – 23, student, b. MA, s/o Walter R. Carlson (MA) and Ruth G. Cohenno (MA); W – 19, student, b. MA, d/o George W. White (MA) and Helen H. Horne (MA)

CARMAN,

John Braisted of Acton, MA m. Ann Tutwiler **Rogers** of N. Sandwich 10/23/2004 in Sandwich

CARR,

Larry Robert of New York, NY m. Kathryn Andrea **Stuntz** of New York, NY 6/21/1987

CARTER,

Almon E. of Sandwich m. Addie L. **Webster** of Sandwich 6/14/1897 in Meredith; H – 22, merchant, b. Sandwich, s/o Dennis F. Carter (Saco, ME) and Olive E. Carter (Sandwich); W – 18, teacher, b. Sandwich, d/o James T. Webster (Sandwich) and Emma Webster (Sandwich)

Almon E. of Sandwich m. Frances A. **Martin** of Sandwich 10/28/1933 in Ctr. Sandwich; H – 25, laborer, b. Sandwich, s/o Almon E. Carter (Sandwich) and Addie L. Webster

(Sandwich); W – 25, nurse, b. Sandwich, d/o J. Frank Martin (Melrose, MA) and Alice Tappan (Sandwich)

Alonzo F. of Sandwich m. Bertha L. **Atwood** of Sandwich 6/14/1896 in Meredith; H – 35, laborer, b. Conway, s/o Nathaniel Carter (Conway); W – 21, b. Sandwich, d/o A. C. Atwood (Sandwich)

Andrew of Sandwich m. Ethel M. **Craig** of Sandwich --/25/1911; H – 36, farmer, b. Cochituate, MA, s/o Warren W. Carter (Cochituate, MA) and Ellen H. Hodge (Sandwich); W – 29, housekeeper, b. Lynn, MA, d/o Arthur Chandler (Lynn, MA) and Nellie Stackpole (Springfield, MA)

David F. of Sandwich m. Elizabeth A. **McBride** of Wolfeboro 5/22/1967; H – 20, carpenter, s/o Almon E. Carter, Jr. and Frances Martin; W – 24, at home, d/o Willard R. Whiting and Ruth P. Young

James Winslow of Sandwich m. Ethel Marie **Wallace** of Sandwich 12/31/1954; H – 17, laborer, b. NH, s/o Almon Ellsworth Carter (NH) and Frances A. Martin (NH); W – 18, at home, b. NH, d/o Ashael Wallace (NH) and Roxy M. Burrows (NH)

Nathaniel of Sandwich m. Lydia A. **Dyere** of Concord 11/30/1893 in Concord; H – 50, laborer, b. Conway, s/o Nathaniel Carter (Conway) and P. Carter (Conway); W – 50, d/o Milton G. Boyce (Canterbury)

CASS,

Earle of Concord m. Caroline **Nudd** of Ctr. Sandwich 5/3/1937 in Center Harbor; H – 24, truck driver, b. Concord, s/o Ralph R. Cass (Concord) and Gertrude Lucia (Milton, VT); W – 19, maid, b. Ctr. Sandwich, d/o Wallace Nudd (Ctr. Sandwich) and Blanche LeClair (Northfield, VT)

CHAMBERS,

Donald M. of N. Sandwich m. Sanja G. **Polic** of N. Sandwich 7/8/2006 in Sandwich

CHAPMAN,

Leonard B. of Sandwich m. Lulu **Thomas** of Philadelphia, PA 1/10/1922 in Sandwich; H – 41, farmer, b. NB, s/o Thomas W. Chapman (NB) and Mary A. Boyd (NB); W – 38, stenographer, b. Allenwood, PA, d/o William Tate and Susan Nye

CHASE,

Bertrand R. m. Lizzie **Morse** 10/23/1910; H – 21, laborer, b. Douglas, MA, s/o Frank A. Chase (Douglas, MA) and Mary J. Tappan (Sweden); W – 41, b. Sandwich, d/o John T. Bickford (Rochester) and Addie Bennett (Sandwich)

Bertrand R. of Sandwich m. Amy C. **Buxton** of Sandwich 7/9/1933 in Wolfeboro; H – 49, farmer, b. Sandwich, s/o Frank A. Chase (Douglass, ME) and Mary J. Tappan (Sandwich); W – 55, d/o Simon P. Buxton (Peabody, MA) and Sarah H. Putnam (Salem, MA)

David K. of Sandwich m. Sally A. **Smith** of Center Harbor 8/26/1965; H – 21, student, s/o Elliott W. Chase and Virginia B. Davis; W – 21, student, d/o Aaron C. Smith and Geraldine L. Bryant

David Robert of N. Sandwich m. Amy Parks **Day** of N. Sandwich 7/27/1997

William L. of Sandwich m. Nellie C. **Watson** of Moultonboro 9/21/1896 in Sandwich; H – 28, farmer, b. Tamworth, s/o Daniel G. Lord (Tamworth) and Susan C. Lord (Moultonboro); W – 29, teacher, b. Moultonboro, d/o Alonzo Watson (Moultonboro) and Ellen G. Watson (Moultonboro)

CHICK,

Frank O. of Sandwich m. Eva M. **Sargent** of Holderness 6/11/1900 in Meredith; H – 21, farmer, b. Moultonboro, d/o

Frank H. Chick (Sandwich) and Lullu M. Chick (Sandwich); W – d/o James M. Sargent (Holderness)

Henry G. of Sandwich m. Elizabeth **Lawrence** of Sandwich 11/6/1887 in Sandwich; H – 72, blacksmith, b. Limington, ME, s/o Nathan Chick (Limington, ME) and Sarah Chick (Limington, ME); W – 68, b. Rochester, d/o John Goodwin (Sandwich) and Lydia Goodwin (Sandwich)

CHILSON,

Herbert A. of Sandwich m. Angie P. **Follett** of Boston, MA 5/15/1889 in Sandwich; H – 42, mill man, b. Cumberland, RI, s/o Asa Chilson (Bellingham, MA) and Amy Chilson (Cumberland, RI); W – 36, bookkeeper, b. Stratton, VT, d/o Benjamin Follett (Cumberland, RI)

CLAIRMONT,

Rene J. of Gilford m. Nancy B. **Evans** of Sandwich 9/24/1968; H – s/o Arthur Clairmont and Evelyn Zimmerman; W – d/o Richard Breed and Camille LaRochelle

CLARK,

Calvin I. of Concord m. Marie L. **Hanson** of Concord 7/7/1935; H – 31, hair dresser, b. Pembroke, s/o Evans C. Clark (Bow) and Eva Edgerly (Hooksett); W – 35, beautician, b. Sandwich, d/o Frank L. Hanson (Sandwich) and Ida M. Priest (Providence, RI)

Joseph P. of Sandwich m. Ann M. **Holmes** of Campton 11/29/1900 in Sandwich; H – 70, farmer, b. Moultonboro, s/o Jonathan Clark (Henniker) and Phebe Clark; W – 61, housewife, b. Thornton, d/o Edmund Bartlett (Campton) and Susan Bartlett (Thornton)

Nathan H. of Salem, MA m. Myrtle V. **Mudgett** of Sandwich 1/1/1966; H – 52, teacher, s/o Arthur E. Clark and Ida F. Nichols; W – 50, nurse, d/o Charles Fannel and Miney Kirstead

Peter G. of Painted Post, NY m. Martha L. **Osberg** of Sandwich 7/17/1976 in Holderness; H – s/o Adelbert G. Clark, Jr. and Mary L. Lowman; W – d/o Calvin J. Osberg and June S. Lander

Sumner B. of Sandwich m. Gladys **Munroe** of Worcester, MA 5/9/1917 in Worcester, MA; H – 27, farmer, b. Sandwich, s/o Charles S. Clark and Nellie B. Brown; W – 21, at home, b. Worcester, MA, d/o Walter Munroe and Cora A. Nichols

Sumner B. of Sandwich m. Violet M. D. **Ward** 10/14/1933 in N. Monroe; H – 44, farmer, b. Sandwich, s/o Charles S. Clark (Sandwich) and Nellie L. Brown (Exeter); W – 38, teacher, b. Monroe, d/o Robert S. Ward (Sheffield, England) and Mary Ward (Dronfield, England)

CLAXTON,

Douglas Carter of Sandwich m. Nancy Doris **Broderick** of Lowell, MA 5/20/1978 in Tamworth; H – s/o Edmund Claxton and Barbara Smith; W – d/o Robert Broderick and Doris Bauer

Edmund S., Jr. of Sandwich m. Marion B. **Eckert** of Marietta, GA 8/25/1973 in Sandwich; H – s/o Edmund S. Claxton and Barbara J. Smith; W – d/o Richard N. Eckert and Helen B. Wentworth

CLEMENT,

Richard D. of New Durham m. Theresa M. **Legault** of Sandwich 5/15/1982

CLEMONS,

Eustis W. of Winthrop, MA m. Marion A. **Card** of Malden, MA 9/29/1945; H – 36, insurance, b. Medford, MA, s/o Harry E. Clemons (Wakefield, MA) and Gladys E. Zurcker (Haverhill, MA); W – 25, insurance clerk, b. Malden, MA, d/o William L. Card (Gaspereau, NS) and Carolyn V. Kenney (Wolfeville, NS)

Frederick A. of Sandwich m. Charlotte E. **Taylor** of Sandwich 12/26/1949; H – 32, woodsman, b. ME, s/o Frederick S. Clemons (ME) and Mary L. Smith (ME); W – 36, housewife, b. ME, d/o Hazel H. Luck (ME)

CLINE,

James A., Jr. of Sandwich m. Audrey K. **King** of Sandwich 10/4/1986

CLOUGH,

Harry O. of Sandwich m. Madeline **Elliott** of Sandwich 4/7/1918 in Moultonboro; H – 23, laborer, b. Cambridge, MA, s/o Ira A. Clough (Tamworth) and Nellie E. Delaney (Ireland); W – 19, at home, b. Sandwich, d/o Elmer Elliott (Tuftonboro) and Maud L. Mitchel (Sandwich)

CLUFF,

Maurice P. of Kennebunkport, ME m. Roxy **Burrows** of Sandwich 1/2/1965; H – 58, carpenter, s/o Nahum J. Cluff and Maud S. Goodwin; W – 42, at home, d/o Newell J. Burrows and Nellie F. Hodge

COCHRAN,

Elwin J. of Ctr. Sandwich m. Ellen M. **Pelchat** of Laconia 11/4/1970 in Sandwich; H – s/o James Cochran and Myrtle Barnes; W – d/o Norman Pelchat and Theresa Collette

James A. of Moultonboro m. Myrtle E. **Barnes** of Sandwich 12/10/1949; H – 19, laborer, b. NH, s/o Clarence J. Cochran (MA) and Mildred Atheran (MA); W – 17, at home, b. NH, d/o Fred E. Barnes (NH) and Florence M. Whiting (NH)

COESPER,
Milo Wilson of Suffield, CT m. Rebecca M. **Blackshear** of Rochester, MI 7/1/1978 in Sandwich; H – s/o Milo G. Coesper and Lois Y. Hicks; W – d/o David S. Blackshear and Marion Speers

COGAN,
Dennis G. of Meredith m. Patricia M. **Covey** of Sandwich 6/29/1969; H – s/o Ernest Cogan and Margaret C. Beach; W – d/o Uradel Covey and Charlotte Brown

COLBY,
William W. of Bow m. Frances D. **Gilman** of Sandwich 6/17/1923 in Sandwich; H – 19, forester, b. Bow, s/o A. Sterling Colby (Bow) and Susie Hoyt (Chichester); W – 16, waitress, b. Sandwich, d/o Edward S. Gilman (Amesbury, MA) and Marjorie Wallace (Sandwich)

COLE,
Michael Lewis of Sandwich m. Theresa Marie **Ottati** of Meredith 3/22/1980

COLLINS,
Lee W. of Meredith m. Sandra M. **Peaslee** of Ctr. Sandwich 12/19/1970 in Sandwich; H – s/o Leland Collins and Marjorie Smith; W – d/o David Peaslee and Mary Noble
Timothy John of Christiana, MA m. Melanie Barbara **Robbins** of Christiana, MA 9/12/1992

CONDIT,
Merrell Edwin of New Lebanon, NY m. Cora Joe **Vittum** of Sandwich 3/22/1952; H – 34, teacher, b. NJ, s/o Henry L. Condit (NJ) and Ruth C. Hance (PA); W – 22, secretary, b. OK, d/o George W. Vittum (KS) and Ethel G. Strong (MA)

CONDON,
Donald E. of Sandwich m. Garaphella **Forristall** of Sandwich 9/22/1949; H – 23, student, b. NH, s/o Wayne O. Condon (NH) and Winona C. Dickey (NH); W – 18, at home, b. MA, d/o William H. Forristall (MA) and Maybelle M. Manning (NH)

CONLEY,
Raymond K., Jr. of Sandwich m. Ruth S. **Laurence** of Sandwich 6/30/1956; H – 32, student, b. MA, s/o Raymond K. Conley (NH) and Edna P. Sharp (MA); W – 31, dental assistant, b. MA, d/o George O. Laurence (England) and May L. Scott (England)

CONLIN,
Robert W. of Concord, MA m. Mary H. **Dolan** of Sandwich 9/4/1971 in Meredith; H – s/o Thomas Conlin and Helen Slyne; W – d/o Richard Dolan and M. Virginia Goodrich

CONVERSE,
Mark Wayne of Sandwich m. Carol Rose **Lavery** of Sandwich 10/11/1997

COOK,
Curtis E. of Sandwich m. Myra T. **Weld** of Sandwich 6/24/1914 in Sandwich; H – 53, farmer, b. Sandwich, s/o Jesse H. Cook (Sandwich) and Emily Beede (Sandwich); W – 28, housekeeper, b. Sandwich, d/o Jonathan Tappan (Sandwich) and Julia Nute (Sandwich)

George O. of Sandwich m. Mary R. **Brown** of Sandwich 6/21/1899 in Sandwich; H – 31, farmer, b. Rock Creek, IL, s/o John O. Cook (Sandwich) and Cynthia Cook (Allenstown); W – 17, b. Sandwich, d/o Moses G. Brown (Errol) and Chestina Brown (NS)

John O. of Sandwich m. Alice W. **Binford** of Sandwich 10/3/1925 in Sandwich; H – 23, farmer, b. Sandwich, s/o George O. Cook (Rock Creek, IL) and Mary Brown (N. Conway); W – 22, telephone operator, b. Fields Corner, MA, d/o William Binford (Baldwin, ME) and Elsie Harris (Canning, NS)

John Otis of Sandwich m. Patricia **Forristall** of Sandwich 9/28/1951; H – 19, woodsman, b. NH, s/o Wilbur Asa Cook (NH) and Edna Ruth Adams (MA); W – 17, at home, b. MA, d/o William H. Forristall (MA) and Maybelle M. Manning (NJ)

John Otis of Sandwich m. Mary Elizabeth **Smith** of Sandwich 5/9/1953; H – 50, laborer, b. NH, s/o George Otis Cook (IL) and Mary E. Brown (NH); W – 61, bookkeeper, b. NH, d/o Charles Omar Smith (NH) and Mary E. Smith

Lawrence Merle of Sandwich m. Dorothy Elizabeth **Tivey** of Sandwich 11/16/1933 in Ctr. Harbor; H – 22, laborer, b. Sandwich, s/o Merle Charles Cook (Moultonboro) and Lucy McCormick (Oxford, NS); W – 21, cook, b. Boston, MA, d/o Albert Tivey (Newton, MA) and Maud Bromlie (Sutton, England)

Merle C. m. Lucy **McCormick** 9/3/1910; H – 18, laborer, b. Moultonboro, s/o Charles C. Cook (Sandwich) and Lizzie A. Bragg (Moultonboro); W – 22, housekeeper, b. NS, d/o Melville McCormick (NS) and Julia Simpson (NS)

Robert W. of Sandwich m. Pamela M. **Copp** of Meredith 6/3/1978 in Meredith; H – s/o Wilbur A. Cook, Jr. and Joan Berry; W – d/o Frederic E. Copp and Jeanine E. Bliss

Wilbur Asa, Jr. of Sandwich m. Joan Nickles **Berry** of Sandwich 11/20/1954; H – 24, farmer, b. NH, s/o Wilbur Asa Cook (NH) and Edna Ruth Adams (NH); W – 18, at home, b. NH, d/o Robert M. Berry (NH) and Marion J. Nickles (NH)

COOLEY,
John Hay, Jr. of Sandwich m. Suzanne D. **Weil** of Sandwich 8/24/1998

COOLIDGE,
Peter B. of Sandwich m. Susan J. **Burney** of Sandwich 9/24/1983
Peter B. of Sandwich m. Sandra J. **Burrows** of Sandwich 8/1/1998

COOMBS,
William P. of N. Gorham, ME m. Sarah M. **Page** of N. Gorham, ME --/--/1933; H – 46, salesman, b. Kingston, s/o William P. Coombs (London, England) and Letitia J. Gowan (Edinburgh, Scotland); W – 43, housewife, b. Poland, ME, d/o J. F. Greenleaf (ME) and Olive G. Rand (ME)

CORLISS,
Arthur E. of Sandwich m. Maude C. **Quimby** of Sandwich 10/26/1914 in Sandwich; H – 43, carpenter, b. Sandwich, s/o Hiram S. Corliss (Sandwich) and Elizabeth Goodwin (Moultonboro); W – 39, nurse, b. Cassville, PQ, d/o Henry M. Quimby (Cassville, PQ) and Clara E. Lee (Fitch Bay, PQ)
Hiram S. of Sandwich m. Henrietta S. **Brown** of Sandwich 5/1/1920 in Sandwich; H – 76, farmer, b. Sandwich, s/o Benjamin Corliss (Sandwich) and Mary Hubbard (Acton, ME); W – 68, housekeeper, b. Devonshire, England
Louis F. of Sandwich m. Marjorie **Thornton** of Portland, ME 8/6/1932; H – 37, farmer, b. W. Dennis, MA, s/o Charles E. Corliss (N. Sandwich) and Jennie M. Fisk (W. Dennis, MA); W – 31, nurse, b. Springfield, ME, d/o Bertrand Thornton (Lincoln, ME) and Nina M. Aldrich (Carroll, ME)

COTE,

Edward Elmer of New Hampton m. Jeanette **Nixon** of Sandwich 6/27/1954; H – 52, carder, b. NH, s/o Albert Cote (Canada) and Jessie Lamond (NH); W – 33, teacher, b. MA, d/o James H. Nixon (Ireland) and Edith Dorr (NH)

CRAM,

Charles S. of Sandwich m. Jennie M. **Hildbold** of Boston, MA 11/19/1897 in Meredith; H – 23, carpenter, b. Rock Island, Canada, s/o L. D. Cram and A. M. Cram (Moultonboro); W – 28, housekeeper, b. Cummington, MA, d/o George F. Fleming and Martha Fleming

Charles S. m. Emma M. **Garland** 11/1/1909 in Sandwich; H – 35, carpenter, s/o Leland D. Cram (Moultonboro) and Maud M. Garland (Moultonboro); W – 28, housewife, b. Moultonboro, d/o Daniel B. Grant (Sandwich) and Lizzie Grant (Moultonboro)

CRORY,

David P. of Sandwich m. Karen Elaine **White** of Tamworth 10/8/1988

Frederick J., Jr. of Durham m. Virginia **Atwood** of Sandwich 10/30/1948; H – 26, teacher, b. Forrest Hills, MA, s/o Frederick J. Crory (Chestnut Hill, MA) and Dorothy Watson (Bridgewater, CT); W – 23, student, b. Woburn, MA, d/o Elbridge Atwood (Woburn, MA) and Helen Parker (Marblehead, MA)

Frederick James, III of Lowell, MA m. Deborah Winifred **McCarthy** of Lowell, MA 6/27/1992

CRUZ,

David P. of Sandwich m. Stephanie **Galfas** of Sandwich 1/15/1995

CUNNINGHAM,
Daniel J. of Sandwich m. Sarah Burnham **Johnston** of Sandwich 5/15/1997

CURLEY,
Leo M. of Shannock, RI m. Sally **Benton** of Sandwich 9/28/1974 in Tamworth; H – s/o Leo M. Curley and Martha W. Cole; W – d/o Richard L. Benton and Nancy Browne

CURRAN,
Benjamin R. of Sandwich m. Heather E. **Hamilton** of Sandwich 9/16/2006 in Center Harbor

CURRIER,
Leon H. of Sandwich m. Emily D. **Hodgdon** of Sandwich 7/29/1896 in Tamworth; H – 24, farmer, b. Sandwich, s/o Howard Currier (Rumney) and Lizze J. Currier (Tuftonboro); W – 21, b. Sandwich, d/o L. Hodgdon (Moultonboro) and Sarah Hodgdon (Sandwich)

CUTLER,
Abbot W. of Sandwich m. Sarah **Holbrook** of Sandwich 1/18/1975 in Sandwich; H – s/o Eric Cutler and Nancy Ware; W – d/o Luther G. Holbrook and Ruth Price

CZADO,
Michael J. of N. Windham, ME m. Brenda J. **Peaslee** of N. Windham, ME 6/11/1983

DANFORTH,
George E. of Sandwich m. Winnie B. **Knowles** of Campton 2/12/1904 in Ashland; H – 29, farmer, b. Sandwich, s/o George W. Danforth (Sandwich) and Annie E. Marston; W – 21, laundress, b. Campton, d/o Daniel Sanborn (Ryegate, VT) and Angeline E. Eaton (Bethlehem)

DARLING,

William of Sandwich m. Nellie P. **Knowles** of Sandwich 12/10/1893 in Sandwich; H – 26, laborer, b. Campton, s/o Abram Darling and Dorothy Darling (NY); W – 18, teacher, d/o Samuel Knowles and Joanna Knowles

DAVEY,

George H. of Sandwich m. Jennie **Vittum** of Sandwich 11/3/1894 in Sandwich; H – 24, laborer, b. NB, s/o Charles Davey (PEI) and Mary Davey (NB); W – 22, housewife, b. Sandwich, d/o Oscar T. Vittum (Sandwich) and Ann Vittum (Sandwich)

DAVIS,

Charles J. of Sandwich m. Charlotte M. **Wallace** of Sandwich 10/17/1920 in Sandwich; H – 38, carpenter, b. Newmarket, s/o James G. W. Davis (Barrington) and Minerva Stackpole (Kennebunkport, ME); W – 64, at home, b. Dunbarton, d/o James O. McCauley (Dunbarton) and Louisa C. Jones (Litchfield)

Charles J. of Sandwich m. Phoebe A. **Elwood** of CT 12/30/1928 in Sandwich; H – 46, farmer, b. Newmarket, s/o James G. W. Davis (Bennington) and M. A. Stackpole (Kennebunk, ME); W – 47, housework, b. CT, d/o M. C. Brown and L. L. Bryne

Charles J. of Sandwich m. Mary L. **Elliott** of Hancock 12/14/1947; H – 65, retired, b. Newmarket, s/o James G. W. Davis (Barrington) and Minerva Stackpole (Kennebunkport, ME); W – 67, at home, b. Burlington, MA, d/o Thomas Elliott (Scotland) and Mary J. Martin (Scotland)

Craig A. of Sandwich m. Heidi A. **Nickerson** of Sandwich 6/5/2002 in Moultonboro

Kenneth C. of Rancho Palos Verde, CA m. Janet A. **Bradfield** of Rancho Palos Verde, CA 9/19/1987

Larry Brian of Moultonboro m. Dorothy Mae **Sturgeon** of Sandwich 12/12/1953; H – 17, lumbering, b. NH, s/o Chester A. Davis (NH) and Ethel J. Frye (NH); W – 18, at home, b. NH, d/o Wilfred J. Sturgeon (ME) and Irma Y. Stokes (ME)

DAY,

Norbert A. of Sandwich m. Margaret J. **Amabile** of Meredith 8/25/1956; H – 38, mechanic, b. NH, s/o Andrew Day (ME) and Kathleen Smith (PA); W – 27, beautician, b. NH, d/o Worcester O. Berry (NH) and Mildred Rand (NH)

DEARBORN,

Allan E. of Sandwich m. Janice L. **Downs** of Tamworth 5/21/1956; H – 22, machine operator, b. NH, s/o Kenneth A. Dearborn (VT) and Sarah B. Davis (NH); W – 19, cashier, b. NH, d/o Clifford F. Downs (NH) and Winnifred W. Weeks (NH)

DEE,

David M. of Boston, MA m. Margaret P. **Watson** of Boston, MA 9/22/1984

DELGADO,

Robert D. of Sandwich m. Rhona A. **Perry** of Epsom 7/1/1967; H – 21, student, s/o Robert Delgado and Marion C. Davis; W – 19, copyholder, d/o Donald Perry and Heather Wills

DEMICK,

William E. of Sandwich m. Dorothy P. **Wing** of Sandwich 5/3/1919 in Sandwich; H – 21, fire warden, b. Fryeburg, ME, s/o William Demick (Manchester) and Minnie L. Osgood (N. Conway); W – 17, at home, b. Lynn, MA, d/o

Charles S. Wing (Lynn, MA) and Dora Preston (Manchester)

DEMING,
Roger of Ctr. Sandwich m. Martha G. **White** of Moultonboro 10/29/1947; H – 26, proprietor, b. Newport, s/o Albert Deming (Newport) and Fanny Ford (Birmingham, England); W – 22, secretary, b. Waltham, MA, d/o Maurice White (Somerville, MA) and Marion Sanderson (Revere, MA)

DENNEY,
Harold C. of Sandwich m. Alice E. **Hilliard** of Winnisquam 12/25/1935; H – 21, laborer, b. Boston, MA, s/o Harry Denney (Meredith) and Edith M. Clark (Sandwich); W – 19, at home, b. Laconia, d/o Oren Hilliard (Laconia) and Eva B. Keith (Haverhill)

DESMARAIS,
Patrick Edward of Leominster, MA m. Melanie E. C. **Gasbarro** of Leominster, MA 9/21/1997

DEVENS,
Richard, IV of Cypress, CA m. Melissa M. **Shaw** of Cypress, CA 5/26/1990

DICEY,
Wendell G. of Tamworth m. Julia M. **Leach** of Sandwich 10/24/1964; H – 20, mill work, s/o Garfield W. Dicey and Helen B. Welch; W – 20, at home, d/o William A. Leach and Dorothy E. Welch

DIFILIPPE,
Jamie D. of Sandwich m. Lori E. **Boucher** of Meredith 8/1/1981

DOANE,
David Hoyt of N. Sandwich m. Gladys Ruth **Ambrose** of N. Sandwich 9/12/1992

DOBYNS,
Christopher D. of E. Lansing, MI m. Susan J. **MacKenzie** of Whitmore Lake, MI 2/25/1981

DODGE,
William Gerald of Sandwich m. Ruth Ivy **Buckingham** of Sandwich 3/17/1978 in Sandwich; H – s/o William E. Dodge and Yvonne Boucher; W – d/o William A. Buckingham and Katherine Robb

DOLAN,
Robert O. of Sandwich m. Joan N. **Auger** of Sandwich 6/28/1980
Robert Owen of Sandwich m. Juliane Eleanor **Richardson** of N. Sandwich 6/4/1994

DORR,
Carl S. of Sandwich m. Edith M. **Moulton** of Sandwich 12/20/1905 in Sandwich; H – 25, b. Sandwich, s/o Henry F. Dorr (Sandwich) and Abbie S. Berry (ME); W – 19, b. Sandwich, d/o Edgar C. Moulton (Newark, VT) and Clara R. Prescott (Sandwich)

DORRICH,
Klaus Dieter of P. Moresby, NG m. Wendy Diane **Wiggins** of P. Moresby, NG 9/16/1978 in Sandwich; H – s/o Ernst Dorrich and Marie Allgeier; W – d/o Kenneth J. Wiggins and Judith Fitzmaurice

DOW,
Charles L. of Sandwich m. Etta **Palmer** of Sandwich 3/17/1913 in Sandwich; H – 52, laborer, b. Tamworth, s/o John C.

Dow (Tamworth) and Augusta Smith (Sandwich); W – 48, housewife, b. Sandwich, d/o Alpheus Vittum (Sandwich) and Alphena Vittum (Sandwich)

Lawrence R. of Conway m. Rachel B. **Nudd** of Sandwich 8/10/1940; H – 23, roller saw-mill, b. Farmington, s/o William Dow and Edith M. Stanley (Parsonsfield, ME); W – 18, housework, b. Sandwich, d/o Wallace Nudd (Sandwich) and Blanche LeClair (Northfield, VT)

Steven F. of Sandwich m. Melissa K. **Benoit** of Sandwich 10/6/2007 in Sandwich

DOWNS,

Barry J. of Meredith m. Susanna B. **Phillips** of Sandwich 6/7/1986

Clifford F., Jr. of Tamworth m. Bonita M. **Swan** of Sandwich 2/3/1962; H – 17, student, s/o Clifford Downs and Winifred Weeks; W – 16, student, d/o Dean E. Swan and Phyliss Bryant

DRAKE,

Benjamin of Ossipee m. Clara **Page** of Sandwich 7/8/1895 in Sandwich; H – 25, barber, b. Ossipee, s/o Charles Drake (Ossipee) and Elizabeth Drake (Ossipee); W – 28, housewife, b. Belgrade, ME, d/o Joel Page (Belgrade, ME) and Maria Page

DREW,

John of Dracut, MA m. Sarah D. **Hoyt** of Sandwich 3/6/1892 in Sandwich; H – 54, blacksmith, b. Tuftonboro, s/o Hezekiah Drew (Tuftonboro) and Mary Drew; W – 58, housewife, b. Alfred, ME

Phillip William of Ossipee m. Frances Josie **Eldridge** of Ossipee 5/17/1941; H – 21, logger, b. Sandwich, s/o William P. Drew (Dover) and Lena M. Tappan (Moultonboro); W – 18, home, b. Tamworth, d/o Clifford D. Eldridge (Ossipee) and Etta M. Colby (Ossipee)

William of Effingham m. Lena M. **Tappan** of Sandwich 8/4/1919 in Effingham; H – 24, lumberman, b. Dover, s/o John Drew (Cambridge, ME) and Mary Fennell (Ireland); W – 26, postmistress, b. Sandwich, d/o Frank Tappan (Sandwich) and Hattie Knowles (Moultonboro)

DROUIN,

Paul A. of Laconia m. Charlotte H. **Nelson** of Sandwich 9/27/1947; H – 20, machinist, b. Laconia, s/o Alfred J. Drouin (Canada) and Cecile B. Bilodeau (Canada); W – 20, nurse, b. Sandwich, d/o Thomas Nelson (Norway) and Henrietta Brown (Quincy, MA)

DUMAS,

Raymond J., Jr. of Sandwich m. Carol L. **Galley** of Lemoyne, PA 6/10/1967; H – 24, student, s/o Raymond J. Dumas and Elizabeth Read; W – 19, student, d/o Charles E. Galley and Florence L. Bush

Raymond Leo of Sandwich m. Elizabeth Randall **Read** of Sandwich 6/18/1938 in Sandwich; H – 24, student, b. Salem, MA, s/o Godfrey Dumas (Three Rivers, Canada) and Lumena LeBlanc (Greenville); W – 25, at home, b. Rehoboth, MA, d/o Leon H. Read (W. Somerville, MA) and Abbie R. Estabrook (Warren, RI)

DUNN,

William L. of Sandwich m. Donna M. **Burrows** of Sandwich 12/18/1983

DUPREY,

Harry M. m. Florence B. **Ward** 12/24/1910; H – 26, lumberman, b. Newport, VT, s/o Theophile Duprey (Canada) and Emma Quimby (Madison); W – 18, b. Wakefield, d/o

Samuel Ward (Wakefield) and Mamie McDonald (Holderness)

DUSTIN,
Robert Gale of Sandwich m. Emily Thompson **Heard** of Sandwich 8/6/1938 in Sandwich; H – 24, forestry, b. Boscawen, s/o Frank B. Dustin (Hebron) and Mary A. Clement; W – 24, at home, b. Sandwich, d/o William A. Heard (Sandwich) and Lillian P. Thompson (Worcester, MA)

DUTTON,
Walter of Deering m. Marguerite **Fellows** of Sandwich 6/20/1932; H – 32, farmer, b. Deering, s/o Edwin Dutton (Stoddard) and Alice Ruffie (Antrim); W – 23, teacher, b. Franklin, d/o Arthur Fellows (Sandwich) and Nellie Foss (Sandwich)

EASTMAN,
Fred, Jr. of Lawrence, MA m. Jessie E. **Woodhead** of Andover, MA 1/15/1956; H – 67, accountant, b. MA, s/o Fred Eastman (WI) and Mary J. Blyth (MA); W – 53, bank teller, b. MA, d/o Edmund S. Woodhead (MA) and Mary E. Meaney (PA)

EATON,
Toby Vining of Sandwich m. Franna Trout **Hamel** of Madison 9/26/1993

ELDREDGE,
Kenneth W. of Tamworth m. Charlene L. **Hawes** of Sandwich 6/28/1964; H – 20, mechanic, s/o Andrew W. Eldredge and Marsha Eldredge; W – 18, at home, d/o Evander F. Hawes II and Louise Elliott

ELDRIDGE,

Hazen A. of Tamworth m. Ellen Elizabeth **Plummer** of Sandwich 11/12/1938 in Tamworth; H – 18, laborer, b. Ossipee, s/o Willie R. Eldridge (Ossipee) and Cora B. Williams (Ossipee); W – 18, at home, b. Sandwich, d/o Clarence R. Plummer (Sandwich) and Luella May Sturgis (Sandwich)

James F. of W. Ossipee m. Kathleen M. **Hawes** of Sandwich 9/4/1966; H – 19, Army, s/o Andrew Eldridge and Marcia Gilman; W – 18, at home, d/o Evander Hawes II and Louise M. Elliott

ELLIOTT,

Anthony C. of N. Sandwich m. Joan M. **Nassif** of Raynham, MA 10/24/1985

Barry P. of N. Sandwich m. Jennifer L. **Kondrotas** of N. Sandwich 10/5/1991

Dennis of Sandwich m. Leona **Batcheldor** of Meredith 8/29/1931; H – 20, laborer, b. Sandwich, s/o Elmer Elliott (Sandwich) and Maude I. ----- (Sandwich); W – 17, at home, b. Meredith, d/o Charles Batcheldor (Meredith) and Alice Quimby (Meredith)

Edward A. of Rumney m. Evelyn S. **Russell** of Sandwich 6/24/1913 in Sandwich; H – 47, manufacturer, b. Rumney, s/o Charles H. Elliott (Rumney) and Laura J. Moulton (Ellsworth); W – 35, teacher, b. Sandwich, d/o Robert Russell (Lawrence, MA) and Sarah Slye (Lowell, MA)

Edwin Lewis of Sandwich m. Marion **Wing** of Sandwich 7/31/1941; H – 27, laborer, b. Sandwich, s/o Lewis C. Elliott (Sandwich) and Sarah A. Pierce (Providence, RI); W – 35, at home, b. Lynn, MA, d/o Charles S. Wing (Fayette, ME) and Dora B. Preston (Springfield, MA)

Elmer of Sandwich m. Maud L. **Mitchell** of Sandwich 5/10/1899 in Plymouth; H – 21, farmer, b. Tuftonboro, s/o John Elliott (Tuftonboro) and Ida Elliott (Sandwich); W – 18, b.

Sandwich, d/o William U. Mitchell (Sandwich) and Asula A. Mitchell (Sandwich)

Elmer of Sandwich m. Lula Elizabeth **Vinal** of Sandwich 6/8/1942; H – 64, farmer, b. Tuftonboro, s/o John Elliott (Tuftonboro) and Ida E. Rowe (Sandwich); W – 44, housekeeper, b. Liverpool, NY, d/o Addison M. Hudson (Ira, NY) and Sarah A. Tall (On the Atlantic Ocean)

Harold of Sandwich m. Evelyn **Roebarge** of Tamworth 4/22/1925 in Sandwich; H – 20, laborer, b. Sandwich, s/o Elmer Elliott (Sandwich) and Maude Mitchell (Sandwich); W – 17, at home, b. Tuftonboro, d/o Lewis Roebarge (Peabody, MA) and Bessie Elliott (Plymouth)

Lewis C. of Sandwich m. Sarah A. **Pierce** of Tamworth 8/26/1905 in Tamworth; H – 21, b. Sandwich, s/o John Elliott (Tuftonboro) and Ida E. Elliott (Sandwich); W – 21, b. Providence, d/o George A. Pierce (MA) and Sarah A. Pierce (MA)

Michael D. of Sandwich m. Colleen J. **Paquette** of Meredith 11/8/1969; H – s/o Preston Elliott and Patricia Steeves; W – d/o Anatole J. Paquette and Charlotte Beede

Michael D. of Sandwich m. Margarey R. **Page** of Lakeport 5/16/1987

Michael D. of Sandwich m. Kathryn A. **Tudor** of Ossipee 7/3/1995

Michael Daniel of Sandwich m. Donna Lee **Morton** of Sandwich 12/18/2004 in Sandwich

Phillip of Sandwich m. Virginia **Forristall** of Sandwich 10/9/1942; H – 21, woodsman, b. Sandwich, s/o Susie M. Elliott (Sandwich); W – 18, at home, b. Framingham, MA, d/o William H. Forristall (Arlington, MA) and Maybelle M. Manning (Rahway, NJ)

Preston of Sandwich m. Patricia **Jackson** of Conway 1/8/1957; H – 28, construction, b. NH, s/o Edwin L. Elliott (NH) and Marion W. Elliott (NH); W – 24, waitress, b. NH, d/o Jerome Steeves (NH) and Helen Brock (NH)

Raymond of Sandwich m. Pamela R. **Ball** of Sandwich 9/1/1961; H – 22, truck driver, s/o Dennis Elliott and Leona Batchelder; W – 19, at home, d/o Littleton Ball and Patricia Remick

Richard Howard of Sandwich m. Elsbeth Minnie **Larrabee** of Laconia 7/28/1951; H – 25, inspector, b. NH, s/o Harold Elliott (NH) and Evelyn I. Roberge (NH); W – 24, secretary, b. NH, d/o Raymond E. Larrabee (NH) and Dorothy T. Vittum (NH)

Sidney of Sandwich m. Lorraine Belle **Hoyt** of Sandwich 12/23/1950; H – 33, craftsman, b. NH, s/o Elmer Elliott (NH) and Maud Mitchell (NH); W – 27, at home, b. NH, d/o Winfred Hoyt (VT) and Hazel Moody (NH)

ELLSWORTH,

John O. of Lahaska, PA m. Karen E. **Brodhead** of Lahaska, PA 11/26/1982

ELY,

Kenyon Brockway of Sandwich m. Rosamond Foss **Powers** of Brookline, MA 6/6/1953; H – 55, inv. council, b. NJ, s/o Lester Hallett Ely (NY) and Marion R. French (MA); W – 35, at home, b. MA, d/o Ralph Emery Foss (MA) and Annie E. Jackson (Canada)

EMERSON,

Denley W. of Sandwich m. Gail M. **Gray** of Belmont 7/22/1945; H – 27, toolmaker, b. Boston, MA, s/o Brigham H. Emerson (Milton, MA) and Marion D. Richards (Boston, MA); W – 25, at home, b. Belmont, d/o Guy L. Hamel (Belmont) and Mildred G. Moulton (Belmont)

Denley W. of Sandwich m. Virginia B. **Rollins** of Sandwich 12/25/1952; H – 34, self-emp., b. MA, s/o B. Homer Emerson (MA) and Marian D. Richards (MA); W – 32, at home, b. MA, d/o William J. Davis (MA) and Beatrice Lowell (ME)

Denley W. of Sandwich m. Elizabeth E. **Marshall** of Sandwich 2/21/1969; H – s/o B. Homer Emerson and Marian D. Richards; W – d/o Mortimer B. Brown and Audrey Seward

ENDICOTT,

George of Worcester, MA m. Vivian **Wood** of Worcester, MA 6/28/1941; H – 51, engineer, b. Beverly, MA, s/o George Endicott (New York, NY) and Ella L. Day (New York, NY); W – 30, school teacher, b. Adrian, MI, d/o Ruel L. Wood (Milton, NY) and Ethel R. Thornton (New Province, IA)

ENGLE,

Robert F. C. of Sandwich m. Janice D. **Stein** of Ossipee 2/10/1968; H – s/o Walter Engle and Amelia Wagner; W – d/o Walter Stein and Dorothy M. Rapp

Walter R., Jr. of Sandwich m. Bonnie **Barnes** of Meredith 3/9/1968; H – s/o Walter R. Engle, Sr. and Amelia Wagner; W – d/o Oliver W. Barnes and Doris M. Carpenter

ENRIGHT,

John E. of Sandwich m. Linda S. **Jacobs** of Sandwich 8/15/1987

EVANS,

Alton Brooks of Tamworth m. Nancy P. **Breed** of Sandwich 8/6/1955; H – 24, construction, b. NH, s/o Almon G. Evans (NH) and Gladys Corbett (NH); W – 18, at home, b. MA, d/o Richard A. Breed (MA) and Camille LaRochelle (MA)

Robert Otis of Moultonboro m. Patricia Aline **Atwood** of Sandwich 9/6/1951; H – 25, laborer, b. TX, s/o Clark G. Evans (NH) and Myrtle Sowell (TX); W – 22, at home, b. NH, d/o Gerald W. Atwood (NH) and Virginia A. Moody (NH)

Timothy J. of Morrison, CO m. B. Alexandria **Applebaum** of Morrison, CO 9/11/1995

FADDEN,
Charles B. of Sandwich m. Annie **Venott** of NS 3/19/1892 in Woodstock; H – 30, teamster, b. Thornton, s/o Joseph Fadden (Lyman) and Harriett Fadden (Alexandria); W – 21, b. NS, d/o Benjamin Venot and Jennie Venot

FARLEY,
Michael Philip of Conway m. Arlene **Sprengling** of Sandwich 4/27/1996

FARMER,
Fred of Sandwich m. Mabel **Burrows** of Sandwich 8/24/1913 in S. Tamworth; H – 37, laborer, b. Piermont, s/o Charles Farmer (Piermont) and Nellie Goodhue; W – 30, housekeeper, b. Sandwich, d/o Charles H. Burrows (Sandwich) and Alice M. George (Sandwich)

FARNSWORTH,
Gary Deane of Ctr. Sandwich m. Susan Janet **Harter** of Ctr. Sandwich 12/12/1992

FAUX,
James H. of Rochester, NY m. Josephine L. **Shepard** of Tilton 8/15/1970 in Sandwich; H – s/o James Faux and Mary E. Harrison; W – d/o F. Harold Shepard and Marjorie Horne

FELCH,
Leverett C. m. Ina **Vittum** 9/9/1909 in Moultonboro; H – 65, carpenter, b. Tamworth, s/o Robert B. Felch (Seabrook) and Catherine P. Felch (Bennington, VT); W – 30, b. Sandwich, d/o Jacob F. Vittum (Sandwich) and Mary O. Vittum (Sandwich)

FELKER,

Onestus A. of Lowell, MA m. Helen S. **Tilton** of Sandwich 10/25/1916 in Center Harbor; H – 19, electrician, b. Lowell, MA, s/o Albion Felker (Lowell, MA) and Gertrude E. Sabine (Nashua); W – 22, at home, b. Moultonboro, d/o Albert H. Tilton (Sandwich) and Clara Tappan (Sandwich)

FELLOWS,

Arthur P. of Sandwich m. Nellie F. **Fellows** of Sandwich 2/9/1901 in Sandwich; H – 25, farmer, b. Sandwich, s/o Charles R. Fellows (Sandwich) and Ora A. Fellows (Sandwich); W – 25, teacher, b. Tamworth, d/o Daniel Foss and Mary E. Foss

Enoch Q. of Sandwich m. Lydia D. **Sanborn** of Center Harbor 6/20/1887 in Sandwich; H – 61, b. Sandwich, s/o John Fellows (Poplin) and Mary J. Fellows (Poplin); W – 48, b. Brunswick, ME, d/o Horace Dunning (Brunswick, ME) and Barbary Dunning (Brunswick, ME)

FERREIRA,

Paul F. of Honolulu, HI m. Jane J. **Briggs** of N. Sandwich 9/5/1947; H – 45, US Treasury, b. Honolulu, HI, s/o August Ferreira (Madeira, Portugal) and Maria Roda (Madeira, Portugal); W – 29, at home, b. Pittsburgh, PA, d/o Richard Briggs (Franklin, MA) and Clara Reynolds (Roxbury, MA)

FINCH,

Christopher M. of Lowell, MA m. Deborah E. **Davock** of Sandwich 7/7/1979 in Chocorua; H – s/o Lucien J. Finch and Margaret Carroll; W – d/o Joseph P. Davock and Nancy Nay

David T. of Sandwich m. Jane G. **Morton** of Sandwich 2/28/1987

FINNEY,
John Milton of Stamford, VT m. Jennifer Johnson **Quimby** of Sandwich 6/18/1994

FISHER,
Gardner Warren of Moultonborough m. Mary Noble **Peaslee** of N. Sandwich 3/6/1993

FITCHETT,
Earl N. of Littleton m. Marion M. **Hutchins** of Sandwich 12/25/1959; H – 55, fireman, s/o Ernest A. Fitchett and Fanny M. Nichols; W – 48, cook, d/o William H. Taylor and Christine E. Skinner

FLANAGAN,
Charles S. of Sandwich m. Myrna E. **Niles** of Meredith 8/5/1961; H – 22, machinist, s/o Paul A. Flanagan and Hilda Colby; W - 23, secretary, d/o Lawton Niles and Dorothy Hackett

FLEISCHMANN,
Andrew H. of N. Sandwich m. Christina A. **Villadolid** of N. Sandwich 6/15/1985
Thomas C. of N. Sandwich m. Kathleen A. **Greene** of N. Sandwich 8/25/2001

FLEMING,
Kevin F. of Meredith m. Patricia A. **Nelson** of Sandwich 12/30/1967; H – 19, millwork, s/o James Fleming and Sarah Rowens; W – 15, student, d/o Kenneth Nelson and Frances Spaulding

FLETCHER,
Robert D. of Sandwich m. Jayne **Mudgett** of Sandwich 3/19/1994

FOGG,

Edwin E. of Sandwich m. Florence **Thompson** of Sandwich 6/25/1933 in N. Sandwich; H- 43, farmer, b. Sandwich, s/o Elias Fogg (Sandwich) and Anna Elmira Beede (Sandwich); W – 34, housewife, b. Ashland, d/o George W. Lambert (Ashland) and Lillian Small (Holderness)

Elias H. of Sandwich m. Elmira A. **Beede** of Sandwich 5/2/1888 in Sandwich; H – 57, farmer, b. Sandwich, s/o John Fogg (Sandwich) and Sarah Fogg; W – 24, b. Sandwich, d/o Josiah A. Beede (Sandwich) and Ann A. Beede (Tilton)

Eugene W. of Sandwich m. Minnie E. **Dimick** of Sandwich 5/7/1902 in Sandwich; H – 27, farmer, b. Sandwich, s/o Hezekiah T. Fogg (Sandwich) and Mary E. Moulton (Ashland); W – 26, housekeeper, b. Conway, d/o Bailey E. Osgood (Fryeburg, ME) and Lizzie Davis (Conway)

Henry O. of Sandwich m. Luella **Durgin** of Moultonboro 4/27/1891 in Sandwich; H – 25, farmer, b. Sandwich, s/o H. T. Fogg and Mary E. Fogg; W – 22, b. Center Harbor, d/o John Fogg and Abbie Fogg

John W. m. Annie I. **Kelley** 9/22/1910; H – 32, farmer, b. Sandwich, s/o H. True Fogg (Sandwich) and Mary Moulton (Sandwich); W – 32, housekeeper, b. NS, d/o Thomas Kelley (NS) and Hannah J. Kelley (NS)

Joseph Alberto of Sandwich m. Dorrit **Brown** of Sandwich 4/6/1942; H – 25, laborer, b. Loudon, s/o Jason Fogg (Gilmanton) and Myrtle Jones (Gilmanton); W – 34, housework, b. Sandwich, d/o Frank W. Brown (Sandwich) and Alice G. Elliott (Sandwich)

Joseph E. of Sandwich m. Deborah A. **Miksch** of Sandwich 10/4/1975 in Freedom; H – s/o Joseph A. Fogg and Dorrit Brown; W – d/o Levin A. Miksch and Alice Colman

Stephen of Sandwich m. Clara H. **Townsend** of Lowell, MA 1/1/1895 in Sandwich; H – 77, farmer, b. Sandwich, s/o Stephen Fogg (Sandwich) and Nancy Fogg; W – 64, housewife, b. Saco, ME, d/o Benjamin Jose (Saco) and Harriet Jose

Wesley H. of Sandwich m. Cora A. **Abbott** of Sandwich 4/24/1893 in Sandwich; H – 22, farmer, b. Sandwich, s/o H. True Fogg (Sandwich) and Mary E. Fogg (Holderness); W – 17, b. Sandwich, d/o R. F. Abbott (Sandwich) and Ann Abbott (Sandwich)

FOISY,

Louis Harold of Ctr. Sandwich m. Patricia Irene **Haynes** of Concord 7/18/1970 in Concord; H – s/o Alfred Foisy and Anna Bouldry; W – d/o Nelson Haynes and Clara L. Sawyer

FOLEY,

James F. of Roslindale, MA m. Dorothy F. **McManus** of Roslindale, MA 12/25/1976 in Sandwich; H – s/o Thomas W. Foley and Marie Wallace; W – d/o Robert W. McManus and Dorothy Curtis

FORD,

Gordon M. of Sandwich m. Elli M. **Hayes** of Sandwich 11/9/1981

FORRISTALL,

William H. of Sandwich m. Helen **Peaslee** of Sandwich 7/12/1945; H – 16, mechanic, b. Framingham, MA, s/o William H. Forristall (Arlington, MA) and Maybelle Manning (Rahway, NJ); W – 16, at home, b. Sandwich, d/o Ralph Q. Peaslee (Sandwich) and Mary E. Moody (Tamworth)

FORSSIUS,

Carl A. of Sandwich m. Sadie J. **Downs** of Sandwich 2/14/1898 in Sandwich; H – 33, fish dealer, b. Sweden, s/o Peter J. Forssius (Sweden) and Sarah C. Forssius (Sweden); W –

43, housekeeper, b. Tamworth, d/o Daniel Downes and Susan Downes (Tamworth)

FOSS,

Charles H. of Sandwich m. Lottie I. **Kimball** of Portland, ME 9/1/1896 in Freedom; H – 52, farmer, b. Sandwich, s/o Enoch Foss (Thornton) and Emma B. Foss (Sandwich); W – 53, housewife, b. Falmouth, ME, d/o Chesley Leighton (Falmouth, ME) and Ruth C. Leighton (Falmouth, ME)

Charles L. of Sandwich m. Nellie F. **Batchelder** of Sandwich 12/24/1891 in Tamworth; H – 25, farmer, b. Tamworth, s/o David B. Foss and Emma A. Foss; W – 24, b. Sandwich, d/o F. F. Batchelder and Sarah F. Batchelder

Frank N. of Sandwich m. Julia **Fleming** of Sandwich 2/25/1896 in Sandwich; H – 52, farmer, b. Bucksport, ME, s/o John B. Foss and Loisa J. Foss; W – 26, housekeeper, b. India

FOSTER,

Robert W. of Moultonborough m. Jane A. **Brewer** of Sandwich 12/9/2001

Sean D. of Sullivan m. Rachel E. **Catalano** of Sandwich 1/18/2006 in Sandwich

FRANK,

Douglas Roy of Sandwich m. Lisa Ann **Cook** of Sandwich 8/6/1988

FRANKLYN,

Percival M. m. Marguerite E. **Newell** 6/30/1909 in Sandwich; H – 28, trainman, b. Geneva, NY, s/o F. J. Franklyn (England) and Eleanor G. Thomas (England); W – 25, teacher, b. Parish, NY, d/o Elijah Newell (England) and Roseanna A. Wilson (Syracuse, NY)

FRASE,
Kimberly K. of Sandwich m. Lauren A. **Ulitz** of Tamworth 5/18/1985

FREEMAN,
Malcolm F., III of Boston, MA m. Nadene J. **Berman** of Boston, MA 10/26/1986
Robert Edwards of White Pigeon, MI m. Margery Garrett **Hoag** of Haveford, PA 8/18/1951; H – 20, student, b. MI, s/o Elmer L. Freeman (ME) and Lorna L. Edwards (WA); W – 19, student, b. MA, d/o Gilbert T. Hoag (ME) and Catherine Harris (PR)

FRENTRESS,
Richard M. of Tucson, AZ m. Daphne A. **Monk** of Tucson, AZ 9/27/1987

FRYE,
Freeman N. of Fossil, OR m. Olive L. **Skinner** of Sandwich 8/30/1890 in Wagner, OR; H – 26, farmer, b. Sandwich, s/o Nathaniel Frye (Sandwich) and Eliza A. Frye (Sandwich); W – 20, b. Sandwich, d/o Daniel M. Skinner (N. Conway) and Sarah Skinner (Sandwich)
Louis W. of Sandwich m. Jennie **Hoyt** of Moultonboro 9/4/1904 in Moultonboro; H – 21, farmer, b. Moultonboro, s/o Ivory Frye (Moultonboro) and Lizzie O. Evans (Peabody, MA); W – 19, b. Moultonboro, d/o Herbert Hoyt (Moultonboro) and Hattie Prime (Moultonboro)
Michael B. of Moultonboro m. Marjorie L. **Nelson** of Sandwich 12/31/1976 in Sandwich; H – s/o Clarence H. Frye and Lucille Y. Tykokee; W – d/o Kenneth W. Nelson and Frances A. Spaulding

FULKERSON,
Davis Rand of Philadelphia, PA m. Jean Ellen **Janson** of Philadelphia, PA 8/1/1992

FULLERTON,
Benjamin J. of Sandwich m. Amanda M. **Ludwick** of Sandwich 5/21/2005 in Sandwich
Dwayne J. of Sandwich m. Tara M. **Staples** of Sandwich 9/22/2001

GALE,
Albert of Sandwich m. Effie S. **Virtue** of Dover --/22/1911; H – 22, farmer, b. Sandwich, s/o Amos Gale (Dover) and Jennie Wade (Moultonboro); W – 22, housekeeper, b. Boston, MA, d/o James Virtue (Scotland) and Agnes Rehord (St. Johns, NB)
Amos of Sandwich m. Jennie **Wade** of Sandwich 11/4/1888 in Sandwich; H – 47, farmer, b. Dover, s/o Daniel R. Gale (Gilmanton) and Lydia Gale (Sandwich); W – 16, b. Moultonboro, d/o Lyman Wade (Moultonboro) and Martha Wade (Center Harbor)

GALFAS,
Peter Mathew of Wyckoff, NJ m. Stephanie **Demme** of Wyckoff, NJ 2/5/1978 in Sandwich; H – s/o Timothy Galfas and Louise Coolidge; W – d/o Frederick P. Demme and Sheila N. Ross

GALL,
John F. of Narbeth, PA m. Mary **Kealy** of Philadelphia, PA 11/27/1971 in Sandwich; H – s/o Charles Gall and Frieda Schiek; W – d/o William Kealy and Mary Burdick

GALLAGHER,
Michael J. of Meredith m. Kimberly **Swan** of Sandwich 8/20/1977 in Sandwich; H – s/o Walter F. Gallagher and Inez Balcom; W – d/o Dean E. Swan and Phyllis Bryant

GALLIVAN,
Thomas Andrew, Jr. of Milton, MA m. Anne **Laverack** of Sandwich 12/14/1972 in Sandwich; H – s/o Thomas A. Gallivan and Helen L. Beavis; W – d/o John W. Laverack and Janet Sabine

GARLAND,
Dexter B. of Sandwich m. Mary A. **Nichols** of Moultonboro 2/24/1900 in Meredith; H – 30, farmer, b. Canada, s/o Nathaniel Garland (Moultonboro) and Mary Garland; W – 18, housewife, b. Moultonboro, d/o F. Nichols (Moultonboro) and Delia A. Nichols (Moultonboro)
Lewis D. of Sandwich m. Ebba O. **Sloberg** of Cambridge, MA 710/1/1914 in Lakeport; H – 19, laborer, b. Sandwich, s/o Seth D. Garland (Moultonboro) and Estella H. Hanson (Sandwich); W – 21, sales girl, b. Cambridge, MA, d/o Charles Sloberg (Sweden) and Ebba ----- (Stockholm, Sweden)
Rufus E. of Sandwich m. Eva S. **Cruckshank** of Milton, MA 10/25/1916 in Milton, MA; H – 22, cook, b. Center Harbor, s/o Seth D. Garland (Tuftonboro) and Estella H. Hanson (Sandwich); W - 23, at home, b. Roxbury, MA, d/o William G. Cruckshank (NS) and Sarah MacAskill (NS)

GARRY,
Franklyn Bernard of Columbus, OH m. Mary Ragan **Adams** of Gainesville, FL 8/16/1986

GAUGHAN,
Matthew M. of Brooklyn, NY m. MaryStarr B. **Hope** of Brooklyn, NY 9/13/2003 in Moultonboro

GAULT,
George F. of Sandwich m. Eva M. **Bagley** of Sandwich 7/26/1899 in Sandwich; H – 48, farmer, b. Salmon Falls, s/o Thomas E. Gault (Concord) and Jane Gault (Lebanon, ME); W – 19, housekeeper, b. Sandwich, d/o Charles M. Bagley (Campton) and Martha Bagley (Sandwich)

GEIB,
Eric F. of Ashland m. Erin R. **Greene** of Ashland 9/15/2007 in Meredith

GEORGE,
Frank Hiram of Moultonboro m. Francis Adelaide **Bryant** of Sandwich 8/1/1952; H – 26, laborer, b. NH, s/o Charles E. George (NH) and Anna E. Hilliard (NH); W – 18, at home, b. NH, d/o Asa William Bryant (NH) and Sylvia L. Avery (NH)
Fred C. of Plymouth m. Alice **Berry** of Sandwich 5/2/1904 in Sandwich; H – 23, painter, b. Canada, s/o Harry J. George and Emma Danforth; W – 19, b. Sandwich, d/o Samuel B. Berry and Louisa Benny

GILLIS,
John W. of Nashua m. Jean **Posey** of Nashua 7/6/1973 in Sandwich; H – s/o John A. Gillis and Hazel Anderson; W – d/o Frank Southworth amnd Aldea Vaillancourt
Paul A. of Sandwich m. Patricia L. **Mathews** of Sandwich 7/25/1973 in Sandwich; H – s/o John A. Gillis and Hazel M. Anderson; W – d/o George W. Mathews and Edna G. Hofman

GILMAN,

Bernard W. of Ctr. Sandwich m. June R. **LaSalle** of Woburn, MA 6/24/1939; H – 24, carpenter, b. Sandwich, s/o Warren Gilman and Alta Atwood; W – 20, at home, b. Woburn, MA, d/o John LaSalle and Martha Norstrom

Clarence W. of Sandwich m. Doris M. **Davis** of Nashua 12/31/1948; H – 22, US Army, b. Sandwich, s/o Wilbur J. Gilman (Fryeburg, ME) and Lena M. Brown (Sandwich); W – 22, office clerk, b. Boston, MA, d/o Charles L. Davis (Nashua) and Mildred Fuller (Lowell, MA)

Dennis W. of Sandwich m. Corinne M. **Plummer** of Moultonboro 8/3/1946; H – 23, carpenter, b. Sandwich, s/o Wilbur J. Gilman (Fryeburg, ME) and Lena M. Brown (Sandwich); W – 21, nurse, b. Ctr. Harbor, d/o Arthur H. Plummer (Ashland) and Nina M. Brett (S. Newbury)

Edward S. of Sandwich m. Marjorie V. **Hall** of Sandwich 8/4/1906 in Sandwich; H – 44, painter, b. MA, s/o Jeremiah Gilman (Franconia); W – 37, housewife, b. Sandwich, d/o Asahel Wallace (Sandwich)

Nathan F. of Sandwich m. Hattie H. **Gannett** of Sandwich 12/25/1888 in Sandwich; H – 40, farmer, b. Sandwich, s/o Elijah D. Gilman (Sandwich) and Phebe Gilman (Conway); W – 26, b. Lyme, d/o William G. Gannett (Tamworth) and Sarah Q. Gannett (Sandwich)

Warren S. of Sandwich m. Alta J. **Atwood** of Sandwich 6/21/1913 in Sandwich; H – 28, blacksmith, b. Sandwich, s/o John C. Gilman (Sandwich) and Maria Beede (Sandwich); W – 22, housekeeper, b. Sandwich, d/o Harry A. Atwood (Sandwich) and Estella E. Burrows (Sandwich)

GISNESS,

William W. of Boston, MA m. Meredith A. **Heard** of Boston, MA 8/25/1990

GLENDAY,
William Frederick of Brooklyn, NY m. Mitzi Ann **Good** of Brooklyn, NY 10/7/2000

GLINES,
David E. of Sandwich m. Addie F. **Parker** of Sandwich 9/17/1895 in Sandwich; H – 30, teamster, b. Sandwich, s/o Asahel Glines (Sandwich) and Lydia Glines; W – 19, housewife, b. Conway, d/o Moses Brown (Conway)

GLOVER,
C. E. of Rumney m. Nellie **Fifield** of Sandwich 10/11/1888 in Sandwich; H – 30, laborer, b. Nashua, s/o F. F. Glover (Rumney) and Lucy Glover (Newmarket); W – 18, b. Sandwich, d/o William Fifield (Tamworth) and M. A. Fifield (Ossipee)

GONZALEZ,
John Joseph of Barre, VT m. Stacey Lyn **Riel** of Barre, VT 7/20/1996

GOODWIN,
Clifton G. of Sandwich m. Myrtie **Vittum** of Sandwich 12/24/1918 in Sandwich; H – 47, mill foreman, b. Haverhill, MA, s/o Charles Goodwin (NS) and Sarah ----- (NS); W – 30, housekeeper, b. Sandwich, d/o Jacob F. Vittum (Sandwich) and Mary O. ----- (Sandwich)
Wendell O. of Brockton, MA m. Edwina P. **Wilkie** of Brockton, MA 6/11/1946; H – 31, teletype op., b. Avon, MA, s/o Charles L. Goodwin (NS) and Ida H. Lofstrom (Brockton, MA); W – 41, clerk, b. Waltham, MA, d/o Charles W. Pennell (Machias, ME) and Emmaline J. Mullen (Machias, ME)

GOOGOO,

John Andrew of Moultonboro m. Elinor Jane **Archibald** of Sandwich 7/5/1952; H – 26, laborer, b. NS, s/o Frank Googoo (Canada) and Mary Ann ----- (Canada); W – 18, at home, b. NH, d/o Everett Archibald (NH) and Violet L. Rowe (VA)

GOTSHALL,

Abbott, Jr. of Sandwich m. Dianne E. **Pierce** of Sandwich 12/27/1962; H – 22, Army, s/o Abbott Gotshall, Sr. and Bertha Woodworth; W – 20, student, d/o Maurice A. Pierce and Alice R. Whiting

GOVE,

Stephen D. of Meredith m. Deborah A. **Brown** of Sandwich 6/7/1975 in Sandwich; H – s/o Robert Gove and Anne Little; W – d/o Frank G. Brown and Jean Leach

GRANT,

Aliston H. of Sandwich m. Sylvia H. **Evans** of Tamworth 1/17/1912 in Portsmouth; H – 20, clerk, b. Plymouth, s/o George A. Grant (Sandwich) and Clara A. Heddle (Sandwich); W – 20, teacher, b. Ossipee, d/o Frank P. Evans (Moultonboro) and Emma I. Clough (Tamworth)

Ernest A. of Sandwich m. Lena M. **Arling** of Tamworth 4/14/1903 in Sandwich; H – 19, farmer, b. Sandwich, s/o Frank H. Grant (Sandwich) and Hattie Abbott (Sandwich); W – 18, b. Tamworth, d/o James G. Arling and Emma Bickford (Tamworth)

Leland H. of Sandwich m. Edith M. **Bryant** of Moultonboro 4/8/1904 in Sandwich; H – 18, farmer, b. Sandwich, s/o Frank H. Grant (Sandwich) and Hattie Abbott (Bristol); W – 16, b. Moultonboro, d/o Walter C. Bryant (Center Harbor) and Jennie Bickford (Moultonboro)

Ned Gordon, Jr. of Ctr. Sandwich m. Margaret Susan **Petersen** of Moultonboro 6/7/1986

Ross A. of Gilford m. Cynthia M. **Nelson** of Sandwich 10/2/1977 in Sandwich; H – s/o George A. Grant, Jr. and Virginia L. Bumpus; W – d/o Kenneth W. Nelson and Frances A. Spaulding

GRAVES,

Clarence E. of Tamworth m. Nellie E. **Whiting** 1/20/1908; H – H – 22, farmer, b. Sandwich, s/o Isaac F. Graves (Sandwich) and Clara B. Wilson (Meredith); W – 18, b. Tamworth, d/o George H. Whiting (Tamworth) and Annie Choate (Sandwich)

Isaac H. F. of Sandwich m. Lizzie B. **Hodgdon** of Sandwich 11/30/1887 in Moultonboro; H – 29, framer, b. Sandwich, s/o Ross Graves (Sandwich) and Mrs. D. Graves (Sandwich); W – 25, b. Sandwich, d/o Alonzo Hodgdon (Sandwich) and Mrs. S. Hodgdon (Sandwich)

Jefferson A. of Cambridge, MA m. Ellen P. **Doughty** of Cambridge, MA 11/10/1973 in Sandwich; H – s/o Richard W. Graves and Margaret J. Young; W – d/o Howard N. Doughty and Frances M. Wilde

Ross M. of Sandwich m. Annie M. **Bemis** of Fryeburg, ME 1/9/1904 in Chatham; H – 26, farmer, b. Sandwich, s/o Aubrey M. Graves (Sandwich) and Louisa S. Sanborn (Tamworth); W – 21, teacher, b. Stowe, ME, d/o Albert L. Bemis (Fryeburg, ME) and Sarah J. Smith (Stow, ME)

Ross M. of Sandwich m. Florentine E. **Prince** of Boston, MA 2/1/1919 in Rochester; H – 42, farmer, b. Sandwich, s/o Aubury M. Graves (Sandwich) and Louise S. Sanborn (Tamworth); W – 42, housekeeper, b. Portland, ME, d/o Silas H. Cram (Portland, ME) and Martha E. Howes (Portland, ME)

Ross M. of Sandwich m. Myrtle G. **Brown** of Sandwich 1/1/1924 in Sandwich; H – 46, farmer, b. Sandwich, s/o Aubury M.

Graves (Sandwich) and Louisa S. Sanborn (Tamworth); W – 40, housekeeper, b. Sandwich, d/o George A. Grant (Sandwich) and Clara A. Heddle (Sandwich)

GRAY,

Charles Henry of Joshua Tree, CA m. Kiki Audrey **Rice** of Sandwich 8/23/1989

Irving of Sandwich m. Mary Etta **Corliss** of Sandwich 1/9/1895 in Sandwich; H – 21, farmer, b. Plymouth, ME, s/o George L. Gray (Plymouth, ME) and Jeanette Gray; W – 20, housewife, b. Sandwich, d/o Hiram Corliss (Sandwich) and Mary Corliss

Richard of Sandwich m. Sylvia B. **Burnham** of Sandwich 2/14/1923 in Sandwich; H – 22, laborer, b. Sandwich, s/o Irving Gray (Plymouth, ME) and M. Etta Corliss (Sandwich); W – 17, tel. operator, b. Sandwich, d/o Charles S. Burnham (Sandwich) and Grace Chase (Bellefontaine, OH)

GRAYHORN,

Herbert S. of Charlestown, MA m. Jessie M. **Craig** of Somerville, MA 7/22/1897 in Meredith; H – 23, book binder, b. St. Johns, NB, s/o Clark Grayhorn (St. Johns, NB) and Sarah Grayhorn (St. Johns, NB); W – 22, b. St. Johns, NB, d/o Charles Craig (St. Johns, NB) and Elizabeth Craig (St. Johns, NB)

GREEN,

Fred of Moultonboro m. Dolly W. **Dearborn** of Sandwich 10/8/1902 in Sandwich; H – 48, painter, b. Moultonboro, s/o Jonathan Green (Moultonboro) and Sarah C. Brown (Tuftonboro); W – 49, housekeeper, b. Sandwich, d/o Nathaniel Vittum (Sandwich) and Lucy H. Vittum (Sandwich)

GREENE,
Christopher W. of Sandwich m. Denise Cathy **Arseneault** of Sandwich 9/6/1986
Eric S. of Sandwich m. Valerie A. **Lavoie** of Sandwich 5/20/2001
William M. of Sandwich m. Susan J. **Hambrook** of Sandwich 6/9/1973 in Meredith; H – s/o Herbert T. Greene and Daphne Hoag; W – d/o Francis G. Hambrook and Mary F. Reeves

GRINNELL,
William Loyd, Jr. of Sandwich m. Karen Jean **Elliott** of Sandwich 7/8/1989

GRISI,
Brian F. of Lake Placid, NY m. Jennifer L. **Bickford** of Tupper Lake, NY 9/21/1991

GUMBERT,
Charles of Waltham, MA m. Florence E. **Crowell** of Allston, MA 6/24/1955; H – 47, machine operator, b. MA, s/o William Gumbert (Lithuania) and Grace ----- (Lithuania); W – 58, beautician, b. MA, d/o George Marshall (MA) and Annie Whitman (NSW)

GURDY,
George of Sandwich m. Emily **Kimball** of Sandwich 10/29/1892 in Sandwich; H – 63, farmer, b. Bristol, s/o Jacob Gurdy (Bristol) and Susan Gurdy (Moultonboro); W – 68, housewife, b. Sandwich, d/o Stephen Ethridge (Sandwich) and Ester Ethridge (Dover)

HALGEDAHL,
Frederick W. of Cedar Falls, IA m. Sandra F. **Watts** of Ontario, Canada 7/22/1976 in Sandwich; H – s/o E. Howard

Halgedahl and Lili Bondi; W – d/o C. Gail Flesher and Ruth E. Timms

HALL,

Jonathan J. of Sandwich m. Christina E. **Dean** of Moultonborough 7/21/2007 in Sandwich

Lawrence Kingsley of Sandwich m. Ednah Wynne **Geer** of Sandwich 12/29/1972 in Sandwich; H – s/o James W. Hall and Laura B. Knipe; W – d/o Hardy H. Phelps and Harriet Joyner

HALLETT,

George Robert of Lakewood, OH m. Katherine Lucille **Van Horn** 9/7/1933 in Ctr. Sandwich; H – 22, auditor, b. Cambridge, OH, s/o Joseph Hallett (MI) and Lillian Grace Barry (OH); W – 24, teacher, b. Madison, WI, d/o Jesse L. Van Horn (KS) and Mary Margaret Hart (Gambier, OH)

HALLIDAY,

Kyle D. of Walnut Creek, CA m. Rachel P. **Cram** of Walnut Creek, CA 7/28/2007 in Sandwich

HAMBROOK,

James Matthew of Sandwich m. Cynthia Jane **Graham** of Sandwich 10/16/1993

HANINGTON,

Herbert, Jr. of Somerville, MA m. Elizabeth W. **Raymond** of Wakefield, MA 10/24/1953; H – 20, machinist, b. MA, s/o Herbert R. Hanington (MA) and Beatrice A. Richards (MA); W – 18, accountant, b. MA, d/o Fred S. Raymond, Sr. (MA) and Bessie Anna Tenney (NH)

HANNA,
William Michael of Portland, ME m. Margaret Rose **Rush** of Portland, ME 7/22/1989

HANSEN,
Carl H. of Sandwich m. Nancy P. **Jones** of Sandwich 9/6/1980

HANSON,
Frank L. of Sandwich m. Ida M. **Priest** of Narragansett, RI 10/25/1890 in Sandwich; H – 20, vet. dentist, b. Sandwich, s/o George O. Hanson (Moultonboro) and ----- (Sandwich); W – 21, b. Narragansett, RI, d/o Charles W. Priest (Germany) and Abbie Priest (Placedale, RI)
William H. of Sandwich m. Minnie E. **Whedon** of Sandwich 3/11/1891 in Sandwich; H – 20, laborer, b. Sandwich, s/o George O. Hanson and Amelia H. Hanson; W – 24, b. VT, d/o John M. Whedon and Mary E. Whedon

HARDING,
Edward of Sandwich m. Laura Jean **Larkin** of Sandwich 6/4/1976 in Sandwich; H – s/o Edward H. Harding and Dorothy Wollenweber; W – d/o H. Nelson Larkin and Lillian O'Neill
Kevin D. of Sandwich m. Ginette **Saucier** of Sandwich 10/14/1990

HARMON,
Frederick of Burton m. Grace A. **Blanchard** of Sandwich 12/28/1892 in Sandwich; H – 27, merchant, b. Aurora, OH, s/o E. C. Harmon (Aurora, OH) and Eliza Harmon (Aurora, OH); W – 20, d/o Charles Blanchard (Sandwich) and Mary J. Blanchard

HART[E],

Elmer B. of Sandwich m. Nellie A. **Atwood** of Sandwich 3/20/1889 in Sandwich; H – 22, clerk, b. Sandwich, s/o Harrison N. Hart (Sandwich) and Lucy E. Hart (Sandwich); W – 20, b. Sandwich, d/o Charles H. Atwood (Sandwich) and Eliza B. Atwood (Tamworth)

Elmer B. of Sandwich m. Ethel A. **Burleigh** of Sandwich 6/9/1897 in Sandwich; H – 34, clerk, b. Sandwich, s/o Harrison N. Hart (Sandwich) and Lucy E. Hart (Sandwich); W – 20, milliner, b. Sandwich, d/o Charles F. Burleigh (Gilmanton) and Olive L. Burleigh (Medway, MA)

Harrison N. of Sandwich m. Lizzie S. **Severance** of Sandwich 1/24/1888 in Sandwich; H – 58, physician, b. Sandwich, s/o John Harte (Conway) and Mary Harte (Sandwich); W – 29, teacher, b. Boston, MA, d/o Sargent F. Severance (Sandwich) and Mary Ann Severance (Gardiner, ME)

Peter D. of Sandwich m. Elizabeth D. **Compton** of Sandwich 7/7/1973 in Meredith; H – s/o Lawrence E. Hart and Gerda Euler; W – d/o Lathrop Compton and Mary M. Cook

HARTMAN,

Vernon D. of Sandwich m. Carol M. **Brock** of Sandwich 7/29/2000

HAWES,

Caspar S. of Sandwich m. Ada B. **Vittum** of Sandwich 6/4/1913 in Sandwich; H – 23, farmer, b. Springfield, MA, s/o William C. Hawes (Springfield, MA) and Dora B. Preston (Auburn); W – 19, teacher, b. Sandwich, d/o Aubrey M. Vittum (Sandwich) and Emily E. Chandler (Lynn, MA)

HAYFORD,

Ernest Arthur of Tamworth m. Elizabeth Delia **Nudd** of Sandwich 5/9/1953; H – 22, retired, b. NH, s/o Arthur L. Hayford (NH)

and Leona M. Speirs (ME); W – 25, housework, b. NH, d/o Wallace Nudd (NH) and Blanche Leclair (VT)

HEALD,
Bruce D. of Meredith m. Helen F. **Forristall** of Sandwich 5/21/1960; H – 24, teacher, s/o Henry Heald and Muriel Day; W – 30, dietician, d/o Ralph Q. Peaslee and Mary E. Moody

HEARD,
Howard B. of Sandwich m. Georgia **Tasker** of Bartlett 11/8/1905 in Bartlett; H – 23, b. Sandwich, s/o Edwin M. Heard (Sandwich) and Nettie L. Barker (Methuen, MA); W – 23, b. Bartlett, d/o William D. Tasker (Bartlett) and Georgianna Sawyer (Lovell, ME)

HEATH,
Albert C. of Sandwich m. Annie E. **Lucas** of Sandwich 4/9/1892 in Sandwich; H – 23, laborer, b. New Hampton, s/o Benjamin H. Heath (Sandwich) and Lydia A. Heath (Sandwich); W – 18, b. Montpelier, VT, d/o Frank Lucas (Boston, MA) and Susan Lucas (Tuftonboro)
Charles E. of Sandwich m. Hazel A. **Blake** of Lowell, MA 10/3/1920 in Epsom; H – 25, chauffeur, b. Sandwich, s/o Benjamin Heath (Sandwich) and Lydia Moulton (Sandwich); W – 27, at home, b. Plymouth, d/o Charles Chandler (Plymouth) and Mary Avery (Plymouth)
Darwin W., Jr. of Boston, MA m. Kristin A. **Smith** of Boston, MA 5/5/1984
Harry Leon of Holderness m. Laura May **Monroe** of Holderness 10/6/1950; H – 28, mechanic, b. NH, s/o George L. Heath (NH) and Anna Lafoe (NH); W – 28, housewife, b. NH, d/o Walter Greenleaf (NH) and Myrtle Page (VT)

HENLE,
Michael Gilman of Oberlin, OH m. Cynthia Hunter **Comer** of Oberlin, OH 12/31/1992

HENSON,
Frank M. of Stamford, CT m. Anne H. **Pinkerton** of Rowayton, CT 10/4/1986

HENSTON,
Forrest of Laconia m. Mildred E. **Martin** of Sandwich 8/7/1919 in Laconia; H – 20, on railroad; W – 17, at home, b. Stoneham, MA, d/o Levi P. Marston (Melrose, MA) and Ella Jefts (Melrose, MA)

HESS,
Jamieson Laurie of Norwich, VT m. Carol Ann **Bando** of Sandwich 5/1/1993

HEWINS,
Alfred of Allston, MA m. Mary **Bullard** of Boston, MA 10/12/1946; H – 41, cashier, b. Dorchester, MA, s/o James Hewins (Medfield, MA) and Anna M. Johanson (Randers, Denmark); W – 44, nurse, b. Cambridge, MA, d/o Henry W. Bullard (Cambridge, MA) and Mary Palmer (Winchester, MA)

HEWITT,
Arthur of Sandwich m. Edith M. **Haley** of Sandwich 5/31/1919 in Moultonboro; H – 35, carpenter, b. Jamaica Plain, s/o John Hewitt (Chelsea, MA) and Katherine Baker (England); W – 28, at home, b. Moultonboro, d/o Harry O. Haley (Tuftonboro) and Flora B. Tilton (Sandwich)

Linwood Arthur of Laconia m. Alice **Gray** of Sandwich 5/16/1944; H – 21, soldier, b. Sandwich, s/o Arthur Hewitt (Jamaica Plain, MA) and Edith Haley (Sandwich); W – 20, shoe worker, b. Sandwich, d/o Richard Gray (Sandwich) and Sylvia Burnham (Sandwich)

HILL,

Carlton M. of Sandwich m. Laura J. **Tibbetts** of Sandwich 7/28/1892 in Sandwich; H – 24, farmer, b. Tamworth, s/o Benjamin M. Hill (VT) and E. H. Hill (Tamworth); W – 20, b. Wolfeboro, d/o Jeremiah E. Tibbetts (Wolfeboro) and Jennie Tibbetts (Dover)

Geoff Alan of Wichita, KA m. Allison Chauncey **Satter** of Wichita, KA 6/25/1994

HIRD,

Stephen A. of Framingham, MA m. Julia M. **Dennett** of Sandwich 8/3/2002 in Sandwich

HOAG,

Albert B. of Sandwich m. Abbie F. **Peaslee** of Sandwich 7/13/1897 in Meredith; H – 24, student, b. Sandwich, s/o Kewis Hoag (Sandwich) and Julia A. Hoag (Dedham, MA); W – 19, teacher, b. Sandwich, d/o Damis Peaslee (Gilmanton) and Harriet W. Peaslee (Sandwich)

Albert Buffum of Sandwich m. Mary Jane **Wilson** of Laconia 3/26/1934; H – 32, manager, b. Sandwich, s/o Albert B. Hoag (Sandwich) and Abbie F. Peaslee (Sandwich); W – 26, nurse, b. Groton, VT, d/o Levi Wilson (Groton, VT) and Jennie Welch (Groton, VT)

Peter C. of Sandwich m. Gloria J. **Eldridge** of Sandwich 10/23/1976 in Sandwich; H – s/o Roland B. Hoag and Barbara Simmonds; W – d/o Roy Eldridge and Jean Campbell

Roland B., Jr. of Sandwich m. Susan A. **Chappell** of Pittsburg 8/10/1968; H – s/o Roland Boyden Hoag, Sr. and Barbara Simonds; W – d/o Colon Chappell and Doris Prescott

Roland Boyden, III of Sandwich m. Heather Lynn **Phelps** of Sandwich 12/16/2000

William G. of Sandwich m. Constance **Tibbetts** of Sandwich 6/14/1959; H – 22, student, s/o Roland B. Hoag and Barbara Simonds; W – 19, student, d/o E. Haven Tibbets and Maude E. Whitehouse

HODGE,

John N. of Sandwich m. Nellie **Burrows** of Sandwich 7/8/1904 in Sandwich; H – 50, farmer, b. Sandwich, s/o Batchelder Hodge (Moultonboro) and Mary A. Smith (Sandwich); W – 38, b. Sandwich, d/o Nathaniel Burrows (Lebanon) and Sarah D. Thompson (Sandwich)

Norman F. of Sandwich m. Effie M. **Nutter** of Sandwich 12/25/1899 in Sandwich; H – 23, farmer, b. Sandwich, s/o John N. Hodge (Sandwich) and Etta M. Hodge (Holderness); W – 30, housekeeper, b. Holderness, d/o Reuben F. Abbott (Tamworth) and Abbie A. Abbott (Sandwich)

Reuben N. of Ctr. Sandwich m. Elizabeth J. **Haggert** of Ctr. Sandwich 6/4/1937 in Ctr. Sandwich; H – 34, insurance agent, b. Ctr. Sandwich, s/o Norman F. Hodge (Ctr. Sandwich) and Effie Mae Abbott (Sandwich); W – 37, nurse, b. Piedmont, NS, d/o James Haggert (Piedmont, NS) and Elizabeth J. Robinson (Piedmont, NS)

Walter E. of Sandwich m. Lois E. **Cram** of Sandwich 11/6/1906 in Sandwich; H – 24, carpenter, b. Sandwich, s/o Charles T. Hodge (Sandwich); W – 25, b. Canada, d/o Leland D. Cram (Moultonboro)

Walter E. of Sandwich m. Mira T. **Cook** of Sandwich 1/21/1930; H – 47, carpenter, b. Moultonboro, s/o Charles T. Hodge (Sandwich) and Hattie Bragg (Sandwich); W – 42, nurse, b. Sandwich, d/o Jonathan Tappan (Sandwich) and Julia F. Nute (Sandwich)

HODSDON,
Marshall S. of Meredith m. Maria Blenda K. **Marken** of Ctr. Sandwich 9/27/1937 in Ctr. Sandwich; H – 35, farmer, b. Somerville, MA, s/o Waldron W. Hodsdon (Somerville, MA) and Marion K. Smith (Cambridge, MA); W – 33, arts & crafts instructor, b. Unnaryd, Sweden, d/o Carl Johansson (Bladinge, Sweden) and Blenda Nilsson (Broronas Fanaholm, Sweden)

HOELL,
John J. of Boston, MA m. Catherine E. **Hope** of Boston, MA 8/4/1990

HOLDEN,
David J. of Boston, MA m. Margaret C. **Harold** of Cleveland, OH 6/27/1939; H – 27, teacher, b. White Plains, NY, s/o Charles E. Holden (New York, NY) and Edna Morgenroth (Brooklyn, NY); W – 29, teacher, b. Worcester, MA, d/o Earle J. Harold (Westland, IN) and Clara E. O'Neal (Milton, IN)

HOLLAND,
Daniel R. of Sandwich m. Lisa K. **Jacobs** of Sandwich 9/7/2002 in Wonalancet
Philip W. of Sandwich m. Vicki L. **Holland** of Sandwich 5/19/2007 in Sandwich

HOLOPAINEN,
Robert J. of Rutland, MA m. Rita M. **Sturgeon** of Sandwich 5/2/1959; H – 20, tester, s/o Vaino J. Holopainen and Francisca M. Handy; W – 19, at home, d/o Wilfred J. Sturgeon and Irma V. Stokes

HOOGEVEEN,
Hans B. H. of Aloha, OR m. Catherine **Crooker** of Aloha, OR 12/12/1987

HORGAN,
John P., Jr. of New Canaan, CT m. Lois Silver **Keates** of New Canaan, CT 1/28/1995

HORNE,
Thomas A. of Sandwich m. Emma J. **Henderson** of Sandwich 6/9/1889 in Tamworth; H – 32, farmer, b. PA, s/o David Horne and Martha Horne; W – 29, b. Sandwich, d/o Smith Henderson and C. H. Henderson

HOSMER,
Peter S. of Sharon, MA m. Nancy B. **Mauch** of Sandwich 8/20/1977 in Sandwich; H – s/o Richard Hosmer and Caroline Farwell; W – d/o Raymond H. Mauch and Frances Traum

HOWARD,
Judson Dillon of Sandwich m. Esther **Currier** of Plymouth 7/9/1941; H – 25, clergyman, b. Kansas City, MO, s/o Charles R. Howard (Tama, IA) and Elsie J. Coon (Plainfield, NJ); W – 24, at home, b. Colebrook, d/o Dean S. Currier (Plymouth) and Emma C. Tenney (Hanover)

HOWE,
Charlie L. of Sandwich m. Margaret H. **Anderson** of Sandwich 8/30/1974 in Chocorua; H – s/o Ray J. Howe and Ina M. Crawford; W – d/o Frank N. Burrows and Hilda B. MacDonald

David Brainerd of Ctr. Sandwich m. Gladys Cynthia **Bean** of Laconia 10/11/1992

David H. of Saco, ME m. Sally F. **Plummer** of Saco, ME 8/25/1984

HOYT,
Charles B. of Sandwich m. Florence **Webster** of Sandwich 10/22/1901 in Sandwich; H – 41, farmer, b. Sandwich, s/o Benjamin B. Hoyt (Sandwich) and Caroline E. Quimby (Sandwich); W – 26, teacher, b. Sandwich, d/o James Y. Webster (Sandwich) and Emma F. Sweatt (Sandwich)

HUCKS,
William Randall of Seattle, WA m. Gretchen C. **Switzer** of Seattle, WA 8/16/1986

HUGNY,
Rollin Philip, Jr. of Washington m. Ruth Joyce **Chapman** of Sandwich 6/17/1950; H – 24, teacher, b. VT, s/o Rollin Philip Hugny (VT) and Lena Clark (Canada); W – 22, teacher, b. MA, d/o Charles B. Chapman (MA) and Nellie R. Harris (MA)

HUNT,
Howard C. of Everett, MA m. Anna **McCrillis** of Sandwich 10/20/1915 in Sandwich; H – 27, div. supervisor, b. Cincinnati, OH, s/o Warder D. Hunt (Cincinnati, OH) and Grace Chapman (London, CT); W – 27, teacher, b. Sandwich, d/o Alonzo McCrillis (Sandwich) and Lulie Clark (Sandwich)

HURD,
Arthur Edgar, Jr. of Laconia m. Patricia Jean **MacDonald** of Sandwich 5/12/1952; H – 21, truck driver, b. NH, s/o Arthur E. Hurd (MA) and Gladys B. Blackey (NH); W – 17, student, b. NH, d/o Ernest E. MacDonald (NH) and Ethel B. Diack (MA)

HUSTON,
Randall L. of Sandwich m. Mary J. **Fowler** of Moultonboro 9/30/2000

HUTCHINS,
Clarence E. of Tamworth m. Marion M. **Taylor** of Tamworth 10/31/1928 in Tamworth; H - 38, farmer, b. Tamworth, s/o William Hutchin (Tamworth) and Augusta Hutchin (Tamworth); W – 17, at home, b. Sandwich, d/o William H. Taylor (Sandwich) and Christine E. Taylor (Sandwich)
Earl U. of Sandwich m. Florence **Wallace** of Sandwich 11/18/1916 in Campton; H – 23, laborer, b. Thornton, s/o Joseph Hutchins and Emma J. Elliott; W – 17, at home, d/o Marcellus C. Wallace (Sandwich) and Harriet L. -----
Edward B. of Sandwich m. Mary Louise **Boone** of Brookline, MA 6/11/1949; H – 21, mechanic, b. NH, s/o Clarence E. Hutchins (NH) and Marion M. Taylor (NH); W – 28, nurse, b. MA, d/o Walter B. Boone (Canada) and Mary A. Jones (England)
Edward C. of Sandwich m. Shirley **Cleasby** of Sandwich 6/20/1965; H – 36, bodyman, s/o Clarence E. Hutchins and Marion Taylor; W – 18, at home, d/o Lauren Lawrence and Sylvia Kimball

IMBACH,
Theodore A. of Towson, MD m. Sindee A. **Sims** of Towson, MD 7/18/1987

INGALLS,
George H. m. Agnes L. **Peaslee** 11/25/1909 in Sandwich; H – 27, machinist, b. MA, s/o George W. Ingalls (Westford, MA) and Lizzie M. Spaulding; W – 21, teacher, b. Sandwich, d/o John N. Peaslee (Sandwich) and Nellie Knowles

INGARI,
Joseph C. of Sandwich m. Rosemarie C. **deMars** of Sandwich 1/2/1987

IRELAND,
John B. of Dunbarton m. Julia D. **Martin** of Sandwich 5/26/1939; H – 42, farmer, b. Dunbarton, s/o Frederick L. Ireland (Dunbarton) and Henrietta McLaren (Greensboro, VT); W – 27, housework, b. Sandwich, d/o Frank Martin (Melrose, MA) and Alice Tappan (Sandwich)

IRVING,
George L. of Sandwich m. Lydia E. **Tibbetts** of Sandwich 10/3/1891 in Sandwich; H – 28, farmer, b. Sandwich, s/o Albert F. Irving and Hannah D. Irving; W – 24, d/o J. D. Tibbetts and Jennie Tibbetts

JACKS,
Duncan A. of Sandwich m. Jamie M. **Wilmarth** of Sandwich 9/26/1987

JACKSON,
Christopher P. of Sandwich m. Sharon Elizabeth **Evans** of Sandwich 12/14/1978 in Casco, ME; H – s/o Howard B. Jackson and Frances Berry; W – d/o Ralph B. Seymour and Nancy Breed
Howard B., Jr. of Sandwich m. Frances Virginia **Berry** of Sandwich 2/28/1953; H – 28, poultryman, b. MA, s/o Howard B. Jackson (RI) and Elizabeth Robinson (MA); W – 19, student, b. NH, d/o Robert M. Berry (NH) and Marion Nichols (NH)
Howard B., Jr. of Sandwich m. Marie A. **Bolduc** of Gilford 7/20/1980

Philip M. of Sandwich m. Patricia **Holland** of Sandwich 5/15/2000

JACOBSON,
Kent A. of Amherst, MA m. Martha H. **Lyon** of Cambridge, MA 9/12/1987

JAMBA,
Michael of Nashua m. Nancy Nay **Davock** of Sandwich 10/21/1978 in Sandwich; H – s/o Michael Jamba and Pauline Homa; W – d/o Garford A. Nay and Roma E. Davis

JANKA,
Luke E. of New York, NY m. Megan M. **Nicolay** of New York, NY 8/11/2007 in Sandwich

JEWELL,
Asahel H. of Ashland m. Winnifred F. **Downs** of Sandwich 10/2/1905 in Moultonboro; H – 19, b. Holderness, s/o Henry A. Jewell (Belmont) and Emma L. Wallace (Thornton); W – 17, b. Tamworth, d/o Edwin F. Downs (Tamworth) and Anna M. Spooner (Haverhill)

JOHNSON,
Paul R. of S. Burlington, VT m. Heidi M. **Larson** of S. Burlington, VT 9/14/1991

JOHNSTON,
Charles C. of Sandwich m. Grace E. **McLendon** of Boxborough, MA 6/30/1990

JONES,
Griffith M., Jr. of Sandwich m. Joanne E. **Graham** of Boston, MA 10/2/1965; H – 35, engineer, s/o Griffith F. Jones, Sr. and

Dorothea Fullagar; W – 28, insurance, d/o Donald F. Ewing and Anna P. Kraatz

Peter G. of Flagstaff, AZ m. Wendy M. **Dixon** of Flagstaff, AZ 6/16/1971 in Sandwich; H – s/o Frank Jones and Bettina Stine; W – d/o William Lovewell and Elnora Brown

JUNICKE,

Dale of Ctr. Sandwich m. Linda E. **Oliver** of Mansfield, MA 2/9/1992

KAMATARIS,

Harry L. of Quincy, MA m. Deborah W. **Anthony** of Quincy, MA 10/1/1983

KAY,

James Hutchinson of Baltimore, MD m. Marion Hoffman **Draper** of Baltimore, MD 8/3/1941; H – 21, surveyor, b. Baltimore, MD, s/o Samuel W. Kay (Philadelphia, PA) and Helen M. Tippett (Baltimore, MD); W – 21, stenographer, b. Baltimore, MD, d/o Albert V. Draper (Oswego, KS) and Marion Hoffman (Baltimore, MD)

KELLER,

Jeremy of Westwood, MA m. Giuliana V. M. **Reed** of Westwood, MA 8/23/1978 in Sandwich; H – s/o John W. Keller and Natalie McL. Coolidge; W – d/o William W. Reed and Giuliana Nardi

KELLEY,

Eric W. of Falmouth, ME m. Anne dePeyster **Valentine** of Falmouth, ME 9/16/1995

Newell R. of Rocky Hill, CT m. E. Maude **Armstrong** of Wollaston, MA 6/2/1937 in Ctr. Sandwich; H – 24, medical student, b. Ludlow, MA, s/o Raymond E. Kelley (Greenwich, MA) and Francis Howe (Beverly, MA); W –

20, student nurse, b. Augusta, ME, d/o George R. Armstrong (Campbell Ford, ON) and Edna Scott (Slaterville, RI)

Thomas of Sandwich m. Sarah **Knowlton** of Sandwich 6/30/1898 in Sandwich; H – 72, farmer, b. Moultonboro, s/o Job Kelley and L. Kelley (Moultonboro); W - --, housekeeper, b. Sandwich, d/o Nathaniel Vittum (Sandwich) and Lucy Vittum (Sandwich)

KEMP,

Arthur D., Jr. of Bolton, MA m. Susan P. **Clattenburg** of Cambridge, MA 7/9/1983

KENNEY,

Arthur R. of New Hampton m. Etta M. **Mudgett** of Sandwich 3/20/1915 in Sandwich; H – 26, farmer, b. New Hampton, s/o John M. Kenney (New Hampton) and Abbie A. Evans (New Hampton); W – 20, housekeeper, b. Sandwich, d/o Fred W. Mudgett (Sandwich) and Ora A. Fogg (Sandwich)

Marshall J. of New Hampton m. Carrie E. **Mudgett** of Sandwich 7/15/1916 in Sandwich; H – 25, farmer, b. New Hampton, s/o John Kenney (Canada) and Abbie A. Evens; W – 20, b. Sandwich, d/o Fred Mudgett (Sandwich) and Ora A. Fogg (Sandwich)

KIMBALL,

Charles J. of Ctr. Sandwich m. Frances **Hurley** of Roxbury, MA 3/12/1933 in Ctr. Sandwich; H – 32, mechanic, b. Boston, MA, s/o Joseph Kimball (Boston, MA) and Anne E. Beardsley (Boston, MA); W – 33, hairdresser, b. Chelsea, MA, d/o John Cummings (Boston, MA) and Nellie Du Van (Boston, MA)

George William of Belmont, MA m. Susan Puckett **Bryant** of Belmont, MA 7/8/1978 in Sandwich; H – s/o George H.

Kimball and Ann M. Shaynd; W – d/o Lynwood S. Bryant and Louise S. Graham

KING,
James A. of Lowell, MA m. Mary E. **McHugh** of Lowell, MA 8/7/1971 in Sandwich; H – s/o James King and Marguerite Tremblay; W – d/o William McHugh and Mary Finnegan

KIRKWOOD,
Douglas H. of Sandwich m. Ann F. **Maksim** of Berkeley, CA 9/17/1966; H – 26, teacher, s/o Samuel B. Kirkwood and Grace H. Hight; W – 28, chemist, d/o George A. Maksim and Frances Frazier

KLECZEK,
Frederick A. of Newmarket m. Ruby M. **Barnes** of Sandwich 3/3/1956; H – 28, USAF, b. NH, s/o Andrew Kleczek (Poland) and Mary Bresideski (Poland); W – 18, mill worker, b. NH, d/o Fred Barnes (NH) and Florence Whiting (NH)

KNOX,
Charles E. of Sandwich m. Emily E. **Nickerson** of Tamworth 9/4/1946; H – 21, student, b. Ossipee, s/o Perley C. Knox (Ossipee) and Florence G. Burrows (Sandwich); W – 19, student, b. Fryeburg, ME, d/o George R. Nickerson (Madison) and Erma L. Alley (Madison)
Charles E. of Sandwich m. Louise M. **King** of Meredith 4/22/1955; H – 29, NE Tel & Tel, b. NH, s/o Perley C. Knox ((NH) and Florence Burrows (NH); W – 20, stenographer, b. NH, d/o Ezra H. King (NH) and Effie Heath (VT)
Charles Edward of Sandwich m. Eleanor Idella **Hurd** of Colebrook 3/29/1958; H – 32, accountant, s/o Perley C. Knox (NH) and Florence G. Burrows (NH); W – 23,

adjuster, d/o Ernest L. DesRosier (MA) and Betsy L. Wright (NH)

Perley C. of Quincy, MA m. Florence G. **Burrows** of Sandwich 6/24/1922 in Sandwich; H – 24, construction foreman, b. W. Ossipee, s/o Charles E. Knox (Berwick, ME) and Mary E. Chesley (Tamworth); W – 18, telephone operator, b. Sandwich, d/o Fred N. Burrows (Sandwich) and Grace E. Skinner (Sandwich)

KOLESAR,

Fred A., Sr. of Oxford, CT m. Ruth E. **Brown** of Oxford, CT 7/28/1973 in Sandwich; H – s/o Charles N. Kolesar and Alice Moren; W – d/o Felix V. Grumuldys and Michanlina Poehailes

LALLY,

Edward J., Jr. of Sandwich m. Charlene E. **McKinney** of Sandwich 10/3/1987

LAMPREY,

John A. of Sandwich m. Gail A. **Dean** of Meredith 2/17/1968; H – s/o Uri Lamprey and Emily S. Adams; W – d/o Amnon Dean and Gretchen Swain

Mark E. of Sandwich m. Holly J. **Follansbee** of Ashland 1/20/1979 in Sandwich; H – s/o Uri Lamprey and Mary Sproat; W – d/o Russell Follansbee and Shirley Jenot

Wilbur H. of Meredith m. Lillian E. **Gilman** of Sandwich 12/15/1946; H – 21, truck driver, b. Melvin Village, s/o Wilbur H. Lamprey (Melvin Village) and Frances L. Harriman (Sandwich); W – 21, at home, b. Sandwich, d/o Wilbur J. Gilman (Fryeburg, ME) and Lena M. Brown (Sandwich)

LANDOFI,
Domenick J., Jr. of Dorchester, MA m. Aileen Barbara **Boudreau** of S. Boston, MA 12/12/1953; H – 25, soldier, b. MA, s/o Domenick J. Landofi (Italy) and Virginia Bonicrureau (Italy); W – 27, waitress, b. England, d/o John Branston (Enagldn) and Winifred L. Branston (England)

LANE,
Prescott Newitt of Everett, MA m. Diane **Minor** of Everett, MA 8/26/1989

LANGFORD,
James R. of South Bend, IN m. Jill A. **Justice** of Corning, NY 7/16/1981

LANGLEY,
Fred of Dover m. Leah Frances **Hardy** of Sandwich 6/28/1930; H – 26, farmer, b. Newmarket, s/o Fred Langley (Dover) and Frances P. Birch (Dover); W – 16, at home, b. Dover, d/o Chester Hardy and Mildred Severance (Biddeford, ME)

LAROWE,
Major Winn of Helena, MT m. Heather Loring **Johnston** of Helena, MT 10/14/2000

LAUGHTON,
Arthur D. of Sandwich and Tamworth m. Pauline M. **Bookhalz** of Tamworth 7/25/1928 in Tamworth; H – 23, truck driver, b. Binock, ME, s/o E. M. Laughton (Orion, ME); W – 21, at home, b. Tamworth, d/o Jacob Borkely (Tamworth) and Emma Cavling (Tamworth)

LAVALLEY,
Kevin Patrick of Black River Falls, WI m. Kristen **Berg** of Black River Falls, WI 7/31/1992

LAWN,

Evan of Sandwich m. Marguerite B. **Kelley** of Colchester, CT 7/21/1953; H – 35, teacher, b. PA, s/o Victor H. Lawn and Dorothy Colby; W – 35, housewife, b. CT, d/o Moses Bailey and Mabel Googins

LAWSON,

George E. of Sandwich m. Marguerite E. **Pignato** of Sandwich 8/8/1968; H – s/o Lorenzo W. Lawton and Eva Lewis; W – d/o Artemus Smith and Jeanne Jacques

LEACH,

Arthur T. of Sandwich m. Caroline **Forristall** of Sandwich 12/28/1949; H – 24, student, b. NH, s/o William T. Leach (NH) and Dorothy Weld (NH); W – 20, at home, b. MA, d/o William H. Forristall (MA) and Maybelle M. Manning (NJ)

David C. of Sandwich m. Nancy A. **Wiggin** of Moultonboro 7/1/1961; H – 22, farmer, s/o William A. Leach and Dorothy E. Weld; W – 19, d/o Raymond P. Freeto and Alberta M. Daigneau

LEAHY,

Jeffrey Vawter of Cambridge, MA m. Amanda Kathryne **Unger** of Cambridge, MA 8/10/1996

LEAR,

Benjamin Hasting of Sandwich m. Deanne Lee **Nedeau** of Meredith 5/28/1994

LEE,

Ansel E. m. Lizabeth C. **Quimby** 12/25/1910; H – 48, merchant, b. Holderness, s/o Walter Lee (Holderness) and Mary F. Corliss (Sandwich); W – clerk, b. Sandwich, d/o John Otis Cook (Sandwich) and Cynthia E. Johnson (Allenstown)

Ansel E. of Sandwich m. Anna L. **Hanson** of Somerville, MA 4/3/1919 in Sandwich; H – 50, merchant, b. Holderness, s/o Walter Lee (Holderness) and Frances Corliss (Sandwich); W – 43, nurse, b. Lanark, IL, d/o Orland C. Hanson (Moultonboro) and Susan E. Cook (Sandwich)

Ansel E. of Sandwich m. Jennie P. **Davey** of Sandwich 6/8/1940; H – 78, farmer, b. Holderness, s/o Walter Lee (Holderness) and Mary F. Corliss (Sandwich); W – 67, housekeeper, b. Sandwich, d/o Oscar T. Vittum (Sandwich) and Annie A. Palmer (Sandwich)

David M. of Largo, FL m. Carol L. **Jowdy** of Ctr. Sandwich 9/1/1991

William B., III of Boston, MA m. Victoria **West** of Boston, MA 9/12/1987

LEHMANN,

William Hugh Campbell, Jr. of Sandwich m. Linda Lawrence **Kunhardt** of Sandwich 7/9/1988

LEIGHTON,

Charles L. of Moultonboro m. Sally Ann **Covey** of Sandwich 1/29/1967; H – 20, machinist, s/o Charles A. Leighton, Jr. and Louise Stacey; W – 17, student, d/o Uradel Covey, Jr. and Charlotte Brown

George W. of Center Harbor m. Lizzie M. **Hanson** of Sandwich 11/12/1887 in Sandwich; H – 20, painter, b. Center Harbor, s/o Alonzo Leighton (Center Harbor) and Sarah Leighton (Canada); W – 22, b. Rocheruk, IL, d/o George O. Hanson (Sandwich) and Amellia Hanson (Sandwich)

LEINWUND,

Ira Jay of New Haven, CT m. Nancy L. **Westneat** of New Haven, CT 6/24/1979 in Sandwich; H – s/o Alan J. Leinwund and Gertrude Buckwalter; W – d/o Francis W. Westneat and Norma L. Rogers

LELAND,
Roger B. of Northboro, MA m. Lorraine J. **Delaney** of Northboro, MA 5/9/1981

LEONARD,
Frank of Pawtucket, RI m. Carrie E. **Hoag** of Sandwich 5/15/1889 in Sandwich; H – 37, bank teller, b. Pawtucket, RI, s/o Charles A. Leonard and Prescilla Leonard: W – 24, teacher, b. Sandwich, d/o N. E. Hoag (Sandwich) and Ann Hoag (Sandwich)

LEROUX,
Larry S. of Meredith m. Mary L. **Nelson** of Sandwich 9/28/1968; H – s/o Armand Leroux and Harriet Harvey; W – d/o Kenneth Nelson and Frances Spaulding

LESTER,
Harold B. of Sandwich m. June Roberts **Pratt** of Keene 12/23/1951; H – 25, student, b. ME, s/o Orlando A. Lester (MA) and Mildred A. Meiser (ME); W – 24, teacher, b. CT, d/o Edson W. Pratt (NH) and Gladys M. Dockman (ME)

LEVY,
Chad W. of Astoria, NY m. Amy G. **Marshall** of Astoria, NY 8/10/2002 in Sandwich

LIBBY,
Rufus A. of New Hampton m. Flora R. **Mudgett** of Sandwich 5/31/1928 in Sandwich; H – 25, radiotheran, b. Brookline, MA, s/o William Libby (New Hampton) and Ruth R. Libby (New Hampton); W – 21, at home, b. Sandwich, d/o F. W. Mudgett (Sandwich) and Ora Fogg (Sandwich)

LIMBERGER,
Donald K. of Sandwich m. Heesun **Kim** of Sandwich 5/23/1987

LINDLEY,
William T. of Sandwich m. June E. **Palmer** of Ctr. Ossipee 1/6/1996

LINDSTROM,
Julius A. m. Lillian S. **Abbott** 12/23/1909 in Sandwich; H – 22, carpenter, b. Sweden, s/o Peter Lindstrom (Sweden) and Matilda Lindstrom (Sweden); W – 36, housekeeper, b. Sandwich, d/o J. Hartwell Smith (Sandwich) and Alice M. Smith (Ossipee)

LITTLE,
Clayton Alton of Laconia m. Joan **Beach** of Sandwich 6/21/1952; H – 25, truck driver, b. NH, s/o Frank H. Little (VT) and Julia E. Hutchins (NH); W – 21, student, b. NH, s/o Watson E. Beach (NH) and Florence E. Hudson (NH)

LITTLEFIELD,
Orace B. m. Beatrice M. **Johnson** 12/17/1936 in Moultonboro; H – 25, laborer, b. Brownfield, ME, s/o Howard I. Littlefield (Brownfield, ME) and Carrie Stover (Brownfield, ME); W – 20, housework, b. Tamworth, d/o Harry S. Johnson (Brownfield, ME) and Alice Kelley (Bridgton, ME)
Paul A. of Tamworth m. Marjorie **Cook** of Sandwich 11/2/1957; H – 29, lumberman, b. NH, s/o Ralph A. Littlefield (ME) and Evelyn M. Briggs (ME); W – 15, b. NH, d/o Wilbur A. Cook (NH) and Edna R. Adams (MA)

LITZELL,
Charles Edward of Sandwich m. Margaret Frances **Dornig** of Sandwich 5/4/1997

LIVELY,
David Glenn of Moultonboro m. Elizabeth J. **Taylorb of Sandwich 11/7/1987**

LOCKHART,
Michael D. of Erie, PA m. Kristina M. **Beach** of Washington, DC 8/9/1991

LOMBARDI,
Gary A. of N. Sandwich m. Ruth J. **Whitney** of Hooksett 7/18/2001

LONDON,
Frank C. of Roxbury, MA m. Pamela H. **Houston** of Roxbury, MA 8/5/1984

LOTTINGER,
Hugh A. of Amherst m. Beth A. **Deming** of Ctr. Sandwich 12/22/1984

LUNT,
Clifton A. of Sandwich m. Emma M. **Cummings** of Amesbury, MA 6/19/1934; H – 39, musician, b. Amesbury, MA, s/o William E. Lunt (Newbury, MA) and Myrtie M. Wiggin (Boston, MA); W – 46, at home, b. Boston, MA, d/o M. Arthur Hugh (Boston, MA) and Martha M. Eldridge (Boston, MA)

LURIA,
Scott L. of Brighton, MA m. Jane E. **Andrews** of Brighton, MA 1/14/1984

MACDONALD,
Ernest E. of Sandwich m. Ethel B. **Diack** of Quincy, MA 7/26/1930; H – 23, laborer, b. Union, s/o Alonzo M.

MacDonald (Wakefield) and Helen F. Bickford (E. Alton); W – 22, bookkeeper, b. Quincy, MA, d/o Alfred Oliver Diack (Scotland) and Jane Wilson (Scotland)

Ernest E. of Sandwich m. Ruth D. **Gebo** of Sandwich 7/8/1955; H – 48, truck driver, b. NH, s/o Alonzo MacDonald (NH) and Helen F. Bickford (NH); W – 45, school teacher, b. VT, d/o John DeCourcy (VT) and Margaret Donovan (VT)

Ernest E., Jr. of Sandwich m. Joyce A. **Haley** of Tuftonboro 5/16/1954; H – 20, laborer, b. NH, s/o Ernest E. MacDonald (NH) and Ethel B. Diack (MA); W – 19, at home, b. NH, d/o Delbert C. Haley (NH) and Muriel C. Roberge (NH)

MACK,

Fred M. of Sandwich m. Nellie E. **Abbott** of Sandwich 9/21/1889 in Sandwich; H – 28, farmer, b. Tamworth, s/o George Mack (Madison) and Lovina R. Mack; W – 18, b. Sandwich, d/o Freeman Abbott and Abbie F. Abbott

Herbert G. of Sandwich m. Clara W. **Hines** of Sandwich 3/30/1887 in Sandwich; H – 24, farmer, b. Tamworth, s/o George Mack (Madison) and Louis Mack (Boston, MA); W – 22, b. Sandwich, d/o Edward Hines (Tamworth) and Almira Hines (Sandwich)

MACLEAN,

John K. of Cambridge, MA m. Grace F. **Henry** of Cambridge, MA 7/20/1991

MACOMBER,

John D. of Cambridge, MA m. Kristin **Hodgkins** of Cambridge, MA 6/11/1983

MADIGAN,

Derek D. of Center Harbor m. Elizabeth J. **Bryant** of Sandwich 7/29/2006 in Laconia

MAGNUS,
Kurt Henry of Bloomfield Hills, MI m. Emily Hodges **Adriance** of Sandwich 8/27/1994

MAGOON,
Levi L. of Sandwich m. Mary A. **Danforth** 4/22/1908; H – 57, farmer, b. Sandwich, s/o Asa Magoon and Mary E. Smith (Sandwich); W – 60, housekeeper, b. Plymouth, MA, d/o John Courtney (Plymouth, MA) and Mary A. Gifford (Plymouth, MA)

MAILLOUX,
Jack J. of Sandwich m. Louise M. **Longley** of Sandwich 8/2/1986

MANGAN,
John R., Jr. of New Haven, CT m. Bronwen **MacArthur** of New Haven, CT 8/2/2003 in Tamworth

MANN,
Charles E. of Sandwich m. Ella **Yeaton** of Sandwich 1/11/1893 in Andover; H – 40, telegraph operator, b. Sandwich, s/o George W. Mann (Moultonboro) and Eliza Skinner (Sandwich); W – 31, b. Andover, d/o Eben Yeaton (Lebanon, ME) and May Tucker (Grafton)

MARDEN,
Melvin F. of Holderness m. Irva B. **Wallace** of Sandwich 2/22/1931; H – 25, farm laborer, b. Medford, MA, s/o Mark K. Marden (Holderness) and Christina Brand (Medford, MA); W – 20, house work, b. New Hampton, d/o Marcellus Wallace (Thornton) and Harriet Smith (New Hampton)

MARRA,
Stephen J. of Sandwich m. Gretchen G. **Geishecker** of Center Harbor 8/14/1999

MARSHALL,
Crofton S. of Sandwich m. Andrea E. **Hoisington** of Sandwich 8/22/1998
Edward H. of Chichester m. Lena M. **Watson** of Sandwich 9/5/1921 in Chichester; H – 30, farmer, b. W. Gloucester, MA, s/o William P. Marshall (W. Gloucester) and Florence N. Harris (Bear River, NS); W – 24, teacher, b. Sandwich, d/o Daniel Watson (Tamworth) and Fannie M. Pitman (Alexandria)

MARSTON,
Charles S. of Sandwich m. Hannah E. **Knowlton** of Tamworth 10/19/1898 in Tamworth; H – 40, farmer, b. Sandwich, s/o W. A. Marston (Tamworth) and Sally Marston (Moultonboro); W – 28, dressmaker, b. Tamworth, d/o Weston Knowlton (Poland, ME) and Hannah Knowlton (Ossipee)
Willis B. of Sandwich m. Adelaide J. **Gilman** of Franconia 10/22/1894 in Franconia; H – 33, farmer, b. Sandwich, s/o Ira Marston (Sandwich) and Sally B. Marston (Sandwich); W – 28, dressmaker, b. Winchester, MA, d/o ----- (Thornton) and ----- (Rockport, MA)

MARTEL,
Elziar of Sandwich m. Beatrice M. **Palmer** of Sandwich 1/9/1916 in Sandwich; H – 23, laborer, b. Canada, s/o Emanuell Martell (Canada) and Adez Boucher (Canada); W – 17, housekeeper, b. Sandwich, d/o James O. Palmer (Sandwich) and Etta A. Vittum (Sandwich)
Haven C. of Sandwich m. Jo-Ann V. **Daigneau** of Sandwich 10/15/1960; H – 19, laborer, s/o Elzear J. Martel and

Beatrice M. Palmer; W – 18, secretary, d/o Ernest J. Daigneau and Louise A. Roucher

James R. of Sandwich m. Jennifer K. **Leiblein** of Sandwich 6/26/1999

Morton C. of Sandwich m. Violet D. **Speckman** of Tamworth 10/6/1956; H – 28, auto mechanic, b. NH, s/o Elgear J. Martel (Canada) and Beatrice Palmer (NH); W – 24, nurse, b. NH, d/o Lester A. Eldridge (NH) and Ida M. Judkins (NH)

Raymond James of Sandwich m. Arline Germaine **Pelchat** of Laconia 5/22/1953; H – 30, poultryman, b. NH, s/o Elzear J. Martel (Canada) and Beatrice M. Palmer (NH); W – 27, knitter, b. NH, d/o George B. Pelchat (Canada) and Anna Rose Chabot (NH)

MARTIN,

Eugene F. of Moultonboro m. Grace A. **Abbott** of Sandwich 8/27/1902 in Sandwich; H – 21, laborer, b. Sandwich, s/o Alden P. Martin (Sandwich) and Margaret Coleman; W – 17, b. Sandwich, d/o Reuben F. Abbott (Tamworth) and Abbie A. Tappan (Sandwich)

Levi P. of Sandwich m. Ethel M. **Peakes** of Sandwich 10/21/1919 in Sandwich; H – 40, farmer, b. Melrose, MA, s/o Jeremiah Martin (Charlestown, MA) and Sarah E. Sprague (Stoneham, MA); W – 39, housekeeper, b. Dedham, MA, d/o John Q. A. Peakes (Scituate, MA) and Mary E. Parker (Cohasset, MA)

Louville K. of Tamworth m. Helen **Weed** of Tamworth 9/12/1940; H – 37, caretaker, b. Tamworth, s/o Lyman L. Martin (Lovell, ME) and Ida M. Kenerson (Tamworth); W – 27, teacher, b. Sandwich, d/o Cleveland Weed (Sandwich) and Lottie M. Vittum (KS)

Wilbur E. of Sandwich m. Dora E. **Peaslee** of Sandwich 6/6/1936 in Tamworth; H – 22, laborer, b, Sandwich, s/o Eugene F.

Martin (Sandwich) and Sarah E. Skinner (Sandwich); W – 19, at home, b. Sandwich, d/o Ruth Peaslee (Sandwich)
Willard Gordon, Jr. of Sandwich m. Margaret Ann **Demos** of Sanbornton 10/1/1988

MASON,
Clinton C. m. Flora V. **Merrow** 9/22/1909 in Ctr. Harbor; H – 27, carpenter, b. Tamworth, s/o Fred C. Mason (Tamworth) and Elta W. Mason (Tamworth); W – 27, housekeeper, b. Somerville, MA, d/o R. J. McPherson (NS) and Mary E. Mahan (Milford, MA)
Philip N., III of Sandwich m. Amy Marie **Brown** of Sandwich 7/11/1998

McBEE,
Burrett E., Jr. of Wallingford, CT m. Deborah R. **Melum** of Glen Head, NY 6/9/1973 in Wonalancet; H – s/o Burrett McBee and Henrietta Gray; W – d/o Jerald H. Melum and Shirley R. Foote

McCARTHY,
Clarence A. of Weirs Beach m. Robin G. **Dustin** of Sandwich 5/23/1987

McCORMACK,
George C. of Holderness m. Frances M. **Wallace** of Sandwich 2/27/1935; H – 25, laborer, b. Campton, s/o Liberius McCormack (Charlottetown, PEI) and Ella M. Ames (Holderness); W – 19, at home, b. Sandwich, d/o Harry Wallace (Sandwich) and Hattie M. Plummer (Sandwich)
George E. of Sandwich m. Linda **Taylor** of Sandwich 9/6/1963; H – 27, carpenter, s/o George C. McCormack and Frances M. Wallace; W – 16, at home, d/o Paul A. Taylor and Marion E. Gray

George E. of Sandwich m. Jean M. **Taylor** of Tamworth 6/27/1975 in Ctr. Conway; H – s/o George C. McCormack and Frances Wallace; W – d/o Irving Rogers and Addie Grace

McCRILLIS,
Henry Bullard of Sandwich m. Constance **Hunt** of Sandwich 6/7/1953; H – 24, welfare worker, b. MA, s/o Neal McCrillis (MA) and Marion Bullard (MA); W – 18, student, b. MA, d/o Kenneth L. Hunt (MA) and Doris E. Perkins (MA)
Neal of Sandwich m. Marion **Bullard** of Wellesley, MA 12/22/1917 in Wayland, MA; H – 27, farmer, b. Sandwich, s/o Alonzo McCrillis and Lulie Clark; W – 24, at home, b. Arlington, MA, d/o Henry W. Bullard and Mary B. Palmer

McDONALD,
Daniel J. of Fryeburg, ME m. Kathleen M. **Hambrook** of Sandwich 8/11/1990

McDONOUGH,
Thomas of Long Island City, NY m. Catherine **O'Donnell** of New York, NY 8/6/1916 in Sandwich; H – 27, groceryman, b. Ireland, s/o Cornelius McDonough (Ireland) and Margaret Morris (Ireland); W – 26, cook, b. Ireland, d/o Thomas O'Donnell (Ireland) and Catherine Reagan (Ireland)

McGRATH,
Michael of Sandwich m. Florence M. **Hall** of Sandwich 5/18/1928 in Somersworth; H – 32, salesman, b. Boston, MA, s/o Michael McGrath (Ireland) and Agnes Doherty (Ireland); W – 38, at home, b. S. Boston, MA

McKISSICK,
Edward of Somerville, MA m. Rose E. **Rockwood** of Cambridge, MA 7/14/1904 in Sandwich; H – 50, machinist, b. Albany,

NY, s/o Edward McKissick (Saco, ME) and Elizabeth McIntire (MA); W – 38, b. Kewanee, IL, d/o Albion Rockwood (Belgrade, ME) and Sarah J. Ricker (Belgrade, ME)

McLEAN,
John S. of Sandwich m. Nina **Benton** of Sandwich 6/28/1980

McMILLEN,
Robert W. of Huntington Beach, CA m. Pamela A. **Emerson** of Reading, MA 6/29/1963; H – 23, commercial driver, s/o Robert W. McMillen and Ruth Nelson; W – 20, student, d/o Denley W. Emerson and Harriet A. Rathbun

McNAMARA,
Stephen James of Sandwich m. Emily Jean **Dorais** of Meredith 9/30/1989

McPHAIL,
Peter W. of Sandwich m. Jacqueline M. **Meredith** of Sandwich 11/8/2003 in Sandwich

MEDER,
Eric James of Waterbury, CT m. Cathleen Anne **Graves** of Waterbury, CT 8/22/1997

MEDVECKY,
John of Largo, FL m. Eva **Sturgeon** of Sandwich 10/19/1963; H – 68, retired, s/o John Medvecky and Anna Medvecky; W – 68, at home, d/o Michael Brezina and Eva Mikus

MEEK,
David Harold of Salem, MA m. Megan Elizabeth **Kelley** of Salem, MA 6/25/1988

MEREDITH,

Clement O. m. Angelina **Weed** 7/23/1913 in Sandwich; H – 36, teacher, b. High Point, NY, s/o Elihu Meridith (High Point, NY) and Prudence M. Lamb (High Point, NY); W – 27, teacher, b. Clintondale, NY, d/o Stephen A. Wood (Dermyter, NY) and ----- (Hanover, MI)

Irving, Jr. of Dover m. Nancy L. **Reed** of Ctr. Sandwich 5/9/1986

MERRILL,

William A. of Salem m. Apphia **Tilton** of Sandwich 12/12/1916 in Sandwich; H – 40, blacksmith, b. Salem, s/o William P. Merrill (Salem) and Wealthy J. Woodbury (Salem); W – 25, at home, b. Moultonboro, d/o Albert Tilton (Sandwich) and Clara Tappan (Sandwich)

MERRIMAN,

Roger B., III of Sandwich m. Harriet R. **Willoughby** of Sandwich 6/29/1968; H – s/o Roger B. Merriman, Jr. and Fredericka Warner; W – d/o Kyle E. Willoughby and Minerva Wallace

Roger B., III of Sandwich m. Patricia A. **Fleming** of Sandwich 9/25/1982

MERRITT,

Edward A. S. of Lenox, MA m. Judith **Bates** of Burlington, MA 8/17/1991

MERRYFIELD,

Clifford of Sandwich m. Christine E. **Taylor** of Sandwich 8/17/1936 in Sandwich; H – 41, carpenter, b. Tuftonboro, s/o Everett Merryfield (Portersville, ME) and Emma I. Nichols (Boston, MA); W – 44, at home, b. Sandwich, d/o Lucien Skinner (Sandwich) and Hattie E. Horne (Sandwich)

Harold of Sandwich m. V. Claire **White** of Windsor, VT 7/3/1922 in Meredith; H – 21, chauffeur, b. Porterfield, ME, s/o

Everett Merryfield (Porterfield, ME) and Emma Nichols (Boston, MA); W – 23, at home, b. Sandwich, d/o Charles M. White (Hallowell, ME) and Hattie M. Bryant (Sandwich)

Norman E. of Sandwich m. Doris L. **Gault** of Sandwich 3/20/1920 in Sandwich; H – 18, laborer, b. Porterfield, ME, s/o Everett Merryfield (Porterfield, ME) and Emma L. Nicol (Charlestown, MA); W – 16, at home, b. Sandwich, d/o George Gault (Somerville, MA) and Eva Bagley (Sandwich)

METCALF,

Winslow H. of Sandwich m. Nancy L. **Lear** of Sandwich 9/25/1948; H – 22, electrician, b. Providence, RI, s/o Edward H. Metcalf (Woonsocket, RI) and Winnifred Winslow (Providence, RI); W – 20, at home, b. Berkeley, CA, d/o Lester A. Lear (Gallipolis, OH) and Isadora Schmidt (Philadelphia, PA)

MICHAEL,

Kevin of Sandwich m. Christina **McHugh** of Meredith 10/8/1994

Monroe of Sandwich m. Bernice A. **Vittum** of Sandwich 3/1/1948; H – 31, expressman, b. New York, NY, s/o Monroe Michael (New York, NY) and Marian Dick (New York, NY); W – 33, postal clerk, b. Manchester, d/o Frank E. Adams (Eden, VT) and Ellen N. Keane (Galway, Ireland)

Philip of N. Sandwich m. Mary L. **D'Este** of Ctr. Sandwich 6/21/1947; H – 24, expressman, b. New York City, s/o Monroe Michael (New York City) and Marion Dick (New York City); W – 25, agriculturist, b. Glen Ridge, NJ, d/o Julian L. D'Este (Salem, MA) and Katherine Goodell (W. Orange, NJ)

Timothy of Sandwich m. Carol L. **Howell** of Moultonboro 9/18/1976 in Sandwich; H – s/o Munroe Michael and

Bernice Adams; W – d/o Hutson K. Howell and Edna F. Thompson

MICHALSKI,
David A. of Sandwich m. Jane E. **Nicoli** of Sandwich 10/15/1983

MIKELINICH,
Kenneth Edward of Sandwich m. Lina Patricia **Atehortua** of Fort Worth, TX 10/18/1999

MILBURY,
William F. of Sandwich m. Holly B. **Cook** of Sandwich 7/31/1982

MILLER,
Arthur P. of Detroit, MI m. Margaret **Marston** of Sandwich 7/29/1926 in Sandwich; H – 24, civil engineer, b. Merchantville, NJ, s/o Burt Miller (Bath, NY) and Caroline Miller (England); W – 25, teacher, b. Sandwich, d/o Charles S. Marston (Sandwich) and Hannah E. Knowlton (Tamworth)

MILLS,
Andrew S. of Sandwich m. Lynn M. **Steiner** of Sandwich 8/25/2001

MINER,
Timothy A. of Sandwich m. Patricia L. **Slothower** of Sandwich 9/27/1980

MITCHELL,
Arthur I. of Ctr. Sandwich m. Madge B. **Hulbert** of Manchester 6/11/1933 in Manchester; H – 57, barber, b. Fitchburg, MA, s/o Simmons A. Mitchell (Wales, ME) and Addie A. Dunn (Lynn, MA); W – 49, saleslady, b. Chicago, IL, d/o Harry E. Curtis (Strafford, VT) and Laura B. Bly (IN)

John Carroll of Yarmouth, ME m. Patricia Ruel **Read** of Sandwich 6/26/1972 in Sandwich; H – s/o Burr C. Mitchell and Margaret M. Pendleton; W – d/o Patrick L. Ruel and Elsie L. Lessard

MOHAN,
Patrick J. of N. Sandwich m. Kimberly B. **Wilson** of N. Sandwich 8/27/2000

MONEYPENNY,
Christopher R. of Tamworth m. Lianne Damon **Prentice** of Sandwich 3/14/1998

MOORE,
Courtenay W. of Moultonboro m. Ann M. **Winchester** of Sandwich 4/21/1984
David W. of Burlingame, CA m. Janet J. **Levesque** of Burlingame, CA 9/8/1984

MORGAN,
Charles H. of Middleton, MA m. Eva Estella **Smith** of Sandwich --/19/1911; H – 25, shoe stitcher, b. Ipswich, s/o John H. Morgan (Salem, MA) and Annie L. Barker (Ipswich, MA); W – 18, b. Boston, MA, d/o John B. Smith (Sandwich) and Lizzie Scott (Boston, MA)
Richard B. of N. Sandwich m. Deborah E. **Gray** of Concord 3/20/1983
Richard R. of Sandwich m. Lisa M. **Tracy** of Hebron, CT 7/23/1995

MORTON,
Lee S. of Sandwich m. Sylvia L. **Robinson** of Meredith 1/16/1988
Michael John of Sandwich m. Nancy Marie **Casella** of Plymouth 8/2/1997

MOSKOWITZ,

Jay I. of Ctr. Sandwich m. Edibeth F. **Merriman** of Ctr. Sandwich 5/16/1984

Jay Irvin of Sandwich m. Jayne Katherine **Greene** of Sandwich 6/18/1978 in Sandwich; H – s/o Raymond L. Moskowitz and Muriel D. Funk; W – d/o Eric E. Geddes and Ella Trudeau

MOULTON,

Arthur P. of Sandwich m. Maud B. **Smith** of Sandwich 11/7/1899 in Sandwich; H – 19, laborer, b. Sandwich, s/o Edgar C. Moulton (Newark, VT) and Clara R. Moulton (Sandwich); W – 16, b. Sandwich, d/o Paul Shabot (Boston) and Mercy B. Shabot (Sandwich)

Edgar C. of Sandwich m. Myrtle **Brown** of Sandwich 5/30/1895 in Sandwich; H – 37, laborer, b. Sandwich, s/o Hiram Moulton and Salome Moulton (Albany); W – 16, housewife, b. Conway, d/o Moses Brown (Conway)

George K. of Sandwich m. Clara P. **Cole** of Porter, ME 3/15/1890 in Sandwich; H – 21, farmer, b. Lake Village, s/o H. H. Moulton (MA) and ----- (Porter, ME); W – 18, b. Porter, ME, d/o Levi Cole (Dorchester) and Hannah Cole (Sandwich)

Isaac A. of Sandwich m. Carrie M. **Tilton** of Moultonboro 1/2/1889 in Center Harbor; H – 22, farmer, b. Sandwich, s/o Daniel Moulton (Sandwich) and Ann Moulton (Sandwich); W – 20, housekeeper, b. Moultonboro, d/o Henry A. Tilton and Sarah J. Tilton

Joseph B. of Sandwich m. Ruth M. **Hodge** of Sandwich 3/1/1919 in Sandwich; H – 19, laborer, b. Sandwich, s/o Edgar C. Moulton (Sandwich) and Myrtle Drown (Conway); W – 18, at home, b. Sandwich, d/o Norman Hodge (Sandwich) and Effie Abbott (Sandwich)

Kendall N. of Meredith m. Pauline S. **Elliott** of Sandwich 5/3/1954; H – 27, weather ob'r, b. NH, s/o George L. Moulton (NH) and Hazel M. Nichols (MA); W – 31, tel. operator, b. NH, d/o Lewis C. Elliott (NH) and Sarah A. Pierce (RI)

MOWATT,

Herman H. of Sandwich m. Daphne **Metcalf** of Sandwich 7/23/1949; H – 26, salesman, b. MA, s/o Frank Allen Mowatt (CT) and Sarah A. Quimby (NH); W – 26, at home, b. RI, d/o Edwin H. Metcalf (RI) and Winifred Winslow (RI)

MUDGETT,

Elisha W. of Sandwich m. Myrtle B. **Fennell** of Tamworth 5/19/1934; H – 23, laborer, b. Sandwich, s/o Jesse A. Mudgett (Sandwich) and Jennie Sturgis (Albany); W – 18, at home, b. Lynn, MA, d/o Charles W. Fennell (PEI) and Miney Kierstead (NB)

Eugene E. of Sandwich m. Eva M. **Davis** of Sandwich 4/6/1898 in Sandwich; H – 23, farmer, b. Sandwich, s/o E. W. Mudgett (Sandwich) and Susan M. Mudgett (Haverhill); W – 16, b. Sandwich, d/o Frank Davis and Rose Bemis Davis (Sandwich)

Eugene R. of Sandwich m. Joan Josephine **Sarni** of Portsmouth 10/15/1955; H – 20, auto mechanic, b. NH, s/o Robert E. Mudgett (NH) and Thelma Mae Watson (MA); W – 20, salesgirl, b. MA, d/o John Leo Sarni (MA) and Mary J. Bonopane (MA)

Francis C. of Sandwich m. Ruth **Shaw** of Moultonboro 5/25/1937 in Center Harbor; H – 24, laborer, b. Sandwich, s/o Jesse A. Mudgett (Sandwich) and Jennie Sturgis (Albany); W – 19, housework, b. Moultonboro, d/o Howard Shaw (Sandwich) and Deldie Bragg (Moultonboro)

Frank L. of Sandwich m. Annie **McInnis** of Sandwich 10/21/1914 in Meredith; H – 20, farmer, b. Sandwich, s/o Elisha W.

Mudgett (Sandwich) and Luella B. Atkins (Sandwich); W – 28, housekeeper, b. Boston, MA, d/o Thomas McInnis (St. John, NB) and Isabel Cochran (St. John, NB)

Fred M. of Sandwich m. Ora A. **Fogg** of Sandwich 7/23/1889 in Sandwich; H – 23, farmer, b. Sandwich, s/o Charles E. Mudgett (Sandwich) and Mary Mudgett (Alton); W – 20, b. Sandwich, d/o H. T. Fogg (Sandwich) and Mary Fogg (Sandwich)

Gary S. of Sandwich m. Laura H. **Miner** of Sandwich 6/19/1999

Irving E. of Sandwich m. Evelyn F. **Taylor** of Sandwich 11/17/1928 in New Hampton; H – 23, farmer, b. Sandwich, s/o Eugene E. Mudgett (Sandwich) and Eva M. Mudgett (Sandwich); W – 19, at home, b. Lynn, MA, d/o ----- (Sandwich) and ----- (Tamworth)

Fred C. of Sandwich m. Marion **Elliott** of Sandwich 6/27/1925 in Sandwich; H – 22, mechanic, b. Sandwich, s/o Fred W. Mudgett (Sandwich) and Ora A. Fogg (Sandwich); W – 19, at home, b. Sandwich, d/o Lewis A. Elliott (Sandwich) and Sadie Pierce (Cranston, RI)

James R. of Sandwich m. Carolyn M. **Conner** of Ctr. Ossipee 4/1/1949; H – 23, equipt. installer, b. NH, s/o Frank L. Mudgett (NH) and Annie McGinnis (MA); W – 21, at home, b. NH, d/o John B. Conner (NH) and Evelyn Sargent (NH)

Jesse A. of Tamworth m. Jennie E. **Sturgess** of Tamworth 11/13/1908; H – 21, farmer, b. Sandwich, s/o Elisha W. Mudgett (Sandwich) and Luella B. Atkins (Sandwich); W – 21, housekeeper, b. Conway, d/o Philip Sturgess (Canada) and Almira E. Sturgess (Albany)

Joel R. of Sandwich m. Frances L. **Glidden** of Moultonboro 9/2/1973 in Moultonboro; H – s/o James Mudgett and Carolyn Conner; W – d/o Ellsworth Glidden and Norma Moulton

Robert E. of Sandwich m. Thelma M. **Walters** of W. Ossipee 10/1/1933 in Fryeburg, ME; H – 21, farmer, b. Sandwich, s/o Eugene E. Mudgett and Eva Davis (Boston, MA); W –

18, at home, b. Dorchester, MA, d/o Jesse M. Walters (Boston, MA)

MULLEN,
Ralph, Jr. of Moultonboro m. Elva Elaine **Taylor** of Sandwich 11/15/1952; H – 26, carpenter, b. ME, s/o Ralph J. Mullen (ME) and Alice E. Tivey (MA); W – 26, at home, b. NH, d/o Charles E. Taylor (MA) and Bernice E. Dodge (NH)

MYKLAND,
James Olav of Ctr. Sandwich m. Susan J. **Borge** of Ctr. Sandwich 5/12/1986

NEDEAU,
Raymond R. of Laconia m. Marjorie E. **Hall** of Sandwich 8/15/1963; H – 18, boarding stockings, s/o Amedee F. Nedeau and Alrita L. Huck; W – 17, stitcher, d/o Ernest F. Hall and Dorothy M. Foss

NELSON,
Herbert E. of Sandwich m. Bernice D. **Jordan** of Laconia 8/9/1947; H – 34, cam filer, b. Quincy, MA, s/o Thomas Nelson (Norway) and Henrietta Brown (Quincy, MA); W – 24, inspector, b. Laconia, d/o Walter Jordan (Fairlee, VT) and Cora Packard (Lebanon)

James E. of Conway m. Ann M. **Nellenback** of Ossipee 6/6/1971 in Sandwich; H – s/o James Nelson and Dorothy Libby; W – d/o Sylvester Nellenback and Galdys Markell

Robert E., Jr. of Sandwich m. Kathryn Stone **DeWitt** of Sandwich 8/8/1998

William T. of Sandwich m. Lena **Thompson** of Sandwich 6/1/1932; H – 23, mechanic, b. Quincy, MA, s/o Thomas Nelson (Norway) and Henrietta Brown (Quincy, MA); W – 24, PO clerk, b. Sandwich, d/o Elmer S. Thompson (Sandwich) and Eva Smith (Sandwich)

NICHOL,

Charles R. of Sandwich m. Nellie J. **Goodwin** of Sandwich 6/16/1897 in Meredith; H – 32, farmer, b. Charlestown, MA, s/o Alexander Nichol (Charlestown, MA) and Lucy A. Nichol (Charlestown, MA); W – 22, teacher, b. Sandwich, d/o Charles Goodwin (Rochester) and Lucinda B. Goodwin (Sandwich)

NIXON,

William Dorr of Sandwich m. Bertha Laurie **Marshall** of Tamworth 6/19/1941; H – 22, machinist, b. Plymouth, MA, s/o James H. Nixon (Berah, Ireland) and Edith M. Dovo (Sandwich); W – 22, bookkeeper, b. Boston, MA, d/o George L. Marshall (Somerville, MA) and Ruth Page (Tamworth)

NOBLE,

Jeffrey A. of Denmark, ME m. Jayne A. **Mudgett** of Sandwich 10/10/1982

NORCROSS,

Charles D. of Tamworth m. Faye V. **Mudgett** of Sandwich 1/27/1962; H – 18, lumber mill, s/o Elmer R. Norcross and Jennie Dorr; W – 17, student, d/o Robert E. Mudgett and Thelma Watson

Milton Arthur of Tamworth m. Regina Lynn **Swan** of Sandwich 3/4/1980

NUDD,

Ronald Eugene of Sandwich m. Irmabelle **Fortier** of Meredith 8/2/1952; H – 21, lumbering, b. NH, s/o Wallace Nudd (NH) and Blanche LeClair (VT); W – 18, at home, b. NH, d/o Albert Fortier (Canada) and Gertrude E. Goss (NH)

Walter of Sandwich m. Mabel Irene **Bickford** of Moultonboro 8/1/1942; H – 26, painter, b. Sandwich, s/o Wallace Nudd (Sandwich) and Blanche D. LeClair (Northfield, VT); W – 19, waitress, b. Moultonboro, d/o Charles M. Bickford (Center Harbor) and Alice M. Hayes (Moultonboro)

Walter E. of Canterbury m. V. Margie **Wallace** of Sandwich 12/18/1891 in Sandwich; H – 23, laborer, b. Canterbury, s/o David K. Nudd and L. J. Nudd; W – 23, b. Sandwich, d/o Asahel Wallace and Caroline T. Wallace

NUNGESSER,

William L., Jr. of Sandwich m. Colleen M. **McDermott** of Sandwich 6/2/1990

NYE,

Joseph Benjamin Harding of Washington, DC m. Jennifer Mackay **Pyle** of Washington, DC 10/23/1993

O'CONNELL,

Declan Anthony of N. Sandwich m. Kathleen Marie **Carney** of N. Sandwich 6/20/1992

O'CONNOR,

James W. of Sandwich m. Sally A. **Fichet** of Sandwich 7/22/2000

O'DONNELL,

Francis Edward of Holderness m. Barbara Jane **Fisher** of Sandwich 6/4/1988

O'GARA,

Robert Michael of Sandwich m. Carissa Audrey **Hull** of Sandwich 2/19/1988

OHMAN,
John Frederick of Dedham, MA m. Sandra **Michael** of Dedham, MA 7/22/1972 in Sandwich; H – s/o Conrad H. Ohman and Madeline C. Moses; W – d/o Philip Michael and Mary L. d'Este

OLESEN,
Per Brix of Copenhagen, Denmark m. Inge **Morup** of Copenhagen, Denmark 3/31/1990

ORTON,
Wayne Liddle of Bahamas m. Anne Boyer **Rozelle** of Nyack, NY 12/7/1972 in Sandwich; H – s/o William H. Orton and Vera M. Liddle; W – d/o Frederick C. Rozelle and Rita C. Anderson

OVALLE,
Arthur of Hudson m. Carolyn J. **Hersey** of Sandwich 12/6/1997

OWENS,
David A. of Red Bank, NJ m. Sandra L. **Hulse** of Red Bank, NJ 8/24/1986

PAGE,
Frank M. of Sandwich m. Ella M. **Abbott** of Sandwich 10/5/1904 in Meredith; H – 24, carpenter, b. Belgrade, ME, s/o Joel R. Page (Belgrade, ME) and Abbie L. Damerin (Belgrade, ME); W – 21, b. Sandwich, d/o Charles H. Abbott (Sandwich) and Ida R. Veazey (Derry)
Hutcheson of Moultonboro m. Louise T. **Jameson** of Sandwich 10/11/1971 in Tamworth; H – s/o George Page and Mary Hutcheson; W – d/o Francis LeClaire and Jeannette Perkins
Joel R. of Sandwich m. Emce V. **Durell** of Kennebunk, ME 3/15/1893 in Sandwich; H – 52, mill man, b. Belgrade, ME,

s/o Saul Page (Belgrade, ME) and Mary A. Page (Kennebunk, ME); W – 42, b. Kennebunk, ME, d/o Daniel Durell (Kennebunk, ME) and Sarah Durell

PALMER,

Archie H. of Sandwich m. Frances **Harriman** of Sandwich 1/1/1919 in Sandwich; H – 17, laborer, b. Sandwich, s/o James O. Palmer (Sandwich) and Etta A. Vittum (Sandwich); W – 21, at home, b. Sandwich, d/o Hiram Harriman (Berlin) and Lottie Car (NS)

Bruce A. of Sandwich m. Michelle **Perry** of Sandwich 8/7/1988

Herbert A. of Sandwich m. Amy **Tappan** of Sandwich 8/1/1893 in Tamworth; H – 28, farmer, b. Sandwich, s/o Ambrose Palmer (Sandwich) and Carrie Palmer (Moultonboro); W – 19, b. Sandwich, d/o A. E. Tappan (Sandwich) and Abbie Tappan (Sandwich)

James O. of Sandwich m. Etta A. **Vittum** of Sandwich 11/14/1899 in Sandwich; H – 41, farmer, b. Sandwich, s/o Ambrose Palmer (Sandwich) and Caroline Palmer (Sandwich); W – 36, housekeeper, b. Sandwich, d/o Alpheus Vittum (Sandwich) and Myra Vittum (Sandwich)

Willard F. of Sandwich m. Lulu B. **Gordon** of Lynn, MA 4/22/1901 in Sandwich; H – 39, farmer, b. Sandwich, s/o Oliver A. Palmer (Sandwich) and Carry L. Palmer (Moultonboro); W – 29, b. Charlestown, MA, d/o G. W. Gordon (Lowell, MA) and Anna D. Gordon (Crown Point, NY)

PAQUETTE,

Thomas D. of Rochester, VT m. Terry E. **Brewer** of Sandwich 8/20/1983

PARKER,

Henry I. of Cambridge, MA m. Marion F. **Scriggins** of Sandwich 9/23/1915 in Sandwich; H – 28, cook, b. Cambridge, MA, s/o James H. Parker (NS) and Nellie O. Sullivan (Cambridge, MA); W – 18, b. Sandwich, d/o Arthur Scriggins (Sandwich) and Flora B. Blackey (Moultonboro)

James W. S. of Ctr. Sandwich m. Ethel F. **O'Brien** of Ctr. Sandwich 10/3/1970 in Tamworth; H – s/o Dennis Parker and Sarah Murphy; W – d/o Frank E. Farnham and Nellie F. Bunker

Steven J. of Sandwich m. Deborah Anne **Myshrall** of Sandwich 8/24/1996

PARRIS,

Leroy A. of Sandwich m. Myrtle G. **McPherson** of Tamworth 5/16/1947; H – 51, woodsman, b. Littleton, s/o James A. Parris (St. John, NB) and Effie M. Dodge (Littleton); W – 36, hairdresser, b. Portland, ME, d/o Ervin W. Grant (Portland, ME) and Phoebe Berry

PARSONS,

John H. m. Ruth **Hoag** 9/4/1927; H – 30, warehouse manager, b. Franklin Park, MA, s/o James W. Parsons (Cornwallis, NS) and Henrietta Pierson (Whitby, ON); W – 23, teacher, b. Woburn, MA, d/o John B. Hoag (Sandwich) and Elizabeth Leiter (Woburn, MA)

PASSOW,

Christian H. of St. Charles, IL m. Honor **Jones** of Englewood, FL 6/2/1990

PATTEN,

Andrew W. of Somerville, MA m. Meta W. **Barton** of Somerville, MA 6/30/1984

PATTERSON,

Albion M. of Augusta, ME m. Mary R. **Hubbard** of Augusta, ME 11/18/1977 in Sandwich; H – s/o Albion H. Patterson and

Myrtle I. Rowe; W – d/o Charles P. Flanders and Ethel M. Lee

PEARSON,

Herman W. of Ashland m. Arlene L. **Thompson** of Sandwich 10/24/1948; H – 47, mgr. of store, b. Madison, s/o Theodore Pearson (Madison) and Carrie Smith (Campton); W – 30, farmerette, b. Sandwich, d/o Arthur G. Thompson (Sandwich) and Lulu Sanborn (Campton)

Herman W. of Sandwich m. Ruth L. **Barnes** of Sandwich 7/26/1967; H – 66, storekeeper, s/o Theodore Pearson and Carrie Smith; W – 29, at home, d/o Fred Barnes and Florence Whiting

PEASLEE,

Charles H. of Sandwich m. Charlotte M. **Avery** of Moultonboro 1/20/1949; H – 23, woodsman, b. NH, s/o Earl Charles Peaslee (NH) and Louise Carter (NH); W – 18, student, b. NH, d/o Roland Jasper Avery (NH) and Doris Towle (NH)

Charles H. of Sandwich m. Dorothy A. **Roberts** of Tamworth 2/3/1957; H – 31, mill work, b. NH, s/o Earle Peaslee (NH) and Louise Carter (NH); W – 20, at home, b. NH, d/o Charles E. Roberts (NH) and Gertrude E. Ripley (NH)

Daniel Charles of Sandwich m. Elaine Lynn **Bryant** of Sandwich 6/26/1976 in Sandwich; H – s/o Robert N. Peaslee and Pauline E. Burrows; W – d/o Milton R. Bryant and Barbara M. Bryant

David J. of Sandwich m. Dora E. **Trask** of Sandwich 6/2/1896 in Sandwich; H – 21, farmer, b. Sandwich, s/o Daniel Peaslee (Gilmanton) and Harriet Peaslee (Sandwich); W – 21, b. Waltham, MA, d/o Charles W. Trask (Danvers, MA)

David J. of Sandwich m. Bernice M. **Frye** of Sandwich 3/10/1913 in Sandwich; H – 36, carpenter, b. Sandwich, s/o Daniel Peaslee (Sandwich) and Harriet W. Fogg (Sandwich); W –

21, housekeeper, b. Lowell, MA,d /o Orrin C. Frye (Sandwich) and Ella G. Wood (Sandwich)

David W. of Sandwich m. Mary Vivian **Spaulding** of Sandwich 5/3/1951; H – 22, truck driver, b. NH, s/o Roscoe D. Peaslee (NH) and Dorothy E. Robinson (MA); W – 20, housework, b. MA, d/o Alexander R. Noble (MA) and Eleanor D. Stevens (NH)

Earl Charles of Sandwich m. Margaretta Joyce **Bickford** of Sandwich 8/12/1951; H – 21, laborer, b. NH, s/o Earl C. Peaslee (NH) and Louise Carter (NH); W – 19, secretary, b. NH, d/o Fred A. Bickford (NH) and Stella Mae Crawford (NH)

Earle C. of Sandwich m. Louise H. **Carter** of Sandwich 12/10/1924 in Sandwich; H – 20, laborer, b. Sandwich, s/o David J. Peaslee (Sandwich) and Dora E. Trask (Waltham, MA); W – 19, at home, b. Sandwich, d/o Almon Carter (Sandwich) and Addie Webster (Sandwich)

Garret E. of Lansing, MI m. Michelle M. **King** of Lansing, MI 12/31/1982

Kerry D. of Sandwich m. Susan J. **Carroll** of Moultonboro 9/17/1999

Robert N. of Sandwich m. Pauline E. **Burrows** of Sandwich 12/1/1951; H – 30, carpenter, b. Sandwich, s/o David J. Peaslee (NH) and Bernice Frye (MA); W – housework, b. Rumney, d/o Nathaniel Burrows (NH) and Edrie Gordon (NY)

Roland of Sandwich m. Dorothy **Demick** of Sandwich 10/1/1923 in Meredith; H – 24, carpenter, b. Sandwich, s/o David J. Peaslee (Sandwich) and Dora Trask (Danvers, MA); W – 22, at home, b. Lynn, MA, d/o C. Sherman Wing (Fayette, ME) and Dora Preston (Manchester)

Roscoe D. of Sandwich m. Dorothy E. **Robinson** of Sandwich 12/25/1922 in Sandwich; H – 21, laborer, b. Sandwich, s/o David Peaslee (Sandwich) and Dora E. Trask (Waltham, MA); W – 17, at home, b. Cambridge, MA, d/o William

Robinson (Portland, ME) and Nettie Quimby (Stewartstown)

PERKINS,

Allan R. of Meredith m. Michelle J. **Blondeau** of Sandwich 7/14/1979 in Meredith; H – s/o Francis S. Perkins and Camillia A. Shaw; W – d/o Gerald Blondeau and Pauline Mondor

George E. of Sandwich m. Addie Y. **West** of Sandwich 9/10/1904 in Sandwich; H – 62, shoemaker, b. Danvers, MA, s/o George Perkins (Wells, ME) and Maria Blackey (VT); W – 45, b. Marblehead, d/o Matthew C. West (Salem, MA) and Mary J. Fellows (Lynn, MA)

Melvin H. of Sandwich m. Georgia A. **Knight** of Ossipee 12/28/1888 in Tamworth; H – 23, laborer, b. Sandwich, s/o George Perkins (Wells, ME) and Maria Perkins (Wells, ME); W – 15, b. Moultonboro, d/o James P. Knight (Moultonboro) and Julia E. Knight (Tamworth)

Ralph H. of Hampton m. Gladys G. **Burrows** of Sandwich 6/24/1914 in Laconia; H – 22, moth work, b. Hampton, s/o George C. Perkins (Hampton) and Rose Cram (New Haven, CT); W – 16, housekeeper, b. Sandwich, d/o John G. Burrows (Sandwich) and Hattie F. Smith (Sandwich)

PETHERBRIDGE,

William C. of Sandwich m. Celia A. **Wood** 6/2/1908; H – 28, physician, s/o W. F. Petherbridge (MD); W – 28, ass't manager, b. Jackson, MI, d/o S. A. Wood (NY) and Ella Wood (Jackson, MI)

PETTENGILL,

Sylvester B. of Sandwich m. Helen E. **Delaney** of Everett, MA 6/18/1896 in Sandwich; H – 34, professional cook, b. Sandwich, s/o H. A. Pettengill (Sandwich) and Polley M.

Pettengill (Sandwich); W – 23, hotel work, b. NS, d/o ----- Delaney (NS)

PFEFFER,
Soren David of Morrisville, VT m. Irene Maria **Facciolo** of Morrisville, VT 9/3/1994

PICKERING,
Ellsworth E. of Meredith m. Elvira Amelia **Nudd** of Sandwich 11/1/1942; H – 21, mill work, b. Newmarket, s/o Everett E. Pickering (New Hampton) and Annie G. Wade (Moultonboro); W – 17, at home, b. Sandwich, d/o Wallace Nudd (Sandwich) and Blanche LeClair (Northfield, VT)

PICONE,
Stephen L. of Sandwich m. Donna L. **Berry** of Sandwich 12/22/1973 in Sandwich; H – s/o Stephen Picone and Olive M. Lawrence; W – d/o Alfred W. Foisy and Anna E. Bouldry
Stephen L. of Sandwich m. Fay P. **Scott** of Conway 9/28/1985

PIERCE,
Maurice A. of Sandwich m. Alice R. **Whiting** of Tamworth 8/22/1936 in Sandwich; H – 26, carpenter, b. Sandwich, s/o James A. Pierce (Cranston, RI) and Nettie Vittum (Sandwich); W – 25, teacher, b. Sandwich, d/o Almon Whiting (Tamworth) and Elizabeth Palmer (Sandwich)
Roger, III of Sandwich m. Felicia P. **Havre** of Plymouth 6/24/1991

PIPER,
David R. of Meredith m. Yvonne A. **MacDonald** of Sandwich 1/29/1955; H – 20, laborer, b. NH, s/o Ralph N. Piper (NH) and Edna Gladys Grant (NH); W – 18, at home, b. NH, d/o Ernest MacDonald (NH) and Ethel B. Diack (MA)

PIRANI,
Karim of San Francisco, CA m. Susan L. **Whitney** of San Francisco, CA 8/6/2005 in Sandwich

PITKIN,
Donald S. of Amherst, MA m. Mary C. **Nichols** of Boston, MA 8/20/1975 in Sandwich; H – s/o Donald S. Pitkin and Dorothy Bacon; W – d/o John G. Coolidge and Mary L. Hill

PITTENGER,
John C. of Winchester, MA m. Susan Elizabeth **Erb** of Winchester, MA 10/3/1987

PITTMAN,
Malcolm G., III of Cambridge, MA m. Ellen R. **Mayer** of Cambridge, MA 8/25/1984

PLASENCIA,
Dale A. of Sandwich m. Allison B. **Stewart** of Moultonboro 1/22/1983

PLIMMER,
Robert S. of N. Sandwich m. Shannon N. **Walsh** of Annapolis, MD 11/19/2006 in Sandwich

PLUMMER,
Clarence R. of Sandwich m. Luella M. **Sturgis** of Sandwich 11/26/1919 in Sandwich; H – 26, millman, b. Sandwich, s/o Wilfred Plummer (Sandwich) and Lizzie E. Webster (Meredith); W – 17, tel. operator, b. Sandwich, d/o Jennie E. Sturgis (Albany)

Frank P. of Sandwich m. Rosa **McBride** of Sandwich 12/25/1912 in Sandwich; H – 70, millman, b. Sanbornton, s/o Jesse Plummer (New Hampton) and Lydia Goss (New Hampton);

W – 36, housewife, b. Ireland, d/o John McBride (Ireland) and Ella Devlin (Ireland)

James H. m. Nettie **Irving** 3/18/1910; H – 23, laborer, b. Sandwich, s/o Wilfred Z. Plummer (Sandwich) and Elizabeth Webster (Sandwich); W – 18, housekeeper, b. Sandwich, d/o George L. Irving (Sandwich) and Ludia Tibbetts (Rochester)

James H. of Sandwich m. Edna B. **Nelson** of Moultonboro 7/20/1935; H – 24, laborer, b. Sandwich, s/o James H. Plummer (Sandwich) and Nettie Irving (Sandwich); W – 22, nurse, b. Moultonboro, d/o Jacob Nelson (Norway) and Leonora Wakefield (Moultonboro)

Wilfred C. of Sandwich m. Elizabeth D. **Nixon** of Sandwich 12/23/1945; H – 31, laborer, b. Sandwich, s/o James H. Plummer (Sandwich) and Nettie E. Irving (Sandwich); W – 27, teacher, b. Plymouth, MA, d/o James H. Nixon (Ireland) and Edith M. Dorr (Sandwich)

Wilfred Z. of Sandwich m. Annie M. **Leary** of Tuftonboro 9/14/1899 in Sandwich; H – 37, farmer, b. Sandwich, s/o Frank Plummer (Sanbornton) and Harriet Plummer (Ashland); W – 40, housekeeper, b. Tuftonboro, d/o David Leary (City of Cork) and Mary A. Leary (Stewartstown)

POHL,

Peter William of Sandwich m. Suzanne Marie **Bourque** of Dover 10/9/1972 in Sandwich; H – s/o Henry Pohl and Kathrine Goemmel; W – d/o Raymond Bourque and Gertrude Laughlin

POOLE,

Clifford of Charlotte, NC m. Lynn Robbins **Kegiah** of Sandwich 7/8/1978 in Sandwich; H – s/o Alonzo H. Poole and Doris Robinson; W – d/o Philip S. Robbins and Ann R. Briggs

POPHAM,
Byron J. m. Agnes F. **Davis** 12/25/1909 in Sandwich; H – 18, laborer, b. Sandwich, s/o James A. Popham (NH) and Betsy H. Gilman (Denmark, ME); W – 22, b. Effingham, d/o Henry E. Davis (Effingham) and Mabel R. Hanson (NH)

PORTER,
David E. of Sandwich m. Sally Anne **Tracy** of Meredith 7/29/1990

POTTER,
Brooks of N. Andover, MA m. Priscilla E. **Moulton** of Boston, MA 8/7/1958; H – 56, lawyer, s/o Albert B. Potter (MA) and Florence Brooks (MA); W – 29, at home, d/o Henry W. Endicott (MA) and Priscilla Maxwell (CT)

POWERS,
Herbert H. of Sandwich m. Mary E. **Fogg** of Sandwich 6/4/1891 in Sandwich; H – 30, engineer, b. Boston, MA, s/o George W. Powers and Johanna M. Powers; W – d/o Albert Fogg

PRESCOTT,
Michael J. of N. Sandwich m. Jennifer A. **Atkinson** of N. Sandwich 4/20/2003 in Sandwich

PRINCE,
Warren F. of Medford, MA m. Marvis P. **Condon** of Sandwich 12/18/1948; H – 21, student, b. Pt. Limon, C.A., s/o Warren F. Prince (N. Chelmsford, MA) and Mary Brown (Hartford, CT); W – 25, waitress, d/o Wayne Condon (Londonderry) and Winona Dickey (Londonderry)

PURVES,
William Carroll of Sandwich m. Robin Elizabeth **Schultz** of Madison, WI 6/18/1989

PYTLIK,
Steven Robert of Higganum, CT m. Kerrie Lee **Cannon** of Higganum, CT 8/16/1997

QUIMBY,
Clifton C. of Sandwich m. Beatrice M. **Annable** of Wolfeboro 11/1/1964; H – 80, retired, s/o Herman Haines Quimby and Amy M. Clark; W – 56, at home, d/o William J. Griffiths and Edith A. Blinkhorn
John S. of Sandwich m. Lucy **Colby** of Campton 1/12/1915 in Laconia; H – 55, farmer, b. Sandwich, s/o Harrison Quimby (Sandwich) and Betsey Severance (Sandwich); W – 48, housewife, b. Campton, d/o Charles Shute (Campton) and Lavina Clark (Campton)
Sherman of Sandwich m. Ursala A. **Watson** of Sandwich 11/16/1887 in Sandwich; H – 30, farmer, s/o Alvah Quimby (Sandwich) and Lucy F. Quimby (Sandwich); W – 38, d/o Thomas Watson (Sandwich) and Julia D. Watson (Sandwich)
Wilbur E. of Sandwich m. Ida M. **Lindstrom** 11/4/1908; H – 21, farmer, b. Sandwich, s/o Ezra Quimby (Sandwich) and Lizzie S. Cook (Sandwich); W – 22, housekeeper, b. Sweden, d/o August Lindstrom (Sweden) and Ida A. Lindstrom (Sweden)
Wilbur Ezra of Sandwich m. Emma Sophia **Karlin** of New Britain, CT 11/2/1938 in Moultonboro; H – 51, carpenter, b. Sandwich, s/o Ezra J. Quimby (Sandwich) and Elizabeth L. Cook (Sandwich); W – 43, cook, b. Bratton, Sweden, d/o Olof M. Karlin (Bratton, Sweden) and Anna R. Olsson (Bratton, Sweden)

QUINN,

Andrew J. of N. Sandwich m. Shannon K. **Cameron** of N. Sandwich 8/19/2000

Thomas B. of Bloomfield, NJ m. Susan L. **Medrick** of Caldwell, NJ 2/14/1991

RACINE,

William A. of Rumney m. Darlene M. **Elliott** of Sandwich 9/24/1983

READ,

Kirke Packard of Sandwich m. Patricia Anne **Ruel** of Meredith 5/17/1953; H – 18, laborer, b. RI, s/o Theodore Otis Read (RI) and Deborah G. Packard (Newfoundland); W – 18, student nurse, b. NH, d/o Patrick Leo Ruel (NH) and Elsie L. Lessard (ME)

Kirke Packard of Sandwich m. Marilyn **Ulrich** of Sandwich 9/4/1978 in Sandwich; H – s/o Theodore O. Read and Deborah G. Packard; W – d/o Charles G. Clements and Rita M. Prescott

Theodore O. of Sandwich m. Geraldine B. **George** of Ctr. Harbor 9/4/1978 in Sandwich; H – s/o Leon H. Read and Abby Esterbrooks; W – d/o John W. Bryant and Madeline Robinson

Theodore O., Jr. of Sandwich m. Pamela G. **Wright** of Meriden, CT 8/22/1964; H – 19, weaver, s/o Theodore O. Read and Deborah Packard; W – 20, student, d/o Jonathan Wright and Barbara Smith

Theodore Otis of Sandwich m. Deborah Packard **Brewer** of Sandwich 8/27/1938 in Sandwich; H – 21, wood worker, b. Rehoboth, MA, s/o Leon H. Read (W. Somerville, MA) and Abbie R. Estabrook (Warren, RI); W – 24, at home, b. St. Anthony's, NF

READER,
Richard Alan of Ashland m. Patti-Ann **Taylor** of Sandwich 10/9/1972 in Sandwich; H – s/o Robert Reader and Phillis Beers; W – d/o Harold E. Taylor and Rita Provencal

RECIO,
Robin Burke of Springfield, VA m. Shannon **Bickford** of Springfield, VA 8/13/1988

REED,
David T. of Tuftonboro m. Eleanor A. **Flanagan** of Sandwich 7/2/1961; H – shoe worker, s/o Frank E. Reed and Mildred F. Whiting; W – 18, at home, d/o Paul Flanagan and Hilda Colby
Lawrence J. of Wethersfield, CT m. Nancy L. **Metcalf** of W. Hartford, CT 7/5/1968; H – s/o John Reed and Nancy Deronne; W – d/o Lester Lear and Isadora Schmidt

REMICK,
A.Dexter m. Dorothy A. **Graves** 12/12/1936 in N. Conway; H - 26, electrician, b. Tamworth, s/o Fred Remick (Tamworth) and Winifred Dooley (Ireland); W – 20, at home, b. Sandwich, d/o Clarence E. Graves (Sandwich) and Nellie Whiting (Tamworth)

RICHARDSON,
F. P. of Moultonboro m. Winifred **Tilton** of Sandwich 9/24/1895 in Sandwich; H – 21, teamster, b. Moultonboro, s/o A. P. Richardson (Madison) and Elsa Richardson; W – 20, housewife, b. Sandwich, d/o Alvin Tilton (Sandwich) and Sarah Tilton
Glen Colin of Sandwich m. Marcella Ruth **Webster** of Sandwich 6/4/1994
Lawrence E. of Concord, MA m. Anne A. **Weed** of Newton, MA 6/24/1922 in Sandwich; H – 28, manufacturing, b.

Concord, MA, s/o Henry P. Richardson (Pittsburgh, PA) and Maria R. Smith (Concord, MA); W – 23, at home, b. Newton, MA, d/o Alonzo Weed (Bangor, ME) and Charlotte Atwater (New Haven, CT)

Verne L. of Sandwich m. Elaine M. **Watts** of Sandwich 9/23/1999

RIPLEY,

William G. m. Edith M. **Bartlett** 12/5/1907 in Sandwich; H – 24, shipper, b. Malden, MA, s/o Henry N. Ripley (Boston, MA) and Sarah L. Jones (MA); W – 21, housewife, b. Lawrence, MA, d/o William Bartlett (Quebec) and Emma Downing (Rummery)

ROBINSON,

Alvin D. of Sandwich m. Laura E. **Lovejoy** of Moultonboro 4/22/1894 in Sandwich; H – 40, farmer, b. Concord, s/o George A. Robinson (Concord) and Harriet A. Robinson (Gilmanton); W – 30, housewife, b. Bridgewater, d/o John Q. Gault (Canterbury) and Emily S. Gault (Bridgewater)

Charles of Sandwich m. Florence E. **Mason** of Moultonboro 6/4/1902 in Sandwich; H – 28, farmer, b. Sandwich, s/o George A. Robinson and Abbie Farrington (Canton, MA); W – 21, b. Moultonboro, d/o William H. Mason (Moultonboro) and Jane A. Morse (Malden, MA)

Charles of Sandwich m. Ruth J. **Hoyt** of Moultonboro --/8/1911; H – 36, farmer, b. Sandwich, s/o George A. Robinson (Sandwich) and Abbie Farrington (Canton, MA); W – 25, b. Moultonboro, d/o Moses E. Hoyt (Sandwich) and Lydia A. Smith (Newmarket)

Gerald W. of New Haven, CT m. Anna S. **Myer** of Cambridge, MA 8/27/1983

RODGERS,

David Paul of Ctr. Sandwich m. Wendy Rae **Buker** of Wolfeboro Falls 8/16/1986

Morton L. of Thornton m. Eileen **Taylor** of Sandwich 9/15/1956; H – 26, carpenter, b. NH, s/o David C. Rodgers (NH) and Nina A. Edgell (NH); W – 18, at home, b. NH, d/o Paul A. Taylor (NH) and Marion E. Gray (NH)

ROSE,
Harry M. of Sandwich m. Helen R. **Buxton** of Lakeville, MA 7/30/1979 in Sandwich; H – s/o Charles H. Rose and Anna Stevens; W – d/o Arthur J. Rotch and Helen G. Lindlington

ROUNER,
Jonathan K. of Brooklyn, NY m. Katrin C. **Noorlind** of Brooklyn, NY 9/22/1984

ROWAN,
Daniel S. of Sandwich m. Cynthia J. **Matckie** of Sandwich 8/8/1987
David K. of Sandwich m. Sheila M. **Perry** of Meredith 7/11/1987

ROWELL,
Frank D. of Sandwich m. Christine **Worthen** of 2/12/2000

RUSSELL,
William W. of Sandwich m. Nellie E. **Craig** of Sandwich 5/16/1916 in Sandwich; H – 34, postmaster, b. Sandwich, s/o Robert Russell (Quebec) and Sarah A. Slye (Montreal, PQ); W – 18, tel. operator, b. Somerville, MA, d/o Charles Craig (St. John, NB) and Ethel A. Chandler (Lynn, MA)

RYAN,
Daniel W. of Sandwich m. Donna R. **Burrows** of Sandwich 6/14/1969; H – s/o John Ryan and Mildred Costa; W – d/o Donald Burrows and Ramona Willoughby

RYDER,
Harris B. of W. Medford, MA m. Alice J. **Watson** of Sandwich 11/1/1924 in Sandwich; H – 37, RR clerk, b. Wellesley Hills, MA, s/o Natt J. L. Ryder (Dunbarton) and Jennie Bailey (Manchester); W – 34, hotels, b. Sandwich, d/o Daniel S. Watson (Tamworth) and Fannie Pitman (Alexandria)

ST. JOHN,
George Oliver of Francestown m. Emily Elaine **Shephard** of Sandwich 6/17/1951; H – 21, laborer, b. NH, s/o A. Oliver St. John (NH) and Carrie G. Johnson (NH); W – 19, millworker, b. NH, s/o Roger F. Shephard (NH) and Ruth Mason Hoyt (NH)

SANCHEZ,
Ricardo B. of Caracas, Venezuela m. Satah E. **Boudreau** of Sandwich 10/6/1977 in Tamworth; H – s/o Bartolome Sanchez and Diane Cassidy; W – d/o Alfred E. Boudreau and Barbara Washburn

SANDERS,
LeRoy of Seattle, WA m. Ruth Hamilton **Hoyt** of Pasadena, CA 12/7/1920 in Sandwich; H – 35, newspaper, b. Salt Lake City, UT, s/o Edmund Sanders (UT) and Jane Gribble (UT); W – 24, at home, b. Pasadena, CA, d/o Albert S. Hoyt (NY) and Minerva Hamilton (NY)

SARGENT,
George H. of Concord m. Victoria M. **Gilman** of Ctr. Sandwich 1/3/1928 in Concord; H – 81, retired, b. Hanover, s/o John Sargent (Gorham) and Ruth Burbank (Plainfield); W – 58, housework, b. Sandwich, d/o Asahel Wallace (Sandwich) and Caroline Wallace (Sandwich)

Steven K. of Sudbury, MA m. Patricia W. **Singer** of Summit, NJ 7/15/1978 in Sandwich; H – s/o David B. Sargent and Anne Hull; W – d/o William C. Singer and Theolinde M. Grosch

SAUNDERS,

Warren T., Jr. of Center Harbor m. Judith L. **Berry** of Sandwich 9/10/1962; H – 21, laborer, s/o Warren T. Saunders and Josephine P. Kakoszki; W – 19, student, d/o Robert M. Berry and Marion Nichols

Warren T., Jr. of Sandwich m. Nancy L. **Ballesteros** of Sandwich 10/12/1968; H – s/o Warren T. Saunders, Sr. and Josephine Kakoszki; W – d/o Louis A. Turner, Jr. and Flora L. Duval

SAWIN,

Edward A., Jr. of Philadelphia, PA m. Sandra D. **Uhle** of Whitemarsh, PA 9/3/1960; H – 23, student, s/o Edward A. Sawin, Sr. and Ethel D. Laughlin; W – 22, student, d/o Charles A. W. Uhle and Janet G. Patterson

SAYERS,

John Kevin of Sandwich m. Marilynn **Cakars** of Sandwich 6/24/1995

SCHLEMMER,

John P. of Sandwich m. Shannon L. **Cameron** of Sandwich 9/30/2006 in Wolfeboro

SCHMIDT,

Robert L. of Sandwich m. Rachel D. **Richard** of Plymouth 8/9/1980

SCHNEIDER,
James Gordon of Kankakee, IL m. Suzina Cecil **Myers** of Sandwich 8/22/1993

SCHOENBURG,
Peter, Jr. of Santa Fe, NM m. Jane W. **McGrath** of Santa Fe, NM 8/8/1981

SCHUMACHER,
Scott A. of Scituate, MA m. Angele K. **Aznavorian** of Duxbury, MA 6/27/1981

SCRIGGINS,
Arthur C. of Sandwich m. Flora B. **Blackey** of Sandwich 1/2/1890 in Sandwich; H – 18, laborer, b. Sandwich, s/o Charles B. Scriggins (Farmington) and Julia A. Scriggins (Sandwich); W – 23, dressmaker, b. Moultonboro, d/o Jeremiah Blackey (Moultonboro) and Abbie Blackey (Albany)
William H. m. Emily J. **Mason** 6/9/1909 in Moultonboro; H – 70, farmer, b. Barnstead, s/o B. Scriggins (Barnstead) and Hannah Davis (Barnstead); W – 65, housekeeper, b. Sandwich, d/o Jesse Mudgett (Sandwich) and Jane Burnham (Sandwich)
William H. of Sandwich m. Addie M. **Foster** of Sandwich 8/13/1916 in Sandwich; H – 77, retired, b. Barnstead, s/o Bradbury Scriggins (Barnstead) and Hannah Davis (Barnstead): W – 52, housekeeper, b. Gilmanton, d/o Ira E. Page (Gilmanton) and Emily Leighton (Gilmanton)

SEARS,
Winthrop M. of Sandwich m. Christie W. **Fowle** of Reading, MA 3/8/1957; H – 63, retired, b. MA, s/o Even W. Sears (MA) and Caroline Roos (MA); W – 54, lecturer, b. ME, d/o Hubbard E. Webber (ME) and Grace Hart (MA)

SEELEY,
Allen K. of Sandwich m. Holli H. **Long** of Sandwich 1/14/1995

SEVERANCE,
Bishop C. m. Glayds E. **Wallace** of Sandwich 1/15/1929; H – 32, laborer, b. Biddeford, ME, s/o Joseph B. Severance (Wolfeboro) and B. F. Cudeford (Kennebunk, ME); W – 20, housework, b. Sandwich, d/o Hattie M. Plummer (Sandwich)

SEVERY,
Merle Eugene of Tamworth m. Teresa Louise **Bookholz** of Tamworth 9/19/1942; H – 20, student, b. Sandwich, s/o William C. Smith (MA) and Enid May Severy (Boston, MA); W – 20, student, b. Tamworth, d/o Edward V. Bookholz (Tamworth) and Ellen P. Whiting (Tamworth)

SEYMOUR,
Ralph B. of Laconia m. Nancy B. **Evans** of Ctr. Sandwich 8/22/1970 in Moultonboro; H – s/o Bertram Seymour and Irene Sherwood; W – d/o Richard Breed and Camille LaRochelle

SHEFFER,
Leonard S. of Palm Harbor, FL m. Polly **Benton** of Palm Harbor, FL 8/28/1977 in Sandwich; H – s/o Leonard E. Sheffer and Susan Benton; W – d/o Richard L. Benton and Nancy Browne

SHELTON,
William G. of Antioch, IL m. Susan **Hoag** of Sandwich 6/15/1969; H – s/o Earl L. Shelton and Mary L. Leiper; W – d/o Roland B. Hoag and Barbara Simonds

SHERWOOD,
Michael A. of Botsford, CT m. Jennifer L. **Bennett** of Alexandria, VA 3/26/1983

SHORE,
Michael Adams of Ctr. Sandwich m. Kelly Susan **Butterfield** of Bow 10/17/1992

SICKLES,
Allen J. of Bangor, ME m. Rose B. **Hall** of Sandwich 8/6/1888 in Laconia; H – 30, lumbering, b. Bangor, ME, s/o William Sickles (Bangor, ME) and Elmira Sickles (Bangor, ME); W – 21, b. Sandwich, d/o John B. Hall (Sandwich) and Almira Hall (Ellsworth)

SIEGEL,
Andrew F. of Brookline, MA m. Barbara A. **Rumsza** of Ambler, PA 8/29/1975 in Sandwich; H – s/o Armand Siegel and Mildred Marks; W – d/o Anthony A. Rymsza and Ann Butchkoska
Jeffrey J. of Webster m. Susan E. **Peaslee** of Sandwich 5/25/1980

SILCOX,
Frederick L. of Meredith m. Jeanne **Campbell** of Sandwich 5/20/1946; H – 26, US Army, b. Lowell, MA, s/o Frederick E. Silcox (Lowell, MA) and Emma Lewis (Hillsboro); W – 20, at home, b. Sandwich, d/o John W. Campbell (Sandwich) and Grace Elliott (Sandwich)
Frederick L. of Sandwich m. Jeanne C. **Silcox** of Sandwich 9/14/1960; H – 40, Army, s/o Frederick E. Silcox and Emma A. Lewis; W – 34, housewife, d/o John W. Campbell and Grace Elliott

SILSBY,
Henry M. of Lunenburg, VT m. Ethel A. **Penniman** of Sandwich 11/25/1899 in Whiteface; H – 29, teamster, b. Lunenburg, VT, s/o Mitchell Silsby (Lunenburg, VT) and Annie Silsby (Lunenburg, VT); W – 16, b. Sandwich, d/o W. S. Penniman (Sandwich) and Addie Penniman (Colebrook)

SIMON,
Gregory Robert of Sandwich m. Heidi Kathryn **Locke** of Clifton Park, NY 8/14/1993

SKINNER,
Cyrus E. of Sandwich m. Addie A. **Angier** of Sandwich 6/15/1903 in Sandwich; H – 52, barber, b. Sandwich, s/o Daniel M. Skinner (Sandwich) and Sarah Stratton (Conway); W – 46, housekeeper, b. Braintree, MA, d/o John French (Braintree, MA) and Mahala Brown (Waterford, ME)

SLOSSON,
Charles A. of Riverside, CT m. Agatha J. **Barton** of Colorado Springs, CO 8/21/1915 in Sandwich; H – 40, insurance, b. Brooklyn, NY, s/o Henry L. Slosson (Geneva, NY) and Agnes Stacey (Geneva, NY); W – 38, broker, b. Bay City, MI, d/o Charles E. Jennison (Baton Rouge, LA) and Florence Birney (Peterborough, NY)

SMITH,
Aaron Clark of Meredith m. Geraldine Louise **Bryant** of Sandwich 8/21/1943; H – 19, farmer, b. Meredith, s/o Nathan C. Smith (Sanbornton) and Blanche E. Clark (Alexandria); W – 18, at home, b. Sandwich, d/o John W. Bryant (Sandwich) and Madeline M. Robinson (Cambridge, MA)

David M. of Chevy Chase, MD m. Katherine S. **McIlvain** of Chevy Chase, MD 8/9/2003 in N. Sandwich

Charles O. of Sandwich m. Mary E. **Pierce** of Sandwich 6/25/1891 in Sandwich; H – 33, tinman, b. Sandwich, s/o James M. Smith and Lydia P. Smith; W – 26, b. Sandwich, d/o Leander Pierce and Caroline Pierce

Demerrit E. of Sandwich m. Eva G. **Burrows** of Sandwich 5/7/1896 in Sandwich; H – 27, farmer, b. Sandwich, s/o Lewis Q. Smith (Sandwich) and Mary E. Smith (Moultonboro); W – 23, b. Sandwich, d/o N. H. Burrows and Sarah D. Burrows (Sandwich)

Edgar W. of Center Harbor m. Hattie E. **Magoon** of Sandwich 9/24/1890 in Center Harbor; H – 35, painter, b. Sandwich, s/o Jacob F. Smith (Moultonboro) and Mary S. Smith (Canada); W – 35, b. Sandwich, d/o Asa Magoon (Sandwich) and Mary E. Magoon (Sandwich)

Ellsworth Wayne of Sandwich m. Jean Martha **Matos** of Devonshire, Bermuda 7/5/1952; H – 17, painter, b. NH, s/o Ellsworth M. Smith (NH) and Olga L. Weeks (NH); W – 19, at home, b. Bermuda, d/o Joseph Matos (Bermuda) and Lillian M. DeSilva (Bermuda)

Frank M. of Sandwich m. Julia M. **Sherman** of Sandwich 6/12/1912 in Sandwich; H – 63, merchant, b. Sandwich, s/o James M. Smith (Sandwich) and Lydia P. Skinner (Sandwich); W – 38, b. Buffalo, NY, d/o D. H. Sherman and Cordelia Robbins (NY)

G. Roland of Sandwich m. Alice Pearl **Davie** of Sandwich 3/3/1915 in Sandwich; H – 19, farmer, b. Sandwich, s/o Samuel B. Smith (Sandwich) and Nellie F. Taylor (Sandwich); W – 19, teacher, b. Sandwich, d/o Henry Davie and Jennie Vittum (Sandwich)

Glenn of Sandwich m. Delima **Morin** of Laconia 1/30/1936 in Laconia; H – 30, merchant, b. Sandwich, s/o Charles O. Smith (Sandwich) and Mary E. Pierce (Sandwich); W – 30, at home, b. Laconia, d/o Alfred O. Morin (Canada) and Leda Labranche (Laconia)

Harrison B. of Sandwich m. Jeanne **McKenzie** of Concord 8/24/1935; H – 25, caretaker, b. CT, Granville Smith (Sandwich) – Guardian; W – 24, teacher, b. Buckie, Scotland, d/o John McKenzie (Scotland) and Margaret Corvie (Scotland)

Harry H. of Sandwich m. Bessie **Blanchard** of Sandwich 10/13/1902 in Sandwich; H – 26, farmer, b. Sandwich, s/o Charles A. Smith (Sandwich) and Margaret Ham (Bethlehem); W – 20, teacher, b. Sandwich, d/o Arven Blanchard (Hopkinton) and Helen Creighton (Sandwich)

Harry H. m. Evelyn H. **Nelson** 12/26/1936 in Moultonboro; H – 60, farmer, b. Sandwich, s/o Charles A. Smith (Sandwich) and Margaret Hale (Bethlehem); W – 26, housework, b. Sandwich, d/o Thomas Nelson (Norway) and Henrietta Brown (Quincy, MA)

J. Alphonso of Sandwich m. H. Anna **Smith** of Sandwich 5/28/1890 in Sandwich; H – 34, merchant, b. Sandwich, s/o James M. Smith (Sandwich) and Lydia P. Smith (Sandwich); W – b. Sandwich, d/o Lewis Q. Smith (Moultonboro) and Mary E. Smith (Sandwich)

John A. of Moultonboro m. Florence **Dearborn** of Sandwich 2/2/1905 in Sandwich; H – 22, b. Moultonboro, s/o Edwin I. Smith (Moultonboro) and Ella M. Cook (Moultonboro); W – 23, b. Sandwich, d/o John Dearborn (Effingham) and Dora Vittum (Sandwich)

Julius H. of Sandwich m. Isabel E. **Smith** of Holderness 5/17/1919 in Holderness; H – 21, chauffeur, b. Sandwich, s/o Willis H. Smith (Sandwich) and Clra M. Mudgett (Franklin); W – 26, teacher, b. Holderness, d/o Henry C. Smith (Holderness) and Flora L. Pulsifer (Campton)

Keneth A. of Sandwich m. Pearl E. **Smith** of Sandwich 5/13/1939; H – 18, student, b. Sandwich, s/o Harry H. Smith (Sandwich) and Bessie Blanchard (Sandwich); W –

17, student, b. Sandwich, d/o George R. Smith (Sandwich) and Alice P. Davey (Sandwich)

Leon A. of Sandwich m. Maude L. **Tilton** of Sandwich 6/28/1913 in Sandwich; H – 39, farmer, b. Sandwich, s/o J. Hartwell Smith (Sandwich) and M. Alice Nute (Ossipee); W – 28, teacher, b. Sandwich, d/o Alvin Tilton (Sandwich) and Mary A. Clement (Sandwich)

Leonard John of Sandwich m. Helena Agnes **Dwyer** of Concord 10/10/1938 in Boscawen; H – 27, teacher, b. Concord, s/o John N. Smith (Newport) and Lulu M. Shedd (Grantham); W – 23, teacher, b. New York, NY, d/o Maurice J. Dwyer (Concord) and Karen Olsen (Norway)

Lewis E. of Sandwich m. Carrie E. **Willey** of Sandwich 3/21/1887 in Sandwich; H – 24, farmer, b. Sandwich, s/o Lewis Q. Smith (Sandwich) and Elizabeth Smith (Moultonboro); W – 21, b. Sandwich, d/o Daniel H. Willey and Susan Willey (Grey, ME)

O. Granville of Sandwich m. Dorothea **Browning** of Lynchburg, VA 11/5/1903 in Sandwich; H – 38, farmer, b. Holderness, s/o Bartlett Smith (Holderness) and Rosina George (Holderness); W – 23, b. Lynchburg, VA, d/o Andrew Richardson (Lynchburg, VA) and Clara S. Petterson (Sweden)

Richard E. of Meredith m. Linda L. **Covey** of Sandwich 8/8/1969; H – s/o Lee E. Smith and Viola Mudgett; W – d/o Uradel Covey and Charlotte Brown

Samuel L. of Sandwich m. Bertha M. **Jaques** of E. Tilton 9/18/1901 in Sandwich; H – 31, farmer, b. Holderness, s/o Bartlett Smith (Holderness) and Rosina George (Sandwich); W – 30, b. E. Tilton, d/o C. Henry Jaques (Tilton) and Rebecca Philbrook (E. Tilton)

Samuel M. of Sandwich m. Janet E. **Burkitt** of Sandwich 7/21/1957; H – 39, laborer, b. NH, s/o George R. Smith (NH) and Alice P. Davey (NH); W – 30, housewife, b. MD, d/o Arthur E. Cummings (MD) and Elizabeth M. Monks (MD)

Samuel Maurice of Sandwich m. Mae Arlene **Locke** of Laconia 9/3/1944; H – 26, truck driver, b. Sandwich, s/o George R. Smith (Sandwich) and Alice P. Davey (Sandwich); W – 20, housework, b. Laconia, d/o Jack Locke (Plymouth) and Ethel Prior (Rutland, VT)

Walter of Newfield, ME m. Gladys **Fisher** of Parsonsfield, ME 5/16/1926 in Sandwich; H – 28, personal business, b. Newfield, ME, s/o Henry Smith (Newfield, ME) and Nancy Story (Wakefield); W – 33, at home, b. Rockland, MA, d/o Eldon Smith (Hanson, MA) and Mary Mitchell (Scotland)

Willis H. of Sandwich m. Clara M. **Mudgett** of Holderness 12/28/1889 in Sandwich; H – 18, farmer, s/o Levi H. Smith and L. M. Smith; W – 16, d/o Harrison Mudgett and L. H. Mudgett

SORELL,

Ames O., Jr. of Sandwich m. Marlene W. **Porter** of Moultonboro 11/24/1968; H – s/o Ames O. Sorell, Sr. and Emma L. Copp; W – d/o Lawrence Porter and Marlene Hodgdon

SPEERS,

William S. of Middletown, DE m. Donna E. **Kinney** of Bedford, MA 8/17/1985

STAFSTROM,

Joel P. of Boulder, CO m. Judith A. **Charles** of Boulder, CO 8/21/1982

STANLEY,

Halsey D. of Beverly, MA m. Esther L. **Kent** of Sandwich 11/20/1913 in Moultonboro; H – 55, real estate & insurance, b. Beverly, MA, s/o William Stanley (Beverly, MA) and Susan H. Dodge (Hamilton, MA); W – 48, b.

Gloucester, MA, d/o Moses L. Griffin (Gloucester, MA) and Mary M. Crouse (NS)

STAPLES,
Larry E. of Sandwich m. Catherine A. **Evans** of Sandwich 3/29/1974 in Sandwich; H – s/o Laurence E. Staples and Florence Townsend; W – d/o Almon G. Evans, Jr. and Shirley C. Webster

STEELE,
George of N. Sandwich m. Charlene **Hawes** of Moultonborough 3/4/2005 in Moultonborough

STEIN,
Stanley N. of Rochester, NY m. Joy V. **Wolf** of Sandwich 8/11/2001

STEWART,
Bret William of Moultonboro m. Courtney M. **Porter** of Moultonboro 9/12/1998

STOCKMAN,
Philip A. of Tuftonboro m. Jean C. **Peaslee** of Sandwich 9/23/1949; H – 23, farmer, b. MA, s/o Frank L. Stockman (NH) and Doris R. Lucas (MA); W – 16, at home, b. NH, d/o Ralph Q. Peaslee (NH) and Mary E. Moody (NH)

STOKES,
Joseph, III of Cambridge, MA m. Ruth Whitson **Stokes** of Cambridge, MA 9/3/1988
Peter W. of Belmont m. Susan C. L. **Murray** of Boston, MA 10/11/1980
Reginald Edwin of Sandwich m. Janice Althea **Peaslee** of Sandwich 11/22/1950; H – 26, pitman, b. NH, s/o Arthur P. Stokes (ME) and Harriet Hutchins (NH); W – 20, at home,

b. NH, d/o Roscoe D. Peaslee (NH) and Dorothy Robinson (MA)

STREETER,
Bradley E. of Sandwich m. Karen A. **Robinson** of Sandwich 8/17/2002 in Tamworth

STUART,
Reginald B. of Gloucester, MA m. Edith A. **Dann** of Gloucester, MA 6/6/1936 in Sandwich; H – 26, letter carrier, b. Gloucester, MA, s/o Lewis R. Stuart (Lanesville, MA) and Gertrude Saunders (Lanesville, MA); W – 27, school teacher, b. Gloucester, MA, d/o Dexter D. Dann (Gloucester, MA) and Anna M. Wonson (Gloucester, MA)

STULL,
David A. of Hampstead m. Peggy L. **Houghton** of Sandwich 12/19/1971 in Sandwich; H – s/o Joseph Stull and Maxine Russell; W – d/o Clifford Haughton and Theodora Hamson

STURGEON,
Fred J. of Sandwich m. Donna J. **Richardson** of Moultonboro 12/14/1963; H – 19, laborer, s/o Wilfred J. Sturgeon and Irma V. Stokes; W – 15, student, d/o Horace L. Richardson and Ernestine E. Berry
Ronald W. of Sandwich m. Beverly A. **Clifford** of Moultonboro 6/2/1956; H – 18, carpenter's helper, b. NH, s/o Wilfred J. Sturgeon (NH) and Erma V. Stokes (ME); W – 20, at home, b. NH, d/o Roland E. Clifford (NH) and Mary E. Berry (NH)
Wilfred of Holderness m. Irma **Stokes** of Sandwich 7/8/1933; H – 20, farmer, b. Van Buren, ME, s/o Edward Sturgeon (Concord, VT) and Ida White (Portland, ME); W – 18, housework, b. Harrison, ME, d/o Arthur Parker Stokes (Harrison, ME) and Harriet Mabel Stokes (Tamworth)

SULLIVAN,

James J. of Sandwich m. Ada E. **Henderson** of Sandwich 12/4/1931; H – 57, farmer, b. Lexington, MA, s/o James Sullivan (Ireland) and Hannah Keleher (Lexington, MA); W – 73, at home, b. Madison, d/o John K. Forest and Eliza Richardson (Bridgton, ME)

SUMNER,

Roland E. of Sandwich m. Bessie E. **Mudgett** of Sandwich 11/9/1937 in Moultonboro; H – 21, woodsman, b. Burlington, VT, s/o George Sumner and Rachel Guyotte (VT); W – 16, at home, b. Sandwich, d/o Jesse Mudgett (Sandwich) and Jennie Stirgis (Albany)

SWAN,

Bernard W. of Sandwich m. Stephanie **Blackstock** of Sandwich 6/19/1982

Dean Edmund of Sandwich m. Phyllis Marion **Bryant** of Sandwich 11/11/1944; H – 18, laborer, b. Percy, s/o Bernard Swan (Bethel, ME) and Helen P. Emery (Percy); W – 17, at home, b. Sandwich, d/o John W. Bryant (Sandwich) and Madeline Robinson (Cambridge, MA)

SWEET,

Gary L. of Harrisville, RI m. Carol J. **Nelson** of Sandwich 9/30/1967; H – 22, carpenter, s/o Lester Sweet and Theora Hathaway; W – 18, bookkeeper, d/o Kenneth Nelson and Frances Spaulding

SZYMUJKO,

Jeffery A. of Bartlett m. Sarah B. **Johnston** of Sandwich 10/24/1981

Jeffery A. of Sandwich m. Meghan E. **Risteen** of Concord 9/16/2007 in Sandwich

TALBOT,

Cecil A. of Sandwich m. Lena May **Cook** of Sandwich 11/20/1928 in Center Harbor; H – 21, laborer, b. Boxhone, IA, s/o Charles A. Talbot (KS) and Ella Talbot (Des Moines, IA); W – 27, housework, b. Sandwich, d/o Georeg O. Cook (Rock Creek, IL) and Mary R. Cook (Conway)

Lawrence William of Sandwich m. Shirley Jean **Daigneau** of Sandwich 10/24/1953; H – 23, mechanic, b. IA, s/o Cecil Arnold Talbot (IA) and Lena May Cook (NH); W – 18, at home, b. NH, d/o Ernest J. Daigneau (NH) and Louise Ann Roucher (MA)

TAPPAN,

Frank H. of Sandwich m. Hattie M. **Knowles** of Sandwich 10/1/1890 in Sandwich; H – 28, farmer, b. Sandwich, s/o John Tappan (Moultonboro) and Sarah Tappan (Sandwich); W – 28, b. Moultonboro, d/o John B. Knowles (Moultonboro) and Betsey Knowles (Newburyport)

Fred of Sandwich m. Abbie **Wakefield** of Moultonboro 12/15/1894 in Sandwich; H – 52, laborer, b. Sandwich, s/o Abram E. Tappan (Sandwich) and Abbie Tappan (Sandwich); W – 19, housewife, b. Canada, d/o Henry Wakefield (Canada) and Ellen Wakefield (Moultonboro)

Fred m. Ina G. **Felch** 11/10/1927; H – 57, farmer, b. Sandwich, s/o Abram E. Tappan (Sandwich) and Abbie F. Graves (Peabody, MA); W – 46, housewife, b. Sandwich, d/o Jacob Vittum (Sandwich) and Mary Vittum (Sandwich)

George H. of Sandwich m. Inez A. **Page** of Sandwich 2/1/1892 in Sandwich; H – 33, farmer, b. Sandwich, s/o Daniel Tappan (Sandwich) and Rhoda Tappan (Sandwich); W – 23, b. Belgrade, ME, d/o Joel R. Page (ME) and Abbie Page (ME)

Lewis R. of Sandwich m. Belle **Sceggell** of Sandwich 7/20/1916 in Sandwich; H – 29, laborer, b. Sandwich, s/o Alfred

Tappan (Sandwich) and Eliza Smith (Sandwich); W – 27, b. Tamworth, d/o James Gilman and Hattie Davis

Walter S. of Sandwich m. Beryl V. **Grant** of Sandwich 2/11/1895 in Sandwich; H – 32, machinist, b. Sandwich, s/o Daniel Tappan (Sandwich) and Rhoda Tappan; W – 20, housewife, b. Sandwich, d/o George Grant (Sandwich) and Clara Grant

TASKER,

Elmer H. of Sandwich m. Evelyn M. **Burleigh** of Sandwich 10/15/1896 in Sandwich; H – 34, druggist, b. Strafford, s/o Levi P. Tasker (Northwood) and Hannah Tasker (Northwood); W – 24, teacher, b. Sandwich, d/o S. H. Burleigh (Sandwich)

Elmer H. of Sandwich m. Evelyn M. **Burleigh** of Sandwich 4/23/1897 in Epsom; H – 35, druggist, b. Strafford, s/o Levi B. Tasker (Northwood) and Hannah P. Tasker (Northwood); W – 25, teacher, b. Sandwich, d/o Samuel H. Burleigh (Sandwich) and Betsy S. Burleigh (Ossipee)

TATUM,

David S. of Yonkers, NY m. Baldura S. **Lindemann** of Sandwich 6/30/1948; H – 69, cost accountant, b. Woodbury, NJ, s/o William Tatum (Woodbury, NJ) and Hannah Leeds (Cinnaminson, NJ); W – 45, pianist, b. Shirley Ctr., MA, d/o Karl Schmidt (Frankfort, Germany) and Edith Kimball (Boston, MA)

TAYLOR,

Charles Edison of Sandwich m. Berenice E. **Dodge** of Mountainview 3/24/1930; H – 18, plumber, b. Lynn, MA, s/o Walter L. Taylor (Sandwich) and Mary A. Wallace (Tamworth); W – 18, at home, d/o Benjamin H. Dodge and Bessie ----- (Livingston)

George H. of Sandwich m. Margaret B. **Boardman** of Sandwich 4/22/1951; H – 23, laborer, b. Orono, ME, s/o Lawrence J. Taylor (ME) and Carlotte E. Whitney (ME); W – 23, housewife, b. NH, d/o Frank N. Burrows (NH) and Hilda MacDonald (NH)

Gurney of Ctr. Sandwich m. Minerva A. **Frazier** of New York, NY 5/17/1986

Harold Edwin of Sandwich m. Rita Marie **Provencal** of Laconia 6/21/1952; H – 28, mechanic, b. NH, s/o Walter L. Taylor (NH) and Agnes Wallace (NH); W – 23, bookkeeper, b. NH, d/o Alfred Provencal (NH) and Blanche M. Martin (Canada)

Paul A. of Sandwich m. Marion E. **Gray** of Sandwich 1/26/1935; H – 25, farmer, b. Sandwich, s/o William H. Taylor (Sandwich) and Christine E. Skinner (Sandwich); W – 21, at home, b. Sanbornton, d/o Irving Gray (Plymouth, ME) and Mary E. Corliss (Sandwich)

Ralph W. of S. Boston, MA m. Hortense **Weed** of Sandwich 8/15/1912 in Sandwich; H – 25, professor, b. S. Boston, MA, s/o Albert J. Taylor (Hermon, ME) and Emma L. Nason (Boston, MA); W – 24,teacher, b. Sandwich, d/o Larkin D. Weed (Sandwich) and Elsie A. Peaslee (Sandwich)

Sumner E. of Parsonsfield, ME m. Alice A. **Mudgett** of Sandwich 1/9/1937 in Center Harbor; H – 25, laborer, b. Parsonsfield, ME, s/o Thomas Taylor (Parsonsfield, ME) and Bessie Wormwood (Somersworth); W – 21, housework, b. Sandwich, d/o Jesse Mudgett (Sandwich) and Jennie Sturgis (Albany)

Walter L. of Sandwich m. Agnes **Wallace** of Sandwich 10/4/1905 in Tamworth; H – 24, b. Sandwich, s/o Charles G. Taylor (Sandwich) and Eliza A. Henderson (Sandwich); W – 19, b. Sandwich, d/o Henry Wallace (ME) and Fannie Wallace (Sandwich)

William H. m. Christine E. **Skinner** 2/18/1909 in Plymouth; H – 23, farmer, b. Sandwich, s/o Augustus F. Taylor (Sandwich) and Dora F. Thompson (Sandwich); W – 17, b. Sandwich, d/o Lucius C. Skinner (Sandwich) and Hattie E. Horne (Sandwich)

William H. of Sandwich m. Jean Marie **Rogers** of Tamworth 4/30/1964; H – 18, mechanic, s/o Paul A. Taylor and Marion Gray; W – 18, mill work, d/o Irving W. Rogers and Addie M. Grace

William H. of Sandwich m. Jane E. **Plummer** of Sandwich 10/8/1977 in Bow; H – s/o Paul A. Taylor and Marion Gray; W – d/o Charles Plummer and Doris Palmer

TEFFT,

Henry Adelbert of Sandwich m. Melina Mary **Sirard** of Franklin 5/24/1958; H – 51, painter, s/o William Tefft (RI) and Alice Tuttle (NH); W – 54, at home, d/o Eugene LaPlante (Canada) and Melina Thession (Canada)

TENNEY,

George W. of Sandwich m. Meline M. **Danforth** of Sandwich 12/25/1894 in Sandwich; H – 29, farmer, b. Boston, s/o Warren E. Tenney (Boston) and Jennet Tenney (Boston); W – 15, housewife, b. Sandwich, d/o George W. Danforth (Sandwich) and Annie E. Danforth (Sandwich)

TEWKSBURY,

Royce A. of Portsmouth m. Margaret J. **Bundy** of Sandwich 11/8/1922 in Sandwich; H – 19, motion picture operator, b. Tamworth, s/o Isaac Tewksbury (Tamworth) and Eva M. Swain (Meredith); W – 16, at home, b. Sandwich, d/o Oscar E. Bundy (Lakeport) and Sadie E. Skinner (Sandwich)

W. Wesley of Sandwich m. Mabel C. **Stocker** of Tamworth 12/22/1923 in Sandwich; H – 44, farmer, b. Albany, s/o J.

H. Tewksbury (Sandwich) and Sarah Hurley (Salem, MA); W – 45, housework, b. Madison, d/o Edwin Henderson (Sandwich) and Ada E. Forrest (Madison)

Wesley of Sandwich m. Nettie **Barnes** of Tamworth 6/18/1901 in Sandwich; H – 22, farmer, b. Albany, s/o James H. Tewksbury (Sandwich) and Sarah Hurley (Salem, MA); W – 18, b. Tamworth, d/o Samuel Barnes (Hiram, ME) and Emma Bean (Stow, ME)

THOMAS,

Alan R. of Upper Darby, PA m. Uni A. **Sprengling** of Sandwich 10/3/1957; H – 33, musician, b. PA, s/o Richard E. Thomas (PA) and Anna M. McHenry (PA); W – 35, musician, b. NH, d/o Martin Sprengling (WI) and Mary C. Schmidt (Germany)

THOMPSON,

Arthur G. of Sandwich m. Ethel M. **Piper** of Campton 9/1/1954; H – 77, retired, b. NH, s/o George W. Thompson (NH) and Lydia Jane Smith (NH); W – 57, housekeeper, b. MA, d/o George W. Kellam (MA) and Ella J. Cowan (MA)

Karl E. of Sandwich m. Florence **Lambert** of Meredith 10/30/1926 in Sandwich; H – 31, merchant, b. Concord, MA, s/o Elmer Thompson (Sandwich) and Eva M. Smith (Sandwich); W – 27, linen mill, b. Ashland, d/o George Lambert (Ashland) and Lillian Small (Holderness)

Lester W. of Tuftonboro m. Edna M. **Nudd** of Sandwich 5/18/1940; H – 27, truck driver, b. Tuftonboro, s/o Simon T. Thompson (Tuftonboro) and Evelyn Bean (Tuftonboro); W – 20, housework, b. Sandwich, d/o Wallace Nudd (Sandwich) and Blanche LeClair (Northfield, VT)

THORNDIKE,

Townsend D. of N. Sandwich m. Melissa J. **Parker** of N. Sandwich 8/25/1984

Townsend Davis of N. Sandwich m. Katherine Anne **Hoyt** of N. Sandwich 10/2/1992

TIBBETTS,

E. Haven of Sandwich m. Maude E. **Whitehouse** of Moultonboro 4/17/1935; H – 24, laborer, b. Sandwich, s/o Henry T. Tibbetts (Benton) and Blanche I. Scriggins (Sandwich); W – 21, at home, b. Moultonboro, d/o Herbert Whitehouse (Moultonboro) and Berenice E. Campbell (Sandwich)

Henry T. of Sandwich m. Nettie **Thompson** of Holderness 7/1/1939; H – 54, carpenter, b. Benton, s/o William Tibbetts (England) and Catherine King (Canada); W – 49, housekeeper, b. NB, d/o William L. Helms (NB) and Augusta Logue (NB)

Paul W. of Sandwich m. Antonia A. **Mazzola** of Ashland 6/24/1939; H – 32, electrical contractor, b. Sandwich, s/o Henry T. Tibbetts (Benton) and Blanche Scriggins (Sandwich); W – 24, at home, b. Quincy, MA, d/o Joseph Mazzola (Isle of Capri, Italy) and Amalia DeMartinia (Naples, Italy)

Willard Ray of Sandwich m. Gwendolin Ashcroft **Handley** of Newton, MA 4/22/1921 in Boston; H – 26, farmer, b. Sandwich, s/o Mildred Tibbetts (Haverhill); W – 21, at home, b. Newton, MA, d/o Alfred H. Handley and Mabelle Ashcroft

TILTON,

Charles O. of Sandwich m. Bessie F. **Haley** of Tuftonboro 1/22/1906 in Tuftonboro; H – 33, farmer, b. Sandwich, s/o Alvin Tilton (Sandwich); W – 32, housewife, b. Tuftonboro, d/o Elijah Haley (Tuftonboro)

John F. of Sandwich m. Sadie M. **Dow** of Sandwich 9/19/1903 in Tamworth; H – 27, telephone inspector, b. Sandwich, s/o Charles E. Tilton (Sandwich) and Fannie E. Ward

(Freedom); W – 20, housekeeper, b. Sandwich, d/o Charles F. Dow and Etta A. Vittum

Orrin H. of Sandwich m. Marion **Messinger** of Boston, MA 12/6/1937 in Moultonboro; H – 30, truck driver, b. Moultonboro, s/o Charles O. Tilton (Sandwich) and Bessie F. Haley (Brockton, MA); W – 34, at home, b. Stoneham, MA, d/o Levi P. Martin (Melrose, MA) and Ella Jefts (Stoneham, MA)

TIMMINS,

John Andrew of Sandwich m. Christine W. **Burrage** of Sandwich 11/22/1952; H – 54, plumber & steam fitter, b. MA, s/o James Timmins (Ireland) and Bridget Corrigan (MA); W – 57, nurse, b. NY, d/o Henry Wendel (NY) and Anna Tetsch (NY)

TITILAH,

Andrew of Winchester, MA m. Thelma M. **Perrault** of Reading, MA 7/18/1959; H – 43, garage owner, s/o Andrew H. Titilah and Annie Rape; W – 43, nurse, d/o Harwood Pruitt and Naomi E. Jarrett

TIVEY,

Edward F. m. Lilla M. **Mudgett** 5/30/1927; H – 20, laborer, b. Everett, MA, s/o Albert B. Tivey (ME) and Maud Brownlie (England); W – 18, b. Sandwich, d/o Eugene E. Mudgett (Sandwich) and Eva Davis (Sandwich)

TONGE,

Peter W. of Greenwood, ME m. Wendelyn M. **Grayson** of Barnstead, England 5/24/2002 in Sandwich

TORSEY,

Guy B. of New Hampton m. Amy M. **Burrows** of Sandwich 11/13/1924 in Concord; H – 54, farmer, b. Meredith, s/o

Winthrop J. Torsey (Haverhill) and Lavina J. Cotton (Holderness); W – 48, housewife, b. Sandwich, d/o John E. Gilman (Sandwich) and Maria C. Beede (Sandwich)

Leon S. of New Hampton m. Dorothy D. **Dearborn** of Sandwich 8/30/1935; H – 40, farmer, b. New Hampton, s/o Guy B. Torsey (Meredith) and Nettie C. Stevens (New Hampton); W – 20, clerk, b. Lester Jct., VT, d/o Earl J. Dearborn (Bristol, VT) and Helen M. Guyer (St. Johnsbury, VT)

TOURIGNY,

Norman J. of Laconia m. Charlotte M. **Peaslee** of Sandwich 12/14/1956; H – 24, tool maker, b. MA, s/o Leo A. Tourigny (MA) and Marie C. Desplaines (MA); W – 26, housewife, b. NH, d/o Roland J. Avery (MA) and Doris Towle (NH)

TOWLE,

Frank L. of Sandwich m. Eliza S. **Graves** of Center Harbor 8/27/1893 in Plymouth; H – 25, clerk, b. Porter, ME, s/o James F. Towle (Porter, ME) and Emma A. Towle (Sandwich); W – 24, b. Sandwich, d/o Joseph S. Graves (Moultonboro) and Sarah Graves (Moultonboro)

TRACY,

Kim of Sandwich m. Paula Jayne **Doyle** of Sandwich 7/9/1994

TRASK,

W. P. of Sandwich m. Eliza B. **Bennett** of Sandwich 10/18/1895 in Tamworth; H – 25, laborer, b. Sandwich, s/o Charles W. Trask (Sandwich) and Arvilla Trask; W – 25, housewife, b. Sandwich, d/o Wyatt F. Bennett (Sandwich) and Mary Bennett

TREEN,
Ira M., Jr. of Norfolk, MA m. Elizabeth A. **Ufhiel** of Islington, MA 9/2/1961; H – 27, laborer, s/o Ira M. Treen, Sr. and Annie N. Matheson; W – 29, housewife, d/o Hans C. Warnick and Marion E. Sanborn

TROMBLEY,
Gerard Joseph of Sandwich m. Kathryn Elizabeth **McDonald** of Sandwich 4/1/1989

TROUT,
Charles H. of Hamilton, NY m. Katherine T. **Griffiths** of N. Sandwich 10/6/1984

TURNER,
Cornelius of Sandwich m. Bertha A. **Canney** of Sandwich 12/29/1892 in Sandwich; H – 29, farmer, b. Bangor, ME, s/o Cornelius Turner (Hamden, ME) and Sarah E. Turner (Veasy, ME); W – 16, b. Sandwich, d/o John P. Canney (Moultonboro) and Olive S. Canney (Sandwich)

TWADDLE,
Stephen M. of Hudson m. Julia E. **Harrington** of Hudson 7/14/1991

UEHLING,
James of New York, NY m. Sylvia L. **Robinson** of New York, NY 10/19/1969; H – s/o Gordon A. Uehling and Alice B. Tumb; W – d/o Joseph S. Robinson and Elizabeth Childs

VACHON,
Lynn of Moultonboro m. Barbara **Burrows** of Sandwich 4/8/1967; H – 34, plumber, s/o Peter J. Vachon and Katherine Bryson; W – 20, beautician, d/o Austin J. Burrows and Thelma Dumas

VAN SICKLE,
Randall David of Chatham, MA m. Margaret Christine **Johnson** of W. Roxbury, MA 10/29/1994

VARNEY,
Freeman of Sandwich m. Sadie F. **Knowles** of Sandwich 10/--/1893 in Tamworth; H – 49, farmer, b. Sandwich, s/o Edward Varney (Sandwich) and Mercy Varney (Sandwich); W – 25, b. Moultonboro, d/o John B. Knowles (Sandwich) and Betsey J. Knowles (Moultonboro)

VAZIFDAR,
Jehangir of Meredith m. Elizabeth S. **Richards** of Sandwich 8/20/1969; H – s/o Sohrah Vazifdar and Mary Wadla; W – d/o Leon Sargent and Mary King

VAZZANO,
Anthony J. of Sandwich m. Susan E. **Wiley** of E. Burke, VT 10/15/1981

VISSER,
William W. of Moultonboro m. Sheila R. **Demme** of Sandwich 5/28/1977 in Tamworth; H – s/o John F. Visser and ----- Vanderzes; W – d/o George Swanson and ----- Grant

VITTUM,
Arthur M. of Sandwich m. S. Pernie **Whitehouse** of Moultonboro 2/6/1916 in Sandwich; H – 18, laborer, b. Sandwich, s/o Aubrey M. Vittum (Sandwich) and Emmaline E. Chandler (Lynn, MA); W – 18, at home, b. Moultonboro, d/o C. C. Whitehouse and Cora Canney

Aubrey M. of Sandwich m. Emeline E. **Chandler** of Boston 9/13/1893 in Moultonboro; H – 19, farmer, b. Sandwich, s/o Lemuel F. Vittum (Sandwich) and C. Vittum

(Sandwich); W – 17, bookkeeper, b. Lynn, MA, d/o A. S. Chandler (Springfield, MA) and Nellie Chandler (Dover)

Carl S. of Sandwich m. Carolyn L. **Peaslee** of Sandwich 10/16/1948; H – 19, carpenter, b. Oklahoma City, OK, s/o George W. Vittum (McPherson, KS) and Ethel Strong (Boston, MA); W – 16, at home, b. Sandwich, d/o Earl C. Peaslee (Sandwich) and Louise Carter

Ernest of Sandwich m. Agnes M. **Ames** of Tamworth --/16/1911; H – 26, farmer, b. Sandwich, s/o Jacob F. Vittum (Sandwich) and Mary O. Vittum (Sandwich); W – 18, b. Tamworth, d/o Zemeri Ames (Tamworth) and Ella Palmer (Sandwich)

Herbert A. of Sandwich m. Alice H. **Clark** of Tamworth 8/8/1906 in Sandwich; H – 24, farmer, b. Sandwich, s/o Jacob F. Vittum (Sandwich); W – 25, b. PEI, d/o Joseph Clark (PEI)

Kenneth David of Sandwich m. Eleanor May **Aldrich** of Lakeport 10/3/1952; H – 29, poultryman, b. OK, s/o George W. Vittum (KS) and Ethel G. Strong (MA); W – 19, office clerk, b. NH, d/o Lewis N. Aldrich (NH) and Marguerite Elliott (NH)

Kenneth Franklin of S. Tamworth m. Frances Viola **Lord** of Wolfeboro 10/27/1934; H – 21, laborer, b. Sandwich, s/o Ernest Vittum (Sandwich) and Agnes Ames (Sandwich); W – 21, cook, b. Wolfeboro, d/o Charles Lord (Effingham Falls) and Gertrude Hoyt (Malden, MA)

Lewis M. of Sandwich m. Bernice R. **Adams** of Manchester 9/4/1937 in Fairlee, VT; H – 27, painter, b. Sandwich, s/o Marshall W. Vittum (Sandwich) and Emma Campbell (Sandwich); W – 22, b. Manchester, d/o Frank E. Adams (Eden, VT) and Ellen N. Keane (Ireland)

Marshall W. of Sandwich m. Emma M. **Campbell** of Sandwich 7/7/1906 in Moultonboro; H – 23, farmer, b. Sandwich, s/o Edmund Vittum (Sandwich); W – 21, b. Sandwich, d/o John N. Campbell (Bedford)

Orrin E. of Sandwich m. Irene C. **Hill** of Sandwich 2/3/1900 in Sandwich; H – 56, farmer, b. Sandwich, s/o Charles Vittum (Moultonboro) and Mahala Vittum (Sandwich); W – 56, housekeeper, b. Sandwich, d/o Ezekiel French (Sandwich) and Bethiah French (Moultonboro)

WADE,

Edwin D. of Sandwich m. Ida M. **Bryant** of Sandwich 8/2/1891 in Sandwich; H – 22, laborer, s/o Lyman M. Wade and Martha A. Wade; W – 25, b. Sandwich, d/o A. P. Martin

Frank of Sandwich m. Ida **Perkins** of Ossipee 5/3/1894 in Sandwich; H – 19, laborer, b. Moultonboro, s/o Lyman M. Wade (Moultonboro) and Martha Wade (Moultonboro); W – 18, housewife, b. Ossipee, d/o Hiram Perkins (Ossipee) and Lizzie Perkins (Ossipee)

Frank M. of Sandwich m. Sadie M. **Clough** of Tamworth 3/13/1902 in Tamworth; H – 24, engineer, b. Moultonboro, s/o Lyman D. Wade (Moultonboro) and Martha Blackey (Center Harbor); W – 18, cook, b. Tamworth, d/o Herbert S. Clough (Tamworth) and Hattie B. Mason (Tamworth)

WAKEFIELD,

Roger W. of Moultonboro m. Dorothy E. **Daigneau** of Sandwich 6/19/1954; H – 18, student, b. NH, s/o Wilfred C. Wakefield (NH) and Frances E. Buxton (MA); W – 17, student, b. NH, d/o Ernest J. Daigneau (NH) and Louise Ann Roucher (MA)

WALLACE,

Asahel A. of Sandwich m. Roxy M. **Burrows** of Sandwich 6/2/1936 in Moultonboro; H – 22, laborer, b. Sandwich, s/o Marcellus Wallace (Thornton) and Harriet Smith (New Hampton); W – 19, at home, b. Sandwich, d/o Newell J. Burrows (Sandwich) and Nellie F. Hodge (Sandwich)

Asahel Andrew of Sandwich m. Ethelyn May **Parris** of Sandwich 9/15/1941; H – 27, laborer, b. Sandwich, s/o Marcellus C. Wallace (Thornton) and Harriett L. Smith (New Hampton); W – 40, clerk, b. Warren, d/o John E. Davis (Haverhill) and Effie L. Annis (Warren)

Asahel Andrew of Sandwich m. Evelyn Mae **Wortman** of Conway 12/20/1950; H – 36, laborer, b. NH, s/o Marcellus Wallace (NH) and Harriet Smith (NH); W – 40, housewife, b. NH, d/o Frank L. Cook (NH) and Alice Tewksbury (NH)

Edward F. of Sandwich m. Charlotte A. **Fairbanks** of Westboro, MA 1/20/1887 in Moultonboro; H – 30, farmer, b. Sandwich, s/o Alfred Wallace and Ann P. Wallace; W – 32, b. Dunbarton, d/o James McCauley (Dunbarton) and Loise McCauley (Litchfield)

Harry of Sandwich m. Effie M. **Hatch** of Sandwich 10/8/1893 in Sandwich; H – 24, farmer, b. Sandwich, s/o Adaline Wallace (Sandwich); W – 15, b. Groveton, d/o George C. Hatch (Groveton) and Augusta Hatch (Montpelier, VT)

Harry m. Hattie M. **Plummer** 11/15/1910; H – 41, farmer, b. Sandwich, s/o Adeline M. Wallace (Sandwich); W – 26, housekeeper, b. Sandwich, d/o Wilfred Z. Plummer (Sandwich) and Lizzie E. Webster (Bedford, MA)

Harry J. m. Mabel T. **Prescott** 5/26/1909 in Sandwich; H – 18, barber, b. Sandwich, s/o W. H. H. Wallace (Sandwich) and Augusta A. Smith (Tamworth); W – 28, housekeeper, b. Sandwich, d/o John D. Prescott (Tamworth) and Mary A. Foley (New Orleans)

Marcellus of Sandwich m. Sadie **Moulton** of Sandwich 1/1/1887 in Sandwich; H – 21, farmer, b. Thornton, s/o Asahel Wallace and Caroline I. Wallace (Sandwich); W – 21, b. Meredith, d/o Hiram Moulton and Salome Moulton

Scott E. of Sandwich m. Mary Joan **Falvey** of Providence, RI 9/28/1932; H – 25, laborer, b, Sandwich. s/o Marcellus Wallace (Thornton) and Harriet Smith (New Hampton); W

– 25, at home, b. Providence, RI, d/o Jeremiah Falvey (Providence, RI) and Joanna Toomey (Providence, RI)

Theodore R. of Sandwich m. Edith F. **Page** of Meredith 12/12/1928 in Concord; H – 24, laborer, b. Sandwich, s/o Marcellus Wallace (Sandwich) and Harriet Wallace (New Hampton); W – 18, at home, b. Meredith, d/o Warren Page (Topsham, VT) and Mela Page (Topsham, VT)

Theodore R. of Sandwich m. Iva **Archer** of Ashland 3/2/1936 in Sandwich; H – 31, laborer, b, Sandwich, s/o Marcellus Wallace (Thornton) and Harriet Smith (New Hampton); W – 24, waitress, b. Sandwich, d/o Enoch Archer (Orford) and Rose Gault (Bridgewater)

William Huston of Elmhurst, IL m. Faith Dunning **Morgan** of Concord, MA 9/2/1950; H – 25, student, b. IL, s/o Leow H. Wallace (KS) and Barbara Keizer (MI); W – 22, at home, b. MA, d/o Reginald Morgan (IL) and Jeanette Morgan (NY)

WALSH,

Francis Damian of Ludlow, MA m. Beth Christina **Garand** of Williamstown, MA 10/9/1992

Stephen Joseph of Franklin, MA m. Dianne Marie **DeGerolamo** of Franklin, MA 6/19/1993

WARNER,

Frederick J. of Ctr. Sandwich m. Maryjane **Pettengill** of Ctr. Sandwich 5/26/1984

WARREN,

Samuel W. of Sandwich m. Jo-Ann **Portanova** of Purchase, NY 2/18/1962; H – 28, advertising, s/o Hamilton Warren and Janet Ward; W – 20, student, d/o John A. Portanova and Carmelia Luongo

WATSON,

Albert S. of Washington, DC m. Margaret C. **Greene** of Ctr. Sandwich 8/23/1947; H – 35, US Govt., b. Chicago, IL, d/o John M. Watson (Smithville, IL) and Dorothy Parson (IN); W – 27, architect, b. Groton, MA, d/o William C. Greene (Brookline, MA) and Margaret W. Eckfelt (New Bedford, MA)

Arthur J. of Sandwich m. Marion E. **Robinson** of Cambridge, MA 5/27/1934; H – 23, carpenter, b. Sandwich, s/o Daniel S. Watson (Sandwich) and Fannie Pitman (Alexandria); W – 21, stenographer, b. Cambridge, MA, d/o William J. Robinson (Portland, ME) and Nettie Quimby (Stewartstown)

Daniel S. of Sandwich m. Fannie M. **Pitman** of Alexandria 7/23/1889 in Sandwich; H – 34, farmer, b. Tamworth, s/o Thomas Watson and Julia D. Watson; W – 20, b. Alexandria, d/o Warren Pitman and Ellen Pitman

Elmer D. of Sandwich m. Florence B. **Atwood** of Sandwich 11/19/1919 in Sandwich; H – 26, laborer, b. Sandwich, s/o Daniel S. Watson (Tamworth) and Fannie Pitman (Alexandria); W – 37, housewife, b. Sandwich, d/o Page Brown (Tamworth) and Angeline Bennett (Grey, ME)

Elmer D. of Sandwich m. Bernice A. **Leach** of Tamworth 8/13/1928 in Moultonboro; H – 34, caretaker, b. Sandwich, s/o Daniel S. Watson (Sandwich) and Fannie Pitman (Alexandria); W – 18, at home, b. Tamworth, d/o William F. Leach (New York, NY) and Alma C. Jeffers (Tamworth)

John C. of Sandwich m. Maria L. **Ward** of Cambridge, MA 10/6/1915 in Sandwich; H – 64, farmer, b. Sandwich, s/o Calvin Watson (Sandwich) and Anna Beede (Sandwich); W – 60, dressmaker, b. Freedom, d/o Sewall Ward (Freedom) and Betsey Parker (Effingham)

WEBB,

John L. of Sandwich m. Eleanor L. **Hall** of Sandwich 4/21/1963; H – 36, service st. operator, s/o John L. Webb and Elizabeth McGinnis; W – 32, teacher, d/o Lawrence K. Hall and Mary Ross

WEBSTER,

Frank H. of Sandwich m. Lizzie **Tappan** of Sandwich 2/26/1889 in Tamworth; H – 32, farmer, b. Sandwich, s/o Samuel L. Webster and Mary Webster (Durham); W – 22, b. Sandwich, d/o Abram E. Tappan (Sandwich) and Abbie Tappan (Sandwich)

Wayne C. of Tamworth m. Janet L. **Bickford** of Sandwich 6/27/1969; H – s/o Chester Webster and Hazel Ames; W – d/o Fred M. Bickford and Ingrid Ingles

WEED,

Charles Ravenel of Minneapolis, MN m. Jennifer Ann **Prestholdt** of Minneapolis, MN 9/6/1997

Chester A. of Sandwich m. Ella C. **Hoag** of Sandwich 6/1/1905 in Sandwich; H – 22, b. Sandwich, s/o Larkin D. Weed (Sandwich) and Elsie A. Peaslee (Sandwich); W – 20, b. Sandwich, d/o Thomas W. Hoag (Sandwich) and Martha E. Hoag (Parsonsfield, ME)

Cleveland of Sandwich m. Lottie M. **Vittum** of Sandwich --/--/1911; H – 21, carpenter, b. Sandwich, s/o Larkin D. Weed (Sandwich) and Elsie Ann P. (Sandwich); W – 27, b. Galva, KS, d/o Charles W. Vittum (Sandwich) and Nannie M. Simpson (Peoria, IL)

F. Herbert of Sandwich m. Edyth S. **Niles** of Cambridge, MA 6/2/1897 in Cambridge, MA; H – 37, broker, b. Sandwich, s/o William M. Weed (Sandwich) and Eliza N. Weed (Sandwich); W – 26, b. Cambridge, MA, d/o Sullivan Niles (N. Jay, ME) and Abbie A. Niles (E. Dixfield, ME)

John J. of Sandwich m. Lucy M. **Smith** of Sandwich 6/21/1905 in Sandwich; H – 20, b. Sandwich, s/o Larkin D. Weed (Sandwich) and Elsie A. Peaslee (Sandwich); W – 21, b. Sandwich, d/o George Hutchins (Meredith) and Lucy M. Smith (Sandwich)

WEEKS,
Ira Merrill, III of Center Harbor m. Katherine Jean **Brown** of Center Harbor 6/13/1970 in Sandwich; H – s/o Ira M. Weeks and Elloyd Harvey; W – d/o Frank Brown and Jean Leach

WELCH,
John W. of Sandwich m. Charlotte J. **Moore** of Laconia 11/23/1957; H – 30, carpenter, b. NH, s/o Edwin Welch (NH) and Sylvia Bickford (NH); W – 25, mill operator, b. NH, d/o Clifford G. Moore (NH) and Marion F. Helms (NY)
Michael W. of Sandwich m. Mary E. **Lamprey** of Sandwich 11/17/1979 in Sandwich; H – s/o John W. Welch and Charlotte J. Moore; W – d/o Uri Lamprey and Mary E. Sproat
Michael W. of Ctr. Sandwich m. Lisa M. **Havlock** of Ctr. Sandwich 6/30/1984
Robert R. of N. Sandwich m. Colleen M. **Swan** of N. Sandwich 5/26/2001

WENTWORTH,
John of Sandwich m. Fanny **Denny** 5/23/1929; H – 52, farmer, b. Hudson, s/o Nathaniel Wentworth (Bingham, MA) and Edwina Greely (Hudson); W – 47, at home, b. Bennington, England, d/o Alfred Ford (Bennington, England) and Fanny Tompkins (England)
John of Sandwich m. Jessie L. **Berry** of Sandwich 1/17/1945; H – 67, game warden, b. Hudson, s/o Nathaniel Wentworth (Brighton, MA) and Martha E. Greeley (Hudson); W – 61,

housewife, b. Hebron, d/o Andrew J. Morgan (Plymouth) and Annie F. Putney

WESCOTT,
Thomas Bond of Montrose, CA m. Kelley Jo **Wahlser** of Montrose, CA 10/4/1997
William L. of Sandwich m. Elisabeth P. **Hunt** of Sandwich 12/29/1956; H – 26, self-employed, b. MA, s/o Merle W. Wescott (ME) and Ruth P. Bond (LA); W – 17, student, b. MA, d/o Kenneth L. Hunt (MA) and Doris E. Perkins (MA)
William L. of Sandwich m. Mary E. **Harris** of Sandwich 3/8/1981

WHEDON,
Oscar A. of Sandwich m. Annie B. **Leavitt** of Sandwich 11/1/1891 in Sandwich; H – 24, buttermaker, b. Sandgate, VT, s/o John M. Whedon and Mary E. Whedon; W – 27, b. Sandwich, d/o Charles E. Mudgett and Mary J. Mudgett

WHEELER,
Robert R. of Baltimore, MD m. Marjorie **Woodbury** of W. Roxbury, MA 9/14/1940; H – 25, teaching fellow, b. Youngstown, OH, s/o Joseph L. Wheeler (Dorchester, MA) and Mabel Archibald (Trinidad, CO); W – 24, secretary, b. W. Roxbury, MA, d/o Ronald S. Woodbury (Boston, MA) and Amy I. Smith (Winchendon, MA)

WHITE,
Frank P. of Sandwich m. Virginia O. **Baron** of Sandwich 10/13/1975 in Sandwich; H – s/o Erskine N. White and Catherine W. Putnam; W – d/o John A. Olsen and Maxine Spry
Fred L. of Sandwich m. Annie W. **Tappan** of Sandwich 10/26/1900 in Meredith; H – 43, farmer, b. Sandwich, s/o James E. White (Northfield) and Sophia Watson

(Sandwich); W – 34, housewife, b. Sandwich, d/o John Tappan (Sandwich) and Augusta Webster (Sandwich)

Keener S., Jr. of Beaver Falls, PA m. Dorothy **Hoag** of Sandwich 2/27/1965; H – 21, Air Force, s/o Keener S. White, Sr. and Leah V. Evans; W – 22, nurse, d/o Roland B. Hoag and Dorothy Sommers

Keener S., III of Sandwich m. Elizabeth Ann **Cook** of Sandwich 1/27/1995

Lawrence A., Jr. of N. Sandwich m. Ruth Anne **Blackeney** of Greenland 12/17/1955; H – 20, student, b. MA, s/o Lawrence A. White and Mae Anderson; W – 22, teacher, b. MA, d/o Charles S. Blackeney and Margaret Beckford

W. Leroy of Sandwich m. Florence A. **Clark** of Sandwich 10/18/1916 in Sandwich; H – 32, lawyer, b. Phillipston, MA, s/o Walter White (Phillipston, MA) and Clara M. Powers (Phillipston, MA); W – 34, at home, b. Sandwich, d/o Charles S. Clark (Sandwich) and Nellie L. Brown (Exeter)

W. Leroy of Sandwich m. Emma **Forster** of Sandwich 11/21/1933 in Ctr. Sandwich; H – 49, lawyer, b. Phillipston, MA, s/o Walter White (Phillipston, MA) and Clara M. Powers (Phillipston, MA); W – 58, at home, b. Richmond, VA, d/o Richard Young (Alexandria, VA) and Susan Stevens (Richmond, VA)

Walter Clark of Sandwich m. Isabelle Victoria **Young** of Bath 7/26/1941; H – 23, laborer, b. Sandwich, s/o Walter L. White (Phillipston, MA) and Florence A. Clark (Sandwich); W – 21, housework, b. Bath, d/o Arthur W. Young (Bath) and Leona A. Noyes (Bath)

Walter Leroy of Sandwich m. Florence Ella **Beede** of Lynn, MA 7/10/1938 in Sandwich; H – 54, lawyer, b. Phillipston, MA, s/o Walter White (Phillipston, MA) and Clara Powers (Phillipston, MA); W – 55, merchant, b. Lynn, MA, d/o Alfred W. Beede (Lynn, MA) and Mary A. Feeny (Lynn, MA)

Walter Leroy of Sandwich m. Katherine Flett **Bryar** of Sandwich 2/27/1944; H – 59, lawyer, b. Phillipston, MA, s/o Walter White (Phillipston, MA) and Clara M. Powers (Phillipston, MA); W – 50, antique dealer and decorator, b. Belmont, MA, d/o George C. Flett (Nelson, NB) and Margretta E. Watson (Boston, MA)

Walter Leroy of Sandwich m. Elizabeth B. **Skinner** of Laconia 9/15/1954; H – 70, retired, b. MA, s/o Walter White (MA) and Clara M. Powers (MA); W – 41, housewife, b. MA, d/o Alvah L. Burrage (MA) and Louise B. Eames (MA)

WHITING,

Raymond V. of Sandwich m. Geraldine S. **Nudd** of Sandwich 1/29/1956; H – 27, laborer, b. NH, s/o Victor L. Whiting (NH) and Mary Davis (NH); W – 19, laborer, b. NH, d/o Wallace E. Nudd (NH) and Blanche Leclair (VT)

WHITMAN,

John Pratt of Boston, MA m. Eleanor Densmore **Wood** of Sandwich 9/21/1916 in Sandwich; H – 45, journalist, b. Louisville, KY, s/o Alfred Whitman (Cambridge, MA) and Mary ----- (Fitzwilliam); W – 43, teacher, b. Hanover, MI, d/o S. Adelbert Wood (Deruyter, NY) and Ella ----- (Hanover, MI)

WICHLAND,

Robert of Sandwich m. Elizabeth A. **DiSalvo** of Sandwich 6/14/2003 in Gilford

V. Robert of Sandwich m. Ruth M. **Asselin** of Sandwich 8/18/1996

WICKS,

Robert D. of Oakland, CA m. Lucy W. **Bullard** of Oakland, CA 8/20/2005 in N. Sandwich

WILCOX,
Phillip N. of Sandwich m. Jeanne **Ryer** of Sandwich 3/5/1987

WILDS,
Arthur H. of Natick, MA m. Fannie S. **Fellows** of Sandwich 9/6/1892 in Somerville; H – 27, teacher, s/o Joseph Wilds and Susane Wilds; W – 24, music teacher, b. Sandwich, d/o Enoch Q. Fellows (Sandwich) and Mary E. Fellows (Sandwich)

WILKINS,
Joseph W. G. of Sandwich m. Elizabeth H. **Kelley** of Sandwich 6/6/1931; H – 65, laborer, b. Middleton, MA, s/o Samuel Wilkins (Middleton, MA) and Elizabeth Mason (W. Swanzey); W – 60, housekeeper, b. NE, d/o Charles H. Kelley (Sandwich) and Sarah E. Norris (IN)
Wilbur C. of Sandwich m. Jennie C. **Garland** of Sandwich 9/28/1904 in Sandwich; H – 21, casemaker, b. Lowell, MA, s/o Clarence B. Wilkins (Middletown, MA) and Ida M. Jones (Lowell, MA); W – 19, b. Tamworth, d/o George D. Garland (Conway) and Ellen M. Hammond (Effingham)

WILLAND,
Howard A. of Sandwich m. Rita M. **Stone** of Gilford 5/4/1974 in Laconia; H – s/o Leander S. Willand and Emma E. Hansen; W – d/o Clarence R. Jones and Josephine A. Muzzey

WILLIAMS,
Bradford C. of Cambridge, MA m. Alice P. **Hamblin** of Cambridge, MA 8/22/1987
Ward B. of Tuftonboro m. Bette Ann **Davis** of Sandwich 12/13/1955; H – 22, draftsman, b. ME, s/o Roger L. Williams (MA) and Bernice Lawrence (MA); W – 17, at

home, b. NH, d/o Forrest E. Davis (NH) and Charlotte Hoag (NH)

WILLOUGHBY,
Kyle E. of Ashland m. Minerva B. **Wallace** of Sandwich 10/16/1945; H – 27, farmer, b. Rumney, s/o Earle B. Willoughby (Holderness) and Eva P. Bacon (Groton); W – 18, student, b. Plymouth, d/o Irva Wallace (Sandwich)

WILSON,
Timothy C. of Irvington, NY m. Carolyn P. **Sawin** of Philadelphia, PA 8/18/1990

WINER,
Kalman A. of Gilmanton m. Linda **Tatelbaum** of Gilmanton 2/2/1975 in Sandwich; H – s/o Harold Winer and Irene Brody; W – d/o Milton Tatelbaum and Harriet Frank

WISHMAN,
William of Sandwich m. Georgia **Burnham** of Sandwich 9/25/1895 in Center Harbor; H – 20, laborer, b. Boston, MA, s/o Charles Wishman (Boston, MA) and Elizabeth Wishman; W – 21, housewife, b. Sandwich, d/o E. W. Burnham (Sandwich) and Susan Burnham

WOODAMAN,
Michael J. of N. Sandwich m. Susan M. **Lance** of N. Sandwich 9/7/1984
Michael Joseph of Sandwich m. Kristine Anne **Hefner** of Sandwich 9/9/1989

WOODBURY,
Charles D. of Milton, MA m. Carolyn F. **Alcock** of Sandwich 7/26/1969: H – s/o Erwin D. Woodbury and Sarah C. Robinson; W – d/o George Alcock and Carolyn Reed

WOODWARD,

Dwight C. of W. Chelmsford, MA m. Carol L. **Daigneau** of Sandwich 5/20/1967; H – 23, pressman, s/o Verne Woodward and Eleanor Hartford; W – 20, secretary, d/o Ernest Daigneau and Louise Roucher

Verne Edson of Haverhill m. Eleanore Marie **Hartford** of W. Ossipee 1/23/1942; H – 23, sta. agent, b. Laconia, s/o Ralph E. Woodward (Warren) and Mildred E. Farrar (Laconia); W – 21, at home, b. Ossipee, d/o Daniel Hartford (Rochester) and Nora F. Knox (Ossipee)

William L. of Sandwich m. Evelyn W. **Gilman** of Sandwich 3/15/1917 in Sandwich; H – 23, farmer, b. Providence, RI, s/o William C. Woodward (Providence, RI) and Lizzie A. Paddock (Providence, RI); W – 18, housekeeper, b. Tamworth, d/o James A. Gilman (Tamworth) and Hattie B. Davis (Tamworth)

WRIGHT,

Jonathan of Sandwich m. Janet F. **Swanson** of Berlin, CT 7/30/1977 in Berlin, CT; H – s/o Harry H. Wright and Jessie Fitzsimmons; W – d/o George J. Fields and Hazel MacPherson

Robert K. of Sandwich m. Judith A. **Orth** of Meredith 8/21/1982

YORK,

George W. of Sandwich m. Helen **Severance** of Sandwich 6/19/1895 in Sandwich; H – 38, laborer, b. Sandwich, s/o George T. York (Sandwich) and Augusta York; W – 42, housewife, b. Boscawen, d/o John Mills and Marion Mills

ZAMORE,

Christopher H. of Cambridge, MA m. Alice C. **Henry** of Cambridge, MA 7/14/1984

Abbott, Cora A. – Fogg, Wesley H.
Abbott, Ella M. – Page, Frank M.
Abbott, Grace A. – Martin, Eugene F.
Abbott, Lillian S. (Smith) – Lindstrom, Julius A.
Abbott, Nellie E. – Mack, Fred M.
Adams, Bernice R. – Vittum, Lewis R.
Adams, Mary Ragan – Garry, Franklyn Bernard
Adriance, Emily Hodges – Magnus, Kurt Henry
Alcock, Carolyn F. – Woodbury, Charles D.
Aldrich, Eleanor May – Vittum, Kenneth David
Amabile, Margaret J. (Berry) – Day, Norbert A.
Ambrose, Gladys Ruth – Doane, David Hoyt
Ames, Agnes M. – Vittum, Ernest
Anderson, Margaret H. (Burrows) – Howe, Charlie L.
Andrews, Jane E. – Luria, Scott L.
Angier, Addie A. (French) – Skinner, Cyrus E.
Angier, Mildred S. – Allen, Melvin C.
Annable, Beatrice M. (Griffiths) – Quimby, Clifton C.
Anthony, Deborah W. – Kamataris, Harry L.
Anthony, Gladys R. – Ambrose, Langdon J.
Applebaum, B. Alexandra – Evans, Timothy J.
Archer, Iva – Wallace, Theodore R.
Archibald, Elinor Jane – Googoo, John Andrew
Arling, Lena M. – Grant, Ernest A.
Armstrong, E. Maude – Kelley, Newell R.
Arseneault, Denise Cathy – Greene, Christopher W.
Asselin, Ruth M. – Wichland, V. Robert
Atehortua, Lina Patricia – Mikelinich, Kenneth Edward
Atkinson, Jennifer A. – Prescott, Michael J.
Atwood, Alta J. – Gilman, Warren S.
Atwood, Bertha L. – Carter, Alonzo F.
Atwood, Dorothy B. – Bryant, Winfield S.
Atwood, Emily E. (Burrows) – Atwood, Daniel D.
Atwood, Florence B. (Brown) – Watson, Elmer D.
Atwood, Nellie A. – Hart, Elmer B.

Atwood, Pauline Alice – Evans, Robert Otis
Atwood, Virginia – Crory, Frederick J., Jr.
Auger, Joan N. – Dolan, Robert O.
Avery, Charlotte M. – Peaslee, Charles H.
Avery, Sylvia L. – Bryant, William A.
Aznavorian, Angele K. – Schumacher, Scott A.

Bagley, Cora B. – Allen, Herman A.
Bagley, Eva M. – Gault, George F.
Ball, Pamela R. – Elliott, Raymond
Ballesteros, Nancy L. (Turner) – Saunders, Warren T., Jr.
Bando, Carol Ann – Hess, Jamieson Laurie
Banks, Tracy Jean – Bradfield, Robert John, III
Barnes, Bonnie – Engle, Walter R., Jr.
Barnes, Myrtle E. – Cochran, James A.
Barnes, Nettie – Tewksbury, Wesley
Barnes, Ruby M. – Kleczek, Frederick A.
Barnes, Ruth L. – Pearson, Herman W.
Baron, Virginia O. (Olsen) – White, Frank P.
Bartlett, Edith M. – Ripley, William G.
Barton, Agatha J. (Jennison) – Slosson, Charles A.
Barton, Meta W. – Patten, Andrew W.
Batchelder, Nellie F. – Foss, Charles L.
Batcheldor, Leona – Elliott, Dennis
Bates, Judith – Merritt, Edward A. S.
Battis, Evelyn B. – Brown, Edgar E.
Beach, Joan – Little, Clayton Alton
Beach, Kristina M. – Lockhart, Michael D.
Bean, Gladys Cynthia – Howe, David Brainerd
Beede, Elmira A. – Fogg, Elias H.
Beede, Florence Ella – White, Walter Leroy
Bemis, Annie M. – Graves, Ross M.
Bennett, Babette Hall – Bowden, David K.
Bennett, Eliza B. – Trask, W. F.
Bennett, Jennifer L. – Sherwood, Michael A.

Benoit, Melissa K. – Dow, Steven F.
Benton, Nina – McLean, John S.
Benton, Polly – Sheffer, Leonard S.
Benton, Sally – Curley, Leo M.
Berg, Kristen – Lavalley, Kevin Patrick
Berman, Nadine – Freeman, Malcolm F., III
Berry, Alice – George, Fred C.
Berry, Donna L. (Foisy) – Picone, Stephen L.
Berry, Frances Virginia – Jackson, Howard B., Jr.
Berry, Jessie L. (Morgan) – Wentworth, John
Berry, Joan Nickles – Cook, Wilbur Asa, Jr.
Berry, Judith L. – Saunders, Warren T., Jr.
Bickford, Janet L. – Webster, Wayne C.
Bickford, Jennifer L. – Grisi, Brian F.
Bickford, Mabel Irene – Nudd, Walter
Bickford, Margaretta Joyce – Peaslee, Earl Charles
Bickford, Shannon – Recin, Robin Burke
Bigelow, Emma L. – Atwood, Albert C.
Bigelow, Mary E. – Burleigh, Thomas E.
Binford, Alice W. – Cook, John O.
Blackeney, Ruth Anne – White, Lawrence A., Jr.
Blackey, Bernice I. – Abbott, Ralph H.
Blackey, Flora B. – Scriggins, Albert C.
Blackshear, Rebecca M. – Coesper, Milo Wilson
Blackstock, Stephanie – Swan, Bernard W.
Blake, Hazel A. (Chandler) – Heath, Charles E.
Blanchard, Bessie – Smith, Harry H.
Blanchard, Grace A. – Harmon, Frederick
Blondeau, Michelle J. – Perkins, Allan R.
Boardman, Margaret B. (Burrows) – Taylor, George H.
Bogre, Susan J. – Mykland, James Olav
Bolduc, Marie A. – Jackson, Howard B., Jr.
Bookholz, Pauline M. (Borkely) – Laughton, Arthur D.
Bookholz, Teresa Louise – Severy, Merle Eugene
Boone, Mary Louise – Hutchins, Edward B.

Boucher, Lori E. – DiFilippe, Jamie D.
Boudreau, Aileen Barbara (Branston) – Landofi, Domenick J., Jr.
Boudreau, Sarah E. – Sanchez, Ricardo B.
Bourque, Suzanne Marie – Pohl, Peter William
Bradfield, Janet A. – Davis, Kenneth C.
Breed, Nancy P. – Evans, Alton Brooks
Brewer, Deborah Packard – Read, Theodore Otis
Brewer, Jane A. – Foster, Robert W.
Brewer, Louisa W. – Bryant, Milton R., Jr.
Brewer, Terry E. – Paquette, Thomas D.
Briggs, Jane J. – Ferreira, Paul F.
Brock, Carol M. – Hartman, Vernon D.
Broderick, Nancy Doris – Claxton, Douglas Carter
Brodhead, Karen E. – Ellsworth, John O.
Brown, Amy Marie – Mason, Philip N., III
Brown, Deborah A. – Gove, Stephen D.
Brown, Dorrit – Fogg, Joseph Alberto
Brown, Florence M. – Atwood, Frank L.
Brown, Henrietta S. – Corliss, Hiram S.
Brown, Katherine Jean – Weeks, Ira Merrill, III
Brown, Mary R. – Cook, George O.
Brown, Myrtle – Moulton, Edgar C.
Brown, Myrtle G. (Grant) – Graves, Ross M.
Brown, Nellie E. – Bickford, Silas H.
Brown, Nellie G. (Stackpole) – Atwood, Albert C.
Brown, Ruth E. (Grumuldys) – Kolesar, Fred A., Sr.
Browning, Dorothea (Richardson) – Smith, O. Granville
Bryant, Diane B. – Abbott, Arthur F.
Bryant, Edith M. – Grant, Leland H.
Bryant, Elaine Lynn – Peaslee, Daniel Charles
Bryant, Elizabeth J. – Madigan, Derek D.
Bryant, Francis Adelaide – George, Frank Hiram
Bryant, Geraldine Louise – Smith, Aaron Clark
Bryant, Ida M. (Martin) – Wade, Edwin D.
Bryant, Phyllis Marion – Swan, Dean Edmund

Bryant, Susan Pickett – Kimball, George William
Bryer, Katherine (Flett) – White, Walter Leroy
Buckingham, Ruth Ivy – Dodge, William Gerald
Buckley, Suzanne Mae – Burrows, Jere Gordon
Buker, Wendy Rae – Rodgers, David Paul
Bullard, Lucy W. – Wicks, Robert D.
Bullard, Marion – McCrillis, Neal
Bullard, Mary – Hewins, Alfred
Bullard, Susan M. – Brown, Lyle A.
Bundy, Margaret J. – Tewksbury, Royce A.
Burkitt, Janet E. (Cummings) – Smith, Samuel M.
Burleigh, Ethel A. – Hart, Elmer B.
Burleigh, Evelyn M. – Tasker, Elmer H.
Burney, Susan J. – Coolidge, Peter B.
Burnham, Georgie – Wishman, William
Burnham, Grace (Chase) – Blackey, Ralph A.
Burnham, Sylvia B. – Gray, Richard
Burrage, Christine W. (Wendel) – Timmins, John Andrew
Burrows, Amy M. (Gilman) – Torsey, Guy B.
Burrows, Barbara – Vachon, Lynn
Burrows, Donna M. – Dunn, William L.
Burrows, Donna R. – Ryan, Daniel W.
Burrows, Edna A. – Bickford, Charles R.
Burrows, Estella J. – Atwood, Harry A.
Burrows, Eva G. – Smith, Demerrit E.
Burrows, Florence O. – Knox, Perley C.
Burrows, Gladys G. – Perkins, Ralph H.
Burrows, Harriet (Foss) – Beede, James H.
Burrows, Mabel – Farmer, Fred
Burrows, Margaret Helen – Boardman, Carlos Weston
Burrows, Mary Lee – Atwood, Gerald A.
Burrows, Nellie – Hodge, John N.
Burrows, Pauline E. – Peaslee, Robert N.
Burrows, Roxy – Cluff, Maurice P.
Burrows, Roxy M. – Wallace, Asahel A.

Burrows, Sandra J. – Coolidge, Peter B.
Butterfield, Kelly Susan – Shore, Michael Adams
Buxton, Amy C. – Chase, Bertrand R.
Buxton, Helen R. (Rotch) – Rose, Harry M.

Cakars, Marilynn – Sayers, John Kevin
Cameron, Shannon K. – Quinn, Andrew J.
Cameron, Shannon L. – Schlemmer, John P.
Campbell, Emma M. – Vittum, Marshall W.
Campbell, Jeanne – Silcox, Frederick L.
Canney, Bertha A. – Turner, Cornelius
Cannon, Kerrie Lee – Pytlik, Steven Robert
Card, Marion A. – Clemons, Eustis W.
Carney, Kathleen Marie – O'Connell, Declan Anthony
Carroll, Susan J. – Peaslee, Kerry D.
Carter, Louise H. – Peaslee, Earle C.
Casella, Nancy Marie – Morton, Michael John
Catalano, Rachel E. – Foster, Sean D.
Cavey, Mary L. – Anderson, William A.
Cawthorne, Ethel E. – Atwood, Walter G.
Chandler, Emeline E. – Vittum, Aubrey M.
Chandler, Nellie G. (Stackpole) – Brown, Warren J.
Chapman, Ruth Joyce – Hugny, Rollin Philip, Jr.
Chappell, Susan A. – Hoag, Roland B., Jr.
Charles, Judith A. – Stafstrom, Joel P.
Chase, Grace – Burnham, Charles S.
Chase, Jill S. – Bickford, Charles R., Jr.
Chase, Marybeth R. – Carleton, Dean W., Jr.
Clark, Alice H. – Vittum, Herbert A.
Clark, Florence A. – White, W. Leroy
Clark, Jeanette T. – Burnham, Charles S.
Clattenburg, Susan P. – Kemp, Arthur D., Jr.
Clay, Sarah E. – Blumberg, Simon N.
Cleasby, Shirley (Lawrence) – Hutchins, Edward C.
Clifford, Beverly A. – Sturgeon, Ronald W.

Clough, Sadie M. – Wade, Frank M.
Cochran, Sheila J. – Ames, Roy M., Jr.
Colby, Lucy (Shute) – Quimby, John S.
Cole, Clara P. – Moulton, George K.
Cole, Rebecca A. – Bourghalem, Farid
Collins, Ada M. – Ambrose, Langdon J.
Combe, Mary A. – Baum, Carl M.
Comer, Cynthia Hunter – Henle, Michael Gilman
Comer, Joanne – Bickford, Fred Eric
Compton, Elizabeth O. – Hart, Peter D.
Condon, Marvis P. – Prince, Warren F.
Conner, Carolyn M. – Mudgett, James R.
Cook, Elizabeth Ann – White, Keener S., III
Cook, Lena May – Talbot, Cecil A.
Cook, Lisa Ann – Frank, Douglas Roy
Cook, Marjorie – Littlefield, Paul A.
Cook, Mira T. (Tappan) – Hodge, Walter E.
Cook, Nancy A. – Brown, Edward I.
Copp, Pamela M. – Cook, Robert W.
Corliss, Mary Etta – Gray, Irving
Covey, Linda L. – Smith, Richard E.
Covey, Patricia M. – Cogan, Dennis G.
Covey, Sally Ann – Leighton, Charles L.
Craig, Ethel M. (Chandler) – Carter, Andrew
Craig, Jessie M. – Grayhorn, Herbert S.
Craig, Nellie E. – Russell, William W.
Cram, Lois E. – Hodge, Walter E.
Cram, Rachel P. – Halliday, Kyle D.
Crawford, Stella M. – Bickford, Fred A.
Crook, Holly B. – Milbury, William F.
Crooker, Catherine – Hoogeveen, Hans B. H.
Crowell, Florence E. (Marshall) – Gumbert, Charles
Cruckshank, Eva S. – Garland, Rufus E.
Cummings, Emma M. (Hugh) – Lunt, Clifton A.
Currier, Esther – Howard, Judson Dillon

D'Este, Mary L. – Michael, Philip
Daigneau, Carol L. – Woodward, Dwight C.
Daigneau, Dorothy E. – Wakefield, Roger W.
Daigneau, Jo-Ann V. – Martel, Haven C.
Daigneau, Shirley Jean – Talbot, Lawrence William
Danforth, Mary A. (Courtney) – Magoon, Levi L.
Danforth, Meline M. – Tenney, George W.
Dann, Edith A. – Stuart, Reginald B.
Davey, Jennie P. (Vittum) – Lee, Ansel E.
Davie, Alice Pearl – Smith, G. Roland
Davis, Agnes F. – Popham, Byron J.
Davis, Bette Ann – Williams, Ward B.
Davis, Beverly F. – Burrows, Robert N.
Davis, Darlene A. – Atwood, Richard A.
Davis, Doris M. – Gilman, Clarence W.
Davis, Eva M. – Mudgett, Eugene E.
Davis, Mamie E. – Bennett, Edward W.
Davis, Nora E. – Burrows, Fred Walter
Davock, Deborah E. – Christopher M. Finch
Davock, Nancy (Nay) – Jamba, Michael
Day, Amy Parks – Chase, David Robert
De Bustamante, Isabel Sanchez – Barnett, Stephen Vincent
Dean, Christina E. – Hall, Jonathan J.
Dean, Gail A. – Lamprey, John A.
Dearborn, Dolly W. (Vittum) – Green, Fred
Dearborn, Dorothy D. – Torsey, Leon S.
Dearborn, Florence – Smith, John A.
Dearborn, Grace L. – Berry, Fred W.
DeGerolamo, Dianne Marie – Walsh, Stephen Joseph
Delaney, Helen E. – Pettengill, Sylvester B.
Delaney, Lorraine J. – Leland, Roger B.
deMars, Rosemarie C. – Ingari, Joseph C.
Demick, Dorothy (Wing) – Peaslee, Roland
Deming, Beth A. – Lottinger, Hugh A.

Deming, Roberta A. – Cahoon, Dennis F.
Demme, Sheila R. (Swanson) – Visser, William W.
Demme, Stephanie – Galfas, Peter Mathew
Demos, Margaret Ann – Martin, Willard Gordon, Jr.
Dennett, Julia M. – Hird, Stephen A.
Dennett, Julia Marie – Belleville, Travis Steven
Denney, Helen Louise – Bickford, Karl H.
Denny, Fanny (Ford) – Wentworth, John
DeWitt, Kathryn Stone – Nelson, Robert E., Jr.
Diack, Ethel B. – MacDonald, Ernest E.
Dimick, Minnie E. (Osgood) – Fogg, Eugene W.
DiSalvo, Elizabeth A. – Wichland, Robert
Dixon, Wendy M. (Lovewell) – Jones, Peter G.
Dodge, Berenice E. – Taylor, Charles Edison
Doland, Mary H. – Conlin, Robert W.
Dorais, Emily Jean – McNamara, Stephen James
Dorning, Margaret Frances – Litzell, Charles Edward
Doughty, Beatrice – Burrows, Lester D.
Doughty, Ellen P. – Graves, Jefferson A.
Dow, Sadie M. – Tilton, John F.
Downs, Janice L. – Dearborn, Allan E.
Downs, Jill S. – Burrows, Bruce J.
Downs, Sadie J. – Forssius, Carl A.
Downs, Winnifred E. – Jewell, Asahel H.
Doyle, Paula Jayne – Tracy, Kim
Draper, Marion Hoffman – Kay, James Hutchinson
Dumas, Thelma – Burrows, Austin G.
Dunbar, Margot – Bleier, Barry B.
Durell, Emce V. – Page, Joel R.
Durgin, Luella (Fogg) – Fogg, Henry O.
Dustin, Robin G. – McCarthy, Clarence A.
Dwyer, Helena Agnes – Smith, Leonard John
Dyere, Lydia A. (Boyce) – Carter, Nathaniel

Eckert, Marion B. – Claxton, Edmund S., Jr.

Eldridge, Frances Josie – Drew, Phillip William
Eldridge, Gloria J. – Hoag, Peter C.
Elliott, Alice E. (Weeks) – Burrows, Phillip F.
Elliott, Alice G. – Brown, Frank W.
Elliott, Darlene M. – Racine, William A.
Elliott, Grace – Campbell, John W.
Elliott, Karen Jean – Grinnell, William Loyd, Jr.
Elliott, Madeline – Clough, Harry O.
Elliott, Marion – Mudgett, Fred C.
Elliott, Mary L. – Davis, Charles J.
Elliott, Pauline S. – Moulton, Kendall N.
Elwood, Phoebe A. (Brown) – Davis, Charles J.
Emerson, Pamela A. – McMillen, Robert W.
Emerson, Virginia B. (Davis) – Burton, Francis A.
Erb, Susan Elizabeth – Pittenger, John C.
Evans, Catherine A. – Staples, Larry E.
Evans, Nancy B. (Breed) – Clairmont, Rene J.
Evans, Nancy B. (Breed) – Seymour, Ralph B.
Evans, Sharon Elizabeth (Seymour) – Jackson, Christopher P.
Evans, Sylvia E. – Grant, Aliston H.
Evans, Wendy L. – Burrows, Jon L.

Facciolo, Irene Maria – Pfeffer, Soren David
Fairbanks, Charlotte A. (McCauley) – Wallace, Edward F.
Falvey, Mary Joan – Wallace, Scott E.
Felch, Bertha M. – Abbott, Arthur F.
Felch, Ina G. (Vittum) – Tappan, Fred
Felch, Martha J. (Grant) – Atwood, John G.
Fellows, Fannie S. – Wilds, Arthur H.
Fellows, Marguerite – Dutton, Walter
Fellows, Nancy M. (Mason) – Blanchard, Charles
Fellows, Nellie F. (Foss) – Fellows, Arthur P.
Fennell, Myrtle B. – Mudgett, Elisha W.
Fichet, Sally A. – O'Connor, James W.
Fifield, Mary A. (Knox) – Campbell, John N.

Fifield, Nellie – Glover, C. E.
Fisher, Barbara Jane – O'Donnell, Francis Edward
Fisher, Gladys – Smith, Walter
Flanagan, Eleanor A. – Reed, David T.
Fleischmann, Ellen L. – Benvenuto, John F.
Fleming, Julia – Foss, Frank N.
Fleming, Patricia A. – Merriman, Roger B., III
Flett, Katherine R. – Bryar, Charles A.
Floyd, Elva L. – Bickford, Carl O.
Fogg, Kathryn Anne – Amaral, Gregory Kevin
Fogg, Mary E. – Powers, Herbert H.
Fogg, Ora A. – Mudgett, Fred M.
Follansbee, Holly J. – Lamprey, Mark E.
Follett, Angie P. – Chilson, Herbert A.
Follett, M. Louise – Brown, Clarence R.
Forbes, Barbara H. – Blumberg, Lawrence J.
Forristall, Caroline – Leach, Arthur T.
Forristall, Garaphelia – Condon, Donald E.
Forristall, Helen P. (Peaslee) – Heald, Bruce D.
Forristall, Patricia – Cook, John Otis
Forristall, Virginia – Elliott, Phillip
Forster, Emma (Young) – White, W. Leroy
Fortier, Irmabelle – Nudd, Ronald Eugene
Foster, Addie M. (Page) – Scriggins, William H.
Fowle, Christie W. (Webber) – Sears, Winthrop M.
Fowler, Mary J. – Huston, Randall L.
Frazier, Minerva A. – Taylor, Gurney
Frye, Bernice M. – Peaslee, David J.

Galfas, Stephanie – Cruz, David P.
Galley, Carol L. – Dumas, Raymond J., Jr.
Gannett, Hattie H. – Gilman, Nathan F.
Garand, Beth Christina – Walsh, Francis Damian
Garland, Agnes J. (Watson) – Carlson, Walter R.
Garland, Emma M. (Grant) – Cram, Charles S.

Garland, Jennie C. – Wilkins, Wilbur C.
Gasbarro, Melanie E. C. – Desmarais, Patrick Edward
Gault, Doris L. – Merryfield, Norman E.
Gebo, Ruth D. – MacDonald, Ernest E.
Geer, Ednah Wynne (Phelps) – Hall, Lawrence Kingsley
Geers, Anna L. – Burrows, Charles G.
Geishecker, Gretchen G. – Marra, Stephen J.
George, Geraldine B. (Bryant) – Read, Theodore O.
Gerli, Madeleine Marie – Bernt, Harold
Gilman, Adelaide J. – Marston, Willis B.
Gilman, Amy M. – Burrows, Charles H.
Gilman, Evelyn W. – Woodward, William L.
Gilman, Frances D. – Colby, William W.
Gilman, Lillian E. – Lamprey, Wilbur H.
Gilman, Lizzie E. – Abbott, Everett H.
Gilman, Victoria M. (Wallace) – Sargent, George H.
Glidden, Frances L. – Mudgett, Joel R.
Good, Mitzi Ann – Glenday, William Frederick
Goodwin, Nellie J. – Nichol, Charles E.
Gordon, Edrie H. – Burrows, Nathaniel
Gordon, Lulu B. – Palmer, Willard F.
Gotshall, Diana F. – Barrie, James M.
Graham, Cynthia Jane – Hambrook, James Matthew
Graham, Joanne E. (Ewing) – Jones, Griffith M. Jr.
Grant, Beryl V. – Tappan, Walter S.
Grant, Myrtie G. – Brown, George E.
Graves, Cathleen Anne – Meder, Eric James
Graves, Dorothy A. – Remick, A. Dexter
Graves, Eliza S. – Towle, Frank L.
Gray, Alice – Hewitt, Linwood Arthur
Gray, Deborah E. – Morgan, Richard B.
Gray, Gail M. (Hamel) – Emerson, Denley W.
Gray, Marion E. – Taylor, Paul A.
Grayson, Wendelyn M. – Tonge, Peter W.
Green, Mayme M. (Bailey) – Abbott, Everett H.

Greene, Erin R. – Geib, Eric F.
Greene, Jayne Katherine (Geddes) – Moskowitz, Jay Irvin
Greene, Kathleen A. – Fleischmann, Thomas C.
Greene, Margaret C. – Watson, Albert S.
Griffiths, Katherine T. – Trout, Charles H.
Grinold, Melinda A. – Bicknell, Brooks E.
Grisco, Donna M. – Burrows, Thomas F.
Guild, Joan Ellen – Burritt, Arthur Ware

Haggert, Elizabeth J. – Hodge, Reuben N.
Haley, Bessie F. – Tilton, Charles O.
Haley, Edith M. – Hewitt, Arthur
Haley, Joyce A. – MacDonald, Ernest E., Jr.
Hall, A. – Bickford, Wyatt T.
Hall, Eleanor L. – Webb, John L.
Hall, Florence M. – McGrath, Michael
Hall, Marjorie E. – Nedeau, Raymond R.
Hall, Marjorie V. (Wallace) – Gilman, Edward S.
Hall, Rose B. – Sickles, Allen J.
Hamblin, Alice P. – Williams, Bradford C.
Hambrook, Kathleen M. – McDonald, Daniel J.
Hambrook, Susan J. – Greene, William M.
Hamel, Franna Trout – Eaton, Toby Vining
Hamilton, Heather E. – Curran, Benjamin R.
Handley, Gwendolin Ashcroft – Tibbetts, Willard Ray
Hanson, Anna L. – Lee, Ansel E.
Hanson, Lizzie M. – Leighton, George W.
Hanson, Marie L. – Clark, Calvin I.
Hardy, Leah Frances – Langley, Fred
Harold, Margaret C. – Holden, David J.
Harriman, Frances – Palmer, Archie H.
Harrington, Josephine – Brown, George W.
Harrington, Julia E. – Twaddle, Stephen M.
Harris, Mary E. – Wescott, William L.
Hart, Lizzie S. (Severance) – Brown, Joel N.

Harter, Susan Janet – Farnsworth, Gary Deane
Hartford, Eleanore Marie – Woodward, Verne Edson
Hatch, Effie M. – Wallace, Harry
Havlock, Lisa M. – Welch, Michael W.
Havre, Felicia P. – Pierce, Roger, III
Hawes, Charlene – Steele, George
Hawes, Charlene L. – Eldredge, Kenneth W.
Hawes, Kathleen M. – Eldridge, James F.
Hayes, Elli M. – Ford, Gordon M.
Hayes, Honora – Berry, Nahum J.
Haynes, Patricia Irene – Foisy, Louis Harold
Heard, Emily Thompson – Dustin, Robert Gale
Heard, Jacqueline Ella – Burns, Michael Evans
Heard, Meredith A. – Gisness, William W.
Heffner, Kristine Anne – Woodaman, Michael Joseph
Henderson, Ada E. (Forest) – Sullivan, James J.
Henderson, Emma J. – Horne, Thomas A.
Henderson, Ethel – Aspinwall, William
Henry, Alice C. – Zamore, Christopher H.
Henry, Grace F. – MacLean, John K.
Hersey, Carolyn J. – Ovalle, Arthur
Hildbold, Jennie M. (Fleming) – Cram, Charles S.
Hill, Elmer R. – Boyd, James S.
Hill, Irene C. (French) – Vittum, Orrin E.
Hilliard, Alice E. – Denney, Harold C.
Hines, Clara W. – Mack, Herbert G.
Hoag, Carrie E. – Leonard, Frank
Hoag, Dorothy – White, Keener S., Jr.
Hoag, Ella C. – Weed, Chester A.
Hoag, Margery Garrett – Freeman, Robert Edwards
Hoag, Ruth – Parsons, John H.
Hoag, Susan – Shelton, William G.
Hodgdon, Emily D. – Currier, Leon H.
Hodgdon, Lizzie B. – Graves, Isaac H. F.
Hodgdon, Patricia M. – Burrows, Phillip T.

Hodge, Nellie F. – Burrows, Newell J.
Hodge, Ruth M. – Moulton, Joseph B.
Hodgkins, Kristin – Macomber, John D.
Hoisington, Andrea E. – Marshall, Crofton S.
Holbrook, Sarah – Cutler, Abbot W.
Holland, Patricia – Jackson, Philip M.
Holland, Vicki L. – Holland, Philip W.
Holmes, Ann M. (Bartlett) – Clark, Joseph P.
Hope, Catherine E. – Broderick, Roric S.
Hope, Catherine E. – Hoell, John J.
Hope, MaryStarr B. – Gaughan, Matthew M.
Houghton, Peggy L. – Stull, David A.
Houston, Pamela H. – London, Frank C.
Howell, Carol L. – Michael, Timothy
Hoyt, Jennie – Frye, Louis W.
Hoyt, Katherine Anne – Thorndike, Townsend Davis
Hoyt, Lorraine Belle – Elliott, Sidney
Hoyt, Ruth Hamilton – Sanders, LeRoy
Hoyt, Ruth J. – Robinson, Charles
Hoyt, Sarah D. – Drew, John
Hubbard, Mary R. (Flanders) – Patterson, Albion M.
Hudson, Florence E. – Beach, Watson E.
Hulbert, Madge B. (Curtis) – Mitchell, Arthur I.
Hull, Adelaide S. – Burrows, Harry L.
Hull, Carissa Audrey – O'Gara, Robert Michael
Hulse, Sandra L. – Owens, David A.
Hunt, Barbara M. – Bryant, Milton R.
Hunt, Constance – McCrillis, Henry Bullard
Hunt, Elisabeth P. – Wescott, William L.
Hurd, Eleanor Idella (DesRosier) – Knox, Charles Edward
Hurley, Frances (Cummings) – Kimball, Charles J.
Hutchins, Marion M. (Taylor) – Fitchett, Earl N.

Ingles, Ingrid E. – Bickford, Fred M.
Irving, Nettie – Plummer, James H.

Jackson, Patricia (Steeves) – Elliott, Preston
Jaclard, Adele H. – Blanchard, George A.
Jacobs, Linda S. – Enright, John E.
Jacobs, Lisa K. – Holland, Daniel R.
Jameson, Louise T. (LeClare) – Page, Hutcheson
Janson, Jean Ellen – Fulkerson, Davis Rand
Jaques, Bertha M. – Smith, Samuel L.
Johnson, Beatrice M. – Littlefield, Orace E.
Johnson, Margaret Christine – Van Sickle, Randall David
Johnston, Heather Loring – Larowe, Major Winn
Johnston, Janet I. (Burnham) – Bickford, Fred M.
Johnston, Sarah B. – Szymujko, Jeffery A.
Johnston, Sarah Burnham – Cunningham, Daniel J.
Jones, Honor – Passow, Christian H.
Jones, Nancy P. – Hansen, Carl H.
Jordan, Bernice D. – Nelson, Herbert E.
Jowdy, Carol L. – Lee, David M.
Justice, Jill A. – Langford, James R.

Karlin, Emma Sophia – Quimby, Wilbur Ezra
Katapodis, Elaine L. – Barghout, Alexander S.
Kealy, Mary – Gall, John F.
Keates, Lois Silver – Horgan, John P., Jr.
Keese, Loretta M. – Buchman, Thomas A., Jr.
Kegiah, Lynn (Robbins) – Poole, Clifford
Kelley, Annie L. – Fogg, John W.
Kelley, Elizabeth H. – Wilkins, Joseph W. G.
Kelley, Marguerite B. (Bailey) – Lawn, Evan
Kelley, Megan Elizabeth – Meek, David Harold
Kent, Esther L. (Griffin) – Stanley, Halsey D.
Kerr, Debbi Lyn – Augustine, Charles Whitney
Khakaura, Cia R. – Bortman, David C.
Kim, Heesun – Limberger, Donald K.
Kimball, Emily (Ethridge) – Gurdy, George

Kimball, Lottie I. (Leighton) – Foss, Charles H.
King, Audrey K. – Cline, James A., Jr.
King, Louise M. – Knox, Charles E.
King, Michelle M. – Peaslee, Garret E.
Kinney, Donna E. – Speers, William S.
Klippert, Terri Lynn – Beal, Douglas Welch
Knight, Georgia A. – Perkins, Melvin E.
Knowles, Hattie M. – Tappan, Frank H.
Knowles, Johanna Beth – Carini, Peter Augustus
Knowles, Nellie P. – Darling, William
Knowles, Sadie F. – Varney, Freeman
Knowles, Winnie B. – Danforth, George E.
Knowlton, Hannah E. – Marston, Charles S.
Knowlton, Sarah (Vittum) – Kelley, Thomas
Kondrotas, Jennifer L. – Elliott, Barry P.
Kroeger, Jane T. – Brown, Donald E.
Kunhardt, Linda Lawrence – Lehmann, William Hugh Campbell, Jr.
Kvamme, Mildred Loretta – Bajowski, John Michael

Lambert, Florence – Thompson, Karl E.
Lamprey, Mary E. – Welch, Michael W.
Lance, Susan M. – Woodaman, Michael J.
Larkin, Laura Jean – Harding, Edward
Larrabee, Elsbeth Minnie – Elliott, Richard Howard
Larson, Heidi M. – Johnson, Paul R.
LaSalle, June R. – Gilman, Bernard W.
Laurence, Ruth S. – Conley, Raymond K., Jr.
Laverack, Anne – Gallivan, Thomas Andrew, Jr.
Lavery, Carol Rose – Converse, Mark Wayne
Lavoie, Valerie A. – Greene, Eric S.
Lawrence, Elizabeth (Goodwin) – Chick, Henry G.
Leach, Bernice A. – Watson, Elmer D.
Leach, Jean F. – Brown, Frank G.
Leach, Julia M. – Dicey, Wendell G.

Leach, Mary – Anair, Roland W., Jr.
Lear, Nancy L. – Metcalf, Winslow H.
Leary, Annie M. – Plummer, Wilfred Z.
Leavitt, Annie B. (Mudgett) – Whedon, Oscar A.
Leete, Helen B. (Barnard) – Bryant, John E. G.
Legault, Theresa M. – Clement, Richard D.
Leiblein, Jennifer K. – Martel, James R.
Levesque, Janet J. – Moore, David W.
Libby, Carol J. (Smith) – Atwood, Hubert L.
Lindemann, Baldura S. (Schmidt) – Tatum, David S.
Lindstrom, Ida M. – Quimby, Wilbur E.
Locke, Heidi Kathleen – Simon, Gregory Robert
Locke, Mae Arlene – Smith, Samuel Maurice
Long, Holli H. – Seeley, Allen K.
Longley, Louise M. – Mailloux, Jack J.
Lord, Frances Viola – Vittum, Kenneth Franklin
Lovejoy, Laura E. (Gault) – Robinson, Alvin D.
Lucas, Annie E. – Heath, Albert C.
Ludwick, Amanda M. – Fullerton, Benjamin J.
Lyon, Martha H. – Jacobson, Kent A.

MacArthur, Bronwen – Mangan, John R., Jr.
MacDonald, Patricia Jean – Hurd, Arthur Edgar, Jr.
MacDonald, Yvonne A. – Piper, David R.
MacGregor, Elizabeth – Bates, Frank Dudley
MacKenzie, Susan J. – Dobyns, Christopher D.
MacMillan, Amy Elizabeth – Canfield, Thomas Matthew
Magoon, Hattie E. – Smith, Edgar W.
Maksim, Ann F. – Kirkwood, Douglas H.
Marken, Maria Blenda K. – Hodsdon, Marshall S.
Marshall, Amy G. – Levy, Chad W.
Marshall, Bertha Laurie – Nixon, William Dorr
Marshall, Elizabeth E. (Brown) – Emerson, Denley W.
Marston, Margaret – Miller, Arthur P.
Martin, Frances A. – Carter, Almon E.

Martin, Helen G. – Bibber, Ross E.
Martin, Julia D. – Ireland, John B.
Martin, Mildred E. – Henston, Forrest
Mason, Emily J. (Mudgett) – Scriggins, William H.
Mason, Florence E. – Robinson, Charles
Matckie, Cynthia J. – Rowan, Daniel S.
Mathews, Patricia L. – Gillis, Paul A.
Matos, Jean Martha – Smith, Ellsworth Wayne
Mauch, Nancy B. – Hosmer, Peter S.
Mayer, Ellen R. – Pittman, Malcolm G., III
Mazzola, Antonia A. – Tibbetts, Paul W.
McBride, Elizabeth A. (Whiting) – Carter, David F.
McBride, Rosa – Plummer, Frank P.
McCarthy, Deborah Winifred – Crory, Frederick James, III
McCarthy, Dorothy – Burrows, Robert N.
McCarthy, Rachel Ann – Bibbs, Michael Derek
McCormick, Lucy – Cook, Merle C.
McCrillis, Anna – Hunt, Howard C.
McDermott, Colleen M. – Nungesser, William L., Jr.
McDonald, Hilda B. – Burrows, Frank N.
McDonald, Kathryn Elizabeth – Trombley, Gerard Joseph
McGrath, Jane W. – Schoenburg, Peter, Jr.
McHugh, Christina – Michael, Kevin
McHugh, Mary E. – King, James A.
McIlvain, Katherine S. – Smith, David M.
McInnis, Annie – Mudgett, Frank L.
McKenzie, Jeanne – Smith, Harrison B.
McKinney, Charlene E. – Lally, Edward J., Jr.
McLendon, Grace E. – Johnston, Charles C.
McManus, Dorothy F. – Foley, James F.
McManus, Mary A. (Kinnie) – Back, Philip J.
McPherson, Myrtle G. – Parris, Leroy A.
Meader, Elizabeth – Brown, Clarence M.
Medrick, Susan L. – Quinn, Thomas B.
Melum, Deborah E. – McBee, Burrett E., Jr.

Mentiply, Margaret – Brown, George E.
Meredith, Jacqueline M. – McPhail, Peter W.
Merriman, Edibeth F. – Moskowitz, Jay I.
Merrow, Flora V. (McPherson) – Mason, Clinton C.
Messinger, Marion (Martin) – Tilton, Orrin H.
Metcalf, Daphne – Mowatt, Herman H.
Metcalf, Nancy L. (Lear) – Reed, Lawrence J.
Michael, Sandra – Ohman, John Frederick
Miksch, Deborah A. – Fogg, Joseph E.
Miller, Carrie Lynne – Brozovich, Shawn Daniel
Miner, Laura H. – Mudgett, Gary S.
Minor, Diane – Lane, Prescott Newitt
Mitchel, Arlene L. (Lee) – Anderson, Wallace W.
Mitchell, Maud L. – Elliott, Elmer
Monk, Daphne A. – Frentress, Richard M.
Monroe, Laura May (Greenleaf) – Heath, Harry Leon
Moody, Virginia E. – Atwood, Gerald W.
Mooney, Florence G. – Bryar, Fred E.
Moore, Charlotte J. – Welch, John W.
Morgan, Faith Dunning – Wallace, William Huston
Morin, Delima – Smith, Glenn
Morrison, Rita D. – Burrows, James M.
Morse, Lizzie (Bickford) – Chase, Bertrand R.
Morton, Donna Lee – Elliott, Michael Daniel
Morton, Jane G. – Finch, David T.
Morup, Inge – Olesen, Per Brix
Moulton, Edith M. – Dorr, Carl S.
Moulton, Priscilla E. (Endicott) – Potter, Brooks
Moulton, Sadie – Wallace, Marcellus
Mudgett, Alice A. – Taylor, Sumner E.
Mudgett, Bessie E. – Sumner, Roland E.
Mudgett, Carrie E. – Kenney, Marshall J.
Mudgett, Clara M. – Smith, Willis H.
Mudgett, Etta M. – Kenney, Arthur R.
Mudgett, Faye V. – Norcross, Charlwes D.

Mudgett, Flora E. – Libby, Rufus A.
Mudgett, Jayne – Fletcher, Robert D.
Mudgett, Jayne – Noble, Jeffrey A.
Mudgett, Lilla M. – Tivey, Edward F.
Mudgett, Lillian F. – Bigelow, Walter R.
Mudgett, Myrtle V. (Fannel) – Clark, Nathan H.
Mudgett, Viola E. – Avery, Guy L.
Munroe, Gladys – Clark, Sumner B.
Murray, Susan C. L. – Stokes, Peter W.
Myer, Anna S. – Robinson, Gerald W.
Myers, Suzita Cecil – Schneider, James Gordon
Myshrall, Deborah Anne – Parker, Steven J.

Nadeau, Regina A. – Burns, David P.
Nassif, Joan M. – Elliott, Anthony C.
Nedeau, Deanne Lee – Lear, Benjamin Hasting
Nellenback, Ann M. – Nelson, James E.
Nelson, Carol J. – Sweet, Gary L.
Nelson, Charlotte H. – Drouin, Paul A.
Nelson, Cynthia M. – Grant, Ross A.
Nelson, Edna B. – Plummer, James H.
Nelson, Evelyn H. – Smith, Harry H.
Nelson, Helen F. – Bryant, Stewart R.
Nelson, Marjorie L. – Burrows, Lester D., Jr.
Nelson, Marjorie L. – Frye, Michael B.
Nelson, Marjorie Lee – Bean, Stephen W.
Nelson, Mary L. – Leroux, Larry S.
Nelson, Patricia A. – Fleming, Kevin F.
Newell, Marguerite E. – Franklyn, Percival M.
Nichols, Martha – Berg, Gunnar
Nichols, Mary A. – Garland, Dexter B.
Nichols, Mary C. (Coolidge) – Pitkin, Donald S.
Nickerson, Emily E. – Knox, Charles E.
Nickerson, Heidi A. – Davis, Craig A.
Nicolay, Megan M. – Janka, Luke E.

Nicoli, Jane E. – Michalski, David A.
Niles, Edyth S. – Weed, F. Herbert
Niles, Myrna E. – Flanagan, Charles S.
Nixon, Elizabeth D. – Plummer, Wilfred C.
Nixon, Jeanette – Cote, Edward Elmer
Noorlind, Katrin C. – Rouner, Jonathan K.
Nudd, Caroline – Cass, Earle
Nudd, Edna M. – Thompson, Lester W.
Nudd, Elizabeth Delia – Hayford, Ernest Arthur
Nudd, Elvira Amelia – Pickering, Ellsworth E.
Nudd, Evalena L. – Ames, Charles E.
Nudd, Geraldine S. – Whiting, Raymond V.
Nudd, Josephine M. – Ayers, Charles M.
Nudd, Rachel B. – Dow, Lawrence R.
Nutter, Effie M. (Abbott) – Hodge, Norman F.

O'Brien, Christina Wells – Angevine, Alain Georges
O'Brien, Ellen F. (Farnham) – Parker, James W. S.
O'Brien, Mabel (Tappan) – Benton, Perrin
O'Donnell, Catherine – McDonough, Thomas
Oliver, Linda E. – Junicke, Dale
Orth, Judith A. – Wright, Robert K.
Osberg, Martha L. – Clark, Peter G.
Ottati, Theresa Marie – Cole, Michael Lewis

Page, Clara – Drake, Benjamin
Page, Edith F. – Wallace, Theodore R.
Page, Inez A. – Tappan, George H.
Page, Margaret R. – Elliott, Michael D.
Page, Sarah M. (Greenleaf) – Coombs, William P.
Palmer, Beatrice M. – Martell, Elziar
Palmer, Etta (Vittum) – Dow, Charles L.
Palmer, June E. – Lindley, William T.
Paquette, Colleen J. – Elliott, Michael D.
Parker, Addie F. (Brown) – Glines, David E.

Parker, Melissa J. – Thorndike, Townsend D.
Parris, Ethelyn May (Davis) – Wallace, Asahel Andrew
Parris, Margaret H. (Burrows) – Anderson, Richard D.
Patrick, Blanche E. – Burrows, Roger N.
Peakes, Ethel M. – Martin, Levi P.
Peaslee, Abbie F. – Hoag, Albert B.
Peaslee, Agnes L. – Ingalls, George H.
Peaslee, Brenda J. – Czado, Michael J.
Peaslee, Carolyn L. – Vittum, Carl S.
Peaslee, Charlotte M. (Avery) – Tourigny, Norman J.
Peaslee, Dora E. – Martin, Wilbur E.
Peaslee, Dorothy W. (Wing) – Brownlie, Albert C.
Peaslee, Helen – Forristall, William H.
Peaslee, Janice Aileen – Stokes, Reginald Edwin
Peaslee, Jean C. – Stockman, Philip A.
Peaslee, Mary Noble – Fisher, Gardner Warren
Peaslee, Sandra M. – Collins, Lee W.
Peaslee, Susan E. – Siegel, Jeffrey J.
Peaslee, Susan J. – Berking, Charles R.
Pelchat, Arline Germaine – Martel, Raymond James
Pelchat, Ellen M. – Cochran, Elwin J.
Pelizza, Susan A. – Carey, Richard A.
Penniman, Ethel A. – Silsby, Henry M.
Perkins, Ida – Wade, Frank
Perrault, Thelma M. (Pruitt) – Titilah, Andrew
Perry, Michelle – Palmer, Bruce A.
Perry, Rhona A. – Delgado, Robert D.
Perry, Sheila M. – Rowan, David K.
Petersen, Margaret Susan – Grant, Ned Gordon, Jr.
Pettengill, Maryjane – Warner, Frederick J.
Phelps, Heather Lynn – Hoag, Ronald Boynton, III
Phillips, Susanna B. – Downs, Barry J.
Pierce, Dianne E. – Gotshall, Abbott, Jr.
Pierce, Mary E. – Smith, Charles O.
Pierce, Sarah A. – Elliott, Lewis C.

Pignato, Marguerite E. (Smith) – Lawson, George E.
Pinkerton, Anne H. – Henson, Frank M.
Piper, Ethel M. (Kellam) – Thompson, Arthur G.
Pitman, Fannie M. – Watson, Daniel S.
Plume, Beatrice – Burrows, Chester J.
Plummer, Corinne M. – Gilman, Dennis W.
Plummer, Elizabeth N. (Nixon) – Anthony, David L.
Plummer, Ellen Elizabeth – Eldridge, Hazen A.
Plummer, Hattie M. – Wallace, Harry
Plummer, Jane E. – Taylor, William H.
Plummer, Janet E. – Cailey, Gloyd R.
Plummer, Rose (McBride) – Bryant, Walter C.
Plummer, Sally F. – Howe, David H.
Polic, Sanja G. – Chambers, Donald M.
Portanova, Jo-Ann – Warren, Samuel W.
Porter, Courtney M. – Stewart, Bret William
Porter, Marlene W. – Sorell, Ames D., Jr.
Posey, Jean (Southworth) – Gillis, John W.
Powers, Rosamond (Foss) – Ely, Kenyon Brockway
Pratt, June Roberts – Lester, Harold B.
Prentice, Lianne Damon – Moneypenny, Christopher R.
Prescott, Mabel T. – Wallace, Harry J.
Prestholdt, Jennifer Ann – Weed, Charles Ravenel
Priest, Ida M. – Hanson, Frank L.
Prince, Florentine E. (Cram) – Graves, Ross M.
Provencal, Rita Marie – Taylor, Harold Edwin
Pyle, Jennifer Mackay – Nye, Joseph Benjamin Harding

Quimby, Edith S. – Burt, Albert E.
Quimby, Jennifer Johnson – Finney, John Milton
Quimby, Lizabeth C. (Cook) – Lee, Ansel E.
Quimby, Maud A. – Bryar, Fred E.
Quimby, Maude C. – Corliss, Arthur E.
Quimby, Rosealie E. – Burrows, Luther J.
Quimby, Sarah P. – Burleigh, Clarence B.

Racine, Darlene Elliott – Burrows, Jon Lester
Randlett, Patricia A. – Burrows, Chester J., Jr.
Raymond, Elizabeth W. – Hanington, Herbert, Jr.
Read, Elizabeth Randall – Dumas, Raymond Leo
Read, Patricia (Ruel) – Mitchell, John Carroll
Reed, Giuliana V. M. – Keller, Jeremy
Reed, Nancy L. – Meredith, Irving, Jr.
Rice, Kiki Audrey – Gray, Charles Henry
Richard, Rachel D. – Schmidt, Robert L.
Richards, Elizabeth S. (Sargent) – Vazifdar, Jehangir
Richardson, Donna J. – Sturgeon, Fred J.
Richardson, Helen Louise (Olden) – Brown, Orin Franklin
Richardson, Juliane Eleanor – Dolan, Robert Owen
Richmond, Paula N. – Adriance, Edwin L.
Riel, Stacey Lyn – Gonzalez, John Joseph
Risteen, Meghan E. – Szymujko, Jeffery A.
Robbins, Melanie Barbara – Collins, Timothy John
Roberts, Dorothy A. – Peaslee, Charles H.
Robinson, Dorothy E. – Peaslee, Roscoe D.
Robinson, Karen A. – Streeter, Bradley E.
Robinson, Madeline M. – Bryant, John W.
Robinson, Marion E. – Watson, Arthur J.
Robinson, Sylvia L. – Morton, Lee S.
Robinson, Sylvia L. – Uehling, James
Rockwood, Rose E. – McKissick, Edward
Roebarge, Evelyn – Elliott, Harold
Rogers, Ann Tutwiler – Carman, John Braisted
Rogers, Jean Marie – Taylor, William H.
Rollins, Virginia B. (Davis) – Emerson, Denley W.
Rosenthal, Dena R. – Bortman, David C.
Rowan, Linda M. – Blackey, Earl R.
Rozelle, Anne Boyer – Orton, Wayne Liddle
Rozelle, Page A. – Bucher, R. Lawrence
Ruel, Patricia Anne – Read, Kirke Packard

Rumsza, Barbara A. – Siegel, Andrew F.
Rush, Margaret Rose – Hanna, William Michael
Russell, Evelyn S. – Elliott, Edward A.
Ryer, Jeanne – Wilcox, Philip N.

Sanborn, Lydia D. (Dunning) – Fellows, Enoch Q.
Sargent, Eva M. – Chick, Frank O.
Sarni, Joan Josephine – Mudgett, Eugene R.
Satter, Allison Chauncey – Hill, Geoff Alan
Saucier, Ginette – Harding, Kevin D.
Sawin, Carolyn P. – Wilson, Timothy C.
Sawyer, M. Elisabeth – Blanchard, Charles E.
Sceggell, Belle (Gilman) – Tappan, Lewis R.
Schultz, Robin Elizabeth – Purves, William Carroll
Scott, Fay P. – Picone, Stephen L.
Scriggins, Marion F. – Parker, Henry L.
Seeley, Pauline Eleanor – Campbell, Everett
Severance, Helen (Mills) – York, George W.
Severance, Lizzie M. – Bryant, Walter C.
Severance, Lizzie S. – Harte, Harrison N.
Shaw, Melissa M. – Devens, Richard, IV
Shaw, Ruth – Mudgett, Francis C.
Shepard, Josephine L. – Faux, James H.
Shephard, Emily Elaine – St. John, George Oliver
Sherman, Julia M. – Smith, Frank M.
Silcox, Joanne C. (Campbell) – Silcox, Frederick L.
Simons, Alice R. (Knowlton) – Brown, Arthur B.
Sims, Sindee A. – Imbach, Theodore A.
Singer, Patricia W. – Sargent, Steven K.
Sirard, Melina Mary (LaPlante) – Tefft, Henry Adelbert
Skinner, Christine E. – Taylor, William H.
Skinner, Elizabeth B. (Burrage) – White, Walter Leroy
Skinner, Grace E. – Burrows, Fred N.
Skinner, Olive L. – Frye, Freeman N.
Skinner, Sarah E. – Bundy, Oscar E.

Sloberg, Ebba O. – Garland, Lewis D.
Slothower, Patricia L. – Miner, Timothy A.
Smith, Eva Estella – Morgan, Charles H.
Smith, Eva M. – Bryant, Edward J.
Smith, G. Ella – Blanchard, Charles O.
Smith, H. Anna – Smith, J. Alphonso
Smith, Hattie (Foss) – Burrows, John G.
Smith, Isabel E. – Smith, Julius H.
Smith, Kristin A. – Heath, Darwin W., Jr.
Smith, Lillian H. – Abbott, Herbert E.
Smith, Lucy M. – Weed, John J.
Smith, Maevina L. (Locke) – Blumberg, Lawrence J.
Smith, Mary Elizabeth – Cook, John Otis
Smith, Maud B. – Moulton, Arthur P.
Smith, Pearl E. – Smith, Kenneth A.
Smith, Sally A. – Chase, David K.
Snow, Nellie M. – Brown, Charles F.
Spaulding, Mary Vivian (Noble) – Peaslee, David W.
Speckman, Violet D. (Eldridge) – Martel, Morton C.
Sprengling, Arlene – Farley, Michael Philip
Sprengling, Uni A. – Thomas, Alan R.
Stacy, Lorraine Priscilla – Atwood, Hubert Loring
Stanton, Mary – Boutwell, Henry W.
Staples, Tara M. – Fullerton, Dwayne J.
Stein, Janice D. – Engle, Robert F. C.
Steiner, Lynn M. – Mills, Andrew S.
Stewart, Allison B. – Plasencia, Dale A.
Stocker, Mabel C. (Henderson) – Tewksbury, W. Wesley
Stokes, Irma – Sturgeon, Wilfred
Stokes, Karen J. – Bennett, Kenneth J.
Stokes, Ruth Whitson – Stokes, Joseph, III
Stone, Rita M. (Jones) – Willand, Howard A.
Strayer, Frances D. – Benton, Richard L., Jr.
Stuntz, Kathryn Andrea – Carr, Larry Robert
Sturgeon, Dorothy Mae – Davis, Larry Brian

Sturgeon, Eva (Brezina) – Medvecky, John
Sturgeon, Rita M. – Holopainen, Robert J.
Sturgess, Jennie E. – Mudgett, Jessie A.
Sturgis, Luella M. – Plummer, Clarence R.
Swan, Bonita M. – Downs, Clifford F., Jr.
Swan, Colleen M. – Welch, Robert R.
Swan, Kimberly – Gallagher, Michael J.
Swan, Regina Lynn – Norcross, Milton Arthur
Swanson, Janet F. (Fields) – Wright, Jonathan
Switzer, Gretchen C. – Hucks, William Randall

Tappan, Amy – Palmer, Herbert A.
Tappan, Annie W. – White, Fred L.
Tappan, Lena M. – Drew, William
Tappan, Lizzie – Webster, Frank H.
Tasker, Georgia – Heard, Howard B.
Tatelbaum, Linda – Winer, Kalman A.
Taylor, Carrie – Britton, Marry
Taylor, Charlotte E. – Clemons, Frederick A.
Taylor, Christine E. (Skinner) – Merryfield, Clifford
Taylor, Eileen – Rodgers, Morton L.
Taylor, Eldora F. – Burrows, Frank N.
Taylor, Elizabeth J. – Lively, David Glenn
Taylor, Elva Elaine – Mullen, Ralph, Jr.
Taylor, Evelyn F. – Mudgett, Irving E.
Taylor, Jean M. (Rogers) – McCormack, George E.
Taylor, Linda – McCormack, George E.
Taylor, Marion M. – Hutchins, Clarence E.
Taylor, Patti-Ann – Reader, Richard Alan
Thomas, Lulu (Tate) – Chapman, Leonard B.
Thompson, Arlene L. – Pearson, Herman W.
Thompson, Florence (Lambert) – Fogg, Edwin E.
Thompson, Lena – Nelson, William T.
Thompson, Nettie (Helms) – Tibbetts, Henry T.
Thornton, Marjorie – Corliss, Louis F.

Tibbetts, Constance – Hoag, William G.
Tibbetts, Laura J. – Hill, Carlton M.
Tibbetts, Lydia E. – Irving, George L.
Tibbetts, Mildred M. – Blanchard, Harry
Tilton, Ann Susan – Brown, Randolph
Tilton, Apphia – Merrill, William A.
Tilton, Carrie M. – Moulton, Isaac A.
Tilton, Helen S. – Felker, Onestus A.
Tilton, Maude L. – Smith, Leon A.
Tilton, Winifred – Richardson, F. P.
Tivey, Dorothy Elizabeth – Cook, Lawrence Merle
Townsend, Clara H. (Jose) – Fogg, Stephen
Townsley, Gladys Mae – Burrows, Luther James
Tracy, Lisa M. – Morgan, Richard R.
Tracy, Sally Anne – Porter, David E.
Trask, Dora E. – Peaslee, David J.
Tudor, Kathryn A. – Elliott, Michael D.

Ufhiel, Elizabeth A. (Warnick) – Treen, Ira M., Jr.
Uhle, Sandra D. – Sawin, Edward A., Jr.
Ulitz, Lauren A. – Frase, Kimberly K.
Ulrich, Marilyn (Clements) – Reed, Kirke Packard
Unger, Amanda Kathryne – Leahy, Jeffrey Vawter

Vachon, Jean P. (Maheux) – Ames, William H.
Valentine, Anne dePeyster – Kelley, Eric W.
Van Horn, Katherine Lucille – Hallett, George Robert
Venott, Annie – Fadden, Charles B.
Villadolid, Christina A. – Fleischmann, Andrew H.
Vinal, Lula Elizabeth (Hudson) – Elliott, Elmer
Virtue, Effie S. – Gale, Albert
Vittum, Ada B. – Hawes, Caspar S.
Vittum, Bernice A. (Adams) – Michael, Monroe
Vittum, Cora Joe – Condit, Merrell Edwin
Vittum, Etta A. – Palmer, James O.

Vittum, Ina – Felch, Leverett C.
Vittum, Jennie – Davey, George H.
Vittum, Lottie M. – Weed, Cleveland
Vittum, Myrtie – Goodwin, Clifton G.
Vittum, Pauline – Ambrose, David G.

Wade, Jennie – Gale, Amos
Wade, Lizzie A. – Blackey, Elijah S.
Wahlsler, Kelley Jo – Wescott, Thomas Bond
Wakefield, Abbie – Tappan, Fred
Walker, Lisamarie – Bennett, Kenneth James
Wallace, Agnes – Taylor, Walter L.
Wallace, Charlotte M. (McCauley) – Davis, Charles J.
Wallace, Dolly C. – Beede, George E.
Wallace, Ethel Marie – Carter, James Winslow
Wallace, Florence – Hutchins, Earl U.
Wallace, Frances M. – McCormack, George C.
Wallace, Gladys E. – Severance, Bishop C.
Wallace, Grace E. – Angier, Ryvers F.
Wallace, Irva B. – Marden, Melvin F.
Wallace, Judith Mary – Batchelder, Lewis Hartwell
Wallace, Minerva B. – Willoughby, Kyle E.
Wallace, V. Margie – Nudd, Walter E.
Walsh, Shannon N. – Plimmer, Robert S.
Walters, Thelma M. – Mudgett, Robert E.
Ward, Florence B. – Duprey, Harry M.
Ward, Maria L. – Watson, John C.
Ward, Violet M. D. – Clark, Sumner B.
Watson, Alice J. – Ryder, Harris B.
Watson, Lena M. – Marshall, Edward H.
Watson, Margaret P. – Dee, David M.
Watson, Nellie C. – Chase, William L.
Watson, Ursala A. – Quimby, Sherman
Watts, Elaine M. – Richardson, Verne L.
Watts, Sandra F. (Flesher) – Halgedahl, Frederick W.

Webster, Addie L. – Carter, Almon E.
Webster, Alice M. – Bagley, Erastus M.
Webster, Betty V. – Bullard, H. Benjamin, IV
Webster, Betty V. – Bullard, Howard B., IV
Webster, Florence – Hoyt, Charles B.
Webster, Marcella Ruth – Richardson, Glen Colin
Weed, Angelina – Meredith, Clement O.
Weed, Anne A. – Richardson, Lawrence E.
Weed, Elizabeth Hoag – Breed, Richard Allen
Weed, Helen – Martin, Louville K.
Weed, Hortense – Taylor, Ralph W.
Weil, Suzanne D. – Cooley, John Hay, Jr.
Weld, Myra T. (Tappan) – Cook, Curtis E.
West, Addie Y. – Perkins, George E.
West, Victoria – Lee, William B., III
Westneat, Nancy L. – Leinwund, Ira Jay
Whedon, Minnie E. – Hanson, William H.
Wheeler, Jean Abbie – Ames, Carl Wilson
White, Georgia A. – Carlson, Walter R., Jr.
White, Karen Elaine – Crory, David P.
White, Martha G. – Deming, Roger
White, V. Claire – Merryfield, Harold
Whitehouse, Maude E. – Tibbetts, E. Haven
Whitehouse, S. Pernie – Vittum, Arthur M.
Whiting, Alice R. – Pierce, Maurice A.
Whiting, Eunice – Brown, Carroll G.
Whiting, Nellie E. – Graves, Clarence E.
Whitney, Ruth J. – Lombardi, Gary A.
Whitney, Susan L. – Pirani, Karim
Wiggin, Nancy A. (Freeto) – Leach, David C.
Wiggins, Wendy Diane – Dorrich, Klaus Dieter
Wilbur, Jo-Anne (Ross) – Alcock, Frederick Paul
Wiley, Susan E. – Vazzano, Anthony J.
Wilkie, Edwina P. (Pennell) – Goodwin, Wendell O.
Wilkins, Laura M. – Bryant, John W., Jr.

Willey, Carrie E. – Smith, Lewis E.
Williams, Mabel E. – Ambrose, Jesse L.
Willoughby, Beatrice – Burrows, Donald H.
Willoughby, Harriet E. – Merriman, Roger B., III
Wilmarth, Jamie M. – Jacks, Duncan A.
Wilson, Kimberly B. – Mohan, Patrick J.
Wilson, Mary Jane – Hoag, Albert Buffum
Winchester, Ann M. – Moore, Courtenay W.
Wing, Dorothy P. – Demick, William E.
Wing, Marion – Elliott, Edwin Lewis
Wolf, Joy V. – Stein, Stanley N.
Wood, Celia A. – Petherbridge, William C.
Wood, Eleanor Densmore – Whitman, John Pratt
Wood, Vivian – Endicott, George
Woodbury, Marjorie – Wheeler, Robert R.
Woodhead, Jessie E. – Eastman, Fred, Jr.
Worthen, Christina – Rowell, Frank D.
Wortman, Evelyn Mae (Cook) – Wallace, Asahel Andrew
Wright, Pamela G. – Read, Theodore O., Jr.

Yeaton, Ella – Mann, Charles E.
Young, Isabelle Victoria – White, Walter Clark

Zuponcic, Bonnie L. – Beckman, Thomas H.

Deaths

ABBOTT,

Frances A., d. 4/21/1934 at 85/7/5; at home; widow; b. Ossipee; Lewis W. Nute (Wolfeboro) and Harriet Hanson (Ossipee)

Lutie B., d. 12/26/1895 at 15/9 in Sandwich; housewife; single; b. Sandwich; R. F. Abbott (Tamworth) and Abbie Tappan (Sandwich)

Lyman, d. 2/20/1898 at 88/10 in Sandwich; mason; married; b. Candia; Joseph Abbott

R. Freeman, d. 11/16/1927 at 82/0/28; farmer; married; b. Sandwich; Lyman Abbott (Candia) and Luro Rowe (Sandwich)

Shuah, d. 10/9/1892 at 79 in Sandwich; housewife; married; b. Sandwich; Daniel Rowe and Jane Bean

ADAMS,

Aquila, d. 10/21/1917 at 85/4/4; retired; widower; b. S. Boston, MA; Isaac Adams (Rochester) and ----- Rayne

Durward, d. 8/8/1923 at 78; lawyer; married; b. Boston, MA; Isaac Adams and Anna Russell (Boston, MA)

Ellen N., d. 10/24/1962 at 81 in Laconia; widow; b. County Galway, Ireland; Thomas Keane and Mary Collins

John R., d. 12/25/1924 at 48/1/5; mechanic; married; b. Boston, MA; Aquila Adams (S. Boston, MA) and Louisa Hayes Emery (Limerick, ME)

Louisa H., d. 7/27/1916 at 77/2/16; housewife; married; b. Limerick, ME; Samuel Emery (ME) and Maria Hayes (ME)

ADRIANCE,

Paula N., d. 11/10/2007 in Dover; Julian Richmond and Edna Apteker

AINGER,

Cyrus E., d. 1/24/1939 at 87/4/15; laborer; widower; b. Braintree, MA; Joseph Ainger (MA)

Grace Edna, d. 10/10/1955 at 68 in Laconia; married; b. Sandwich; Eugene Wallace and Mary E. Estes

Pliny Archie, d. 7/19/1951 at 79 in Laconia; single; b. Sandwich; Edson C. Ainger and Emma Heddle

Ryvers F., d. 3/16/1971 at 87 in Sandwich; widower; b. NH; Cyrus Ainger and Emma Hiddle

ALCOCK,

George A., Jr., d. 5/17/2007 in Stuart, FL; George Alcock and Isabel Manning

AMBROSE,

Celia N., d. 9/20/1914 at 22/6/23; single; b. Sandwich; Langdon C. Ambrose (Sandwich) and Hattie E. Tilton (Sandwich)

Ellen P., d. 2/27/1903 at 57/9/25 in Sandwich; housewife; married; b. Sandwich; Elden McGaffey (Sandwich) and Mehitable Neally (Sandwich)

Hattie E., d. 12/23/1922 at 59/8/13; at home; married; b. Sandwich; David Tilton (Sandwich) and Susan W. Hill (Sanford, ME)

Jesse L., d. 6/14/1969 at 76 in Laconia; widower; b. NH; Langdon Ambrose and Hattie Tilton

Langdon C., d. 7/19/1944 at 88/6/23 in Sandwich; farmer; widower; b. Sandwich; Oliver L. Ambrose (Sandwich) and Mary Jane Cotton (Moultonboro)

Langdon Jesse, d. 12/19/1988 in Sandwich; Jesse Ambrose and Mable Williams

Mabel W., d. 6/17/1946 at 53/11/28 in Laconia; housewife; married; b. Knoxville, TN; Frederick Williams (Utica, NY) and Agnes Brooker (Bloomingdale, TN)

Oliver C., d. 2/24/1907 at 80/4/11; farmer; widower; b. Sandwich; Jesse Ambrose (Sandwich) and Sarah Lee (Moultonboro)

AMES,
son, d. 5/6/1925 at 0/0/0; b. Sandwich; Harold Ames (Brockton, MA) and Charlotte Hoag (Sandwich)
Barbara Charlotte, d. 9/8/1998 in Meredith; b. Lynn, MA; Raymond Muise and Margaret Golden

ANDERSON,
Constance B., d. 1/29/1975 at 74 in Wolfeboro; housewife; married; b. MA; Henry Boyer and Mabel Conant
Richard D., d. 5/20/1974 at 44 in Laconia; carpenter; married; b. MA; Frank Anderson and Lena Page
Wallace W., d. 8/30/1978 at 78 in Wolfeboro; clergyman; married; b. NJ; Alfred W. Anderson and Edna Soule

ANGIER,
Emma J., d. 3/27/1933 at 84/0/27; housewife; married; b. Laconia; William Haddle (Scotland) and Louisa Hadley (Sandwich)

ARTHMANN,
Kathryn Esther, d. 2/24/1998 in Wolfeboro; b. Mt. Pleasant, IA; Hiram Gilbert and Jennie Cook

ATKINS,
Aria, d. 9/22/1936 at 77/4/25; single; b. Sandwich; Henry Atkins and Lucy Coffin
Lucy, d. 10/24/1903 at 85/5/11 in Sandwich; housewife; widow; b. Sandwich; John Cofran (Henniker) and Rhoda Hoyt (Sandwich)
Rhoda E., d. 4/22/1925 at 73/11/22; housekeeper; single; b. Sandwich; Henry Atkins (Claremont) and Lucy Coffren (Sandwich)

ATWOOD,

son, d. 6/5/1913 at 0/0/1; b. Sandwich; W. S. Gilman (Sandwich) and Alta J. Atwood (Sandwich)

Agusta A., d. 8/22/1908 at 69/2/12; farmer; married; b. Sandwich; Joseph J. Batchelder (Raymond) and Arvilla Webster (Sandwich)

Albert C., d. 11/27/1917 at 73/6/6; farmer; married; b. Sandwich; Ira Atwood (Sandwich) and Eliza Godfrey (ME)

Annie, d. 11/4/1923 at 64/6/4; at home; married; b. Sandwich; Alpheus Hall (Sandwich) and Drusilla Avery (Campton)

Charles H., d. 10/17/1910 at 67/8/0; blacksmith; married; b. Sandwich; Harrison Atwood and Sarepa Hatch (Tamworth)

Daniel D., d. 8/14/1936 at 86/10/22; retired; widower; b. Sandwich; Harrison Atwood (Sandwich) and Sarepia Hatch (Sandwich)

Edwin J., d. 6/6/1941 at 84/11/27; laborer; single; b. Sandwich; John G. Atwood (Sandwich) and Sarah J. Webster (Sandwich)

Eliza A., d. 3/6/1906 at 93/4/25; housewife; widow; b. Rye Beach; John Godfrey

Eliza B., d. 12/23/1913 at 69/4/17; housewife; widow; b. Tamworth; L. D. Stevenson (Tamworth) and Lucy B. Miers (Essex, MA)

Emily E., d. 4/24/1929 at 58/2/5; at home; married; b. Sandwich; James Burrows (ME) and Sophia Wallace (Sandwich)

Emma L., d. 4/8/1902 at 56/7/8 in Sandwich; housewife; married; b. Canada; Stephen Place (Scotland) and Sarah Partlow (England)

Ethel E., d. 2/19/1959 at 85 in Methuen, MA; widow; b. Marlboro, MA; Edward Cawthorne and Georgiana Crosby

Frank L., d. 3/12/1914 at 51/5/14; foreman; married; b. Sandwich; Harrison Atwood (Gray, ME) and Augusta A. Batchelder (Sandwich)

Gerald W., d. 1/19/1981 in Laconia; Frank Atwood and Florence Brown

Harrison, d. 3/26/1897 at 82/0/25 in Sandwich; farmer; married; b. Sandwich; Philip Atwood (Sandwich) and ----- Colby (Sandwich)

Harry A., d. 2/21/1924 at 56/7/27; blacksmith; married; b. Sandwich; Albert C. Atwood (Sandwich) and Janette Mason (Sandwich)

Ira, d. 10/18/1895 at 82/6/19 in Sandwich; farmer; married; b. Sandwich; Philip Atwood (Sandwich) and Elizabeth Dustin (Sandwich)

John, d. 7/10/1912 at --; farmer; widower; b. Sandwich; Philip Atwood (Gray, ME) and A. Batchelder (Sandwich)

John Frank, d. 6/16/1939 at 75/3/6; plummer; widower; b. Sandwich; John G. Atwood (Sandwich) and Sarah Webster (Sandwich_

John G., d. 9/6/1909 at 72/5/21; blacksmith; married; b. Sandwich; Ira Atwood (Sandwich) and Eliza A. Godfrey (Rye)

M. J., d. 11/18/1888 at 45/10; married; b. Sandwich; Nathan Mason (Sandwich) and Charlotte ----- (Sandwich)

Martha, d. 5/13/1911 at 75; housekeeper; widow; b. Sandwich

Martha G., d. 3/1/1892 at 78/8 in Sandwich; housewife; widow; b. Tamworth; Chase Wedgewood (Chichester) and Martha Mitchell (Lewiston)

Myra L., d. 10/30/1924 at 66/3/22; housewife; married; b. Somersworth; John T. Lothrop (Somersworth) and Lydia Hanson (Somersworth)

Nellie G., d. 10/20/1936 at 78/5/22; housewife; widow; b. Lynn, MA; Timothy Stackpole (Lynn, MA) and Elizabeth Hurd (Lynn, MA)

Sarah J., d. 3/10/1900 at 66/11/8 in Sandwich; housewife; married; b. Sandwich; Nehemiah Webster (VT) and Betsy Bennett (Sandwich)

Sarepta, d. 1/10/1902 at 83/7/18 in Sandwich; housewife; widow; b. Sandwich; David Hatch (Tamworth) and Susan Colbern (ME)

Walter G., d. 9/24/1941 at 65/11/12; carpenter; married; b. Sandwich; Charles Atwood (Tamworth) and Eliza Stevenson (Tamworth)

AUGER,
Maurice J. C., d. 6/29/2006 in Ctr. Sandwich; Charles Auger and Marie Menard

AVERY,
son, d. 1/12/1925 at 0/0/0; b. Sandwich; Guy Avery (Rumney) and Viola Mudgett (Sandwich)
Jennie B., d. 11/14/1952 at 59 in New York, NY; married; b. NS; Henry Manning and Ruth Carter
Lauretta R., d. 2/2/1920 at 0/3/2; b. Sandwich; Arthur W. Avery (Rumney) and Jennie B. Manning (Halifax, NS)
Nellie B., d. 12/30/1947 at 70/1/10 in Ctr. Sandwich; married; b. Sandwich; Arven Blanchard (Hopkinton) and Helen Creighton (Sandwich)
Walter H., d. 1/30/1957 at 79 in Sandwich; widower; b. Taunton, MA; William Avery
Willis K., d. 10/16/1918 at 0/7/3; b. Sandwich; Arthur W. Avery (Rumney) and Jennie B. Manning (NS)

BABB,
Fred W., d. 5/8/1954 at 77 in Sandwich; divorced; b. Blanford, MA; Mordica Babb and Harriett Church

BACON,
Abagail, d. 2/17/1889 at 86/11/5; housewife; widow; b. Sandwich; ----- Plumer and Anna Hoag

BAER,
Florida E., d. 9/17/1986 in Wolfeboro; Clarence Wyble and Sarah Grey

Raymond J., d. 11/13/1987 in Conway; Raymond Baer and Maria Unterweger

BAGLEY,
Martha A., d. 2/21/1890 at 41/9/5 in Sandwich; housewife; widow; b. Sandwich; David Mudgett (Sandwich) and Catherine Philbrook (Rye)

BAILEY,
Walter L., d. 3/28/1978 at 84 in Ossipee; minister; married; b. OR; John Bailey and Ruth Lovell
Winona R., d. 1/20/1992 in Wolfeboro; John W. Platt and Mary M. Milliron

BALCH,
Henry G., d. 3/22/1975 at 73 in Sandwich; transportation R.R.; married; b. MA; Franklin G. Balch and Lucy R. Bowditch
Mary B., d. 12/24/2002 in Laconia; John P. Benson and Sarah B. Whitman

BANCROFT,
Charlotte, d. 2/7/1899 at 69 in Sandwich; housewife; widow; b. Londonderry; Joseph Eaton (Londonderry) and Abigail Chase (Haverhill, MA)

BARKER,
Cora Marston, d. 9/17/1951 at 71 in Laconia; single; b. NY; Julia Marston
Julia E., d. 11/11/1897 at 50/2/9 in Sandwich; housewife; married; b. Sandwich; Ira Marston (Tamworth) and Sarah B. Webster (Sandwich)

BARNES,
Florence M., d. 10/1/1971 at 70 in Laconia; widow; b. NH; Charles Whiting and Jennie Wade

Fred, d. 10/25/1944 at 62/0/6 in Sandwich; farmer; married; b. Tamworth; Samuel Barnes and Emma Bean

BARNEY,
Marion, d. 6/10/1968 at 85 in Sandwich; married; b. MN; Oscar C Green and Alice Huff
William P., d. 3/17/1970 at 75 in Sandwich; widower; b. GA; Charles Gorham Barney and Frances Pope

BASKER,
Daniel, d. 12/3/1920 at 25/0/1; lumberman; Daniel Basker and Mary A. Fraser

BATCHELDER,
Alva H., d. 2/16/1937 at 88/10; farmer; widower; b. Sandwich; Joseph Batchelder (Raymond) and Arcella Webster (Sandwich)
J. J., d. 7/28/1899 at 89 in Sandwich; laborer; widower; b. Raymond; B. Batchelder and ----- Brown
L. J., d. 12/9/1921 at 88/8/20; retired; widow; b. Strafford; Joseph Roberts and Lydia Goss
Lydia, d. 3/9/1919 at 75/10/8; housewife; married; b. Sandwich; Tyler Rogers (Moultonboro) and Sarah Swain (Strafford)
Mrs. Joseph, d. 12/9/1887 at 69; married; b. Sandwich; Nehemiah Webster (VT) and A. Fogg (Sandwich)
R. S., d. 6/12/1915 at 68/9/7; farmer; married; b. Sandwich; George Batchelder (Raymond) and Abigail Tilton (Sandwich)
Robert H., d. 9/25/2004 in Laconia; Henry S. Batchelder and Nellie Hughes

BATES,
Frances G., d. 11/25/2005 in Sandwich; James Rendall and Frances Strong

Helen B., d. 12/22/1995 in Sandwich; b. New London, CT; Frederick Hermes and Katherine Brunke

Robert E., d. 4/3/2000 in Wolfeboro; Rufus Bates and Edna Allen

Wilhelmina J., d. 10/5/1995 in Laconia; b. Netherlands; Gerard Vandeene and Jacoba Dehaas

BEACH,

Edith K., d. 2/7/1936 at 79/7/17; at home; widow; b. Sunderville, VT; Patrick Kelley and Mary O. Grout

Florence E., d. 12/28/1992 in Laconia; Delbert Hudson and Eva M. Keyes

Watson E., d. 3/10/1977 at 77 in Laconia; woodsman, farmer; married; b. NH; John J. Beach and Edith M. Kelley

BEAN,

Abbie F., d. 1/15/1911 at 76/8/26; housekeeper; single; b. Sandwich; Gilman Bean (Sandwich) and Rebecca Avery (Ellsworth)

Celinda M., d. 1/14/1905 at 86/9/28; housekeeper; widow; b. Dunbarton; John Miller and Margaret McCauley

Clara Ann, d. 6/6/1938 at 86/5/24; housekeeper; widow; b. Sandwich; Stephen Vittum (Sandwich) and Ruth Tappan (Sandwich)

Edith May, d. 11/17/1890 at 11/5/5 in Sandwich; b. Sandwich; Lorenzo Bean (Sandwich) and Clara A. Vittum (Sandwich)

Ernest Warren, d. 5/3/1990 in Albany; Eddie W. Bean and Eva Hatch

G. Clarke, d. 9/6/1987 in Hanover; George Tinney Bean and Elizabeth Clarke

Lorenzo D., d. 4/17/1918 at 74/9/2; farmer; married; b. Sandwich; Nicholas M. Bean (Sandwich) and Celinda M. Miller (Dunbarton)

Mary, d. 8/5/1896 at 76/6 in Sandwich; housewife; widow; b. Berwick, ME

Nicholas M., d. 3/31/1899 at 80/10/12 in Sandwich; farmer; married; b. Sandwich; Phillip Bean (Sandwich) and Betsy Moulton (Sandwich)

BEANE,
Arthur, Jr., d. 12/16/1972 at 59 in Ctr. Sandwich; teacher; married; b. MA; Arthur Beane, Sr. and Ruth Richards
Richards, d. 8/2/1983 in Rutland, VT

BEATON,
John, d. 4/10/1912 at 43/10; salesman; single; b. Scotland

BEATTIE,
Ernest R., d. 12/11/2006 in Laconia; Ralph Beattie and Ethel Richardson
Ethel W., d. 11/25/1990 in Meredith; George H. Richardson and Addie M. Wheeler

BECKMAN,
Harry, d. 9/16/1981 in Sandwich; Julius Beckman and Florence Stubee
Martha Jane, d. 10/2/2006 in Philadelphia, PA; William Smith and Helen Humphrey

BEDARD,
Maria G., d. 5/29/1930 at 0/2/6; b. Laconia; Ferdinand Bedard (Lyndonville, VT) and Frances Webster (Sandwich)

BEEDE,
Aaron, d. 12/5/1899 at 79/11/22 in Sandwich; farmer; married; b. Sandwich; Elisha Beede (Sandwich) and Sally Flanders (Fremont)
Abbie B., d. 3/18/1901 at 53/10/15 in Sandwich; housekeeper; single; b. Sandwich; Parker Beede (Sandwich) and Achsah Bradbury (Buxton, ME)

Abbie E. R., d. 10/14/1930 at 90/11/13; widow; b. Dover; Jeremiah Roberts (Dover) and Hannah J. Beede (Dover)

Abbie M., d. 7/16/1893 at 75/4/16 in Sandwich; Aaron Beede and Polly Burleigh

Abigail, d. 4/2/1900 at 83/0/2 in Sandwich; single; b. Sandwich; Jonathan Beede

Amy R., d. 8/3/1943 at 80/7/20 in Boston, MA; single

Annie E., d. 2/1/1896 at 28/0/26 in Sandwich; housework; single; b. Sandwich; Aaron Beede (Sandwich) and Mary McGaffey (Sandwich)

Augusta A., d. 10/9/1915 at 76/5/17; housewife; married; b. Sanbornton; Timothy Sullivan (Ireland) and Betsy Chapman (Sanbornton)

Daniel G., d. 1/15/1894 at 79/6/5 in Sandwich; teacher; married; b. Sandwich; Thomas Beede (Sandwich) and Susana Rogers (Sandwich)

Ellen, d. 8/18/1916 at 74; single; b. Sandwich; Parker Beede (NH) and Oxie Bradbury (ME)

George, d. 2/12/1895 at 57/9/18 in Sandwich; farmer; married; b. Sandwich; Parker Beede (Sandwich) and Achsah Bradbury (Buxton, ME)

Harriett M., d. 4/12/1958 at 85 in Laconia; married; b. Sandwich; Daniel Foss

J. Edwin, d. 10/17/1915 at 77/1/8; farmer; widower; b. Sandwich; Josiah Beede (Sandwich) and Almira Paine (Center Harbor)

James H., d. 6/15/1969 at 93 in Wolfeboro; widower; b. NH; Edwin Beede and Augusta Sullivan

Mabel G., d. 2/24/1942 at 68/9/26 in Newton, MA; housewife; married; b. Worcester, MA; George E. Merrill (Bangor, ME) and Adelaide Reed (Cambridge, MA)

Parker, d. 2/10/1890 at 86/2/26 in Sandwich; farmer; widower; b. Sandwich; Elijah Beede and Anna Felch (Seabrook)

Ruth R., d. 2/24/1888 at 74/3/7; widow; b. Sandwich; Isaac Smith and Nancy Straw

Syntha Hodge, d. 12/1/1892 at 81/5/22 in Sandwich; housewife; widow; b. Sandwich; William Hodge (Deering, ME) and Joanna Hill (Deering, ME)

BENNETT,
Arthur R., d. 4/21/1958 at 84 in Ctr. Harbor; widower; b. Sandwich; Wyatt F. Bennett and Mary A. Hancock
Charles F., d. 9/23/1902 at 76/10 in Sandwich; farmer; b. Sandwich; John Bennett (Sandwich) and Lucinda Fogg (Sandwich)
Mary A., d. 11/14/1898 at 51/9/29 in Sandwich; housewife; married; b. Cornwall, England; William R. Hancock and Elizabeth M. -----
Robert, d. 10/6/1906 at 39/11/2; contractor; married; b. PEI; Robert Bennett (Birmingham, England) and Sarah E. Bennett (Birmingham, England)
Sally P., d. 3/4/1905 at 76/1/16; housekeeper; widow; Philip Atwood and Mary Elliott
Willie H., d. 6/13/1893 at 17/1/20 in Sandwich; b. Sandwich; Wyatt F. Bennett (Sandwich) and Mary A. Hancock (England)

BENZ,
Doris L., d. 4/13/1984 in MA
Edith Louise, d. 10/27/1956 at 89 in Laconia; widow; b. Oldham, England; Amos Foster and Mary Ann Jackson

BERRY,
Marion Josephine, d. 1/14/1997 in Meredith; b. Candia; Herbert Nickles and Etta Noble
Nahum J., d. 7/14/1927 at 64/8/28; farmer; married; b. Bridgewater, MA; Aaron Berry (ME) and Abigail Johnson (MA)
Robert Morgan, d. 8/15/1997 in Ctr. Sandwich; b. Farmington; Elverton C. Berry and Jesie L. Morgan

BICKFORD,

daughter, d. 11/10/1922 at 0/0/1; b. Sandwich; Fred A. Bickford (E. Haverhill) and Stella Crawford (N. Holderness)

Addie, d. 1/2/1894 at 31/3/2 in Sandwich; housewife; married; b. Sandwich; Wyatt Bennett (Sandwich) and Helen ----- (Sandwich)

Charles R., d. 6/1/1973 at 65 in Sandwich; carpenter; married; b. NH; Roy F. Bickford and Maybelle L. Brown

Elizabeth F., d. 1/9/1906 at 70/10/13; housewife; widow; b. Sandwich; Hugh Beede (Sandwich) and Mary Worthing

Fred Alberta, d. 2/17/1993 in Sandwich; b. Haverhill; Nathan Bickford and Abbie Avery

Freeman A., d. 1/21/1899 at 76/0/24 in Sandwich; pressman; widower; b. Dearborn, ME; Stephen Bickford (Dearborn, ME)

James H., d. 4/15/1888 at 85/4/15; farmer; widower; b. Dover; James Bickford and Rebecca -----

Linwood, d. 11/1/1918 at 15/2/4; single; b. Sandwich; George Bickford

Martha, d. 3/3/1891 at 83/5 in Sandwich; single; b. Durham

Noah M., d. 10/9/1907 at 65/9; farmer; married; b. Somersworth; J. B. Bickford (Somersworth) and S. Wentworth

Roy F., d. 1/31/1940 at 64/1; farmer; married; b. Meredith; Moses Bickford (Meredith) and Arieanna Bickford (Meredith)

Sarah, d. 8/16/1887 at 79/2/26; married; b. Milton; Joseph Richardson (Milton) and Lois Lee

Stella Crawford, d. 9/26/1988 in Ossipee; Henry Crawford and Emma McDonald

Vesta A., d. 10/26/1910 at 82/2/21; housewife; married; b. Ossipee; Robert Lord

Wyatt, d. 9/11/1914 at 69/7/27; b. Conway

BIGELOW,
Bernice L., d. 9/11/1906 at 0/2/6; b. Sandwich; Walter R. Bigelow (Sandwich) and Lilla Mudgett (Sandwich)
Lilla, d. 7/5/1906 at 18; housewife; married; b. Sandwich; Erastus Mudgett and Susan Tibbetts
Samuel, d. 6/17/1939 at 70/8/10; hot. man; divorced; b. Lyndon, VT; William Bigelow (Lyndon, VT) and Emma Place (Burlington, VT)
William B., d. 8/7/1888 at 52/10; farmer; married; b. Lyndon Ct., VT; Rufus Bigelow and Nancy Prescott

BIGGART,
William Lang, d. 10/12/1949 at 61 in Sandwich; married; b. Bloomfield, NJ; William Biggart and Netta Moore

BIGGS,
John M., d. 9/3/2000 in Laconia; John Biggs and A. Davidson

BILODEAU,
Malcolm F., d. 11/24/1957 at 53 in Sandwich; married; b. Haverhill, MA; Arthur G. Bilodeau and Edith L. West

BIRCH,
Marie E., d. 11/14/2007 in Laconia; William Mullens and Lottie Eike
Myra S., d. 11/24/1983 in Sandwich; Guy L. Smith and Minnie Thorne

BISHOP,
Dorothy E., d. 9/4/1991 in Wolfeboro; Marvin Wood and Lillian Stahler
John S., d. 5/8/1981 in Laconia; David Bishop and Etta Davies

BLACKEY,

son, d. 4/27/1892 at 0/7/15 in Sandwich; b. Sandwich; Elijah Blackey (Sandwich) and Lizzie Wade (Center Harbor)

son, d. 11/3/1895 at – in Sandwich; b. Sandwich; Elijah Blackey (Sandwich) and Lizzie Wade (Moultonboro)

Daniel, d. 9/6/1922 at 73/4/5

Elijah S., d. 1/28/1922 at 74/6/21; carpenter; divorced; Ira Blackey and Sarah Stewart

Emily F., d. 8/15/1900 at 84/11/2 in Sandwich; housewife; widow; b. Augusta, ME; William Irving (Scotland) and ----- (China, ME)

Ira, d. 8/8/1888 at 80/4/19; farmer; widower; b. Sandwich; Thomas Blackey and Mary Webster (Thornton)

John N., d. 6/15/1893 at 83/3/27 in Sandwich; farmer; b. Sandwich; Thomas Blackey (Portsmouth) and Mary Webster (Linden, VT)

Sarah S., d. 4/13/1888 at 73/5/12; married; b. Thornton; Caleb Smart (Thornton) and Hannah Libbey (Gorham, ME)

BLANCHARD,

Alice N., d. 4/18/1938 at 81/7/17; at home; widow; b. Sandwich; Arthur Quinby (Sandwich) and Lavinia Bryer (Tamworth)

Arven, d. 10/22/1907 at 56/10/9; merchant; married; b. Hopkinton; A. Blanchard (Billerica, MA) and Mary Carter (Warner, MA)

Charles, d. 5/8/1918 at 82/3/11; merchant; widower; b. Sandwich; Augustine Blanchard (Sandwich) and Betsy P. Ambrose (Moultonboro)

Charles, d. 11/7/1918 at 67/10/7; farmer; married; b. Eaton; Thomas Blanchard (Sandwich) and Sarah L. Vittum (Sandwich)

Clara F., d. 6/11/1940 at 72/1/8

Georgia E., d. 10/6/1936 at 83/9/9; widow; b. Sandwich; James M. Smith (Sandwich) and Lydia F. Skinner (Sandwich)

Harry, d. 4/11/1959 at 79 in Meredith; married; b. Sandwich; Arvin Blanchard and Helen Creighton

Helen Susan, d. 10/10/1930 at 89/0/28; housewife; widow; b. Sandwich; Edward Creighton (Sandwich) and Susan Scarlett (Sandwich)

Howard W., d. 10/2/1914 at 46/4/24; farmer; single; b. Sandwich; James B. Blanchard and Sarah D. Webster (Sandwich)

James B., d. 12/26/1891 at 71/2/4 in Sandwich; married; b. Sandwich; Benjamin Blanchard (Loudon) and Hannah Buzzell (Sandwich)

Joshua, d. 3/11/1889 at 30; none; single; b. Sandwich; J. W. Blanchard (Sandwich) and Lucy R. Elles (MA)

Lucy R., d. 5/10/1892 at 78 in Sandwich; housewife; widow; b. Brighton; John Ellis

M. Jennie, d. 8/4/1900 at 60/9/27 in Sandwich; housewife; married; b. Sandwich; John Donovan (Sandwich) and Jane Brown (Sandwich)

Mary, d. 6/2/1888 at 92/1/13; widow; b. Warner, MA; Joel Carter (Warner, MA) and Sarah Jenkins (Warner, MA)

Mildred M., d. 10/21/1960 at 86 in Laconia; widow; b. Benton; William Tibbetts and Kate King

Mildred T., d. 9/11/1928 at 43/4/11; at home; single; b. Sandwich; Arven Blanchard (Hopkinton) and Nellie S. Creighton (Sandwich)

Nancy, d. 1/19/1917 at 82/7/23; housewife; married; b. Sandwich; Nathan Mason (Sandwich) and Charlotte P. Quimby

Sarah D., d. 12/19/1914 at 82/3/1; housekeeper; widow; b. Sandwich; Jacob Webster (Sandwich) and Nancy F. Dinsmore (Conway)

BLODGETT,

Helen B., d. 11/24/1992 in Portchester, NY; John Burrows and Harriet Foss

BLONDEAU,

Annette P., d. 4/5/1979 at 17 in Holderness; student; single; b. NH; Gerald A. Blondeau and Pauline D. Mondor

BLUMBERG,

Estella Clay, d. 6/1/1936 at 47/10/10; at home; divorced; b. Sandwich; Henry Clay (Thornton) and Almena Pettengill (Sandwich)

Lawrence J., d. 3/17/1964 at 52 in Sandwich; b. Sandwich; Simon N. Blumberg and Estella Clay

Lewis C., d. 2/18/1940 at 0/3/22; b. Plymouth; Lawrence Blumberg (Sandwich) and Louise Carter (Sandwich)

Louise, d. 10/31/1939 at 34/11; housewife; married; b. Sandwich; Almon E. Carter (Sandwich) and Addie S. Webster (Sandwich)

BODGE,

Chester L., d. 7/5/1911 at 0/1/2; b. Sandwich; Harry E. Bodge (Moultonboro) and Annie M. Glidden (Tamworth)

Edgar F., d. 10/11/1906 at 1/10/12; b. Sandwich; Harry E. Bodge (Moultonboro) and Annie Glidden (Tamworth)

BONATAKIS,

Andrew, d. 7/4/2003 in West Islip, NY; Joseph Bonatakis and Anna Demetropoulos

Mary Frances, d. 1/6/1993 in Sandwich; b. Hamden, NY; Clarence Betsinger and Lina Shafer

BONNYMAN,

Harold R., d. 1/19/2003 in Laconia; Charles Bonnyman and Margaret Tabor

Winifred M., d. 12/15/1984 in Wolfeboro; Arnold Welles Catlin and Martha Morris

BOOTY,
daughter, d. 9/30/1984 in Sandwich; Geoffrey Rollins Booty and Helen Todd Platt

BOWER,
Adam H., d. 7/30/1925 at 85; carpenter; widower; b. Shelburn, NS

BOWES,
Harriet M., d. 10/9/1960 at 76 in Sandwich; widow; b. Lunenburg, NS; Charles MacGregor and Rhoda Silver

BOWLER,
Barbara J., d. 5/21/2006 in Concord; Arthur Brown and Jennie Watkins

BREED,
Elsie Wilbur, d. 10/4/1998 in N. Sandwich; b. Raynham, MA; Ralph O. Wilbur and Eva Gardner

BREWER,
Robert W., d. 7/12/1985 in Hanover; Raymond Brewer and Elizabeth Roberts

BRINTON,
Loring A., d. 3/29/2007 in Peoria, AZ; Lionel Brinton and Ellen Anthony

BROWN,
son, d. 3/11/1887 at 0/0/1; b. Sandwich; ----- Brown
daughter, d. 8/9/1901 at 0/5 in Sandwich; b. Sandwich; Charles F. Brown (Sandwich) and Nellie Snow (Sandwich)
Alice Gertrude, d. 4/23/1954 at 67 in Sandwich; widow; b. NH; John Elliott and Ida S. Rowe

Alice Knowlton, d. 10/7/1986 in Clinton, SC; Clinton Knowlton and Sarah Tilton

Angeline T., d. 8/14/1933 at 84/6/11; housewife; widow; b. Bath, ME; Charles Bennett (Sandwich) and Sally Atwood (Sandwich)

Arthur Butler, d. 3/10/1986 in Clinton, SC: Andrew J. Brown and Ida Bodine

Charles F., d. 11/29/1913 at 69/0/11; farmer; widower; b. Sandwich

Charles W., d. 6/3/1908 at 36; laborer; single; b. Sandwich; Frank Brown (Sandwich) and Harriet Bennett (Sandwich)

Clarence M., d. 9/24/1971 at 67 in Laconia; married; b. NH; Frank Brown and Alice Elliott

Clayton, d. 11/25/1901 at 1/11/7 in Sandwich; b. Sandwich; Charles F. Brown (Sandwich) and Nellie M. Snow (Sandwich)

Daniel O., d. 5/26/1920 at 61/0/26; farmer; married; b. Sandwich; David J. Brown (Sandwich) and Sarah Felch (Tamworth)

David Clyde, d. 7/17/1954 at 16 in Sandwich; single; b. Meredith; Glenn Brown and Dorothy Ambrose

David J., d. 1/25/1895 at 62/5/3 in Sandwich; farmer; widower; b. Sandwich; Daniel Brown (Sandwich) and Margaret Jewell (Sandwich)

Elizabeth M., d. 6/4/1988 in Meredith; Ganville Meader and Rheuamma B. Peach

Elmer W., d. 3/18/1913 at 27/5/27; manager; married; b. Sandwich; Arven B. Brown (Sandwich) and Addie Bennett (Sandwich)

Frank Granville, d. 2/2/1989 in Sandwich; Clarence M. Brown and Elizabeth Meader

Frank W., d. 2/14/1923 at 54/1/0; carpenter; married; b. Sandwich; J. Page Brown (Sandwich) and Angeline Bennett (Gray, ME)

G. F., d. 1/27/1907 at 88/1; farmer; widower; b. ME; John Brown (Erroll) and Hepsibeth ----- (Scotland)

George E., d. 12/3/1954 at 72 in Concord; widower; b. Sandwich; Charles F. Brown and Harriet Bennett

Gertie L., d. 9/26/1891 at 16/10/26 in Sandwich; single; b. Sandwich; C. F. Brown (Sandwich) and Harriet Bennett (Sandwich)

Harriet H., d. 9/16/1888 at 44/6; married; b. Sandwich; John W. Bennett (Sandwich) and Lucinda Fogg (Sandwich)

Henry A., d. 11/13/1957 at 66 in Sandwich; married; b. Indian Lakes, NY; William T. Brown and Ida Stevens

James F., d. 2/4/2007 in Sandwich; Frank Brown and Jean Leach

Janet M., d. 3/13/2004 in Sandwich; William Munro and May Muller

John P., d. 12/12/1908 at 68/0/14; farmer; married; b. Nottingham; Joseph Brown and Abigail Langley

Joshua, d. 10/15/1917 at 70/4/2; machinist; married; b. England; Edward Brown (England) and Ellen Barrett (England)

Margaret C., d. 109/1945 at 63/8 in Laconia; housewife; married; b. Scotland; ----- Carmichael

Mary E., d. 10/7/1942 at 79/11/20 in Sandwich; at home; widow; b. Sandwich; Hezekiah T. Fogg (Sandwich) and Mary E. Moulton (Sandwich)

Mary M., d. 9/25/1903 at 1/4/27 in Sandwich; b. Sandwich; Charles F. Brown (Sandwich) and Nellie Snow (Sandwich)

Mary Senior, d. 4/17/1966 at 70 in Wolfeboro; married; b. Waterbury, CT; William Davies and Cora Terrill

Nellie N., d. 11/2/1909 at 29/10/2; housewife; married; b. Sandwich; James Snow (Strafford) and Lucy Clark (Sandwich)

Warren J., d. 2/6/1902 at 59/5/6 in Sandwich; farmer; married; b. Sandwich; Russell Brown (Sandwich) and Lydia S. Mason (Sandwich)

BROWNLIE,

Albert C., d. 12/13/1941 at 46/2/4; laborer; widower; b. Everett, MA; John Brownlie (London, England) and Caroline Dickinson (London, England)

Dorothy W., d. 10/10/1930 at 29/2/23; housewife; married; b. Lynn, MA; Charles S. Wing (Fayette, ME) and Dora Preston (Manchester)

Fred W., d. 10/10/1937 at 51/0/20; painter; married; b. Charlestown, MA; John Brownlie (England) and Caroline Dickinson (England)

Leonard, d. 4/9/1962 at 83 in Laconia; single; b. London, England; John Brownlie and Caroline Dickerson

Lilly C., d. 8/25/1962 at 74 in Ctr. Harbor; widow; b. Sweden; John Beck and Augusta Stark

Marie, d. 5/23/1974 at 86 in Haverhill, MA; at home; widow; b. MA; John F. Kerry and Margaret Donovan

BRYANT,

Alton D., d. 9/27/1971 at 86 in Laconia; married; b. NH; Edmund Bryant and Mary Davis

Charles H., d. 2/27/1891 at 50/2/17 in Sandwich; laborer; married; b. Sandwich; Alvin Bryant (Sandwich) and Mary Wallace (Littleton)

Clarence E., d. 2/19/1924 at 73/3/6; laborer; married; b. Sandwich; Jewell Bryant (Sandwich) and Mary A. Brown (Sandwich)

Dorothy A., d. 11/7/1983 in Laconia; Frank Atwood and Florence Brown

E. J., d. 6/6/1936 at 60/4/25; retired; widower; b. Sandwich; C. E. Bryant (Sandwich) and Mary Helen Martin (Sandwich)

Eva M., d. 3/15/1925 at 44/10/13; housewife; married; b. Sandwich; Charles H. Smith (Sandwich) and Margaret Hale (Bethlehem)

Jennie M., d. 4/10/1897 at 28/4/3 in Sandwich; housewife; married; b. Moultonboro; Oliver C. Bickford (Moultonboro) and Eliza M. Hutchins (Eaton)
John W., d. 12/28/1974 at 71 in Sandwich; contractor; married; b. NH; Walter G. Bryant and Elizabeth Severance
Josephine S., d. 8/23/1984 in Ossipee; Daniel C. Smith and Adelaide L. Bicknell
Lynwood S., d. 3/16/2005 in Sandwich; Royal Bryant and Mary Jane Bradbury
Madeline B., d. 6/6/1980 in Laconia; William J. Robinson and Nettie L. Quimby
Mary Ann, d. 6/18/1888 at 79/0/28; married; b. Littleton; David Wallace (Littleton) and Nancy Palmer (Littleton)
Mary Ann, d. 10/2/1908 at 88/5/19; housewife; widow; b. Sandwich; Bradbury Brown
Mary E., d. 1/30/1916 at 36/3/4; housewife; married; b. Sandwich; John W. Severance (Sandwich) and Helen M. Mills (Lakeport)
Mary Helen, d. 5/11/1931 at 77/7/2; housewife; widow; b. Tamworth; Alden P. Martin (Tamworth) and Sarah Vittum (Sandwich)
Mary O., d. 5/6/1957 at 79 in Laconia; married; b. Oxford, PA; John Oakford and Agnes B. Irvin
Milton R., Sr., d. 8/12/1988 in Sandwich; John W. Bryant, Sr. and Madelyn Robinson
Rita, d. 3/17/1933 at 0/0/11; b. Sandwich; William A. Bryant (Sandwich) and Sylvia T. Avery (Rumney)
Rose McBride, d. 2/7/1951 at 71 in Laconia; widow; b. Ireland
Shirley C., d. 11/11/1928 at 1; b. Sandwich; Winfield S. Bryant (Sandwich) and Dorohy Atwood (Sandwich)
Sylvia A., d. 10/2/1974 at 68 in Hanover; retired; widow; b. NH; Arthur Avery and Florence Soule
Walter C., d. 3/26/1942 at 75/8/22 in Sandwich; painter; married; b. Moultonboro; William Bryant (Moultonboro)

William Asa, d. 9/29/1948 at 46/11/20 in Sandwich; married; b. Sandwich; Walter C. Bryant (Moultonboro) and Elizabeth Severance (Sandwich)
Winfield S., d. 8/8/1982 in Laconia; Walter Bryant and Elizabeth Severance

BRYAR,
Daniel, d. 2/10/1907 at 70/0/11; laborer; widower; b. Tuftonboro; Daniel Bryar (Sandwich) and Rosalie Jewell (Sandwich)
Maude Q., d. 11/22/1913 at 38/4/26; housewife; married; b. Sandwich; Stan F. Quimby (Sandwich) and E. S. Nickerson (Tamworth)

BRYER,
Annie F., d. 9/6/1911 at 47/0/10; housewife; married; b. S. Boston, MA
Betsey, d. 2/21/1899 at 97/9 in Sandwich; housewife; married; b. Sandwich; John Hackett (Sandwich) and Abigail Sinclair (Sandwich)
Betsey S., d. 11/22/1889 at 90/5; housewife; married; b. Sandwich; Andrew Bean (Sandwich) and Betsey Sinclair (Sandwich)
Daniel, d. 11/20/1892 at 87/4 in Sandwich; farmer; widower; b. Sandwich; Jered Bryer and Polly Hall
David, d. 7/8/1890 at 85/3 in Sandwich; farmer; widower; b. Sandwich; James Bryer (Sandwich)
Francis M., d. 8/26/1888 at 29/8/8; married; b. Meredith; Samuel F. Nichols and Lois Kelly
Frank A., d. 8/6/1942 at 78/5/18 in Concord; auctioneer; married; b. Sandwich; David Bryer (Sandwich) and Mary Gilman (Sandwich)
James, d. 2/2/1887 at 83/1/27; b. Tamworth
James R., d. 1/6/1923 at 87/1/29
Rhoda E., d. 2/9/1924 at 84/0/5; housewife; widow; b. Sandwich; John Bennett (Sandwich) and Lucinda Fogg (Sandwich)

Rosilla, d. 5/13/1892 at 80/6 in Sandwich; housewife; married; b. Tuftonboro; David Jewell and ----- Clough

BUKER,

Benjamin J., d. 9/13/1979 at 18 hrs. in Hanover; b. NH; Kim B. Buker and Rita M. Horn

BULLARD,

Gardner P., d. 7/27/1964 at 74 in Sandwich; b. Arlington, MA; Henry W. Bullard and Mary Palmer

Mary Palmer, d. 10/11/1950 at 85 in Sandwich; widow; b. Winchester, MA; Wilson Palmer and Harriet Currier

BUNDY,

Elizabeth E., d. 4/2/1905 at 59/2/10; housewife; married; b. Moultonboro; Dana Buzzell and Augusta Moulton (Moultonboro)

BUNKER,

Doris A., d. 12/7/1949 at 48 in Laconia; married; b. NH; George Davey and Jennie Vittum

Violet E., d. 2/25/1991 in Sandwich; Charles A. Worrsam and Emily Clark

BURGHARDT,

Jacob J., d. 9/24/2002 in Sandwich; Philip Burghardt and Elisabeth Riegel

BURLEIGH,

Charles F., d. 3/24/1926 at 81/2/28; farmer; married; b. Belmont; Charles F. Burleigh and Mary Bean (Sanford, ME)

Chester H., d. 10/5/1892 at 25 in Sandwich; farmer; single; b. Meredith; Charles F. Burleigh (Gilmanton) and Olive S. Hutchins (Medway)

Frank E., d. 2/27/1889 at 46/6/15; hotelkeeper; married; b. Sandwich; Thomas Burleigh (Sandwich) and Therza Pierce (Thornton)

John C., d. 7/17/1896 at 68/1/1 in Sandwich; hotel keeper; married; b. Sandwich; John Burleigh (Sandwich) and Pr. C. Prescott (Holderness)

Mary, d. 4/19/1896 at 83 in Sandwich; housewife; widow; b. Sanford, ME; Jedediah Bean and Mercy Thurston

Olive L., d. 12/16/1928 at 83/3/19; housewife; widow; b. Medway, MA; Moses Hutchins and C. Miranda

Sally, d. 7/13/1890 at 84 in Sandwich; housewife; widow; b. Ossipee; Ebenezer Hodsdon (Berwick) and Sally Wentworth (Berwick)

Samuel H., d. 7/17/1908 at 73/3/13; farmer; married; b. Sandwich; John Burleigh (Sandwich) and Priscila Prescott (Holderness)

Sarah Q., d. 12/18/1953 at 89 in Winthrop, ME; widow; b. Sandwich; Joseph Quimby and Nancy Fogg

Theresa, d. 3/3/1902 at 97/4/8 in Sandwich; housewife; widow; b. Thornton; Samuel Pierce and Mary Sargent

Thomas, d. 8/5/1887 at 83/2; farmer; married; b. Sandwich; Samuel Burleigh (Sandwich) and Ruth Prescott (Sandwich)

Thomas E., d. 6/12/1904 at 36/0/21; hotel keeper; married; b. Sandwich; Frank E. Burleigh (Sandwich) and Emily Ambrose (Sandwich)

BURNHAM,

Edward W., d. 6/21/1916 at 72/0/29; stone mason; married; b. Sandwich; Aaron Burnham (Sandwich) and Betsey Watson (Sandwich)

Grace C., d. 5/12/1953 at 75 in Laconia; divorced; b. OH

Jewell, d. 4/24/1907 at 5/0/15; scholar; b. Sandwich; C. S. Burnham (Sandwich) and Grace Chase (OH)

John C., d. 12/19/1909 at 74/5; farmer; single; b. Sandwich; Aaron Burnham (Sandwich) and Betsy H. Watson (Sandwich)

BURNS,

Arthur C., d. 3/26/1995 in Meredith; b. Philadelphia, PA; Ben E. Burns and Mary Johnson

Lois V., d. 6/27/1999 in Laconia; Robert Vreeland and Laura Bockoven

Margaret L., d. 9/24/1974 at 87 in Lexington, MA; ret. phys. ed. teacher; single; b. NH; Robert Burns and Caroline Sargent

Richard Tipton, Dr., d. 7/7/1993 in Plymouth; b. Philadelphia, PA; Ben Burns and Mary Johnson

Sarah Ruth, d. 9/17/1958 at 67 in Sandwich; single; b. Plymouth; Robert Burns and Caroline Sargent

BURROWS,

Adelaide S., d. 7/31/1982 in Sandwich; Alonzo Hull and Emma Brown

Anna Geers, d. 11/28/1953 at 28 in Laconia; married; b. NH; Lawrence M. Geers and Ada Berg

Beatrice D., d. 12/18/1981 in Wolfeboro; Stephen Doughty

Beatrice V., d. 10/13/1977 at 62 in Laconia; mill worker; married; b. NH; Percy Plume and Grace Cross

Charles G., d. 11/7/1972 at 48 in Laconia; mail carrier; widower; b. NH; Nathaniel Burrows and Edrie Gordon

Charles H., d. 3/12/1922 at 61/6/25; farmer; married; b. Sandwich; Nathaniel Burrows (Lebanon) and Sarah D. Thompson (Sandwich)

Chester J., Sr., d. 5/22/1978 at 64 in Sandwich; handyman; widower; b. NH; Newell J. Burrows and Nellie F. Hodge

Clayton P., d. 9/6/1928 at 2/9; b. Sandwich; Frank N. Burrows (Sandwich) and Hilda McDonald (Wolfeboro)

Edith S., d. 2/9/1903 at 0/0/5 in Sandwich; b. Sandwich; Fred N. Burrows (Sandwich) and Grace E. Skinner (Moultonboro)

Edrie H., d. 2/17/1979 at 76 in Laconia; housewife; widow; b. NY; Jesse Gordon and Martha Nourie

Eldora F., d. 1/4/1992 in Laconia; William Taylor and Christen E. Skinner

Florence K., d. 3/4/1957 at 79 in Laconia; widow; b. Sandwich; Fred N. Burrows and Grace E. Skinner

Frank N., d. 9/11/1992 in Meredith; b.Sandwich; Newell Burrows and Nellie Hodge

Fred N., d. 3/23/1949 at 72 in Concord; widower

Grace E., d. 12/19/1937 at 53/11/5; housewife; married; b. Moultonboro; Charles E. Skinner (Sandwich) and Jennie Torrey (Sandwich)

Harry L., d. 11/1/1959 at 79 in Wolfeboro; married; b. Sandwich; James Burrows and Sophia Wallace

James, d. 6/8/1929 at 97/3/15; farmer; widower; b. Lebanon, ME; James B. Burrows

John L., d. 3/11/1920 at 56/7/5; farmer; divorced; b. Sandwich; James W. Burrows (Lebanon, ME) and Sophia E. Wallace (Sandwich)

Lester D., Jr., d. 11/17/1977 at 54 in Laconia; lumberman; married; b. NH; Lester D. Burrows, Sr. and Beatrice Doughty

Lester D., Sr., d. 9/26/1975 at 70 in Sandwich; state employee; married; b. NH; Harry L. Burrows and Adelaide Hull

Luther J., d. 5/5/1971 at 63 in Sandwich; married; b. NH; Harry Burrows and Adalaide Hull

Michael, d. 12/28/1962 at 0/0/2 in Laconia; b. Laconia; Richard Burrows and Joanne Baragona

Nathaniel H., d. 4/10/1900 at 64/8/2 in Sandwich; farmer; married; b. Lebanon, ME; J. Burrows and Abigail Goodwin

Nathaniel H., d. 5/14/1971 at 67 in Sandwich; married; b. NH; Charles Burrows and Amy Gilman

Nellie F., d. 10/16/1964 at 84 in Ctr. Harbor; b. Sandwich; John Hodge and Edna Berry

Newell J., d. 5/5/1961 at 88 in Sandwich; married; b. Sandwich; James Burrows and Sophia Wallace
Nora Davis, d. 12/16/1987 in Laconia; Alva Davis and Florence Wiggin
Peter, d. 7/12/1982 in Laconia; Fred W. Burrows and Nora E. Davis
Robert N., d. 6/26/2003 in Lebanon; Nathaniel Burrows and Edrie Gordon
Sarah D., d. 5/19/1902 at 66/9 in Sandwich; housewife; widow; b. Sandwich; Samuel Thompson (Farmington) and Betsey Seavey (Rye)
Sophia E., d. 11/8/1912 at 71/1/16; housewife; married; b. Sandwich; G. Wallace (Sandwich) and F. Penniman (Sandwich)

BUTLER,
Grace, d. 5/14/1888 at 79/5; married; b. Sandwich; Thomas Vittum (Sandwich) and Sally Weed (Sandwich)
Moses, d. 10/24/1889 at 84/3/27; farmer; married; b. Sandwich; William Butler and Abagail Copp
Phebe A., d. 8/27/1893 at 59/6 in Sandwich; b. Sandwich; Moses Butler (Sandwich) and Grace Vittum (Sandwich)
Susan R., d. 5/21/1905 at 62/5/10; invalid; single; b. Sandwich; Moses Butler (Standish, ME) and Grace Vittum (Standish)

CAMPBELL,
Everett, d. 12/19/1998 in Laconia; b. Sandwich; John Campbell and Grace Ida Elliott
John N., d. 3/8/1905 at 56/6/20; farmer; married; b. Bedford, MA; Abner Campbell and Mary Butterfield
John W., d. 7/11/1945 at 57/5/28 in Sandwich; laborer; married; b. Sandwich; John N. Campbell (Londonderry) and Bernie Campbell (Londonderry)

Lottie M., d. 2/21/1901 at 20/4/26 in Sandwich; single; b. Sandwich; John N. Campbell (Bedford) and Byrne Bancroft (Londonderry)
Mrs. B. E., d. 4/25/1899 at 50/11/15 in Sandwich; housewife; married; b. Londonderry; James Bancroft (Londonderry) and Charlotte Eaton (Londonderry)
Pauline Eliner, d. 9/24/2004 in Laconia; Rupert Bragg and Blanche M. George

CANNEY,
Emma B., d. 3/14/1915 at 49/8/4; divorced; b. Rutland, VT; John T. Beach (Salisbury, VT) and C. Goldthwaite

CARLISLE,
Margaret E., d. 9/21/1965 at 69 in Concord; b. Boston, MA; Amos Carlisle and Elizabeth McDonald

CARLSON,
Andrew J., d. 7/18/1938 at 82/9/21; gardner; widower; b. Ojjaby, Sweden
Walter R., Sr., d. 9/29/1990 in Sandwich; Andrew J. Carlson and Irene M. Holmstrom

CARON,
Kathleen Anne, d. 10/31/1998 in Sandwich; b. Manchester; Donald F. Caron and Irene Chamberland

CARTER,
Almon Ellsworth, d. 1/17/1987 in Sandwich; Almon Ellsworth Carter, Sr.
Betsey L., d. 2/19/1893 at 56/7/19 in Sandwich; housewife; married; b. Albany; Asa Brown (Conway) and Abigail Head (Conway)
Dennis F., d. 1/20/1899 at 54 in Sandwich; merchant; married; b. Saco, ME; Caswell Carter (ME) and Julia Whitten (ME)

Frances M., d. 6/2/1987 in Laconia; James F. Martin and Alice M. Tappan
Grace L., d. 4/2/1952 at 53 in Laconia; never married; b. NH; Alonzo F. Carter and Bertha Atwood
James W., d. 2/28/1984 in Manchester; Almond E. Carter and Frances Martin
Lawrence J., d. 3/21/1914 at 0/2/21; b. Ashland; Almon E. Carter (Sandwich) and Addie L. Webster (Sandwich)
Winifred A., d. 8/27/1913 at 40/9/5; single; b. Laconia; Russell H. Carter (Holderness) and Laura A. Durgin (Laconia)

CARTLAND,
daughter, d. 11/25/1887 at 0/0/½; b. Sandwich; Joseph Cartland (Parsonsfield, ME)
daughter, d. 11/25/1887 at 0/0/1–½; b. Sandwich; Joseph Cartland (Parsonsfield, ME)
Dora E., d. 2/14/1894 at 30/4/2 in Sandwich; housewife; married; b. Parsonsfield; Timothy Eastman (Cornish, ME) and Asenath Day (Cornish, ME)
Eunice, d. 11/15/1894 at 64/5 in Sandwich; housewife; married; b. Windham, ME; Mark Knight (Alfred, ME) and Mercy Douglas (Durham, ME)
Harriet E., d. 12/23/1962 at 87 in Laconia; widow; b. Lynn, MA; Robert C. MacLean and Emma Austin
John B., d. 3/4/1905 at 80/6; minister; widower; b. Parsonsfield, ME; Silas Cartland (Parsonsfield, ME) and Annie Brackett (Parsonsfield, ME)
Joseph J., d. 1/18/1956 at 81 in Tamworth; married; b. E. Parsonsfield, ME; John Cartland and Eunice Cartland

CASS,
Edward Wesley, d. 4/11/1997 in Manchester; b. Wolfeboro; Clayton Cass and Helen Woodward

CASWELL,
James W., d. 7/16/1991 in Laconia; Herbert H. Caswell and Grace Parker

CATLIN,
Clarence Wilfred, d. 8/13/1978 at 76 in Hartford, CT; secretary; married; b. CT; Clarence C. Catlin and Annie Bidwell

CAWLEY,
Arnold W. C., d. 10/16/2006 in Laconia; Frank Cawley and Winifred Catlin

CAWTHORNE,
Edwin M., d. 12/1/1943 at 95/4/7 in Sandwich; retired; widow; b. Northboro, MA; David Cawthorne (Leeds, England) and Sophia Wheelock (Leominster, MA)

CHAMBERLAIN,
LeRoy W., d. 2/3/1983 in Laconia

CHARLET,
Henry, d. 5/3/1969 at 68 in Laconia; married; b. France; Celestine Charlet and Mary Penette

CHASE,
Altie E., d. 6/6/1894 at 33/6 in Sandwich; farmer; single; b. Sandwich; Sarah Quimby
Amy C., d. 6/11/1948 at 69 in Sandwich; married; b. Danvers, MA; Simon P. Buxton (Peabody, MA) and Sarah H. Putnam (Salem, MA)
Belinda S., d. 12/15/1897 at 82/9/6 in Sandwich; housewife; widow; b. Tamworth; Nicholas Ham and Hannah Chase
Betsy, d. 9/3/1908 at 80/5/13; housewife; married; b. Albany; Nathaniel Carter (Parsonsfield) and Patience Colamey (New Durham)

Dean Elliott, d. 8/22/1993 in Sandwich; b. Wolfeboro; Charles S. Chase and Abigale Elliott
Jennie, d. 1/9/1919 at 64/6/18; at home; single; b. Sandwich; Jonathan Chase (Meredith) and Sally Smith (Sandwich)
Jonathan, d. 4/10/1892 at 72/6 in Sandwich; blacksmith; widower; b. Meredith; Daniel Chase and May Vittum
Samuel, d. 6/20/1912 at 89; farmer; widower; b. Conway; Gilbert Chase (Conway) and Phoebe Carr

CHATEL,
Norman W., d. 8/25/2001 in Meredith; Eugene Chatel and Edith Barett

CHICK,
Margaret Ann, d. 2/24/1948 at 5/7/20 in Sandwich; b. Wolfeboro; Ralph Drown (Eaton) and Emmaline Abbott (Wilcard, VT)

CHILD,
Marshall B., d. 9/2/1952 at 35 in Sandwich; married; b. E. Peru, ME; Perley K. Child and Helen D. Howard

CHINN,
Joseph, d. 7/9/1982 in Laconia; Arthur W. Chinn and Mary E. Dimes

CHITTICK,
Clara J., d. 10/5/1925 at 53/2/21; at home; widow; b. Worcester, MA; William Thompson (Burlington, VT) and Eliza J. Slye (St. Johns, PQ)

CLAFFEY,
Ruth, d. 4/25/1894 at 80/6 in Sandwich; housewife; widow; b. Tamworth; Josiah Prescott (Tamworth)

CLARK,

Charles S., d. 2/21/1934 at 77/0/8; farmer; widower; b. Sandwich; Langdon G. Clark (Sandwich) and Ann Beede (Sandwich)

Charlotte S., d. 9/16/1899 at 61/8/24 in Sandwich; housewife; married; b. Holderness; Nason Smith (Holderness) and Mary Carter (Sandwich)

Emily, d. 12/22/1888 at 24/8/15; single; b. Sandwich; John Clark (Sandwich) and Grace Vittum (Sandwich)

Frances Olive, d. 4/20/1969 at 79 in Keene; married; b. MA; Jeremiah Martin and Sarah Sprague

Grace E., d. 2/28/1899 at 69/9 in Sandwich; housewife; widow; b. Sandwich; Samuel F. Vittum (Sandwich) and M. C. Kenniston (Albany)

Herman M., d. 7/13/1929 at 67/10/13; farmer; married; b. Sandwich; Joseph P. Clark and ----- Smith

John, d. 5/24/1890 at 81/9 in Sandwich; farmer; single; b. Sandwich; Robert Clark (Newington) and Sally Davis (Portsmouth)

John N., d. 3/8/1893 at 27/2/9 in Sandwich; laborer; b. Holderness; Joseph Clark (Moultonboro) and Charlotte Smith (Holderness)

John R., d. 11/3/1920 at 61/0/21; farmer; single; b. Sandwich; John Clark (Sandwich) and Grace E. Vittum (Sandwich)

Joseph P., d. 2/19/1917 at 87/0/23; farmer; widower; b. Moultonboro; Jonathan Clark and Phebe -----

Langdon G., d. 1/28/1899 at 79/11/5 in Sandwich; farmer; widower; b. Sandwich; Robert Clark (Newington) and Sallis Davis (Kittery, ME)

Nellie L., d. 3/23/1930 at 64/8/25; housewife; widow; b. Sandwich; Levi Smith (Sandwich) and Samantha Miller (Canada)

Sumner B., d. 5/9/1948 at 58/8/24 in Hanover; married; b. Sandwich; Charles S. Clark (Sandwich) and Nellie Brown (Exeter)

CLARKSON,
Annie Belle, d. 10/9/1978 at 100 in Ossipee; school teacher; widow; b. MA; Joseph Richardson and Clara Pettigrew

CLAY,
Almena, d. 3/18/1926 at 67/1/17; housewife; married; b. Sandwich; Hosea Pettengill (Ringe) and Polly Skinner (Sandwich)
Basil L., d. 11/17/1981 in Moultonboro; Flora McBean
Dorothy Carson, d. 12/19/1987 in Wolfeboro; William Carson and Louise A. Cook
Henry N., d. 10/16/1932 at 80/2/22; undertaker; widower; b. Leominster, MA; Nathan Clay and Eliza Durgin

CLEAVES,
Helen B., d. 7/31/1982 in Wolfeboro; Joseph S. Burton and Emma C. Whitney
James H., d. 4/29/1977 at 86 in Meredith; stock broker; married; b. MA; Edward Cleaves and Emma -----

CLEMENT,
Mary G., d. 5/21/1891 at 83/9/22 in Sandwich; housewife; married; b. New Market; Eben Smith (New Market) and Sally Smith (New Market)

CLIFFORD,
Mary Kimball, d. 8/19/1983 in Franklin

CLOUGH,
Lucy M., d. 11/15/1896 at 64 in Sandwich; housewife; widow; b. Sandwich; Jonathan Tappan and Dorothy Heard

CLUFF,
Roxy, d. 10/23/2004 in Laconia; Newell Burrows and Nellie Hodge

COBURN,
John F., d. 11/6/2006 in Ctr. Sandwich; Dean Coburn and Eleanor Laing

COFFIN,
Francis, d. 6/26/1890 at 91/1/21 in Sandwich; farmer; widower; b. Sandwich; John Coffin (Rutland) and Rhoda Hoit (Weare)

COGAN,
Susan D., d. 4/8/1895 at 78 in Sandwich; single; b. Sandwich; William Cogan (Durham) and Susan Durgin (Durham)

COLBY,
Gertrude Ann, d. 3/2/1998 in Wolfeboro; b. Claremont; John Francis Colby and Ada F. Ayers

COMMON,
Jack David, d. 6/2/1998 in Sandwich; b. Dayton, OH; John D. Common and Alice Firthmiller

CONGDON,
Arthur S., Jr., d. 5/17/1997 in Laconia; b. Glenridge, NJ; Arthur S. Congdon, Sr. and Margaret Koeniger
William Ward, d. 11/13/1984 in Sandwich; Arthur S. Congdon, Jr. and Ruth Jenkins

CONLEY,
Raymond K., Jr., d. 9/7/1995 in Laconia; b. Springfield, MA; Raymond S. Conley, Sr. and Edna P. Sharp

COOK,

Abbie, d. 11/27/1927 at 90/0/14; housekeeper; single; b. Sandwich; Jesse Cook

Charles C., d. 9/5/1945 at 83/6/24 iun Sandwich; carpenter; widower; b. Sandwich; Jesse H. Cook (Sandwich) and Emily Beede (Sandwich)

Curtis E., d. 2/22/1923 at 61/9/15; farmer; married; b. Sandwich; Jesse Cook (Sandwich) and Emily J. Beede (Sandwich)

Cynthia, d. 7/16/1934 at 0/0/25; b. Sandwich; Wilbur A. Cook (Sandwich) and Edina Adams (Athol, MA)

Cynthia K., d. 10/17/1901 at 69/6 in Sandwich; housekeeper; widow; b. Allenstown; John Johnson (Allenstown) and Esther Holt (Pembroke)

Edna A., d. 1/5/1974 at 67 in Wolfeboro; house mother; single; b. MA; John Adams and Grace Terry

Emily B., d. 9/10/1934 at 99/7/21; at home; widow; b. Sandwich; James Beede and Cynthia Hodge

George Otis, d. 1/20/1950 at 81 in Sandwich; widower; b. Rock Creek, IL; John O. Cook

J. Otis, d. 1/4/1981 in Laconia; George Cook and Mary Brown

Jesse, d. 5/3/1900 at 91/3/22 in Sandwich; farmer; widower; b. Sandwich; Joel Cook (Sandwich) and E. Maxfield (Sandwich)

Jesse H., d. 1/29/1912 at 84/3/4; farmer; married; b. Sandwich; Sally Cook (Sandwich)

John, d. 6/6/1887 at 91/4/8; farmer; married; b. Sandwich; Joel Cook and Elizabeth Maxfield

John O., d. 10/18/1893 at 61/9/5 in Sandwich; farmer; b. Sandwich; John Cook (Sandwich) and Sarah Sinclair (Sandwich)

Lucy E., d. 9/12/1922 at 86/9/23; at home; single; b. Sandwich; Jesse Cook (Sandwich) and Patience G. Smith (Sandwich)

Mary R., d. 6/5/1931 at 49/1/4; housewife; married; b. N. Conway; Moses G. Brown (Erroll) and Christina Robbins (PEI)

Mary S., d. 10/13/1979 at 87 in Meredith; teacher-retired; married; b. NH; Charles O. Smith and Mary Pierce
Sarah H., d. 9/22/1890 at 95/8/10 in Sandwich; housewife; widow; b. Sandwich; Ebenezer Sinclair (Sandwich) and Mercy Hoag (Sandwich)

COOKE,
Batchelder, d. 6/21/1891 at – in Sandwich; married

COOLIDGE,
Anna L., d. 2/9/1985 in Meredith; William B. Cabot and Elizabeth Parker
Joseph B., d. 8/8/1928 at 66/2/22; retired arch.; married; b. Boston, MA; Joseph R. Coolidge (Boston, MA) and Julia Gardner (Boston, MA)
Joseph R., d. 9/22/1936 at 49/9/9; retired; married; b. Boston, MA; Joseph R. Coolidge (Boston, MA) and Mary Hill (Boston, MA)
Joseph R., d. 9/1/1999 in Manchester; Joseph Coolidge and Anna Cabot
Julia, d. 1/20/1999 in Laconia; Joseph Coolidge and Anna Cabot
Mary Hamilton, d. 10/6/1952 at 89 in Groton, MA; widow; b. Boston, MA; Hamilton A. Hill and Mary E. Robbins
Mary Hill, d. 8/8/1978 at 79 in Sandwich; housewife; married; b. MA; Arthur D. Hill and Henryette McLain
Oliver Hill, d. 1/17/1992 in Meredith; J. Randolph Colidge and Mary H. Hill

CORLISS,
Arthur, d. 9/16/1939 at 69/9/4; basket maker; married; b. Sandwich; Hiram Corliss (Sandwich) and Elizabeth Goodwin (Moultonboro)
Benjamin, d. 8/29/1895 at 87/12/29 in Sandwich; farmer; married; b. Sandwich; Joseph Corliss (Weare) and Mary Hubbard (Acton, ME)

Charles E., d. 7/12/1922 at 55/5/8; teacher; married; b. Sandwich; Hiram S. Corliss (Sandwich) and Sarah E. Goodwin (Moultonboro)
Elizabeth, d. 10/12/1966 at 84 in Ctr. Harbor; single; b. Sandwich; Herman Corliss and Elizabeth Goodwin
George H., d. 8/15/1934 at 73/4/0; retired; widower; b. N. Sandwich; Benjamin Corliss (Weare) and Mary Hubbard (Acton, ME)
Hiram S., d. 11/24/1926 at 82/7/12; farmer; married; b. Sandwich; Benjamin Corliss (Sandwich) and Mary Hubbard (Acton, ME)
Mary, d. 1/22/1892 at 77/2 in Sandwich; housewife; married; b. Acton, ME; Samuel Hubbard and Olive Wakefield
Sarah E., d. 3/29/1917 at 72/6/27; housewife; married; b. Moultonboro; John Goodwin (Moultonboro) and Mary Smith (Moultonboro)

CORSACK,
Howard, d. 6/4/1995 in Concord; b. Brooklyn, NY; Charles Corsack and Sylvia Yagman

COSEBOOM,
Ethel C., d. 3/11/1986 in Ossipee; Pry Cost and Effie Grosnickle

COTTON,
Marjorie M., d. 9/9/1967 at 65 in Sandwich; b. Schenectady, NY; Alexander Maxwell and Lena Hilton

COUNIHAN,
Madeline A., d. 5/21/1981 in Laconia; Felix Hagan and Katherine Long

CRAM,

Emma M., d. 10/3/1932 at 51/4/16; housewife; married; b. Moultonboro; Daniel Grant (Sandwich) and Elizabeth Evans (Moultonboro)

L. D., d. 6/8/1895 at 62/2/11 in Sandwich; farmer; married; b. Moultonboro; Stephen Cram (Manchester) and ----- (Hooksett)

CRANSTON,

Agnes T., d. 12/14/1969 at 95 in Sandwich; widow; b. MA; Lot W. Taylor and Sarah S. Sears

CROCKETT,

Elizabeth, d. 4/19/1948 at 81/4/29 in Sandwich; divorced; b. Ctr. Sandwich; Wesley Burnham and Susan Smith

CRONIN,

Alice, d. 4/30/1979 at 86 in Concord; widow; b. MA; Robert West and Mary Attridge

Timothy, d. 11/7/1955 at 69 in Sandwich; married; b. Ireland; Timothy Cronin and Mary Connolly

CROOKER,

Charles W., Rev., d. 8/29/1994 in Sandwich; b. Malden, MA; Charles E. Crooker and Marguerite Wescott

CROWELL,

Francis L., d. 1/13/1955 at 57 in Plymouth; married; b. Lebanon; Frank Crowell and Abbie Weston

Frank L., d. 12/19/1938 at 75/3/18; laborer; widower; b. Campton; Harum Crowell (Hyde Park, VT) and Marilla Brown (Sandwich)

Fred H., d. 2/7/1953 at 80 in Sandwich; widower; b. Campton; Harem Crowell and Marilla Brown

Mary E., d. 11/26/1939 at 72/1/24; at home; married; b. Sandwich; Edw. W. Burnham (Sandwich) and Susan Smith (Sandwich)

CURRIER,

son, d. 8/18/1899 at 0/0/10 in Sandwich; b. Sandwich; Leon Currier (Sandwich) and Emily Hodgdon (Sandwich)

Elizabeth, d. 3/15/1915 at 66/6/25; housewife; married; b. Tuftonboro; Daniel Bryer (Tuftonboro) and Rosilla Jewell (Sandwich)

Emily V., d. 12/15/1963 at 88 in Sandwich; widow; b. Sandwich; Leonidas Hodgdon and Susan Webster

Howard H., d. 2/27/1936 at 88/4/21; retired; widower; b. Rumney; Erastus Currier (Durham) and Sarah Smart

Leon H., d. 10/21/1935 at 63/7/16; farmer; married; b. Sandwich; Howard Currier (Rumney) and Elizabeth Bryar (Tuftonboro)

Lewis H., d. 4/6/1972 at 68 in Wolfeboro; carpenter; married; b. NH; Leon Currier and Emily Hodgedon

CURTIS,

William Fitch, d. 11/5/1934 at 56/6/20; married

CURTISS,

Anna Sherman, d. 10/13/1955 at 78 in Groton, CT

CUSHING,

Carrie I., d. 6/11/1938 at 77/7/8; housewife; widow; b. Sandwich; Lemuel F. Vittum (Sandwich) and Clemena Wallace (Sandwich)

Joseph L., d. 9/2/1929 at 79/6/23; retired; widower; b. MA; Daniel Cushing (Providence, RI) and Elizabeth Leavitt (Meredith)

DANFORTH,

George W., d. 10/6/1888 at 38/8/27; farmer; married; b. Sandwich; Milton Danforth (Sandwich) and Lydia ----- (Sandwich)

Noah, d. 5/19/1888 at 86; carpenter; widower; b. Sandwich; Stephen Danforth (Meredith) and Betsey Johnson

Rodney, d. 1/21/1914 at 68; farmer; single; b. Sandwich; Milton Danforth and Lydia Brown

DARLING,

son, d. 10/23/1894 at 0/0/1 in Sandwich; b. Sandwich; William Darling (Campton) and Nellie Knowles (Haverhill)

Grace L., d. 10/10/1900 at 1/7/18 in Sandwich; b. Sandwich; Will Darling (Campton) and Nellie P. Knowles (Haverhill, MA)

Hazel, d. 2/16/1898 at 0/0/19 in Sandwich; b. Sandwich; Will D. Darling (Campton) and Nellie P. Knowles (Haverhill)

DAVEY,

Edna F., d. 8/3/1921 at 12/3/6; student; b. Sandwich; George W. Davey (NB) and Jennie Vittum (Sandwich)

Lawrence, d. 7/2/1926 at 19/5/6; laborer; single; b. Sandwich; Henry E. Davey (NB) and Jennie Vittum (Sandwich)

DAVIE,

Bernard, d. 5/14/1905 at 0/2; b. Sandwich; Henry Davie (PEI) and Jennie Vittum (Sandwich)

Bertha, d. 6/21/1905 at 0/2/7; Henry Davie (NB) and Jennie Vittum (Sandwich)

Henry, d. 2/8/1910 at --; laborer; married

Philip C., d. 1/18/1965 at 68 in Ashland; b. Sandwich; George Davie and Jennie Vittum

DAVIS,

son, d. 12/3/1917 at 0/0/1; b. Sandwich; Charles J. Davis (Newmarket) and Katherine Holland (Newmarket)

son, d. 6/29/1951 at 0/0/1; b. Laconia; Lelia Davis
Charles J., d. 12/28/1948 at 66/5/21 in Laconia; married; b. Newmarket; James G. W. Davis (Barrington) and Minerva Stackpole (Kennebunk, ME)
Charlotte, d. 11/8/1927 at 73/1/24; housewife; married; b. Dunbarton; James McCauley (Dunbarton) and Louisa Jones (Litchfield)
Charlotte H., d. 8/8/1986 in Wolfeboro; Albert B. Hoag and Abigail Peaslee
Forrest Elsworth, d. 9/23/1993 in Laconia; b. Wakefield; Fred H. Davis and Bertha McDonald
Frank W., d. 11/19/1938 at 78/6/20; laborer; widower; b. Lakeport; Samuel Davis (Lakeport) and Mary Pickering (Meredith)
Frederick H., d. 12/31/1948 at 87/11/9 in Sandwich; widower; b. Jackson; Jonathan Davis
Helena S., d. 3/9/1959 at 73 in Wolfeboro; widow; b. New York, NY; Lewis Stone and Louise Titus
Horace E., d. 2/12/1943 at 74/9/24 in Laconia; stone mason; married; b. Lyman, ME; Lorenzo T. Davis (Lyman, ME) and Malisia Grant (Dexter, ME)
Katherine, d. 1/21/1919 at 31/7/2; housewife; married; b. Newmarket; James E. Holland (England) and Alice E. Hersom (Newmarket)
Nester W., d. 3/14/1983 in Ossipee
Phoebe A., d. 4/18/1945 at 62/7/5 in Sandwich; housewife; married; b. Lyme, CT; Christopher Brown (Haddam, CT) and Laura A. Bougue (Bolton Notch, CT)

DEARBORN,
Eliza, d. 6/5/1895 at 87/0/4 in Sandwich; housewife; widow; b. Sandwich; Joseph Flanders (Poplin) and Sarah Webster (Poplin)

John M., d. 11/24/1897 at 57/11 in Sandwich; farmer; married; b. Effingham; Shepard Dearborn (Effingham) and Emeline Mason (Tamworth)

Ruth R., d. 9/14/1961 at 87 in Sandwich; married; b. New Rochelle, NY; John Dampman and Mary Beattie

William O., d. 9/8/1966 at 85 in Laconia; widower; b. Lowell, MA; Charles Dearborn and Mary Kelly

DEBUSTAMANTE,

Isabel G. Sanchez, d. 3/30/2003 in Laconia; Gustavo Sanchez DeBustamante and Grace Luke

DELANO,

Robert Elmer, d. 2/7/1998 in Laconia; b. Dorchester, MA; Elmer Delano and Nell Donovan

DELGADO,

Marion D., d. 6/5/2000 in Ctr. Sandwich; J. Stanley Davis and Marion Cantine

Robert, d. 2/27/1991 in Wolfeboro; Pablo Delgado and Carmen Torres

DEMAR,

Samuel D., d. 7/31/1974 at 72 in Sandwich; optician; single; b. Russia; Isadore Demarsky and Etta -----

DEMING,

Martha G., d. 9/15/2001 in Yuma, AZ; Maurice White and Marion Sanderson

Roger, d. 3/4/1999 in Sandwich; Elbert Deming and Fannie Ford

DENISON,

Harold Francis, d. 7/21/1995 in Plymouth; b. Hartford, CT; William R. Denison and Madelyn Campane

DENNEY,
George, d. 2/5/1901 at 92 in Sandwich; farmer; widower

DEVERE,
Peter F., d. 9/28/2002 in Sandwich; Frederick E. Devere and Dorothy Daland

DINSMORE,
Samuel, d. 10/3/1888 at 72/3/22; wheelwright; married; b. Effingham; John Dinsmore (Conway) and Theodora Garland (Ossipee)

DIX,
Evelyn, d. 2/10/1964 at 82 in Nashua; b. Chelsea, MA; Johnson D. Quimby and Caroline Peaslee
Thomas M., d. 6/3/1942 at 58/3/6 in Everett, MA; salesman; married; b. Chelmsford, MA; Royal Dix (Billerica, MA) and Mary Marshall (Chelmsford, MA)

DOANE,
Gladys R., d. 1/6/2001 in Sandwich; Arnold Anthony and Ruth Berry

DOBYNS,
Barbara Johnston, d. 1/10/1997 in Lebanon; b. Utica, NY; John E. Johnston and Georgia Pomeroy
Lester L., d. 10/12/1989 in Sandwich; Harry C. Dobyns and Grace Magers

DODGE,
female, d. 12/12/1893 at 49 in Sandwich; housewife; Jerry Glidden and Abby Scott (Sandwich)
Ruth Ivy, d. 4/5/2004 in N. Sandwich; William A. Buckingham and Eva Robb

DONOVAN,

Charles W., d. 5/24/1921 at 90/0/8; farmer; married; b. Sandwich; John Donovan (Sandwich) and Jane M. Brown (Sandwich)

Mary S., d. 12/24/1921 at 86/4/16; retired; widow; b. Sandwich; James Norris and Lucinda Stevenson

DOOLITTLE,

Elsie A., d. 11/24/1977 at 89 in Wolfeboro; housewife; widow; b. NY; Charles P. Augur and Isabelle Murray

DORR,

Charles A., d. 2/23/1896 at 2/2/18 in Sandwich; b. Chicago, IL; Orrin J. Dorr (Sandwich) and M. J. McSoley (Wisconsin)

Mary M. B., d. 5/23/1897 at 76/1/2 in Sandwich; housewife; married; b. Tamworth; Charles Wedgewood (Saco, ME)

Samuel H., d. 9/25/1897 at 75 in Sandwich; farmer; widower; b. Newfield, ME; James Dorr and Abigail Young

DOUGHTY,

Howard N., d. 2/17/1970 at 66 in Littleton; married; b. NJ; Howard N. Doughty, Sr. and Ellen Flitner

DOUGLASS,

Frank L., d. 11/22/1928 at 45/3/2; laborer; married; b. Albany; Charles Douglass

DOW,

Charles F., Sr., d. 2/6/1973 at 55 in Wolfeboro; mechanic; married; b. NH; Charles Dow and Eva M. Morse

Edith M., d. 12/2/1977 at 91 in Laconia; housewife; widow; b. NH; Edgar Moulton and Clara Prescott

Elsbeth, d. 3/9/1996 in Plymouth; b. Hartford, CT; William O'Brien and Ethel Farnham

Etta A., d. 10/13/1940 at 78/1/20; housewife; widow; b. Sandwich; Alpheus Vittum (Sandwich) and Elmira Vittum (Sandwich)

DOWNS,
Daniel, d. 6/2/1905 at 89/4/16; farmer; widower; b. Fryeburg, ME; Uriah Downs (Alfred, ME)
Susan, d. 2/8/1905 at 78/10/23; housekeeper; married; b. Tamworth; Phineas Johnson (Tamworth) and Dolly James (Tamworth)

DRAKE,
Eliza M., d. 9/5/1953 at 86 in Laconia; single; b. Ossipee; Charles L. Drake and Belinda Sceggell
Olin A., d. 11/20/1960 at 37 in Sandwich; married; b. Ashland; Luther Drake and Minnie Boynton

DUFFY,
Sarah Annette, d. 7/15/1994 in Rochester, MN; b. Denver, CO; James F. Ransom and Annette Mowat

DUMAS,
Elizabeth R., d. 10/6/1981 in Sandwich; Leon H. Read and Abby Estherbrooks

DUNBAR,
Emma J., d. 8/19/1894 at 36 in Sandwich; clerk; single; b. Boston; Abraham Dunbar (Boston) and Emily Sullivan (Boston)

DUNTLEY,
Martha J., d. 5/10/1900 at 88/8/3 in Sandwich; housewife; married; b. Sandwich; Eliphalet Prescott (Sandwich) and Mary Jewell

DUNTLY,
Alpheus C., d. 9/12/1908 at 85; farmer; widower; b. Sandwich

DURGIN,
Charles C., d. 5/3/1915 at 58/8/23; salesman; widower; b. E. Andover; Charles A. Durgin
Jane H., d. 11/17/1895 at 75/3 in Sandwich; housewife; widow; b. Wolfeboro; Paul Varney (Farmington) and Sarah Varney (Wolfeboro)

DUSTIN,
Emily H., d. 8/27/2000 in Laconia; William Heard and Lillian Thompson
Robert G., d. 11/16/2001 in Meredith; Frank Dustin and Mary Clement

DYER,
Emma B., d. 6/28/1902 at 66/3/2 in Sandwich; widow; ----- Pottle
Priscilla F., d. 3/21/1992 in Wolfeboro; Frank G. Feeley and Edith Noble

EASTMAN,
Charles E., d. 2/26/1919 at 65/2; farmer; married; b. Ashland; Charles E. Eastman (Holderness) and Priscilla J. Abbott (Holderness)
Nellie F., d. 8/14/1936 at 68/7/6; housewife; widow; b. Sandwich; Dana Watson (Sandwich) and Amanda Wallman (Searsmont, ME)

EATON,
Ellen M., d. 4/29/1912 at 68/3; housekeeper; widow; b. Tamworth; L. M. Abbott and Shuah Freeman
George L., d. 5/2/1952 at 78 in Sandwich; b. Laconia; James L. Eaton and Mary Abbott

Lawrence H., d. 7/22/1986 in Concord; Charles Eaton and Laura Van Valkenburgh
Meredith V., d. 11/5/2007 in Sandwich; Howard Vining and Ruth Case

EDGERLY,
Charlotte E., d. 9/1/1895 at 47/0/28 in Sandwich; housewife; married; b. Boston; George W. Redding

ELLIOTT,
son, d. 9/11/1900 at 0/1/22 in Sandwich; b. Sandwich; Elmer Elliott (Tuftonboro) and Maud Mitchell (Sandwich)
Edwin Lewis, d. 12/30/1993 in Meredith; b. Sandwich; Lewis Elliott and Sarah Adeline Pierce
Elmer, d. 3/9/1958 at 80 in Sandwich; widower; b. Sandwich; John Elliott
George F., d. 12/9/1965 at 81 in Laconia; b. Sandwich; John Elliott and Ida Rowe
Harold, d. 7/15/1993 in Meredith; b. N. Sandwich; Elmer Elliott and Maude Mitchell
Ida E., d. 4/13/1935 at 77/7/13; housewife; widow; b. Sandwich; David Rowe (Sandwich) and Susan Tappin (Sandwich)
John G., d. 10/12/1917 at 74/2/3; farmer; divorced; b. Tuftonboro; Albert Elliott and Mehitable -----
Lewis C., d. 11/25/1959 at 76 in Wolfeboro; married; b. Sandwich; John Elliott and Ida Rowe
Lorraine, d. 5/16/2004 in Wolfeboro; Winifred P. Hoyt and Hazel Moody
Marion W., d. 10/9/1985 in Wolfeboro; Sherman Wing and Dora Wing
Maude L., d. 8/18/1938 at 57/8/19; housewife; married; b. Sandwich; ----- Mitchell
Melvin, d. 11/23/1917 at 11/4/19; b. Sandwich; Elmer Elliott (Sandwich) and Maud Mitchell (Sandwich)

Preston B., d. 9/15/2002 in Sandwich; Edwin L. Elliott and Marion Wing

Sarah A., d. 1/7/1962 at 77 in Wolfeboro; widow; b. RI; George Pierce and Sarah Andrews

Virginia, d. 2/9/1965 at 42 in Ctr. Harbor; married; b. Framingham, MA; William Forristall and Maybelle Manning

ENGEMANN,

Hedwig, d. 7/27/1939 at 74/10/6; housewife; widow; b. Russia; Paul Beyer (Germany) and Emilie Bruckirch (Germany)

ESTES,

Henry Atkins, d. 1/22/1952 at 76 in Sandwich; never married; b. Sandwich; Wiliam H. Estes and Mary Atkins

Mary A., d. 4/16/1916 at 69/4/21; housewife; married; b. Lynn, MA; Henry Atkins (Claremont) and Mary Dow

William H., d. 10/21/1918 at 79/1/17; farmer; widower; b. Sandwich; Caleb Estes and Mehitable Watson

ETH[E]RIDGE,

Chancellor S., d. 2/17/1939 at 85; blacksmith; divorced; b. Lawrence, MA; Martin Etheridge

Charles H., d. 8/5/1915 at 67/8/5; hotel proprietor; married; b. Sandwich; Lewis Ethridge and Mary Goodwin

Lewis B., d. 6/6/1902 at 82/5/15 in Sandwich; farmer; married; b. Sandwich; David Ethridge (Sandwich) and Polly Watson (Dover)

Martin R., d. 1/16/1898 at 85/4/1 in Sandwich; shoe m'f'r; widower; b. Ashland; Nathaniel Ethridge (Sandwich) and ----- Kimball (Sandwich)

Mary A., d. 6/29/1904 at 80/5/27; housewife; widow; b. Rochester; John Goodwin (Rochester) and Lydia Bickford

Walter H., d. 6/16/1910 at 60/2/17; mill operative; married; b. Rumford, ME; Martin Ethridge (Sandwich) and Mary J. Ethridge (Tamworth)

EVANS,

Elizabeth D., d. 10/15/1922 at 76/0/12; at home; single; b. Concord; Franklin Evans and Sarah Davis

Mrs. P. L., d. 10/12/1921 at 92/11/19; retired; widow; b. Barnstead; W. J. George (Northfield) and ----- Ayres

FALLS,

Wilson S., d. 1/27/1945 at 61/1/9 in Hartford, CT; married

FARLEY,

Marcia Wilcox, d. 8/24/1995 in Laconia; b. Dunellen, NJ; Albert C. Wilcox and Mary C. Lingo

FARMER,

Mabel A., d. 10/12/1914 at 29/10/27; housewife; married; b. Sandwich; Charles H. Burrows (Sandwich) and Alice M. George (Sandwich)

FAROY,

Florence I., d. 12/19/1926 at 54/3/6; housewife; married; b. Cambridge, MA; Henry E. Jackson (MA) and ----- Whitney (Boston, MA)

FELCH,

Annie S., d. 5/30/1893 at 48 in Sandwich; housewife; b. Boston; John Welch

Eliza E., d. 9/3/1896 at 53 in Sandwich; housewife; married; b. Sandwich; Warren Dearborn and Eliza Flanders

Osman B., d. 10/20/1901 at 65/11/6 in Sandwich; farmer; married; b. Holderness; Simeon Felch and Susan Smith

William H., d. 9/18/1902 at 62/5/1 in Sandwich; widower; b. Sandwich; Simeon Felch and Susan Smith

FELLOWS,

Benjamin F., d. 4/9/1897 at 62/4/28 in Sandwich; farmer; married; b. Sandwich; John Fellows (Sandwich) and Mary B. Quimby (Sandwich)

Benjamin F., d. 8/31/1970 at 66 in Lawrence, MA; married; b. NH; Arthur P. Fellows and Nellie Foss

Charles R., d. 4/24/1939 at 91/1/7; farmer; widower; b. Sandwich; John Fellows (Sandwich) and May B. Quinby (Sandwich)

Charles R., d. 3/28/1968 at 65 in Meredith; married; b. NH; Arthur P. Fellows and Jennie Goodrich

Christopher C., d. 4/3/1888 at 68/1; apothecary; married; b. Sandwich; John Fellows (Poplin) and Mary J. Quimby (Sandwich)

Dorothy S., d. 9/11/1903 at 83/3/22 in Sandwich; housewife; widow; b. Danbury; Caleb Flanders (Amesbury) and Mehitable Searle

Eva LeMoine, d. 2/21/1984 in Laconia; William LeMoine and Clara Belanger

Lydia D., d. 5/6/1891 at 53/9/17 in Sandwich; housewife; married; b. Brunswick; ----- Dunning (Brunswick)

Mary B., d. 4/9/1893 at 80/1/14 in Sandwich; housewife; b. Sandwich; Johnson Quimby (Ware) and Mary Callin (ME)

Mary E., d. 1/21/1887 at 60/11/10; married; b. Sandwich; Joseph Quimby (Sandwich) and Elizabeth Fullerton (Sandwich)

Ora A., d. 11/28/1924 at 72/6/5; at home; married; b. Tamworth; Benjamin B. Lock (Suncook) and Julia M. Currier (Tamworth)

FIFIELD,

William J., d. 7/29/1897 at 64/8 in Sandwich; farmer; married; b. Tamworth; Harrison Fifield and Eliza Varney (Ossipee)

FISHER,
Chester P., d. 8/29/1986 in Wolfeboro; Charles Fisher and Augusta Bratt
Mary V., d. 6/11/1994 in Laconia; b. Bradford, MA; Alexander Roscoe Noble and Eleanor Stevens

FISK,
Cynthia J., d. 5/19/1933 at 86/11/4; at home; widow; b. W. Dennis, MA; Alexander Baker (S. Yarmouth, MA) and Sarah D. Crowel (W. Dennis, MA)

FITTS,
Evelena, d. 5/31/1967 at 88 in Wolfeboro; b. Canada; Henry Quimby and Clara Lee

FLAHERTY,
John F., Jr., d. 5/30/1980 in Sandwich; John F. Flaherty, Sr. and Mildred Curley

FLANDERS,
Otis, d. 7/14/1888 at 26; farmer; single; b. Sandwich; Charles Flanders (Sandwich) and P. Vittum (Sandwich)

FLETCHER,
Ethel M., d. 9/17/1967 at 76 in Sandwich; b. Boston, MA; Edmund Fletcher and Helen Hovey
Ida H., d. 8/27/1978 at 91 in Laconia; bookkeeper; widow; b. RI; Edward V. Hatch and Etta Boyd

FLETT,
George C., d. 7/23/1920 at 60/11/29; printing; married; b. Nelson, NB; William Flett (Nelson, NB) and Helen Robertson (Gloucester, Scotland)

FLOYD,

daughter, d. 2/20/1937 at 0/0/0; b. Sandwich; Carl O. Bickford (Meredith) and Elva Floyd (Tamworth)

Grant A., d. 11/3/1986 in Laconia; Perley Floyd and Nettie Grant

Regina D., d. 2/8/1987 in Pensacola, FL; Elbert Deming and Fannie Ford

FOGG,

son, d. 11/2/1903 at 0/0/2 in Sandwich; b. Sandwich; Eugene W. Fogg (Sandwich) and Minne L. Osgood (N. Conway)

Albert, d. 6/10/1889 at 63/10/8; farmer; married; b. Sandwich; Samuel Fogg (Sandwich) and Sally Palmer (Sandwich)

Anna E., d. 2/28/1944 at 80 in Concord; housewife; widow; J. Edwin Beede and Augusta A. Sullivan

Annie I., d. 1/24/1919 at 40/0/19; housewife; married; b. NS

Clara H., d. 1/17/1913 at 71; housewife; widow; b. Hollis, ME; Benjamin B. Jose (Saco, ME) and H. B. Anderson (Saco, ME)

Dorrit Brown, d. 2/2/1997 in Laconia; b. N. Sandwich; Frank W. Brown and Alice G. Elliott

Edwin, d. 5/14/1943 at 53/3/16 in Concord; farmer; married; b. Sandwich; Elias H. Fogg (Sandwich) and Annie Beede (Sandwich)

Eugene W., d. 3/11/1942 at 69/6/23 in Laconia; basket maker; widower; b. Sandwich; Hezekiah Fogg (Sandwich) and Mary E. Moulton (Sandwich)

Harriet S., d. 2/14/1894 at 73/9/4 in Sandwich; housewife; married; b. Boston; Edward Barber (ME) and Ruth ----- (MA)

Hezekiah True, d. 10/27/1889 at 65/9/23; farmer; married; b. Sandwich; John Fogg (Sandwich) and Sally Webster (Sandwich)

John W., d. 10/29/1953 at 76 in Plymouth; widower; b. Sandwich; Hezekiah Fogg and Mary Moulton

Joseph Alberto, d. 12/6/1998 in Sandwich; b. Loudon; Jason Fogg and Myrtle Estelle Jones

Joseph Errol, d. 11/13/1996 in Laconia; b. Meredith; Joseph A. Fogg and Dorrit Brown

Mary E., d. 1/16/1919 at 80/11/22; housewife; widow; b. Holderness; Aaron M. Moulton (Sandwich) and Sarah E. Eastman (E. Concord)

Mary Lydia, d. 12/21/1951 at 85 in Plymouth; married; b. Andover; John Seavey and Druscilla Stewart

Samuel, d. 7/18/1889 at 88; farmer; widower; Stephen Fogg (Exeter) and Nancy Batchelder (Raymond)

Stephen, d. 5/17/1912 at 94/4/17; farmer; married; b. Sandwich; Stephen Fogg (Exeter) and N. Batchelder (Raymond)

FOISY,

Alfred W., d. 11/28/2006 in Ctr. Sandwich; Louis Foisty and Emily Whittle

Anna E., d. 10/3/2007 in Sandwich; Harold Bouldry and Lucy Woodbury

FOLCH-PI,

Willa B., d. 11/16/2002 in Concord; Charles W. Babcock and Helen G. Robinson

FOLSOM,

Huldah, d. 12/25/1889 at 80; housewife; widow; b. Tamworth; ----- Downs

FORBES,

Sylbert U., d. 4/1/2005 in Meredith; Ryvers Ainger and Grace Wallace

Walter Aaron, Jr., d. 3/8/1995 in Sandwich; b. Winchendon, MA; Walter A. Forbes, Sr. and Ida -----

FORBUSH,

C. S., d. 6/20/1910 at 76/3/5; machinist; married; b. Peterboro; Luke Forbush and Nancy A. Carey

Mary Jane, d. 12/11/1929 at 92/5/14; at home; widow; b. Somersworth; M. R. Etheridge (Ashland) and Mary J. Mason (Tamworth)

FORD,

Edmund M., d. 9/8/1937 at 73/3/20; scale sealer; married; b. Morgan, VT; Hobart Ford (CT) and Lucy Morse

Elizabeth B., d. 10/29/1963 at 57 in Hartford, CT; married; b. Newton, MA; Carl G. Beede and Mabel G. Merrill

Lucy F., d. 10/30/1913 at 0/0/3; b. Sandwich; Edmund M. Ford (Cabot, VT) and Grace L. Smith (Burke, VT)

Nelson Grant, d. 2/3/1933 at 67/5/24; married

FORRISTALL,

Maybelle, d. 3/4/1968 at 74 in Sandwich; married; b. NJ; James Manning

FORSTER,

Emma, d. 5/19/1943 at 72/5/28 in Sandwich; housewife; divorced; b. Alexandria, VA; Joseph Steavens (Safe Harbor, PA) and Mary Young (Safe Harbor, PA)

FOSS,

son, d. 2/24/1887 at 0/0/1; b. Sandwich; Charles H. Foss (Sandwich) and Hattie F. Dudley (Weston, MA)

son, d. 6/5/1893 at 0/0/2 in Sandwich; b. Sandwich; Charles L. Foss (Tamworth) and Nellie S. Fogg (Sandwich)

son, d. 11/20/1920 at 0/0/0; b. Sandwich; Millard R. Foss (Moultonboro) and Doris A. Davis (Sandwich)

Almira B., d. 9/13/1889 at 81/10/14; housewife; widow; b. Sandwich; Jacob Blake (Thornton) and Louisa Whipple (Moultonboro)

Anne Josephine, d. 1/21/1959 at 70 in Wolfeboro; married; b. Hartford, CT; James McCarthy and Catherine Hayes
Blake, d. 9/16/1898 at 85/2/24 in Sandwich; farmer; married; b. Strafford; Simon Foss (Strafford) and Sarah Blake
Charles H., d. 6/20/1924 at 80/7/24; farmer; widower; b. Sandwich; Enoch Foss and Almira Blake
Frank N., d. 4/9/1912 at --; laborer; married; b. Bucksport, ME; John B. Foss and Loisa J. -----
John B., d. 6/16/1891 at 79 in Sandwich; farmer; widower; b. Sandwich; Isaac Foss (Loudon)
John L., d. 4/26/1966 at 88 in Meredith; widower; b. New Britain, CT; John L. Foss and Elizabeth Marston
Lucinda, d. 9/1/1887 at 84; widow; b. Sandwich
Sally, d. 9/24/1898 at 91 in Sandwich; housewife; widow; b. Gilford; Jacob Morse (Raymond) and Ruth Currier (Kingston)

FOSSIUS,
Charles A., d. 3/24/1918 at 52; farmer; married; b. Sweden; ----- Fossius (Sweden)

FRANK,
Lindsey A., d. 3/5/2002 in Sandwich; Douglas Frank and Lisa Cook

FRANKE,
Evelyn M., d. 3/6/1980 in Wolfeboro; James A. Chalmers and Alice L. Dunton

FRENCH,
Freeman E., d. 11/10/1916 at 66/9/19; farmer; married; b. Sandwich; Ezekiel F. French (Sandwich) and Bethia Paine (Moultonboro)
George N., d. 9/8/1909 at 68/3; clerk; married; b. Sandwich; Hiram E. French (Sandwich) and Mary L. Norris (Meredith)

Mary Jane, d. 10/16/1898 at 89/7/29 in Sandwich; housewife; widow; b. Meredith; Stephen Norris (Raymond) and Sarah Libby (Gilford)

FROST,

Alice May, d. 7/14/1945 at 81/2/7 in Sandwich; retired teacher; single; b. MA; Leslie P. Frost (MA) and Eliza F. White (Sandwich)

Lilla N., d. 4/23/1930 at 75/6/6; teacher; single; b. Waltham, MA; Leonard P. Frost (Barre, VT) and Eliza F. White (Sandwich)

FRYE,

Hattie F., d. 11/10/1891 at 25/9/17 in Sandwich; single; b. Sandwich; Nathaniel Frye (Tuftonboro) and Eliza A. Tappan (Sandwich)

Isaac H., d. 5/30/1899 at 76 in Sandwich; farmer; married; Isaac Frye (Salem, MA) and Annie Bowman (Cape Cod)

Lizzie C., d. 3/16/1893 at 53/0/8 in Sandwich; housewife; married; b. Wolfeboro; James Evans (Moultonboro)

Nathaniel, d. 12/20/1898 at 82/7/4 in Sandwich; farmer; married; b. Tuftonboro; Obediah Frye (Eliot, ME) and ----- (Tuftonboro)

GALE,

Albert C., d. 1/2/1951 at 62 in Hartford, VT; married; b. Sandwich; Amos Gale and Jennie Wade

Amos, d. 5/20/1922 at 82/5/0; farmer; divorced; b. Dover

Lydia, d. 2/15/1891 at 84 in Sandwich; housewife; widow; b. Sandwich; Paul Hume

GANNETT,

Sarah Q., d. 11/24/1895 at 59/5 in Sandwich; housewife; married; b. Sandwich; John S. Quimby (Sandwich) and Nancy Marston (Sandwich)

GARDNER,
Robert C., d. 9/12/2003 in Sandwich; Alfred Gardner and Hazel Cuthburtson

GARLAND,
Dexter, d. 2/4/1914 at 43/5/10; laborer; widower; b. Canada; Nathaniel B. Garland (Moultonboro) and Mary A. Ward (Bolton, PQ)
George D., d. 5/9/1901 at 61/6/8 in Sandwich; farmer; married; b. Jackson; Eben Garland (Conway) and Abigail Chase (Conway)
George N., d. 8/11/1972 at 85 in Laconia; caretaker; single; b. NH; Seth D. Garland and Estella H. Hanson
Hannah E., d. 8/25/1931 at 68/612; at home; widow; b. Sandwich; George O. Hanson (Ctr. Harbor) and Amelia R. Flanders (Amesbury, MA)
Nathaniel, d. 8/7/1908 at 77/7/6; farmer; married; b. Moultonboro; Dexter B. Garland (Moultonboro) and Abigal Hanscome (Moultonboro)
Peter B., d. 4/14/1887 at 88; laborer; single
Seth D., d. 7/2/1913 at 46/2/16; blacksmith; married; b. Tuftonboro; Nathaniel B. Garland (Moultonboro) and Mary A. Ward (Holland, VT)
Winfield S., d. 10/12/1959 at 76 in Sandwich; married; b. Wolfeboro; Eli Garland and Adalaide Tibbetts

GAUDETTE,
Edmund Emile, d. 10/16/1996 in Wolfeboro; b. Lowell, MA; Edmund J. Gaudette and Dorothy St. Onge

GAULT,
Eva M., d. 5/21/1924 at 42/9; housework; married; b. Sandwich; Charles Bagley (NH) and Martha Mudgett (NH)

George, d. 10/3/1934 at 83/11/4; laborer; widower; b. Ctr. Sandwich; Thomas Gault

Jane, d. 1/5/1908 at 80/8/29; housewife; widow; b. Lebanon, ME; ----- Brock (Lebanon, ME) and Experience Libby (Lebanon, ME)

Thomas E., d. 5/1/1902 at 76/3/9 in Sandwich; farmer; married; b. Concord; Eastman Gault (Concord) and Sally ----- (Concord)

GEISS,

Fannie A., d. 12/29/1968 at 73 in Sandwich; widow; b. Germany; Alois Althammer and Franciska Toschel

Joseph, d. 11/13/1968 at 70 in Laconia; married; b. West Germany; Louis Geiss and Rosalie Weidinger

GEORGE,

Annie P., d. 10/17/1909 at 69/11/17; housewife; married; b. Portsmouth; E. P. Roach (Portsmouth) and Ruth Coffin (Portsmouth)

Charles P., d. 2/11/1910 at 77/2/18; farmer; married; b. Sandwich; Daniel George (Sandwich) and Mary Plummer (Sandwich)

Clare Edith, d. 5/23/1949 at 71 in Laconia; single; b. Portsmouth; John George

D. Wilson, d. 12/7/1930 at 90/10/16; married

Eliza M., d. 8/17/1913 at 76/2; housewife; widow; b. Sandwich; Joseph Gilman (Sandwich) and Mary Leavitt (Holderness)

John A., d. 8/22/1910 at 77/10/22; widower; b. Barnstead; Noah J. F. George (Sandwich) and Loirus Ayers

Lydia M., d. 5/5/1931 at 82/5/12

GEPHART,

Sarah Lou, d. 12/6/1988 in Sandwich; Clyde Taylor and Pearl Perkins

GIFFORD,

Dorothea Belcher, d. 6/30/1994 in Wolfeboro; b. Dresden, Germany

Robert L., Sr., d. 4/1/1978 at 83 in Sandwich; engineer (retired); married; b. MA; Nathaniel Gifford and Elizabeth Murray

GILL,

Gertrude Neff, d. 1/24/1933 at 34

GILMAN,

A. S. A., d. 4/2/1910 at 56/1/5; farmer; married; b. Sandwich; Elijah D. Gilman (Sandwich) and Phoebe Annis (Madison)

Alta Atwood, d. 1/17/1952 at 60 in Concord; widow; b. Ctr. Sandwich; Harry Atwood and Estelle Burrows

Charles A., d. 3/21/1890 at 63/8 in Sandwich; farmer; married; Aba Gilman (Sanbornton) and Lucy P. Chase (Sanbornton)

Charles A., d. 8/7/1923 at 80/6/0; shoemaker; married; b. Sandwich; Joseph Gilman and May Moulton

Edward, d. 5/18/1919 at 56/11/18; painter; married; b. Winchester, MA; Jeremiah Gilman (Thornton) and Delia C. Poliguin (Rockport, MA)

Edward H., d. 10/6/1903 at 53/8/15 in Sandwich; machinist; single; b. Lakeport; Ezekiel Gilman (Gilford) and Adeline Young (Gilmanton)

Eleanor, d. 3/20/1918 at 86/5/15; housewife; widow; b. Parsonsfield, ME; Joseph Q. Prescott (Sandwich) and Eliza Parker (Newfield, ME)

Elijah T., d. 1/29/1889 at 73/8/24; farmer; married; b. Sandwich; Jonathan Gilman (Sandwich) and Sally Dinsmore (Conway)

Emma F., d. 2/9/1939 at 81/3/27; at home; widow; b. Sandwich; David Tilton (Sandwich) and Susan Heald (Salmon Falls, ME)

Frank N., d. 5/5/1935 at 87/8; widower; b. Sandwich; Elijah Gilman (Sandwich) and Phoebe Annis (Albany)
George A., d. 6/20/1924 at 49/9; farmer; single; b. Sandwich; John Gilman (Sandwich) and Maria Beede (Sandwich)
Hattie M., d. 12/4/1931 at 69; housewife; married; William Gannett (Tamworth) and ----- Quimby (Sandwich)
James A., d. 11/30/1934 at 57/8/10; laborer; single; b. Denmark, ME; John F. Gilman (Denmark, ME) and Harriette Richardson (Denmark, ME)
John C., d. 10/30/1928 at 79/4/19; farmer; married; b. Sandwich; Joseph Gilman (Sandwich) and Mary Leavitt (Sandwich)
John F., d. 9/21/1932 at 69/1/25; stone mason; widower; b. Denmark, ME; Fairfield Gilman (Denmark, ME) and Harriet Richardson (Denmark, ME)
Keziah P., d. 6/28/1928 at 83/10; at home; widow; Thomas Curtis (England) and Deborah Kingsbury (Dedham, MA)
Laura E., d. 3/3/1903 at 56/10/25 in Sandwich; housewife; married; b. Tuftonboro; Charles Libby (Moultonboro) and Alvira Caverly (Tuftonboro)
Lewis C., d. 3/3/1890 at 35 in Sandwich; farmer; single; b. Sandwich; David Gilman (Sandwich) and Maria Lewis (Sandwich)
Maria E., d. 11/10/1928 at 83/0/7; housewife; married; b. Sandwich; James Beede and S. Cynthia Hodge
Owen L., d. 2/22/1923 at 67/11/23; farmer; married; b. Sandwich; John F. Gilman (Sandwich) and Betsy Bryar (Tamworth)
Phebe, d. 4/13/1897 at 80/1/20 in Sandwich; housewife; widow; b. Eaton; ----- Amis
Rebecca, d. 3/6/1891 at 78 in Sandwich; housewife; widow; b. Sandwich; Stephen Atwood (Sandwich)
Warren Stanley, d. 12/17/1950 at 65 in Sandwich; married; b. Ctr. Sandwich; John Gilman and Mary Beede

GIRTY,

Dorothy M., d. 9/15/1989 in Sandwich; A. Morgan, Jr. and Lois Herman

Everett Charles, d. 4/12/1988 in Sandwich; William K. Girty and Wilimena Alperman

GIVENS,

Jane Wright, d. 2/18/1997 in Laconia; b. Corpus Christi, TX; Thomas N. Givens and Lois A. Williamson

GLIDDEN,

Ralph C., d. 1/1/2001 in Sandwich; Ralph Glidden and Florence Day

Ralph C., Jr., d. 1/22/2005 in Sandwich; Ralph Glidden Sr. and E. Louise Syler

GLINES,

Addie Francilla, d. 10/7/1955 at 77 in Nashua; married; b. NH; Moses Q. Brown and Christine Robbins

Asahel, d. 9/19/1902 at 71/4/5 in Sandwich; farmer; married; b. Moultonboro; Asa Glines (Moultonboro) and Deborah Leonard (Moultonboro)

David, d. 10/24/1956 at 91 in Concord; widower; b. Sandwich; Asahel Glines and Lydia Ann Foss

Lydia A., d. 3/12/1903 at 74/6/15 in Sandwich; housewife; widow; b. Sandwich; David Foss (Thornton) and L. Richardson (Sutton, VT)

GLOVER,

David M., d. 8/27/1946 at – in Ossipee; single; b. Sandwich

GOLDTHWAIT,

Fred W., d. 2/12/1975 at 92 in Laconia; married; b. MA; Charles S. Goldthwait and Ida M. Berry

GOODWIN,
Clifton J., d. 11/29/1943 at 67/1/16 in Laconia; farmer; married; b. Haverhill, MA; Charles Goodwin and Sarah Brooks
Frank L., d. 3/3/1896 at 32/0/27 in Sandwich; farmer; single; b. Sandwich; Charles E. Goodwin (Rochester) and L. B. Goodwin (Sandwich)
James B., d. 2/9/1902 at 83/4/5 in Sandwich; farmer; married; b. Rochester; John Goodwin (Rochester) and Lydia Bickford (Dover)
Lucinda B., d. 8/9/1916 at 78/1/22; housewife; widow; b. Sandwich; Jesse Mudgett (Sandwich) and Jane Burnham (Sandwich)
Myrtie M., d. 2/15/1958 at 69 in Wolfeboro; widow; b. Sandwich; Jacob E. Vittum and Mary O. Vittum
William J., d. 10/3/2003 in Meredith; William Goodwin and Jennie Culler

GORDON,
Anna D., d. 6/16/1920 at 73/7/8; housekeeper; widow; b. Crown Point, NY; Darius Sanborn (Bethlehem) and ----- Crossman
Belle L., d. 4/4/1916 at 76/8; housekeeper; widow; Samuel Crawford
George W., d. 3/31/1912 at 75/9/9; prov. dealer; married; b. Lowell, MA; William Gordon and Dorothy Beede

GORHAM,
May A. K., d. 9/9/1970 at 81 in Ctr. Harbor; single; b. CT; Edwin S. Gorham and Carrie F. -----

GOTSHALL,
Abbott, d. 5/7/1988 in Laconia; Thomas D. Gotshall and Mary Abbott
Mary A., d. 11/30/2001 in Sandwich; Abbott Gotshall and Bertha Woodworth

Mary E., d. 10/29/1938 at 65/11/26; housewife; married; b. Boston, MA; William T. Abbott (Waterboro, ME) and Frances Hoyt (Boston, MA)

GOULD,

Ezra, d. 2/26/1888 at 79/6; hotel keeper; married; b. Sandwich; William Gould (Dover) and Hannah Bean

Mary Jane, d. 5/31/1890 at 75/4 in Sandwich; housewife; single; b. Windham, ME; William Frieze

GRANT,

Aliston H., d. 1/26/1979 at 87 in Wolfeboro; carpenter; married; b. NH; George A. Grant and Clara Heddle

Aristus W., d. 10/6/1935 at 88/7/6; dentist; married; b. Sandwich; Wentworth Grant (Newington) and Lavina Gates (Newington)

Clara A., d. 3/16/1922 at 66/1/2; housewife; married; b. Sandwich; William Heddle (Quebec) and Louisa Q. Hadley (Sandwich)

Daniel B., d. 2/2/1914 at 80/4/15; farmer; married; b. Tuftonboro; Wentworth Grant (Tuftonboro) and Lovina Gates

Elizabeth A., d. 10/1/1947 at 88/7/18 in Sandwich; widow; b. Sandwich; Charles Bennett (Sandwich) and Sarah Atwood (Sandwich)

Frank, d. 1/21/1934 at 80/11/11; laborer; widower

Frank H., d. 3/5/1921 at 71/4/2; farmer; married; b. Sandwich; Wentworth Grant (Ossipee) and Lavina Gates (Newington)

George A. M., d. 12/10/1933 at 79/10/10; carpenter; widower; b. Sandwich; Wentworth Grant (Madbury)

Syliva E., d. 4/15/1983 in Meredith; Allston Evans and Idella Clough

GRAVES,

Aubrey M., d. 2/23/1920 at 76/8/25; farmer; married; b. Sandwich; Ross C. Graves (Sandwich) and Dorothy Vittum

Daniel V., d. 1/31/1921 at 72/6/26; farmer; single; b. Sandwich; Ross M. Graves (Sandwich) and Dorothy Vittum (Sandwich)
Dorothy, d. 3/27/1908 at 86/3/2; housewife; widow; b. Sandwich; Moses Vittum (Sandwich) and Sally Vittum (Sandwich)
Isaac Frye, d. 1/31/1949 at – in Sandwich; married; b. Sandwich; Ross M. Graves and Dorothy Vittum
Lizzie B., d. 6/24/1949 at 83 in Sandwich; widow; b. Sandwich; Leonidas Hodgdon and Susan A. Webster
Myrtle G., d. 5/4/1949 at 66 in Sandwich; married; b. Sandwich; George Grant and Clara Heddle
Nellie Edith, d. 2/6/1951 at 58 in Laconia; married; b. Tamworth; Frank Whiting and Annie Choate
Oliver, d. 7/25/1894 at 38/4 in Sandwich; farmer; married; b. Sandwich; Russell Graves (Sandwich) and Mary Libbey (Sandwich)
Ross M., d. 2/17/1960 at 83 in Meredith; widower; b. Sandwich; Aubry Graves and Louise Sanborn
Russell, d. 8/26/1888 at 68; married; Joseph Graves and Betsey Vittum

GRAY,
Charles H., d. 10/5/1895 at 67/2 in Sandwich; painter; single; b. Monmouth; Richard Gray (Monmouth) and Elizabeth Fowler (Saco, ME)
George L., d. 2/18/1918 at 21/9/27; machinist; single; b. Sandwich; Irving Gray (Plymouth, ME) and Mary Etta Corliss (Sandwich)
George L., d. 1/6/1932 at 83/11/2; retired farmer; married; b. Plymouth, ME; Richard Gray (Monmouth, ME) and Elizabeth Fowler (Monmouth, ME)
Grace M., d. 9/30/1908 at 2/5; b. Sandwich; Irving Gray (Plymouth) and Etta Corliss (Sandwich)
Gracie May, d. 4/2/1895 at 0/1/3 in Sandwich; b. Sandwich; Irving Gray (Plymouth, ME) and Etta Corliss (Sandwich)

Irving, d. 8/25/1966 at 91 in Meredith; widower; b. Plymouth, ME; George Gray and Jeanette Tarbox

Jannette T., d. 1/23/1935 at 86/10/3; housework; widow; b. Biddeford, ME; Jastham Tarbox (Biddeford, ME) and Diana Fletcher (Biddeford, ME)

Julia G., d. 4/26/1913 at 0/0/4; b. Sandwich; Irving H. Gray (Strafford) and Gladys C. Pease (Gilmanton)

Mary Etta, d. 1/10/1937 at 64/0/26; at home; married; b. Sandwich; Hiram Corliss (Sandwich)

Sarah Ann, d. 9/11/1903 at 1/10/20 in Sandwich; b. Sandwich; Lysander D. Gray (Madison) and Annie Twombly (Madison)

GREELEY,

Donna P., d. 10/29/1970 at 93 in Wolfeboro; widow; b. NH; John Pelkey and Margaret McKenzie

GREEN,

daughter, d. 4/3/1933 at –; b. Sandwich; Wilber J. Green (Moultonboro) and Mina E. Towle (Center Harbor)

Annie Valora, d. 10/22/1960 at 78 in Wolfeboro; married; b. New Hampton; Charles Pickering and Jennie M. Chase

GREENE,

Herbert T., d. 10/24/2006 in Ossipee; William C. Greene and Margaret W. Eckfeldt

Margaret E., d. 7/18/1975 at 85 in Laconia; ret. teacher; married; b. NH; Thomas H. Eckfeldt and Grace Weed

William C., d. 9/7/1978 at 88 in Wolfeboro; professor; widower; b. MA; Herbert E. Greene and Harriet S. Chase

GREGSON,

Marie E., d. 10/11/1970 at 89 in Ctr. Harbor; widow; b. NY; Henry Biscoff and Eva Parker

GURDY,
George, d. 8/4/1898 at 67/4/10 in Sandwich; farmer; married; b. Bristol; Jacob Gurdy (Bartlett) and Sarah Doton (Moultonboro)
Sarah R., d. 2/15/1891 at 54 in Sandwich; housewife; married; b. Sandwich; Ebenezer Dale (Wilton) and Mehitable Beede (Sandwich)

GUTCHESS,
Franklin J., d. 12/24/2000 in Ctr. Sandwich; Harold Gutchess and Freda Goelke

HACKETT,
George E., d. 6/15/1893 at 25/10/11 in Sandwich; b. Sandwich; Albert F. Hackett (Sandwich) and Susan A. Smith (Sandwich)
Susan A., d. 11/26/1909 at 87; housewife; widow; b. Sandwich; John Smith (Sandwich) and Eliza W. ----- (VT)

HAHN,
Andrew Joseph, d. 8/31/1953 at 0/2 in Sandwich; b. NJ; Erwin L. Hahn and Marion E. Failing

HALEY,
Flora Belle, d. 10/28/1954 at 88 in Rochester; widow; b. NH; Alvin Tilton and Mary Abbie Clement
Harry O., d. 5/6/1946 at 80/0/11 in Laconia; farmer; married; b. Tuftonboro; William Hale (Tuftonboro) and Betsy F. Thompson (Ossipee)

HALL,
daughter, d. 8/26/1948 at 2 hrs. in Laconia; b. Laconia; Ernest Hall (Revere, MA) and Dorothy Foss (Lynn, MA)
Alpheus, d. 1/24/1891 at 69/6 in Sandwich; farmer; married; b. Thornton; John Hall and Polly Mussey

Dorothy Foss, d. 6/17/1972 at 61 in Laconia; shoe worker; widow; b. MA; Albert Foss and Emelie W. Moore
Ednah W., d. 9/15/1986 in Arlington, VA; Hardy Hardison Phelps and Harriet Joyner
Ernest F., d. 8/30/1960 at 57 in Sandwich; married; b. Revere, MA; Jess Hall and Martha -----
John B., d. 11/25/1892 at 82 in Sandwich; farmer; married; b. Thornton; Jeremiah Hall (Moultonboro) and Ruth Rice (Sandwich)
Joseph, d. 6/10/1943 at 7/2/1 in Laconia; b. Sandwich; Ernest F. Hall (Revere, MA) and Dorothea M. Foss (Lynn, MA)
Laurence K., d. 2/8/1979 at 92 in Meredith; ret. YMCA sec.; married; b. KA; James W. Hall and Laura Knipe
Mary R., d. 8/22/1971 at 81 in Laconia; married; b. MO; John Rose and Mary Schakleford
Moses A., d. 5/5/1930 at 84; farmer; single; b. Sandwich; Alpheus Hall (Sandwich) and Rosilla Avery (Thornton)
Rozilla, d. 12/11/1893 at 77/2/7 in Sandwich; housewife; b. Campton; Stephen Avery

HALLETT,
Paul B., d. 5/5/1934 at 26/4/19; minister; married; b. Cambridge, OH; Joseph Hallett (OH) and Lillian Barry

HAM,
J. Herbert, d. 8/7/1925 at 55; single
Laura E., d. 3/13/1910 at 63/0/11; housekeeper; single; b. Sandwich; Penn Hamm and Mary Cavis

HAMBROOK,
Mary Frances, d. 12/23/2004 in Sandwich; Howell H. Reeves and Justina L. Smith

HAMMOND,

Emily S., d. 11/13/1999 in Sandwich; John Adams and Emily Heinze

John Arnold, d. 6/1/1994 in Wolfeboro; b. Raymond; John Hammond and Hattie Carew

HANSEN,

Marion, d. 2/18/2002 in Falmouth, ME; Chester Howe and Annie C. Thompson

HANSON,

Amelia R., d. 2/16/1909 at 68/4/11; housewife; married; b. MA; Jesse Flanders (Plaistow) and Lydia Battis

Annie, d. 3/26/1933 at 84/10/8; housewife; widow

Charles, d. 9/8/1893 at 76/11/8 in Sandwich; farmer; Jonathan Hanson (Tuftonboro) and Hannah Wiggin (Tuftonboro)

Charles F., d. 1/27/1895 at 46/1/1 in Sandwich; farmer; single; b. Holderness; James W. Hanson (Moultonboro) and Sarah Sturtevant (Center Harbor)

Frank L., d. 2/22/1941 at 71/1/27; painter; married; b. Sandwich; George O. Hanson (Moultonboro) and Amelia Flanders (NH)

Frank W., d. 9/12/1933 at 58/0/0; farmer; single; Alonzo Hanson

George N., d. 2/17/1926 at 30/1/6; chauffeur; divorced; b. Sandwich; Frank L. Hanson (Sandwich) and Ida M. Priest (Peace Dale, RI)

George O., d. 7/29/1920 at 74/6/16; farmer; widower; b. Moultonboro; Charles Hanson (Moultonboro)

Harry L., d. 11/10/1890 at 17/11/10 in Sandwich; single; b. Winchester, MA; Ruel W. Hanson (Moultonboro) and Vandelia Bean (Great Falls)

Henrietta P., d. 6/16/1945 at 98/11/21 in Newton, MA; widow; b. Sandwich; Tillotson Pierce (Campton) and Almira Holmes (Campton)

James A., d. 1/4/1922 at 77/10/28; farmer; married; b. Holderness; James W. Hanson (Moultonboro) and Sally Sturtivant (Center Harbor)
Richard M., d. 12/29/1916 at 72/2/25; teaming; married; b. Carroll; Charles Hanson (Moultonboro) and Mary True (Center Harbor)
Ruel W., d. 1/18/1910 at 68/9/8; farmer; widower; b. Moultonboro; James W. Hanson and Sally Sturtevant
Sally, d. 5/17/1889 at 67 in Sandwich; housewife; widow; b. Center Harbor; John Sturtevant (Center Harbor)

HARDING,
Dorothy Wollenweber, d. 6/18/1994 in Sandwich; b. Denver, CO; Dr. Louis C. Wollenweber, Sr. and Bessie Brannen

HARKNESS,
Edith Alice, d. 8/19/1951 at 80 in Sandwich; single; b. Chicago, IL; Edson J. Harkness and Marianne Bates

HARRIS,
Mary E., d. 11/15/1887 at 55/10/19; widow; Thomas B. Weeks (Gilmanton) and Philenda Way (Lempster)

HART,
Elmer B., d. 5/22/1939 at 76/9/6; merchant; widower; b. Sandwich; Dr. H. N. Hart (Sandwich) and Lucy Beede (Sandwich)
Ethel A., d. 6/20/1930 at 53/1/20; at home; married; b. Sandwich; Charles F. Burleigh (Gilmanton) and Olive Hutchins (W. Medway, MA)
Harrison A., d. 8/2/1894 at 0/3/27 in Sandwich; b. Sandwich; Elmer B. Hart (Sandwich) and Nellie Atwood (Sandwich)
Harrison N., d. 8/1/1889 at 61/2; physician; married; b. Sandwich; John Hart (Conway) and Mary C. Gilman (Sandwich)

Joseph P., d. 5/6/2000 in Wolfeboro; ----- and Elizabeth Hart
Nellie A., d. 4/12/1894 at 24/5/26 in Sandwich; housewife; married; b. Sandwich; Charles Atwood (Sandwich) and Eliza Stevenson (Tamworth)
Stickney B., d. 10/23/1916 at 11/0/1; student; b. Sandwich; Elmer B. Hart (Sandwich) and Ethel M. Burleigh (Sandwich)

HARVEY,
Mary G., d. 8/26/1935 at 59/11/18; housewife; married; b. Lowell, MA; Ezra Grant (Saco, ME)

HASKELL,
James Leland, d. 8/21/1994 in Laconia; b. Boston, MA; Theodore W. Haskell and Clara Ripley

HASLEY,
Margaret, d. 3/21/1907 at 72/7; housewife; widow; b. Ireland; David Hurley (Ireland) and Sarah Webb

HATCH,
George C., d.10/29/1897 at 67/10/27 in Sandwich; carpenter; married; b. Groveton; Alpheus Hatch (Groveton) and Lucinda Marshall
Lydia C., d. 6/16/1898 at 78/11 in Sandwich; housewife; widow; b. Tuftonboro; Obediah Frye (Eliot, ME) and Lydia Caverly (Tuftonboro)

HAUGHTON,
Clifford B., Jr., d. 4/17/1970 at 53 in Sandwich; married; b. FL; Clifford B. Haughton, Sr. and Lewise Collins

HAWES,
Ada F., d. 7/4/1917 at 1/8/9; b. Sandwich; Casper S. Hawes (Springfield, MA) and Ada Vittum (Sandwich)

HEALY,

Marjorie D., d. 8/23/2000 in N. Sandwich; Willard Dow and Blanche Lincoln

Raymond John, d. 7/17/1997 in Laconia; b. New York, NY; Joseph Healy and Emily O'Brien

HEARD,

Edwin M., d. 7/26/1928 at 74/7/26; retired mer.; married; b. Sandwich; William A. Heard (Wayland, MA) and Ann E. Marston (Sandwich)

Emily M., d. 9/13/1908 at 75/4/26; housewife; widow; b. Sandwich; Moulton Marston (Moultonboro) and Ann M. Ambrose (Moultonboro)

Lillian, d. 1/28/1964 at 88 in Concord; b. Worcester, MA; William Thompson and Eliza Slye

Mary S., d. 6/6/1982 in Sandwich; J. Watts Stovall and Lucy -----

Nettie Louisa, d. 10/20/1945 at 86/3/24 in Laconia; at home; widow; b. Methuen, MA; Charles O. Barker (Londonderry) and Dorothy Flanders (Danbury)

Stuart W., d. 11/3/2000 in Meredith; William Heard and Lillian Thompson

William, d. 3/24/1942 at 81/7/10 in St. Petersburg, FL; merchant; married; b. Sandwich; William A. Heard (Wayland, MA) and Emily Marston (Ctr. Sandwich)

William A., d. 4/15/1901 at 73/7/21 in Sandwich; banker; married; b. Wayland, MA; William Heard (Wayland, MA) and Susan Mann (Oxford)

HEATH,

Albert C., d. 12/25/1892 at 23/8/16 in Sandwich; married; b. New Hampton; Benjamin H. Heath (Sandwich) and Ludia A. Moulton (Holderness)

HEDDLE,
Louisa, d. 2/24/1888 at 65/3; married; b. Sandwich; Winthrop Hadley (Sandwich) and Sebil Worthen (Canaan)

HIGGINS,
Ella M., d. 1/25/1892 at 38/6/14 in Sandwich; housewife; single; b. NS

HIGHT,
H. Wadsworth, d. 9/8/1958 at 79 in Wolfeboro; married; b. Winchester, MA; Henry W. Hight and Nettie Swan

HILL,
David H., d. 11/25/1889 at 55/11/13; lawyer; married; b. N. Berwick; Oliver Hill (N. Berwick) and Lucinda ----- (Cornish, ME)
Harriet J., d. 7/30/1915 at 80/6/1; widow; b. Canada; James Thompson (England) and Ester Farranee (England)
Mary Abbie, d. 5/19/1908 at 61/8/1; housewife; single; b. Sandwich; Robert Hill and R. H. Hill
Samuel A., d. 4/8/1920 at 79/10/7; farmer; single; b. Sandwich; Robert Hill (ME) and R. H. Hill (Sandwich)
Walter F., d. 11/21/1914 at 39/2/10; carpenter; married; b. N. Brookfield, ME; Hiram J. Hill (Spencer, MA) and Irene C. French (Sandwich)

HILTON,
Eliza M., d. 3/19/1887 at 59/9; married; b. Moultonboro; Nathaniel Ambrose (Moultonboro) and Irene Brown (Ossipee)
Gilman, d. 10/19/1937 at 72/5/14; farmer; single; b. Sandwich; John N. Hilton (Sandwich) and Louise Ricker (Boston, MA)
J. E., d. 12/29/1905 at 80/8/15; farmer; widower; b. Sandwich

Louisa, d. 11/16/1902 at 68/9/26 in Sandwich; housewife; married; David Ricker (Moultonboro) and Catherine Vittum (Sandwich)

Newman J., d. 10/15/1906 at 65/1/23; farmer; widower; b. Sandwich; John H. Hilton (Sandwich) and Sophia Severance (Sandwich)

HINDS,

Edward S., d. 9/30/1892 at 64/1 in Sandwich; farmer; married; b. Portland; Nathaniel Hinds (Tamworth) and Eraline Beverly (Sanborn)

Loveland, d. 3/11/1919 at 67/5/15; farmer; single; b. Sandwich; Edward S. Hinds (Tamworth) and Almira A. Mudgett (Sandwich)

HOAG,

stillborn son, d., 3/20/1960 at – in Laconia; b. Laconia; William G. Hoag and Constance Tibbets

Abbie P., d. 11/19/1944 at 66/0/13 in Branford, CT; widow; b. Sandwich; Samuel Peaslee

Albert B., d. 2/13/1925 at 52; physician; married; b. Sandwich; Lewis Hoag (Sandwich) and Julia Estes (Dedham)

Alice N., d. 9/26/1958 at 80 in Laconia; single; b. Tamworth; Thomas W. Hoag and Martha Cartland

Almena V., d. 7/11/1888 at 63/2; married; b. Sandwich; Reuben Hurd and Mary Varney

Arthur T., d. 11/13/1926 at 58/0/17; laborer; single; b. Sandwich; Lewis Hoag (Sandwich) and Julia Estes (Danvers, MA)

Elizabeth L., d. 8/21/1948 at 85/9/24 in Ctr. Sandwich; married; b. N. Woburn, MA; David W. Leslie (Deering) and Ellen Hall (NS)

Elizabeth S., d. 7/18/1937 at 83/7/11; retired; single; b. Sandwich; Russell Hoag (Sandwich) and Naomi Beede (Sandwich)

Lelia, d. 1/2/1899 at 1/1/3 in Sandwich; b. Sandwich; Albert B. Hoag (Sandwich) and Abbie F. Peaslee (Sandwich)

Lewis, d. 1/3/1913 at 89/4/25; farmer; married; b. Sandwich; John Hoag (Sandwich) and Comfort Morrell (Brunswick, ME)

Martha E., d. 10/22/1920 at 67/4/23; at home; widow; b. Parsonsfield, ME; John B. Cartland (Parsonsfield, ME) and Cynthia Winslowe (Westbrook, ME)

Nathan F., d. 2/14/1914 at 89/0/2; farmer; married; b. Sandwich; John Hoag (Sandwich) and Comfort Morrill (Waterville)

Russell, d. 4/24/1897 at 79/11/19 in Sandwich; farmer; widower; b. Sandwich; James Hoag (Sandwich) and Ruth Scribner (Sandwich)

Thomas W., d. 7/28/1920 at 73/2/18; farmer; married; b. Sandwich; Russell Hoag (Sandwich) and Naomi Beede (Sandwich)

HODGE,

Benjamin B., d. 2/13/1898 at 77/10 in Sandwich; farmer; married; b. Moultonboro; Thomas Hodge (Derry) and H. Batchelder (Moultonboro)

Charles, d. 4/2/1942 at 87/4/2 in Sandwich; farmer; widower; b. Sandwich; Charles W. Hodge (Moultonboro) and Elizabeth Garland (Rochester)

Charles W., d. 6/17/1909 at 86/2; farmer; married; b. Moultonboro; Thomas Hodge (Moultonboro) and H. Batchelder (Moultonboro)

Effie M., d. 7/19/1932 at 62/10/17; housewife; married; b. Holderness; Freeman Abbott (Sandwich) and Abbie Tappan (Sandwich)

Elizabeth J., d. 4/20/1982 in Meredith; James Haggart and Jane Robinson

Hattie E., d. 7/8/1941 at 78/11/20; housewife; married; b. Moultonboro; Alonzo Bragg (Sandwich) and Mary Cook (Moultonboro)

John N., d. 2/1/1916 at 59/6/9; farmer; married; b. Sandwich; Benjamin B. Hodge (Moultonboro) and Mary Smith (Sandwich)

Mira T., d. 6/13/1975 at 88 in Ossipee; nurse; widow; b. NH; Jonathan Tappan and Julia Nute

Nellie F., d. 3/25/1920 at 53/6/7; housekeeper; widow; b. Sandwich; Nathaniel H. Burrows (Lebanon, ME) and Sarah D. Thompson (Sandwich)

Norman Francis, d. 1/1/1954 at 76 in Moultonboro; widower; b. Sandwich; John N. Hodge and Ruth Berry

Reuben Norman, d. 9/30/1990 in Sandwich; Norman Hodge and Effie Abbott

Walter Elmer, d. 1/28/1951 at 65 in Sandwich; married; b. Moultonboro; Charles R. Hodge and Hattie E. Bragg

HODSDON,

Florence T., d. 1/29/1986 in Meredith; Rev. Charles Turner and Olive Brock

Grant W., d. 7/23/1970 at 68 in Laconia; married; b. ME; Herbert A. Hodsdon and Lucy Charles

Lucy W., d. 7/1/1954 at 81 in Moultonboro; widow; b. Chatham; Norman Charles and Esther Walker

HOLLAND,

Philip Anthony, d. 8/1/1994 in Laconia; b. New Hampton; Frank Holland and Jennie Vossahlik

HOLT,

Benjamin B., d. 7/20/1899 at 83/4/26 in Sandwich; farmer; married; b. Sandwich; Ezekiel Holt (Sandwich) and Polly Burleigh (Sandwich)

HOLWELL,

Edith Eckert, d. 3/3/1994 in N. Sandwich; b. Amesbury, MA; Robert Leonard Eckert and Eleanor Sargent

HORNE,
Amasa, d. 1/13/1892 at 76/10 in Sandwich; farmer; widower; b. Sandwich; ----- (Dover) and ----- (Dover)
Emma, d. 4/20/1892 at 62/11/4 in Sandwich; housewife; married; b. Searsmont; ----- (ME)
Emma J., d. 8/8/1931 at 71/1/24; housewife; married; b. Sandwich; Smith Henderson (Sandwich) and C. Dow (Tuftonboro)
John F., d. 11/28/1911 at 78; farmer; married; b. Sandwich; Paul Horne (Dover) and Christine Watson (Sandwich)
Marcia E., d. 1/30/1918 at 83/0/10; housewife; widow; b. Searsmont, ME; John Weelman (Searsmont, ME) and Eliza Bennett (Searsmont, ME)
Otis B., d. 2/28/1895 at 78 in Sandwich; farmer; widower; b. Sandwich; Paul Horne (Dover) and Christena Watson (Dover)
Thomas, d. 3/30/1932 at 74/11/9; farmer; widower; b. PA; David Horne (PA)

HOUSTON,
John, d. 5/14/2000 in Ossipee; David Houston and Martha Fraser

HOWARD,
Marion P., d. 10/5/1962 at 79 in Sandwich; single; b. Boston, MA; James Howard and Annie Pember

HOWARTH,
James Oberland, d. 4/18/1950 at 90 in Laconia; widower; b. Andover, MA; Oberland B. Howarth

HOWE,
David B., d. 12/9/2000 in Laconia; Chester H. Howe and Annie C. Thompson

Elizabeth M., d. 12/28/1991 in New London, CT; Burton S. Wood and Elizabeth Kinney

Harris Winchester, d. 6/14/1987 in San Diego, CA; Chester Harris Howe and Annie Thompson

Margaret A., d. 6/3/1993 in Sandwich; b. Sandwich; Frank Burrows and ----- McDonald

Ray J., d. 7/23/1976 at 78 in Sandwich; heavy equipment operator; widower; b. VT; Carl T. Howe and Mary M. Webb

HOYT,

Calvin, d. 12/17/1891 at 81/9/23 in Sandwich; farmer; married; b. Sandwich; George Hoyt and Mary Hoyt

Caroline B., d. 8/3/1908 at 84/6/10; housewife; widow; b. Sandwich; John S. Quimby (Sandwich) and Nancy M. Marston (Sandwich)

Charles B., d. 3/11/1938 at 78/3/9; farmer; widower; b. Sandwich; Burleigh Hoyt (Sandwich) and Caroline Quimby (Sandwich)

Florence Weed, d. 2/15/1934 at 58/7/28; housewife; married; b. Sandwich; James Y. Webster (Sandwich) and Emma Swett (Sandwich)

George S., d. 9/14/1934 at 80/8/6; married

James E., d. 6/30/1956 at 81 in Laconia; widower; b. Moultonboro; Moses E. Hoyt and Lydia Smith

Lydia C., d. 12/13/1934 at 80/8/15; widow; b. Ctr. Sandwich; Joseph Wentworth (Sandwich) and Sarah P. Jones (Brookline, MA)

Moses E., d. 4/17/1921 at 87/7/21; carpenter; widower; b. Sandwich; Moses Hoyt (Henniker) and Sally Pupper (Sandwich)

Ruth E., d. 5/29/1945 at 72/11/3 in Laconia; housewife; widow; b. Moultonboro; James Y. Webster (Sandwich) and Emma F. Swett (Sandwich)

Ruth Moulton, d. 12/9/1951 at 86 in Lakeport; married; b. NH; Daniel Moulton and Ann Skinner

Sarah L., d. 10/18/1906 at 78/4/17; housewife; widow; b. Sandwich; Henry Vittum (Sandwich) and Lydia Leach (Moultonboro)

Wentworth, d. 11/30/1897 at 15/9/17 in Sandwich; single; b. Sandwich; George S. Hoyt (Sandwich) and Lydia Wentworth (Sandwich)

HUGHES,

Bernadette A., d. 5/21/2005 in Omaha, NE; William Keough and Alice Cox

HULL,

Lorenzo B., d. 9/5/1909 at 68/9/24; watch maker; married; b. Plymouth; Nathaniel Hull (Plymouth) and Mahala Kelley (Plymouth)

HUNT,

Anna M., d. 11/14/1977 at 90 in Laconia; housewife; married; b. NH; Alonzo McCrillis and Lulie Clark

HUNTRESS,

Josephine, d. 3/30/1895 at 55/9/4 in Sandwich; housewife; widow; b. Sandwich; Tillotson Pierce (Corinth, VT) and Almira Holmes (Campton)

HURD,

William A., d. 5/13/1963 at 64 in Tamworth; married; b. Freedom; William Hurd and Enna Danforth

HURLEY,

Esther F., d. 11/23/1979 at 84 in Wolfeboro; teacher – public sch.; widow; b. NH; J. Choate Furness and Lillian Appleton

John J., d. 3/15/1976 at 80 in Sandwich; teacher; married; b. NH; John J. Hurley and Margaret Cullity

HUSE,
Lizzie, d. 1/27/1887 at 61; married; b. ME; Peter Bryer and Ruth Bean

HUTCHINS,
Clarence E., d. 1/19/1957 at 66 in Sandwich; married; b. Tamworth; Noah Hutchins and Augusta Downs
Edward C., d. 5/24/1983 in Hanover; Clarence E. Hutchins and Marion Taylor
Minnie J., d. 8/15/1925 at 56/1/25; housewife; married; b. Columbus, OH; Joseph Jeffrey (St. Mary, OH) and Celia Harris (NY)
Sarah A., d. 4/3/1891 at 65 in Sandwich; housewife; married; b. Madison; George Mack and Mary Keniston

HYSON,
Helen B., d. 2/25/1965 at 80 in Sandwich; b. Salem, MA; Arthur Copp and Sarah Gardner

INGLES,
Eric G., d. 4/3/1969 at 72 in Wolfeboro; married; b. Sweden; Charles Ingleson and Emma Peterson

IPPOLITO,
Vincent J., Sr., d. 2/17/1993 in Sandwich; b. Lawrence, MA; Alexander Ippolito and Vincenza Viana

IRVING,
Albert, d. 2/12/1891 at 73 in Sandwich; farmer; widower; William Irving (Scotland) and Hannah Balbe (Augusta)
Arthur L., d. 9/18/1894 at 0/1/25 in Sandwich; b. Sandwich; George Irving (Sandwich) and Lydia Tibbetts (Wolfeboro)
George L., d. 3/3/1926 at 62/8/22; laborer; divorced; b. Sandwich; Albert Irving (Sandwich) and Hannah Heard (Sandwich)

Mary Jane, d. 8/27/1958 at 55 in Concord; widow; b. Sandwich; George Irving and Lydia Tibbetts

JACKSON,
Alida, d. 6/20/1951 at 80 in Concord; divorced; b. Sandwich; Edward Marston and Ellen Smith
Euphemia, d. 1/9/1939 at 44/7/10; housewife; married; b. Frizzleton, NS; ----- McDonald (Frizzleton, NS) and Martha Ingraham (Frizzleton, NS)
Maria A., d. 7/2/2006 in Manchester; Charles Burris and Bertha Machnig

JACOBS,
Joseph H., d. 12/17/1962 at 62 in Marlboro; married; b. Barnstead; Coran M. Jacobs and Lettie Hillsgrove

JACQUES,
Oleana, d. 3/13/1964 at 65 in Sandwich; b. Berlin; Napoleon Jacques and Melina Nourrie

JAMESON,
William D., d. 6/25/1970 at 55 in Sandwich; married; b. PA

JENNINGS,
Fred M., d. 11/4/2000 in Augusta, ME

JOHNSON,
Donald, d. 4/2/1981 in Laconia
Sarah, d. 10/27/1913 at 84/4/2; housewife; widow; b. Acton, ME; Joseph Sanborn and Mary -----

JOHNSTON,
Richard B., d. 9/24/1975 at 48 in Laconia; forestry; married; b. NJ; Charles C. V. Johnston and Myra Smith

JONES,

Eugene F., d. 10/23/1904 at 31/7/3; inspector; widower; b. Cambridge, MA; Joseph M. Jones (Pittsfield, M) and A. L. Milner (NS)

Griffith M., d. 1/18/1964 at 68 in Hartford, VT; b. Bayonne, NJ; John Jones and Gertrude -----

JOSE,

Edward Henry, d. 9/29/1914 at 69/5/2; lawyer; married; b. Dayton, ME; Benjamin B. Jose (Dayton, ME) and Harriet Patterson (Dayton, ME)

Edwin H., d. 3/5/1999 in Laconia; Edwin Jose and Nancy Swift

KEEFE,

Wayne F., d. 9/17/1991 in Sandwich; Walter F. Keefe and Patricia Finlay

KEITH,

Anna Spooner, d. 1/29/1949 at 77 in Haverhill; married; b. Haverhill; William Spooner and Susan Tibbetts

James, d. 7/17/1954 at 79 in Haverhill; widower; b. Canada; Andrew Keith and Catherine E. Wright

KELLEY,

Thomas P., d. 12/26/1901 at 76/2/26 in Sandwich; farmer; married; Job Kelley (Moultonboro) and Lois Blackey (Moultonboro)

KENDALL,

Philip A., d. 8/11/1995 in Temple; b. Boston, MA; Alexander Kendall and Mary Shannon

KENLY,

Henry C., d. 1/18/1972 at 76 in Ctr. Sandwich; retired; married; b. VA; William L. Kenly and Julie Closson

Ruth Burdick, d. 8/21/1989 in Ossipee; Clark Burdick and Elizabeth L. Peckham

KEVIN,
Ruth J., d. 2/5/1991 in Plymouth; Robert Kevin and Ruth Hazlett

KIMBALL,
Alden L., d. 9/9/1971 at 53 in Laconia; married; b. ME; Calvin Kimball and Marian Coombs
Clarissa, d. 10/18/1887 at 94/5/17; widow; b. Center Harbor; P. Sturtevant and Sally Senter
James J., d. 10/25/1889 at 77; farmer; married
Mildred, d. 2/15/1978 at 72 in Wolfeboro; receptionist; widow; b. MA; Fred Barton

KING,
Mary A., d. 10/22/1978 at 86 in Sandwich; laborer – manuf.; married; b. MA; Dennis McCarthy and Margaret -----

KINGMAN,
Morton A., d. 9/10/1929 at 74/3/19; retired; married; b. MA; Lewis A. Kingman (Mansfield, MA) and M. J. Alderman (Westfield, MA)

KIRKWOOD,
Grace H., d. 9/17/1996 in N. Sandwich; b. Winchester, MA; Henry Wadsworth Hight and Grace Higham
Samuel Brown, d. 3/2/1994 in Wolfeboro; b. Seattle, WA; Samuel Kennedy Kirkwood and Edith Brown

KNIGHT,
James P., d. 4/5/1932 at 79/10/8; farmer; widower; b. Moultonboro; ----- Knight and Sarah Goodwin (Moultonboro)

William, d. 9/30/1920 at 84/4/27; pipe fitter; widower; b. Glessop, England; William Knight (England)

KNOX,
Perley Cecil, d. 12/5/1954 at 56 in Sandwich; married; b. NH; Charles Edward Knox and Mary Elliott Chesley
Thomas Y., d. 9/19/1902 at 83/0/27 in Sandwich; farmer; widower; b. Ossipee

KURTH,
Richard A., d. 2/18/1972 at 82 in Wolfeboro; musician; married; b. MA; Richard Kurth and Jane McKenna

LADIEU,
Francine Piche, d. 10/8/1983 in Sandwich; Francis J. Piche and Catherine McShea

LAMBERT,
Alfred E., d. 7/20/1993 in Laconia; b. E. Boston, MA; Alfred E. Lambert and Alma S. Gunn

LANE,
Irene T., d. 11/17/1887 at 82/1/15; widow; John Tucker and Rebecca Bowker

LANGLEY,
Effie M., d. 7/25/1956 at 77 in Franklin; widow; b. Sandwich; Russell Bryer and Rebekah Bryer
Rufus H., d. 10/3/1942 at 71/1/22 in Tilton; mgr. of retail store; married; b. Cambridge, MA; Margaret MacDonald (Scotland)

LANGNER,
Edward G., d. 5/24/1991 in Meredith; William Langner and Eva Boehn

Wilhelmina E., d. 10/5/1991 in Laconia; Emil Ruben and Freda Schilling

LARSON,

Frederick C., d. 9/21/1976 at 83 in Wolfeboro; industrial engineer; married; b. MA; John P. Larson and Birgitta Jensen

LARSSON,

Thure L. F., d. 4/17/1951 at 85 in Sandwich; widower; b. Arvika, Sweden; Lars G. Larsson and Eugenia Sandelin

LAVERACK,

Janet, d. 2/5/2001 in Sandwich; Stephen Sabine and Mary Lawrence

LAWRENCE,

Agnes C., d. 4/28/1988 in Laconia; Eugene Sullivan and Arvilla Chandler

Etta M., d. 11/15/1931 at 45/7/10; housewife; married; b. Brownfield, ME; Albhsa Rogers (Brownfield, ME) and Mary O. Moulton (Sebago, ME)

Glenn W., d. 5/3/1983 in Meredith; Edwin Lawrence and Ellen March

Mark D., d. 10/16/1895 at 39/9 in Sandwich; blacksmith; married; b. Albany; George Lawrence and Jane Willey

LAWSON,

George E., d. 6/12/1970 at 75 in Ctr. Harbor; married; b. MA; Alphonse Lawson

LEACH,

Dorothy E., d. 1/11/2003 in Meredith; Max Weld and Myra Tappan

Earl Stanley, d. 10/12/1996 in Plymouth; b. Sandwich; William A. Leach and Dorothy Weld

Ernest W., d. 6/28/1932 at 0/11/10; b. Sandwich; William Leach (Concord) and Dorothy Weld (Manchester)

Raymond C., d. 9/6/1936 at 0/1/7; b. Sandwich; William Leach (Concord) and Dorothy Weld (Manchester)

Sally Jean, d. 5/11/1953 at 0/1 in Laconia; b. Laconia; Arthur T. Leach and Caroline Forristall

William A., d. 7/29/1986 in Meredith; Arthur Leach and Bertha Lindberg

LEAR,

Lester A., d. 8/17/1987 in Laconia; Alonzo Lear and Corrine Woolweaver

LEAVENS,

Mary, d. 1/14/1956 at 82 in Laconia; single; b. Concord; Albert Leavens and Emily French

LEE,

Ansel E., d. 4/2/1948 at 86/2/7 in No. Sandwich; married; b. Holderness; Walter Lee (Holderness) and Mary Frances Corlis (No. Sandwich)

David G., d. 9/27/1912 at 38/1/14; laborer; divorced; David G. Lee (Moultonboro) and Louise Elliott (Campton)

Elizabeth, d. 2/5/1915 at 59/3/8; clerk; married; b. Sandwich; John Otis Cook (Sandwich) and Cyntha Johnson (Allenstown)

Jennie Davey, d. 6/12/1954 at 81 in Sandwich; widow; b. Sandwich; Oscar T. Vittum and Ann Palmer

Moulton M., d. 5/13/1907 at 72/11/16; laborer; b. Sandwich; J. A. Lee (Moultonboro) and Lucy Marston (Sandwich)

Oliver E., d. 2/5/1931 at 84/9/18; farmer; single; b. Sandwich; Jonathan Lee (Moultonboro) and Nancy Bean (Sandwich)

Valinda Ann, d. 6/18/1914 at 83/8/5; housekeeper; widow; b. Corinth, VT; Jim Wilson (Corinth, VT) and Belinda Almon (Corinth, VT)

LEHMANN,
Sara K., d. 7/26/1998 in Laconia; b. Campbelltown, PA

LEIGHTON,
Charlotte E., d. 8/3/1916 at 70/2/2; housewife; widow; b. Gilmanton; Samuel D. Folsom (Gilmanton) and Eunice Folsom (Sanbornton)
James S., d. 2/5/1916 at 81/0/23; carpenter; married; b. Columbia, ME; Aaron Leighton (Columbia, ME) and Eliza F. Worcester (Indian River, ME)

LEWIS,
Arthur H., Sr., d. 6/29/1975 at 82 in Laconia; machinist-farmer; married; b. MA; John H. Lewis and Mary Corkhill
John S., d. 8/12/1923 at 63/7/3; printer; married; b. Liverpool, England; John Lewis (Liverpool, England) and Isabella Burrows (Liverpool, England)
Philomene L., d. 11/13/1980 in Laconia; Rene LeBlanc and Josephine Santerre

LIBBY,
Hanson, d. 6/3/1892 at 83/10/7 in Sandwich; farmer; widower; b. Tuftonboro; Daniel Libby (Tuftonboro) and Mary Abbott (Tuftonboro)

LILLIE,
Eliza F., d. 8/13/1911 at 85/11/15; housekeeper; widow; Parker Prescott (VT) and Mary Vittum (Sandwich)

LINDLEY,
Louise Rose, d. 12/19/1993 in Laconia; b. Ridgefield Park, NJ; Eugene Lauber and Anna Maria McGoff

LINNEMAYR,
Klaus, d. 12/24/1995 in Sandwich; b. Austria; Erich Linnemayr and Emma Steigler

LINSCHEER,
Franklin G., d. 8/2/1985 in Moultonboro; Willem G. Linscheer and Johanna -----

LITTLE,
Blanch I., d. 10/8/1975 at 90 in Wolfeboro; housewife; married; b. NH; Frank Scriggins and Carrie Blackey
Jay A., d. 8/18/1975 at 15 in Swanzey; student; single; b. NH; Clayton A. Little and Joan Beach

LOMBARD,
Cynthia, d. 3/25/1894 at 71/11/29 in Sandwich; housewife; widow; b. Sandwich; Samuel Thompson (Farmington) and Betsey Seavey (Rye)

LONDON,
Joshua, d. 6/6/1917 at 49/11/14; black; servant; single; b. NC; ----- (slaves in South)

LONG,
Walter Fairfield, d. 10/11/1950 at 71 in Sandwich; married; b. Billerica, MA; John S. Long and Mary A. Kellogg

LOVEJOY,
William F., d. 12/27/1900 at 55 in Sandwich; carpenter; single; b. Wayne, ME; Hubbard Lovejoy (Wayne, ME) and Lucia Burgess (Wayne, ME)

LOVERING,

Bessie E., d. 8/24/1956 at 74 in Center Harbor; widow; b. NB; Arthur Canning and Charlotte Ellison

Frank S., d. 12/25/1942 at 81/7/12 in Wolfeboro; physician; married; b. Freedom; John N. Lovering (Freedom) and Elizabeth S. Piper (Tuftonboro)

Josephine May, d. 5/29/1954 at 82 in Laconia; widow; b. NH; Moses E. Hoyt and Lydia A. Smith

LUCAS,

Edith J., d. 12/21/1906 at 32/6/8; housewife; widow; b. Tuftonboro; Francis J. Lucas and Susan F. Grant

MACDONALD,

Alonzo M., d. 8/30/1960 at 84 in Laconia; married; b. Wakefield; Malcolm MacDonald

Ethel Bennie, d. 7/28/1954 at 48 in Laconia; married; b. MA; Oliver Diack and ----- Wilson

Myrtle C., d. 10/18/2001 in Portsmouth; William Brown and Margaret Miller

Helena F., d. 12/7/1963 at 77 in Sandwich; widow; b. Wolfeboro; Alonzo Bickford and Harriet Beecher Stowe

MACDOUGALL,

Alice G., d. 4/3/1934 at 60/11/5; married; b. Sandwich; Daniel G. Beede (Sandwich) and Abbie E. Roberts (Dover)

Hamilton C., d. 3/16/1945 at 86/5 in Wellesley, MA; retired professor; married; b. Warwick, RI; Alexander MacDougall (Scotland) and Ann F. Briggs (RI)

MACK,

Albert, d. 8/11/1905 at 17/6; laborer; single; b. Sandwich; Frank Mack (Sandwich) and Lydia Tibbetts (Rochester)

Fred M., d. 6/8/1908 at 59/2/25; farmer; divorced; b. Tamworth; George Mack (Madison) and Lois Chase (Conway)

George, d. 11/23/1894 at 76 in Sandwich; farmer; widower; b. Sandwich

Lois R., d. 5/30/1891 at 69/11/21 in Sandwich; housewife; married; b. Madison; Oliver Chase (Concord) and Abigail Kennett (Freedom)

MACKENNY,

Frank L., d. 5/14/1922 at 65/2/0; painter; married; b. Grand Manan, Canada; Edward MacKenny

MAGOON,

Leslie, d. 1/16/1912 at 62/3/5; farmer; married; b. Sandwich; Asa Magoon and Eliza Smith

Mary A., d. 6/25/1937 at 95/2/18; retired; widow; b. Cheltonville, MA; John Courtney (England) and Mary A.Gifford (England)

Mary E., d. 11/9/1906 at 79/1/12; housewife; widow; b. Sandwich; Levi Smith (Sandwich) and Betsey Moulton (Sandwich)

MANN,

George W., d. 9/24/1888 at 86; carpenter; married; b. Sandwich; James Mann and Alice Treig (Moultonboro)

Mary H., d. 5/11/1897 at 83/6/21 in Sandwich; housewife; widow; b. Tuftonboro; Obediah Frye (Kittery, ME) and Lydia Caverly (Tuftonboro)

MANNING,

Virginia V., d. 4/2/1978 at 60 in Laconia; housewife; widow; b. NH; George W. Vittum and Ethel Strong

MARDEN,
Iva B., d. 4/29/1980 in Laconia; Marcellus Wallace and Harriet Smith

MARINO,
Leonard H., d. 10/11/2003 in Lebanon; Leonard Marino and Viola Galawszka

MARRA,
Frank J., d. 8/16/2006 in Laconia; Angelo Marra and Nichotta Disalvo

MARSH,
Lewis Webster, d. 6/3/1994 in Laconia; b. Salem, MA; Warren Marsh and Robina Stevenson

MARSHALL,
Crofton William Basil, d. 6/27/1994 in Sandwich; b. Ealing, England; William Johnston Marshall and Margaret Sankey

MARSTON,
Adelaide J., d. 8/30/1947 at 81/3/11 in Concord; widow; b. Winchendon, MA; Jeremiah Gilman (Thornton) and Delia Poloquin (MA)
Caleb M., d. 9/9/1893 at 90/2/4 in Sandwich; farmer; b. Moultonboro; John Marston (Hampton) and Nancy Wiggin (Hampton)
Carry A., d. 4/18/1897 at 29/10/6 in Sandwich; housewife; married; b. Sandwich; Charles H. Atwood (Sandwich) and Eliza B. Stevenson (Tamworth)
Celestia M., d. 12/30/1902 at 61/2/17 in Sandwich; housewife; married; b. Tamworth; Ira Marston (Tamworth) and Sally Webster (Moultonboro)

Charles S., d. 2/3/1924 at 65/10/20; farmer; married; b. Sandwich; Ira Marston (Tamworth) and Sallie Webster (Moultonboro)
Elisha, d. 9/11/1902 at 101/0/2 in Sandwich; farmer; widower; b. Moultonboro; John Marston (Hampton) and Nancy Moulton (Hampton)
Emma E., d. 10/17/1907 at 56/10/9; housewife; widow; b. Ware, MA; R. Cummings (Ware, MA) and Emeline Record (Ware, MA)
Enoch Q., d. 2/1/1904 at 56/8/11; physician; married; b. Sandwich; Elisha Marston (Moultonboro) and Lucy S. Ferris (Bath, ME)
Grace, d. 12/9/1888 at 3/1/10; b. Sandwich; Enoch Q. Marston and Emma E. Commings (Weare, MA)
Grace Stanton, d. 9/29/1955 at 89 in Watertown, MA
Ira, d. 11/24/1890 at 77/1/7 in Sandwich; farmer; married; b. Tamworth; Ebenezer Marston (Hampton) and Abigail Marston (Parsonsfield)
John A., d. 12/9/1910 at 81/3/7; farmer; widower; b. Sandwich; Caleb M. Marston and Betsey Ambrose (Sandwich)
Moulton H., d. 12/25/1894 at 88/11/16 in Sandwich; widower; b. Moultonboro; John Marston (Hampton) and Nancy Moulton (Hampton)
Sarah B., d. 9/20/1893 at 75/11/27 in Sandwich; housewife; b. Moultonboro; Isaac Webster (Sandwich) and Sarah Watson (Sandwich)
Willis B., d. 2/7/1945 at 83/9/0 in Lowell, MA; farmer; married; b. Sandwich; Ira Marston (Tamworth) and Sally Webster (Moultonboro)

MARTEL[LE],
Beatrice M., d. 12/23/1965 at 66 in Ctr. Harbor; b. Sandwich; James Palmer and Etta Dow
Donald, d. 3/27/1938 at –; b. Sandwich; Elzear Martelle (St. Monique, Canada) and Beatrice Palmer (Sandwich)

Elzear, d. 10/4/1965 at 72 in Wolfeboro; b. Canada; Manuel Martel and Addie Boucher
Forest E., d. 6/22/1986 in Wolfeboro; Elzear Martel and Beatrice Palmer
Linda Lee, d. 11/22/1963 at 0/0/1 in Laconia; b. Laconia; Haven Martel and Jo-Ann Daigneau
Raymond, d. 5/20/2004 in Laconia; Elzear Martel and Beatrice Palmer

MARTIN,
child, d. 8/26/1941 at 6 hrs.; b. Laconia; Wilbur Martin (Sandwich) and Dora Peasley (Sandwich)
Alden P., d. 12/10/1889 at 67/1/6; farmer; married; b. Sandwich; Samuel Martin (Sandwich) and Betsey Watson (Sandwich)
Annie E., d. 1/18/1895 at 36/5/15 in Sandwich; housewife; single; b. Boston
Eugene F., d. 3/13/1956 at 76 in Sandwich; married; b. Sandwich; Alden Martin and Margaret J.
Harry L., d. 9/12/1894 at 12/1 in Sandwich; b. Sandwich; Alden Martin (Sandwich) and Margaret Coleman (PA)
James F., d. 7/4/1965 at 80 in Sandwich; b. Melrose, MA; Jerimiah Martin and Sarah E. Sprague
Jeremiah, d. 9/7/1924 at 78/6/17; shoemaker; widower; b. Bingham, ME; Levi P. Martin (Wakefield) and Lucinda Langley (Bingham, ME)
Jeremiah, d. 2/7/1940 at 67/6/11; laborer; single; b. Melrose, MA; Jeremiah Martin (Bingham, ME) and Sarah Sprague (Stoneham, MA)
John, d. 1/1/1979 in Quincy, MA; James F. Martin and Mary A. Tappan
Julia G., d. 12/24/1910 at 0/1/21; b. Sandwich; James P. Martin and Mary A. Tappan (Sandwich)
Mary Alice, d. 7/3/1967 at 81 in Franklin; b. Sandwich; Jonathan Tappan and Julia Nute

Sarah Bertha, d. 4/26/1941 at 64/3/23; housework; single; b. Sandwich; Alden P. Martin (Sandwich) and Margarett Coleman (Chester, PA)
Sarah E., d. 5/23/1977 at 90 in Laconia; housewife; widow; b.; NH; Charles Skinner and Jennie -----
Wilbur Eugene, d. 9/30/1993 in Laconia; b. Sandwich; Eugene Martin and Sarah Skinner

MASON,
Amos W., d. 8/21/1888 at 63/11/22; farmer; married; b. Sandwich; William Mason (Sandwich) and Sophia M. Wingate (Farmington)
Charles Clinton, d. 11/4/1954 at 72 in Laconia; married; b. NH; Fred O. Mason and Mary Etta Whiting
Charlotte Q., d. 3/16/1900 at 96/6/21 in Sandwich; housewife; widow; b. Sandwich; Moses Quimby (Weare) and Hannah Thrasher (Sandwich)
David T., d. 6/3/1892 at 71/6/3 in Sandwich; carpenter; married; b. Sandwich; Edward Mason (Newmarket) and Sarah Thrasher (Sandwich)
Etta, d. 6/27/1941 at 78/6/22; housewife; married; b. Ossipee; George C. Whitting (Ossipee) and Ellen Johnson (Tamworth)
Eupheme, d. 11/27/1892 at 67/11 in Sandwich; housewife; widow; b. Sandwich; Jere P. Moulton (Moultonboro) and Joanna Hodge (Sandwich)
John A., d. 3/18/1899 at 59 in Sandwich; farmer; married; b. Sandwich; David T. Mason (Sandwich) and Roxanna Hatch (Tamworth)
Luther J., d. 11/11/1932 at 68/10/13
William, d. 11/3/1888 at 93/7; farmer; married; Simeon Mason and Abigail Mason

MAUCH,
Henry, d. 5/10/1964 at 78 in Sandwich; b. Patterson, NJ; Marsell Mauch and Magalein Baum

MAXWELL,
John M., d. 6/27/1967 at 78 in Laconia; b. Scotland; Samuel R. Maxwell and Mary Agnew

MAYER,
John Eric, d. 1/15/1988 in Santa Barbara, CA; John C. Mayer and Dorothy Ehrich

McBEE,
Burrett, d. 11/6/1985 in Laconia; William Hunter McBee and Alice Eaton
Henrietta G., d. 8/8/2000 in Laconia; William Gray and Henrietta Seelye

McCANNA,
Clare Foy, d. 4/22/1984 in Sandwich; James A. Foy and Nora Murray

McCARTHY,
Beverly J., d. 8/6/1985 in Wolfeboro; Robert McClure and Dover -----

McCAULEY,
John A.,d . 4/24/1932 at 83/8/27
Louisa C., d. 11/26/1900 at 78/6/26 in Sandwich; married; b. Litchfield; Benjamin Jones (Litchfield) and ----- Powell (Litchfield)

McCLEAN,
Eva Maria, d. 5/24/1949 at 75 in Laconia; b. NH; John F. Keyes and Lucinda Kimball

McCLOSKY,
William, d. 3/3/1937 at 76/2/12; farmer; divorced; b. Haverhill, MA; Butrick McClosky and Isabelle -----

McCORMACK,
Arthur W., d. 6/13/1988 in Sandwich; Charles P. McCormack and Charlotte Wakefield
George C., d. 9/4/1985 in Wolfeboro; Libarius McCormack and Ella Ames

McCORMICK,
Emma J., d. 5/7/1925 at 46/4; at home; married; b. Charlestown, MA; Charles Hill (Sandwich) and Harriet Thompson (Sandwich)
Frances M., d. 1/31/1975 at 59 in Hanover; housewife; married; b. NH; Harry Wallace and Hattie Plummer

McCRACKEN,
Barbara S., d. 3/19/1991 in Laconia; Homer I. Silvers and Mae V. Adams

McCRILLIS,
daughter, d. 9/13/1918 at 0/0/1; b. Sandwich; Neal McCrillis (Sandwich) and Marion Bullard (Arlington, MA)
Alonzo, d. 10/18/1938 at 80/2/16; civil eng.; married; b. Sandwich; William McCrillis (Sandwich) and Mary Watson (Tamworth)
James H., d. 9/--/1893 at 78 in Sandwich; b. Sandwich
Lulu M., d. 3/4/1942 at 81/10/28 in Norwood, MA; housewife; widow; b. Sandwich; Langdon G. Clark (Sandwich) and Anne M. Beede (Sandwich)
Margaret, d. 10/26/1969 at 80 in Ossipee; single; b. NH; Alonzo McCrillis and Lulie Clark

Marion B., d. 7/3/1971 at 77 in Sandwich; widow; b. MA; Henry Bullard and Mary Palmer
Neal, d. 3/3/1955 at 64 in Boston, MA; married; b. Sandwich; Alonzo McCrillis and Lulie Clark
William, d. 5/24/1895 at 74/0/24 in Sandwich; farmer; married; b. Sandwich; Neal McCrillis (Sandwich) and Abigail Foss

McDANIEL,
Eliza, d. 12/9/1896 at 83/9 in Sandwich; housewife; widow; b. Albany; Uriah McDaniel and ----- (Madison)
Uriah, d. 12/22/1927 at 75/0/7; farmer; widower; b. Albany; Sewall McDaniel (Albany)

McDANIELS,
daughter, d. 11/28/1895 at – in Sandwich; b. Sandwich; Uriah McDaniels (Albany) and Nellie Nichols (Moultonboro)
Nellie, d. 9/24/1909 at 54/0/4; housewife; married; b. Moultonboro

McGAFFEY,
Caroline, d. 5/12/1900 at 84/2/9 in Sandwich; housewife; single; b. Sandwich; Neil McGaffey (Sandwich) and Peggy McCrillis
Carrie M., d. 6/28/1898 at 42/0/2 in Sandwich; housewife; widow; b. Sandwich; Elijah T. Eastman (Sandwich) and Phebe Annis (Eaton)
George, d. 9/5/1892 at 44 in Sandwich; farmer; married; b. Sandwich; Elden McGaffey (Sandwich) and Mehitable Nealey (Tamworth)
Irene, d. 9/12/1888 at 74; milliner; single; b. Sandwich; Neal McGaffey (Sandwich) and Peggy McCrillis (Sandwich)
Mehitable, d. 1/28/1890 at 74 in Sandwich; housewife; widow; b. Sandwich; Amos Neally (Tamworth) and Anna Head (Tamworth)

McGLAUFLIN,
Elizabeth, d. 5/23/1902 at 76/4/9 in Sandwich; housewife; widow; b. W. Swanzey; Martin Mason (W. Swanzey)

McGOWAN,
T. H., Jr., d. 9/3/1937 at 16/6/17; schoolboy; single; b. Woburn, MA; Thomas H. McGowan (Woburn, MA) and Lorette Lafferty (Woburn, MA)

McGUIRE,
James, d. 4/30/1904 at 90

McINTIRE,
Lydia F., d. 10/31/1905 at 56; single; b. Lynn, MA

McLELLAN,
Rita, d. 2/23/1932 at 0/0/27; b. Plymouth; Barton McLellan (Canada) and Mabel Nugent (Bloomfield, VT)

MENSCH,
Karen M., d. 2/15/2002 in Sandwich; Robert C. Jensen and Laura M. Sliney

MEREDITH,
Irving, Jr., d. 10/20/2001 in Sandwich; Irving Meredith and Lois Woodley
Nancy L., d. 11/21/1995 in Sandwich; b. Berkeley, CA; Lester A. Lear and Isadora Schmidt

MERRILL,
Belinda, d. 6/5/1893 at 76/6/18 in Sandwich; housewife; b. Moultonboro; David Adams (Moultonboro) and Dolly Bradbury

MERRIMAN,
Frederika W., d. 2/23/1995 in Needham, MA; b. Lincoln, MA; Henry Warner and Henrietta Slade
Harriett R., d. 5/19/1970 at 21 in Boston, MA; married; b. NH; Kyle E. Willoughby and Minerva B. Wallace
Roger Bigelow, Jr., d. 5/27/1994 in Needham, MA; b. Cambridge, MA; Roger Bigelow Merriman and Dorothea Foote

MERRYFIELD,
Christine, d. 7/15/1941 at 49/5/22; housework; widow; b. Sandwich; Lucian Skinner (Sandwich) and Hattie Horne (Sandwich)
Clifford, d. 1/5/1940 at 44/6/22; carpenter; married; b. Tuftonboro; Everett Merryfield (ME) and Emma Nichols (Charlestown, MA)

MESSER,
Annie L., d. 11/27/1951 at 77 in Moultonboro; widow; b. Sandwich; Abram Tappan and Addie Graves

METCALF,
Winslow H., d. 9/4/1978 at 52 in Laconia; retired; divorced; b. RI; Edward H. Metcalf and Winifred Winslow

MICHAEL,
Anthony A., d. 4/15/1963 at 14 in Sandwich; single; b. Laconia; Monroe Michael and Bernice Adams
Marion D., d. 12/31/1973 at 84 in Ctr. Harbor; housewife; widow; b. NY; Philip F. Dick and Elizabeth -----

MIKULIS,
George P., d. 11/18/1978 at 34 in Sandwich; co-owner Depot Rest.; married; b. MA; Benjamin M. Mikulis and Nellie Antonovich

MILBURY,
Lorraine G., d. 6/27/2004 in Manchester; Herman Tilton and Gertrude Martin

MILLS,
Maryellen M., d. 5/12/1999 in Boston, MA; John McManus and Margaret Mooney

MINER,
Louisa Post, d. 1/12/2004 in Sandwich; Carr Cemper Sutton and May Daugherty
Robert F., d. 12/13/2002 in Laconia; James Miner and Virginia Hatch

MITCHELL,
Mrs. U., d. 11/6/1896 at 54/2 in Sandwich; housewife; widow; b. Tamworth; Parker Prescott and Polly Vittum (Sandwich)

MONTGOMERY,
Nancy F., d. 1/21/2006 in Portsmouth; Philip C. Fenn and Mary E. Ford

MOODY,
Elmer P., d. 7/13/1971 at 73 in Wolfeboro; married; b. NH; William Moody and Mabel Moore
Margaret R., d. 8/21/2002 in Ossipee; Rose McBride
Raymond E., d. 11/2/1929 at 7/5/28; b. Sandwich; Elmer P. Moody (Albany) and Margaret McBride (Somersworth)

MOORE,
Gideon, d. 1/11/1898 at – in Sandwich; farmer; b. Moultonboro; John P. Moore (NY) and Eliza A. Farrar (Gilmanton)
Henry W., Jr., d. 9/11/2006 in Laconia; Henry Moore and Rosamond Ritchie

MOORE-JUMPER,
Davida T., d. 2/3/2001 in Sandwich; David Moore and Denette Thomas

MOORHOUSE,
Alfred Blanchard, d. 11/11/1986 in Wolfeboro; Alfred Hampden Moorhouse and Alice Maud Blanchard
Alice M., d. 9/19/1942 at 68/4 in Brookline, MA; treasurer; married; b. Sandwich; Arven Blanchard (Sandwich) and Nellie S. Creigthton (Sandwich)

MORGAN,
Alexis, d. 11/29/2004 in Cambridge, MA; Patrick Morgan and Maud Cabot
Dorothy R., d. 8/9/2003 in N. Sandwich; William Rising and Janie Leffel
Robert L., d. 4/6/1976 at 61 in Hartford, VT; potter; married; b. CA; Charles A. Morgan and Kathryn Potter

MORSE,
George W., d. 6/24/1918 at 92/1/14; farmer; widower; b. Sandwich; Benjamin Morse and ----- Thresher
Hannah J., d. 2/4/1910 at 68/11; housekeeper; married; b. Tamworth; Alry Jewell and Jane Rowe

MORTON,
H. Clifford, d. 11/19/1979 at 71 in Laconia; research chemist; married; b. CT; John Morton and Alice Lamphier

MOSES,
Raymond G., d. 7/16/1974 at 82 in Wolfeboro; ret. Army officer; married; b. NY; James J. Moses and Minerva Rich

MOULTON,

Alvah, d. 1/24/1892 at 76/11/24 in Sandwich; farmer; married; b. Sandwich; John Moulton

Ann E., d. 7/29/1913 at 82/9/21; housewife; married; b. Sandwich; Joseph Skinner (Sandwich) and Betsey Cornley (Tuftonboro)

Clara, d. 3/23/1889 at --; housewife; married; b. Sandwich; Asa S. Prescott and Mary Wallace

Daniel, d. 1/20/1920 at 86/1/11; carpenter; widower; b. Sandwich; Jeremiah Moulton and ----- Rice

Eliza, d. 1/17/1891 at 87/7/17 in Sandwich; housewife; widow; b. Henniker; George Hoyt (Henniker) and Mary Hoyt (Henniker)

Elsy, d. 8/10/1889 at 78/8; housewife; widow; b. Sanbornton; ----- Blaisdell and ----- Sanborn

George, d. 1/22/1919 at 71/6/10; farmer; widower; b. Holderness; Aaron M. Moulton (Sandwich) and Sarah E. Eastman (E. Concord)

George R., d. 6/25/1894 at 25 in Sandwich; farmer; married; b. Laconia; Hiram Moulton (Albany) and Saloma Beols (Munson, MA)

Giles L., d. 7/24/1901 at 62/6/24 in Sandwich; farmer; single; b. Sandwich; John Moulton (Ashland) and Eliza Hoyt (Sandwich)

Herbert E., d. 1/3/1935 at 84/6/9; retired; married; b. Albany; Moses P. Moulton and Louisa A. Rice (Sandwich)

Jeremiah P., d. 8/11/1888 at 90; farmer; widower; b. Moultonboro

John, d. 1/7/1887 at 90/9/3; farmer; married; b. Sandwich; Reuben Moulton (Rye) and Mary ----- (Rye)

Julia A., d. 8/15/1938 at 78/5/2; housewife; widow; b. Sandwich; David Tilton (Sandwich) and Susan W. Hill (Sanford, ME)

Julia D., d. 8/31/1906 at 81/1/16; widow; b. Tamworth; Ebenezer Marston (Parsonsfield, ME) and Abigail Marston (Brownfield, ME)

Louisa, d. 2/4/1974 at 86 in Franconia; school teacher; single; b. NH; Edward Moulton and Julia Tilton
Nancy M., d. 9/9/2002 in Laconia; Stanley Miles
Pauline S., d. 4/21/1999 in Laconia; Lewis Elliott and Sara Pierce
Sally, d. 4/30/1895 at 89 in Sandwich; housewife; widow
Saloma S., d. 2/2/1911 at 85/5/28; housekeeper; widow; b. Southbridge; William Beals (England) and Mary Smith

MOWATT,
Herman H., d. 9/26/1976 at 53 in Ottawa, Canada; self employed; married; b. MA; Frank A. Mowatt and Sarah Quimby

MUDGETT,
Bruce, d. 2/19/1939 at 0/5; b. Sandwich; Fred C. Mudgett (Sandwich) and Marion Elliott (Sandwich)
Carolyn M., d. 4/28/1988 in Laconia; John Conner and Evelyn Sargent
Charles, d. 7/7/1939 at 78/8/21; foreman; married; b. Sandwich; Charles Mudgett (Sandwich) and Mary Wallingford (Alton)
Charles E., d. 4/17/1904 at 75/10; farmer; widower; b. Sandwich; Orlando Mudgett and Nancy Hinds
David, d. 3/17/1889 at 92/8; farmer; widower; b. Sandwich; Elisha Mudgett and Sarah -----
Donald Merton, Sr., d. 4/19/1993 in Laconia; b. N. Sandwich; Eugene Mudgett and Eva Davis
Elisha W., d. 9/16/1911 at 70/2/29; farmer; married; b. Sandwich; Jesse Mudgett (Sandwich) and Jane Burnham (Sandwich)
Elisha W., d. 5/8/1975 at 64 in Laconia; farmer-logger; single; b. NH; Jessie Mudgett and Jennie Sturges
Elnora, d. 6/15/1926 at 1/3/0; b. Sandwich; Jesse A. Mudgett (Sandwich) and Jennie Sturgis (Albany)
Emma Melissa, d. 4/1/1954 at 86 in Laconia; widow; b. NH; Hezekiah T. Fogg and Mary B. Moulton

Ernest M., d. 1/24/1929 at 0/7/24; b. Sandwich; Eugene E. Mudgett (Sandwich) and Eva M. Davis (Sandwich)

Eugene E., d. 11/21/1930 at 56/1/1/3; farmer; married; b. Sandwich; Erastus Mudgett (Sandwich) and Susan M. Tibbetts (Rye, VT)

Eva May, d. 10/30/1941 at 58; housewife; widow; b. Ctr. Sandwich; Frank Davis (Lakeport) and Rose Belle Willey (Ctr. Sandwich)

Evelyn F. T., d. 10/24/1984 in Sandwich; Walter Taylor and Mary Agnes Wallace

Frank L., d. 2/7/1966 at 71 in Sandwich; married; b. Sandwich; Elisha Mudgett and Luella Atkins

Fred C., d. 10/23/1965 at 63 in Laconia; b. Sandwich; Fred W. Mudgett and Anne Fogg

Fred W., d. 2/23/1948 at 82/2/2 in New Hampton; widower; b. Sandwich; Charles E. Mudgett (Sandwich) and Mary Wellingford (Sandwich)

Helen E., d. 12/26/1936 at 9/7/7; childhood; b. Sandwich; Jessie Mudgett (Sandwich) and Jennie Sturgis (Sandwich)

Henry E., d. 7/18/1902 at 13/7/25 in Sandwich; student; single; b. Sandwich; Elisha W. Mudgett (Sandwich) and Luella B. Atkins (Sandwich)

Irving, d. 10/31/1972 at 66 in Hanover; farmer; married; b. NH; Eugene Mudgett and Eva Davis

James E., d. 1/18/1914 at 75/10/21; married; Moses Mudgett (Sandwich) and Clarissa A. Eaton

James R., d. 1/24/1979 at 53 in Wolfeboro; N.E. Telephone; married; b. NH; Frank L. Mudgett and Annie McInnis

Jennie E., d. 11/25/1943 at 56/11/12 in Pittsfield; housewife; widow; b. Albany; Philip Sturgis (Canada) and Elmira Douglas (Conway)

Jesse, d. 7/14/1902 at 90/4/22 in Sandwich; farmer; widower; b. Sandwich; Elisha Mudgett (Weare) and Sarah Webster (Weare)

Jesse, d. 6/21/1939 at 52/1/26; farmer; married; b. Sandwich; Elisha Mudgett (Sandwich) and Luella Atkins (Sandwich)

Linwood C., d. 11/2/1930 at 0/1/16; b. Sandwich; Fred C. Mudgett (Sandwich) and Marion L. Elliott (Sandwich)

Luella, d. 10/4/1917 at 64/2/12; widow; b. Sandwich; Henry Atkins and Lucy Coffin

M. Olive, d. 2/4/1921 at 77/4/24; retired housewife; widow; b. Meredith; David Cotton and Isabel Boynton (Meredith)

Marion E., d. 10/14/1969 at 63 in Keene; widow; b. NH; Louis Elliott and Sarah Pierce

Mary J., d. 3/13/1899 at 71/7 in Sandwich; housewife; married; b. Alton; R. Wallingford and Rebecca Richards

Ora A., d. 2/22/1940 at 71/11/18; housewife; married; b. Sandwich; True Fogg (Sandwich) and Mary Moulton (Sandwich)

Richard E., d. 3/30/1947 at 51/9/14 in Springfield, MA; married; b. Ctr. Sandwich; Charles H. Mudgett (Ctr. Sandwich) and Emma Fogg (Ctr. Sandwich)

Robert E., d. 1/17/1986 in Sandwich; Eugene E. Mudgett and Eva May Davis

Sadie E., d. 9/23/1893 at 3/9/24 in Sandwich; b. Sandwich; Fred W. Mudgett (Sandwich) and Ora A. Fogg (Sandwich)

Thelma Walters, d. 1/23/1993 in Sandwich; b. Dorchester, MA; ----- and Jessie Walters

MUNROE,

Vera A., d. 6/17/1968 at 71 in Sandwich; married; b. ME; John Bragdon and Alice Huff

MYKLAND,

Olav, d. 3/2/1986 in Laconia; Olav Mjaavatn and Gunhild Jensdatten

MYSTROM,
Clara S., d. 9/7/1918 at 83/7/11; housekeeper; widow; Peter Peterson (Sweden) and Anna Anderson (Sweden)

NEBESAR,
Robert A., d. 7/19/2006 in Laconia; Robert J. Nebesar and Anne Dvorak

NEFF,
Frank Anton, d. 6/22/1938 at 70/6/3; store; married; b. Boston, MA; Frank A. Neff (Baden-Baden, Germany) and Philipina Volk (Baden-Baden, Germany)
Maria B., d. 7/13/1948 at 75/5/2 in Sandwich; widow; b. NY; Thomas D. Bauer (Friendship, NY) and Hannah Sherman (NY)

NELSON,
Charles H., d. 11/24/1926 at 7/4/7; b. Sandwich; Thomas Nelson (Norway) and Henrietta Brown (Quincy, MA)
Harold, d. 10/19/1942 at 63/6/2 in Laconia; laborer; single; b. Norway; John Nelson (Norway) and Sophia Hendrickson (Norway)
Henrietta B., d. 10/5/1974 at 88 in Wolfeboro; retired; widow; b. MA; Joshua Brown and Henrietta Day
John, d. 7/13/1923 at 82/4/19; blacksmith; widower; b. Norway; Ole Nelson (Norway)
Kenneth Warren, d. 6/15/1988 in Sandwich; Thomas Nelson and Henrietta Brown
Thomas, d. 11/13/1940 at 58/7/5; laborer; married; b. Norway; John Nelson (Norway) and Sophia Henderson (Norway)

NEWCOMB,
John E., d. 12/23/1992 in Laconia; Willard E. Newcomb and Clare Wilson

NICHOLS,
daughter, d. 6/25/1901 at – in Sandwich; b. Sandwich; Celia H. Nichols (Sandwich)
Charles F., d. 7/16/1905 at 55/1/2; carpenter; single; b. Moultonboro; Simeon F. Nichols (Moultonboro) and Lois P. Kelley (Meredith)
Margaret Ann, d. 1/7/1959 at 74 in Wolfeboro; married; b. South Cove, NS; Neil MacInnis and Jessie McAuley
William D., d. 11/2/2006 in Lebanon; William Deming and Mabel Turck

NICKERSON,
Wallace, d. 10/7/1891 at ¼ in Sandwich; b. NS; Jerome Nickerson (NS) and Elthea Wentzel (NS)

NICOLL,
Charles Randolph, d. 12/24/1950 at 86 in Sandwich; married; b. Charlestown, MA; Alexander Nicoll and Lucy Morley
Nellie J., d. 5/27/1958 at 83 in Wolfeboro; widow; b. Sandwich; Charles Goodwin and Lucinda Mudgett

NIXON,
Edith M., d. 3/3/1959 at 80 in Gilford; widow; b. Sandwich; Henry F. Dorr and Abbie S. Berry
James H., Jr., d. 2/17/1968 at 51 in Laconia; single; b. MA; James Nixon and Edith Dorr

NORTON,
Fred L., d. 11/29/1966 at 81 in Laconia; widower; b. Watertown, MA; Harrison Norton and Elmyra Nigers

NOVAK,
John W., d. 4/28/1959 at 33 in Hartford, VT; married; b. Englewood, NJ; Joseph Novak and Laura Nemsqoo

NUDD,
Blanch L., d. 10/15/1963 at 69 in Sandwich; married; b. Northfield, VT; Domino LeClair
Frederick L., d. 11/13/1939 at 0/0/28; b. Sandwich; Wallace Nudd (Sandwich) and Blanche LeClair (Northfield, VT)
Wallace E., d. 2/1/1968 at 72 in Laconia; widower; b. NH; Walter Nudd and Marjorie Gilman

NUNGESSER,
Catherine E., d. 1/17/2007 in Meredith; George Simons and Elizabeth Ryan

NUTTER,
Armine, d. 10/7/1910 at 76; housekeeper; single; b. Sandwich; Daniel Nutter (Sandwich) and Betsey Cook (Sandwich)
Emma, d. 9/22/1889 at 0/2/23; b. Sandwich; Benjamin M. Nutter (Sandwich) and Effie Abbott (Holderness)

O'BRIEN,
Lawrence, d. 4/1/1948 at 61/3/15 in Sandwich; divorced; b. Boston, MA; Lawrence O'Brien (Cardican, Wales) and Joan Sheen (Boston, MA)
William Farnham, d. 2/11/1993 in Sandwich; b. Cranston, RI; William J. O'Brien and Ethel Farnham
William J., d. 3/10/1955 at 67 in Wolfeboro; married; b. Providence, RI; William A. O'Brien and ----- Mulholland

O'CONNOR,
Paul D., d. 1/28/2006 in Sandwich; Edward O'Connor and Eileen Gavin

O'NEIL,
Letitia A., d. 10/11/2004 in Laconia; Charles J. O'Connor and Letitia A. Gallagher

OLAFSEN,
Arthur H., d. 7/19/1990 in Laconia; Harry Olafsen and Ragnhild Olsen

OLIVIER,
James M., d. 7/16/1961 at 62 in Plymouth; married; b. New Bedford, MA; George L. Olivier
James M., Jr., d. 7/10/2006 in Winchester, MA; James M. Olivier and Etta L. Baker
Louise B., d. 7/17/1961 at 60 in Plymouth; married; b. Atlantic City, NJ; Harry E. Baker and Etta Hall

ORDWAY,
Otis O., d. 8/11/1916 at 70/9/11; clergyman; married; b. Hamilton, MA; Luther Ordway (VT) and Mary E. Larcom (Beverly, MA)

OTTO,
George Myers, d. 2/11/1954 at 82 in Sandwich; married; b. Appleton, WI; John Henry Otis and Ana Marie Ver Hagen

PACKARD,
Mary S., d. 5/25/1947 at 79/1/6 in Ctr. Sandwich; single; b. Niagara, NY; Joshra Packard (Enfield, MA) and Margaret Packard (St. David, Canada)

PAGE,
Abbie L., d. 5/24/1888 at 46/7/19; married; b. Belgrade, ME; William A. Damren (Belgrade, ME) and Lois P. Gilman (Mt. Vernon, ME)
Hutcheson, d. 3/20/1985 in Franklin; George Page and Mary Hutcheson
Louise L., d. 7/10/1982 in Sandwich; Joseph E. LeClair and Mary J. Perkins

PAINE,

Lucy, d. 2/24/1895 at 73/8/3 in Sandwich; housewife; widow; b. Sandwich; Joseph Kimball (Center Harbor) and Clarissa Sturtevant (Center Harbor)

PALMER,

Herbert, d. 5/9/1938 at 73/10/28; farmer; widower; b. Sandwich; Ambrose Palmer (Sandwich) and Carolyn Moulton (Moultonboro)

James O., d. 7/21/1904 at 45/9/29; farmer; married; b. Sandwich; Oliver A. Palmer (Sandwich) and Carrie L. Moulton (Moultonboro)

Julia A., d. 12/26/1909 at 87/3/14; housewife; single; b. Sandwich; James Palmer (Sandwich) and Nancy Weed (Sandwich)

Willard F., d. 5/29/1920 at 67; merchant; married; b. Sandwich; Oliver A. Palmer (Sandwich) and Caroline Moulton (Moultonboro)

PARKER,

daughter, d. 6/11/1918 at 0/0/0; b. Laconia; H. L. Parker (Cambridge) and Marion F. Scriggins (Sandwich)

Ethel F., d. 6/13/1975 at 81 in Meredith; housewife; married; b. RI; Frank E. Farnham and Nellie B. Bunker

James W. S., d. 4/22/1976 at 81 in N. Tarrytown, NY; produce farmer; widower; b. MA; Dennis Parker and Sarah Murphy

Marion E., d. 6/11/1918 at 21/1/27; housewife; married; b. Sandwich; Arthur C. Scriggins (Sandwich) and Flora B. Blackey (Sandwich)

Robert H., d. 2/6/1948 at 83/5/24 in Sandwich; widower; b. Huron, ON; John Parker (Canada) and Martha Little (Canada)

PARSONS,
Barbara S., d. 4/2/2003 in Sandwich; Harold Smith and Minnie Downie

PATERSON,
Edna M., d. 10/19/1964 at 67 in Laconia; b. Orange, NJ; William Menzel and Mabel Jagger

PEARSALL,
Drew I., d. 5/24/2002 in Sandwich; Raymond Pearsall and Dorothy Illingworth

PEARSON,
Herman W., d. 5/5/1983 in Laconia

PEASE,
Florence M., d. 10/2/1966 at 74 in Woburn, MA; widow; b. Somerville, MA; Trevellyn Dougmore and Martha Russell

PEASLEE,
son, d. 1/7/1928 at 0/0/5; b. Sandwich; Ralph Peaslee (Sandwich) and Mary E. Moody (Tamworth)
Bernice Marion, d. 3/14/1950 at 58 in Sandwich; married; b. Lowell, MA; Orrin C. Frye and Ella G. Wood
Burton F., d. 6/13/1920 at 0/2/11; b. Sandwich; David J. Peaslee (Sandwich) and Bernice Frye (Lowell, MA)
Daniel, d. 2/11/1910 at 76/2/29; farmer; married; b. Gilmanton; David Peaslee (Pittsfield) and Ruth Burnham (Sandwich)
David J., d. 3/10/1952 at 76 in Sandwich; widower; b. Sandwich; Daniel Peaslee and Harriett Fogg
David W., d. 1/8/1985 in Laconia; Roscoe Peaslee and Dorothy E. Robinson
Donald, d. 2/10/1932 at 0/0/9; b. Sandwich; Ralph Peaslee (Sandwich) and Mary E. Moody (Tamworth)

Dora E., d. 2/11/1910 at 35/7/9; housekeeper; married; b. Waltham; Charles W. Trask (Danvers, MA) and Arvilla M. Hackett (Sandwich)

Doris Marion, d. 2/1/1949 at – in Sandwich; single; b. Sandwich; Roscoe Peaslee and Dorothy Robinson

Earl C., d. 10/3/1934 at 30/6/19; mechanic; married; b. Sandwich; David Peaslee (Sandwich) and Dora Trask

Elizabeth D., d. 2/14/1992 in Sandwich; Andrew F. Doe and Mary Hoyt

Harriet, d. 12/14/1915 at 83/9/8; housewife; widow; b. Sandwich; John Fogg (Sandwich) and Sarah Webster (Sandwich)

Heather L., d. 4/4/2000 in Laconia; Andrew Peaslee and Cheryl Baker

John N., d. 11/8/1912 at 57/2/14; farmer; married; b. Sandwich; David Peaslee (Pittsfield) and L. Burnham (Sandwich)

Kerry D., d. 12/6/1999 in Boston, MA; David Peaslee and Mary Noble

Lucinda, d. 4/17/1893 at 80 in Sandwich; housewife; b. Sandwich; Aaron Burnham (Ware) and Sarah Emery (Ware)

Mary, d. 1/30/1890 at 73 in Sandwich; invalid; widow; b. Sandwich; Aaron Peaslee and Sarah Pope

Mary E., d. 10/11/1935 at 88/0/11; housewife; widow; b. Sandwich; Stephen Vittum (Sandwich) and Ruth Tappan (Sandwich)

Nellie D., d. 7/16/1915 at 49/7/17; married; b. Manchester; Ezra Kimball (Lowell, MA) and Mary A. Wilson (Lowell, MA)

Pauline E., d. 2/27/2002 in Concord; Nathaniel Burrows and Edrie Gordon

Ralph Q., d. 12/5/1967 at 58 in Sandwich; b. Sandwich; David J. Peaslee and Dora Trask

Ralph Quimby, Jr., d. 11/22/1998 in N. Sandwich; b. N. Sandwich; Ralph Q. Peaslee, Sr. and Elizabeth Moody

Robert Nelson, d. 9/30/1994 in N. Sandwich; b. Sandwich; David J. Peaslee and Bernice M. Frye

Roland, d. 2/9/1958 at 57 in Tamworth; single; b. Sandwich; David J. Peaslee

Roscoe D., d. 11/9/1967 at 66 in Sandwich; b. Sandwich; David J. Peaslee and Dora Trask

Ruth M., d. 2/8/1918 at 20/9/18; at home; single; b. Sandwich; David J. Peaslee (Sandwich) and Dora E. Trask (Waltham, MA)

Samuel, d. 7/1/1909 at 71/2/9; farmer; married; b. Sandwich; David Peaslee (Pittsfield) and Ruth Burnham (Sandwich)

PELKEY,

Nancy E., d. 10/11/1914 at 52/4/24; housekeeper; married; b. Mapleton, ME; Benjamin Hughes and Ruth Cushing

PELKIE,

Raymond E., d. 9/3/1970 at 24 in Sandwich; married; b. NH; Emerson R. Pelkie and Pauline Bowley

PENNIMAN,

Sarah E., d. 3/2/1928 at 74/11/28; housewife; married; b. Moultonboro; Charles L. Glines (Moultonboro) and Elmira Gurdy

White H., d. 5/20/1938 at 84/2/14; farmer; widower; b. Sandwich; Robert Penniman and ----- Wallace (Sandwich)

PERCIVAL,

Albert, d. 1/4/1955 at 80 in Conway; single; b. Campton

PERKINS,

Alfred T., d. 3/16/1910 at 58/1/21; farmer; single; b. Sandwich; George Perkins (Wells, ME) and Maria S. Blackey (VT)

Everett S., d. 2/1/1920 at 65/9/27; shoemaker; widower; b. Wells, ME; George Perkins (Norfolk, ME) and Maria Blackie (Wells, ME)

George, d. 6/3/1888 at 73/7/10; married; b. Weld, ME; Foris Perkins (Weld, ME) and Abigail Furbush (Weld, ME)
George E., d. 4/8/1922 at 79/11/13; shoemaker; married; b. Sandwich; George Perkins (Wells, ME) and Maria M. Blocky (Strafford, VT)
Georgiana M., d. 12/1/1937 at 63/11/4; at home; widow; b. Tamworth; James P. Knight (Tamworth) and Julia Clough
Harold C., d. 9/25/1895 at – in Sandwich; b. Sandwich; Alston W. Perkins (Jackson) and Ella M. Bryor (Sandwich)
Herbert L., d. 8/24/1959 at 69 in Wolfeboro; single; b. Sandwich; Melvin E. Perkins and Georgia A. Knight
Mariah, d. 9/26/1906 at 84/1/1; housewife; b. Lyndon, VT; Thomas Blackey (Portsmouth) and Mary Webster (Sandwich)
Melvin E., d. 11/14/1916 at 51/4/11; carpenter; married; b. Sandwich; George Perkins (Wells, ME) and Maria Blackey
Millett Fish, d. 1/2/1951 at 53 in Laconia; married; b. Wolfeboro; Sam Perkins and ----- Chamberlain

PETERSON,
Eleanor F., d. 1/3/2006 in Laconia; Charles Houston and Ellen Merrifield

PETTENGILL,
Abbie M., d. 2/27/1888 at 34/0/8; single; b. Sandwich; Hosea A. Pettengill (Sandwich) and Polly M. Skinner (Sandwich)
Ernest, d. 4/10/1893 at 14/3/14 in Sandwich; single; b. Sandwich; J. Burleigh (Sandwich) and Almena Pettengill (Sandwich)
Helen, d. 1/31/1939 at 67/9/22; housework; widow; b. NS; Patrick Delaney (NS) and Sophia Powell (NS)
Helen A., d. 3/8/1952 at 54 in Laconia; married; b. MD; John G. Sloan and Anne Essinger

Hosea A., d. 4/2/1889 at 80/6; tinsmith; married; b. Sandwich; Asa Pettengill (Sandwich) and Hannah Webster (Sandwich)
Polly M., d. 10/29/1896 at 78/11/20 in Sandwich; housewife; widow; b. Sandwich; E. Skinner (Sandwich) and Abagail Moulton
Sylvester B., d. 4/14/1932 at 70/1/0; chef; married; b. Sandwich; Hosea Pettengill (Sandwich) and Pauline Skinner (Sandwich)

PHILBIN,
Mary Theresa, d. 10/29/1998 in Laconia; b. New York, NY; George Williams and Hanora Blake

PHILLIPS,
Clarinda B., d. 12/25/2003 in N. Sandwich; Wardell Burr and Mary -----

PICKTHALL,
Mary N. W., d. 7/20/1926 at 69/11/0; housewife; married; b. Sandwich; Charles Weed (Sandwich) and Sarah F. McCrillis (Sandwich)
Richard E., d. 8/27/1933 at 80/0/26; retired; widower; b. Charlestown, MA; Mary Ann Snowden

PICONE,
Stephen, d. 7/13/1972 at 65 in Laconia; warehouseman; married; b. MA; Frank Picone and Maria Delucia

PIERCE,
Alice W., d. 6/6/1982 in Laconia; Almon J. Whiting and Elizabeth Palmer
Caroline E., d. 12/18/1912 at 82/4/18; housewife; widow; b. Sandwich; N. Burleigh (Sandwich) and Hannah Heath (Whitefield, ME)

Ellsworth, d. 3/31/1926 at 63/6/25; mkt. garden.; married; b. N. Reading, MA; Prescott Pierce (Lowell, MA) and Almira Jones (Wilmington, MA)
Frank K., d. 10/18/1904 at 53/3/14; machinist; married; b. Sandwich; Leander Pierce (Thornton) and Caroline Burleigh (Sandwich)
George Albert, d. 10/14/1936 at 84/5/23; widower; b. Rehoboth, MA; Ellen MacFarland (Scotland)
Jane, d. 11/26/1897 at 87/8 in Sandwich; single; b. Thornton; Samuel Pierce (Chester) and Mary Sargent (Thornton)
Leander, d. 11/21/1896 at 75/5/26 in Sandwich; farmer; married; b. Thornton; Samuel Pierce and Mary Sargent
Maurice A., d. 12/25/1980 in Hanover; James Pierce and Nettie Vittum
Nettie Grace, d. 4/5/1933 at 49/9/27; at home; married; b. Sandwich; Cyrus Vittum (Sandwich) and Lizzie Dodge (Beverly Farms, MA)

PLUMER,
Ella C., d. 8/7/1888 at 26/8/8; dressmaker; married; b. Sandwich; Arven Blanchard (Hopkinton) and Nellie S. Creighton (Sandwich)
Lydia, d. 8/3/1889 at 78/10/11; housewife; widow; b. Sandwich; Samuel Corliss (Sandwich) and Abagail Gilman (Sandwich)
William, d. 9/21/1887 at 81/3/8; farmer; married; b. Sandwich; Richard Plummer and Annie Hoag

PLUMMER,
son, d. 4/16/1926 at 0/0/0; b. Sandwich; Clarence Plummer (Sandwich) and Luella M. Sturgis (Sandwich)
daughter, d. 1/12/1935 at 0/0/0; b. Laconia; Clarence R. Plummer (Sandwich) and Luella Sturgis (Sandwich)
daughter, d. 12/25/1939 at 0/0/0; b. Sandwich; Clarence Plummer (Sandwich) and Luella Sturgis (Sandwich)

Annie M., d. 6/5/1938 at 84/1/21; housewife; married; b. Tuftonboro; Daniel Leary (Ireland) and Mary Swett (USA)

Clarence R., Jr., d. 8/13/1965 at 71 in Manchester; b. Sandwich; Wilfred Plummer and Elizabeth Webster

Edna, d. 4/19/1982 in Laconia; Jacob Nelson and Lenora Wakefield

Edward J., d. 3/17/1925 at 1/3/26; b. Sandwich; Clarence Plummer (Sandwich) and May Sturgis (Sandwich)

Frank P., d. 12/25/1916 at 78/5/22; millman; married; b. Sanbornton; Jesse Plummer (New Hampton) and Lydia Goss (New Hampton)

Harriet, d. 5/6/1910 at 65/6; housewife; married; b. Sandwich; Daniel M. Moulton (Sandwich) and Hulda Quimby (Sandwich)

James H., d. 6/26/1958 at 71 in Wolfeboro; married; b. Sandwich; Wilfred Plummer and Lizzie Webster

James H., Jr., d. 1/23/1989 in Laconia; James H. Plummer, Sr. and Nettie Irving

Jessie M., d. 8/29/1903 at 21/0/10 in Sandwich; single; b. Sandwich; Wilfred Plummer (Sandwich) and Lizzy Webster (Meredith)

Lizzie, d. 3/22/1894 at 30/1 in Sandwich; housewife; married; b. Meredith; Charles Webster (Sandwich) and Marilla Bartlett (Center Harbor)

Luella, d. 12/30/1939 at 37/2/21; housewife; married; b. Sandwich; Eli J. Plant (W. Ossipee) and Jennie Sturgis (Albany)

Mabel, d. 4/17/1964 at 63 in Manchester; b. Bartlett; William Nute and Laura Wentworth

Roy Jesse, d. 11/18/1930 at 0/5/4; b. Sandwich; Clarence B. Plummer (Sandwich) and ----- Sturgis (Sandwich)

Wilfred C., d. 9/4/1966 at 51 in Rye; married; b. Sandwich; James H. Plummer and Nettie Irving

Wilfred Z., d. 5/24/1940 at 79/6/9; farmer; widower; b. Sandwich; Frank Plummer (Marblehead, MA) and Harrett Moulton (Campton)

POHL,
Henry, d. 2/3/1967 at 59 in Sandwich; b. E. Prussia; William Pohl and Mina Neumann
Katherine G., d. 5/8/1996 in Laconia; b. Germany

POTTER,
Paul B., d. 4/20/1988 in Wolfeboro; John Potter and Bertha I. Barber

POWERS,
Elisabeth, d. 6/9/1996 in Manchester; b. Annapolis, MD; Morris Gilmore and Mary Isemann
Grant James, d. 1/12/1978 at 79 in Sandwich; artist; married; b. PA; William Powers and Katherine MacDonald

PRESCOTT,
Asa S., d. 6/24/1909 at 75/6; shoemaker; married; b. Sandwich; Newell Prescott and Ruth Smith (Sandwich)
Eliza, d. 10/31/1891 at 85/3/20 in Sandwich; housewife; widow; b. ME; Caleb Parker (ME) and Marguret Horne (ME)
John D., d. 2/29/1904 at 77/1/28; widower; b. Sandwich; Parker Prescott (Sandwich) and Mary Vittum (Sandwich)
Mary, d. 5/11/1911 at 83/2/2; housekeeper; widow; b. Sandwich; William Wallace (Sandwich) and Sally Bryant (Sandwich)
William, d. 2/26/1928 at 55/9/20; farmer; single; b. San Francisco; John D. Prescott (Tamworth) and Mary Foley (New Orleans, LA)

PRUETT,
James E., Jr., d. 8/19/1988 in Manchester; James E. Pruett, Sr. and Ruth Connelly

PURVES,
Paul G., d. 10/13/1986 in Sandwich; Walter Purves and Brenda Cannole

QUIMBY,
daughter, d. 6/26/1907 at --; b. Sandwich; W. Quimby (Sandwich) and Edith Durgin (Randolph, MA)
Agnes L., d. 1/9/1961 at 80 in New York, NY; married; b. MA; William Allison and Isabel -----
Amy M., d. 8/5/1929 at 71/2/5; at home; widow; b. Sandwich; L. G. Clark (Sandwich) and Ann Beede (Sandwich)
Betsy W., d. 4/24/1914 at 80/1/18; housekeeper; widow; b. Sandwich; John S. Severance (Sandwich) and Rhoda Webster (Sandwich)
Caleb, d. 12/19/1901 at 74/1/16 in Sandwich; blacksmith; married; b. Sandwich; Smith Quimby (Sandwich) and Nancy Marston (Moultonboro)
Charles, d. 2/1/1896 at 92/1/3 in Sandwich; farmer; married; b. Sandwich; Johnson Quimby (Sandwich) and Polly Collins (Shapleigh, ME)
Clara E., d. 11/17/1945 at 90/8/1 in Sandwich; housewife; widow; b. Stanstead, Canada; Ede W. Lee and Delinda A. Wilson
Clifton C., d. 10/5/1971 at 87 in Laconia; married; b. NH; Herman Quimby and Amy Clark
Daniel, d. 4/17/1891 at 75 in Sandwich; farmer; widower; b. Sandwich; Isaac Quimby (Sandwich) and Lydia Maxfield (Sandwich)
Edith M., d. 7/14/1953 at 74 in Lawrence, MA; widow; b. Randolph, MA; John C. Durgin and Mary F. Este
Edward E., d. 3/27/1947 at 90/5/4 in Laconia; widower; b. Sandwich; Caleb Quimby (Sandwich) and Susan Donovan (Sandwich)

Eunice A., d. 1/5/1895 at 1/10/22 in Sandwich; b. Sandwich; Herman H. Quimby (Sandwich) and Amy M. Clark (Sandwich)

George F., d. 1/28/1891 at 0/7/25 in Sandwich; b. Sandwich; Herman Quimby (Sandwich) and Amy Clark (Sandwich)

Georgia B., d. 1/7/1897 at 14/4 in Sandwich; single; b. Sandwich; Ezra J. Quimby (Sandwich) and Lizzie L. Cook (Sandwich)

Grace M., d. 2/21/1937 at 72/10/21; at home; married

Harrison M., d. 4/10/1898 at 66/10 in Sandwich; farmer; married; b. Sandwich; John S. Quimby (Sandwich) and Nancy Marston (Moultonboro)

Herman H., d. 12/14/1895 at 40/4/6 in Sandwich; farmer; married; b. Sandwich; John M. Quimby (Sandwich) and Sarah Haines (Sandwich)

Ida W., d. 2/1/1936 at 50/0/3; housewife; married; b. Sweden; Carl Linstrum (Sweden)

John M., d. 1/2/1904 at 83/8/9; farmer; widower; b. Sandwich; John S. Quimby (Sandwich) and Nancy Marston (Sandwich)

John S., d. 8/17/1940 at 81; farmer; married; b. Sandwich; Harrison Quimby (NH) and Bessie Quimby (NH)

Johnson D., d. 5/9/1929 at 91; widower; b. Sandwich; Charles Quimby (Sandwich) and Susan S. ----- (Wolfeboro)

Joseph H., d. 10/6/1906 at 79/8/4; carpenter; married; b. Sandwich; John Quimby (Sandwich) and Jane Webster (Sandwich)

Lewis, d. 2/6/1888 at 81/4; farmer; widower; b. Sandwich; John Quimby and Jane Webster

Lucy, d. 108/1957 at 92 in Laconia; widow; b. Campton; ----- Shute

Minnie B., d. 8/20/1913 at 55/11/13; housewife; married; b. Sandwich; James Blanchard (Sandwich) and Sarah Webster (Sandwich)

Sarah S., d. 9/12/1895 at 77/1/17 in Sandwich; housewife; married; b. Moultonboro; Josiah Haines (Raymond) and Sally Sturtevant (MA)

Susan B., d. 2/12/1918 at 84/1/23; housewife; widow; b. Sandwich; John Donovan (Sandwich) and Jane Brown (Sandwich)

Susan S., d. 2/5/1896 at 91/5/1 in Sandwich; housewife; widow; b. Wolfeboro; William Fullerton (Wolfeboro) and Meribe Stanley

Susie M., d. 7/24/1895 at 36/10/11 in Sandwich; housewife; married; b. Deerfield; David Gerrish (Deerfield) and Susan Tilton (Deerfield)

Wilbur E., d. 10/5/1964 at 77 in Laconia; b. Sandwich; Ezra Quimby and Elizabeth Cook

William F., d. 10/7/1900 at 6-/2/6 in Sandwich; farmer; married; b. Sandwich; Charles Quinby (Sandwich) and Susan Fullerton (Tuftonboro)

Winfield S., d. 5/18/1933 at 64/6/18; cook; married; b. Sandwich; John Quimby (Sandwich) and Caroline Peaslee (Sandwich)

QUINBY,

Etta S., d. 11/26/1941 at 87/5/27; housewife; widow; b. Tamworth; Robert Nickerson (Albany) and Mary Ann Quinby (Sandwich)

Mabel Ida, d. 7/24/1960 at 86 in Laconia; single; b. N. Sandwich; Stanley F. Quinby and Etta Nickerson

Robert S., d. 7/30/1954 at 65 in Hanover; married; b. Sandwich; Stanley Quinby and Etta Nickerson

Stanley F., d. 9/2/1938 at 91/4/4; farmer; married; b. Sandwich; Charles Quinby (Sandwich) and Susan Fullerton (Wolfeboro)

Stella E., d. 8/19/1971 at 85 in Sandwich; widow; b. MA; Felix Murray and E. B. Cheeseboro

QUINLAN,
Isabel T., d. 10/10/1967 at 72 in Hanover; b. Chicago, IL; Frederick Tucker and Fannie Van Kirk

QUIRK,
Thomas F., d. 1/12/1910 at 23/1/9; reporter; single; b. Waltham, MA; Patrick F. Quirk (Ireland) and Catherine Murray (Ireland)

RAINS,
Claude W., d. 5/30/1967 at 77 in Laconia; b. London, England; William C. Raines and Eliza Cox
Rosemary, d. 12/31/1964 at 47 in Sandwich; b. Wilkes-Barre, PA; John McGroarty and Mary C. Connole

RAMIREZ,
Elizabeth A., d. 10/6/2006 in N. Sandwich; David Ramirez and Marguerite Smith
Robert G., d. 9/26/1987 in Sandwich; George Barclay and Elizabeth E. Ramirez

RAND,
William H., d. 2/6/1937 at 57/10/9; butcher; married; b. Laconia; Benjamin Rand (Charlestown, MA) and Luella Sanborn (Sanbornton)

RANSOM,
Annett Mowatt, d. 10/9/1996 in Wolfeboro; b. Swampscott, MA; Frank A. Mowatt and Sarah A. Quimby
James Frederick, d. 7/19/1983 in Littleton; Willard G. Ransom and Edna Lischer
John H., d. 1/23/1946 at 2/2/6 in Ridge, CO; b. Denver, CO; James F. Ransom (Davenport, IA) and Annette Mowatt (Swampscott, MA)

RAYMOND,
Lillian, d. 5/24/2005 in Laconia; William Youngson and Phoebe Squires

READ,
Deborah P., d. 12/3/1977 at 64 in Laconia; housewife; married; b. Newfield
Geraldine B., d. 11/30/2006 in Meredith; John Bryant and Madeline Robinson
Kirke P., d. 6/13/1999 in Brunswick, ME; Alvin Brewer and Deborah Packard
Leon Henry, Jr., d. 4/5/1983 in Burnsville, NC
Theodore O., d. 3/13/2005 in Laconia; Leon Read and Abigail Randall

REEVES,
Howell H., d. 1/28/1960 at 74 in Sandwich; widower; b. Tampico, IL; Joseph Reeves and Frances Brewer

REICHERT,
Hermann A., d. 1/28/1977 at 87 in Meredith; mason; married; b. Germany; Hermann Reichert and Emma -----

REIFENBERGER,
Lloyd A., d. 12/6/2000 in Laconia; Andrew Reifenberger and Henrietta Klaige

REILLY,
Dorothy R., d. 6/9/1991 in Sandwich; Kerr Rainsford and Christina Nichols
Noel M. P., d. 4/22/1991 in Laconia; ----- Reilly and ----- Prouse

REMICK,
Emily S., d. 8/11/1986 in Sandwich; Raymond Seanway and Catherine -----

Nelson Atwood, d. 9/13/1985 in Ossipee; James Remick and Cora Atwood

REYNOLDS,
Ida G., d. 1/29/1969 at 93 in Wolfeboro; single; b. MA; Edward Reynolds and Idalena Richards

RICE-GRAY,
Kiki A., d. 11/13/2007 in Joshua Tree, CA; Earnest Kiekenapp and Edith -----

RICHARDS,
son, d. 1/18/1921 at 0/0/0; b. Sandwich; Blair Richards (Framingham, MA) and Alice M. Brown (Braintree, MA)
Henry H., Jr., d. 11/1/1986 in Meredith; Henry Howe Richards, Sr. and Julia Coolidge
Mary C., d. 8/12/1966 at 48 in Sandwich; married; b. Lawrence, MA; Charles H. Choate and Pauline Culver

RICHARDSON,
Clement S., d. 12/23/1970 at 76 in Wolfeboro; married; b. MA; Joseph Richardson and Clara Pettigrew

RICKER,
Catherine, d. 9/26/1890 at 75/10 in Sandwich; housewife; widow; Tilton Vittum (Sandwich) and Phebe Beadbry

ROBBINS,
Ann R., d. 2/12/2003 in Wolfeboro; Richard Briggs and Clara Reynolds
Philip Senter, d. 6/19/1998 in Nashua; b. Keene; Perley Robbins and Mabel Senter

ROBERGE,
Lewis, d. 10/15/1970 at 0/0/2 in Laconia; b. NH; Ernest L. Roberge and Beverly DeWitt

ROBERTS,
Hannah F., d. 3/3/1890 at 89/0/24 in Sandwich; housewife; widow; b. Poplin; Moses Beede (NH) and Miriam Peaslee (NH)

ROBERTSON,
Charles L., Jr., d. 3/27/2007 in Sandwich; Charles Robertson, Sr. and Dorothy Downing

ROBINSON,
daughter, d. 5/6/1905 at --; b. Sandwich; Charles Robinson (Sandwich) and Florence Mason (Moultonboro)
Abbie F., d. 12/23/1911 at 75/11/5; housewife; married; b. Canton, MA; N. Farrington (Milton, MA) and Ruth Home (Milton, MA)
Ellen M., d. 10/24/1893 at 41/3/4 in Sandwich; b. Sandwich; Joseph Gilman (Sandwich) and Mary Moulton (Sandwich)
George, d. 3/5/1917 at 80/3/21; farmer; widower; b. New Durham; Meshach Robinson and Betsey Sinclair
Nettie Louise, d. 7/24/1955 at 74 in Sandwich; widow; b. Fitchbay, Canada; Henry Quimby and Clara Lee
William John, d. 9/30/1949 at 75 in Sandwich; married; b. Portland, ME; John Robinson and Netta Moore

ROBY,
Robert E., d. 9/11/1991 in Sandwich; Edwin Roby and Elsie Brown

ROGERS,

Caroline, d. 12/3/1892 at 68/6/29 in Sandwich; housewife; married; b. Tamworth; Jedediah Felch (Seabrook) and Mary Moulton (N. Berwick)

Etta, d. 3/10/1934 at 72/2/15; housewife; widow; b. Sandwich; H. T. Fogg (Sandwich) and M. Moulton (Holderness)

Gorham D., d. 9/4/1929 at 72/9/21; M.D.; widower; b. MA; E. D. Rogers (Newbury, MA) and Betsy A. Rogers (Newbury, MA)

Horatio T., d. 10/6/1922 at 76/4/15; farmer; married; b. Sandwich; Tyler Rogers (Moultonboro) and Sally Swain (Strafford)

Ida L., d. 5/10/1939 at 55/6/6; housewife; married; b. Somerville, MA; James B. Rand (Rye) and Minnie E. Doane (Truro, MA)

James S., d. 7/27/1915 at 0/0/2; b. Plymouth; James S. Rogers (Newbury, MA) and Ida L. Rand (Somerville, MA)

James S., d. 10/15/1946 at 61/7/8 in Laconia; retired; widower; b. Byfield, MA; Dr. Rogers (Byfield, MA) and Mary Eaton

Tyler, d. 9/29/1893 at 77/7/14 in Sandwich; farmer; b. Sandwich

ROSE,

Elizabeth Dryden, d. 4/30/1978 at 72 in Sandwich; housewife; married; b. MA; Archibald Ramage and Christina Ramage

Harry M., MD, d. 11/4/1986 in Meredith; Charles Hosmer Rose and Annie Beatrice Stevens

ROTH,

Clara W., d. 4/16/1985 in Concord, ME; Henri Wenson and Annie Bennett

Julius, d. 10/15/1971 at 63 in Sandwich; married; b. NY; Morris Roth and Jennie Blair

ROUNER,

Leroy S., d. 2/11/2006 in Lebanon; Arthur Rouner and Elizabeth Stephens

ROWE,

David S., d. 4/18/1898 at 70/4 in Sandwich; farmer; married; b. Sandwich; David B. Rowe (Sandwich) and Fannie Coffin (Sandwich)

Melvina P., d. 12/8/1921 at 86/5/16; retired; widow; Philip Atwood and Mary Elliott

RUSSELL,

Marlene Ann, d. 10/13/1933 at 0/0/10; b. Sandwich; William Wesley Russell (Sandwich) and Nellie Craig (Somerville, MA)

Robert, d. 7/31/1913 at 70/9/29; harnessmaker; married; b. Quebec; John Russell (Ireland) and Margaret Daly (Ireland)

Robert Tillison, d. 7/23/1953 at 68 in Sandwich; married; b. Sandwich; Robert Russell and Sarah Slye

Sarah, d. 12/2/1932 at 81/6/27; widow

RYDER,

Eleanor Marie, d. 3/11/1997 in Laconia; b. Boston, MA; Edmund Q. Cole and Laura Lynn

Philip Kenneth, d. 10/11/1986 in Sandwich; Marshall A. Ryder and Elizabeth Robb

SAMPSON,

George, d. 8/12/1922 at 84/10/2; retired; married; b. Bridgewater, MA; Pearson H. Sampson (Braintree, MA) and Hannah Perkins (Bridgewater, MA)

SANBORN,
Emma H., d. 7/28/1900 at 48 in Sandwich; teacher; single; b. Sandwich; Tristan Sanborn (Sanbornton) and Hannah Burleigh (Sandwich)
Ida M., d. 8/30/1932 at 76/5/15; retired; widow; b. Holderness; Cyrus Plaisted and Eliza Rowe
Lewis, d. 8/11/1901 at 80/2/7 in Sandwich; farmer; widower; b. Sandwich; Amos Sanborn (Sandwich) and Lavania -----
Loiza, d. 5/16/1887 at 74/2/23; married; b. Wells, ME; Forest Perkins (Wells, ME) and Abigeil ----- (Wells, ME)

SANDERS,
Eliza W., d. 4/11/1900 at 84/3/1 in Sandwich; housewife; widow; b. Sandwich; Orlando Mudgett (Sandwich) and Nancy Hinds (Tamworth)

SARGENT,
Leon Frank, d. 8/17/1988 in Sandwich; Frank H. Sargent and Evelyn Burroughs
Mary K., d. 7/27/2000 in Laconia; Dr. John King and Eliza Mcvey
Ruth M. K., d. 2/8/1998 in Laconia; b. Hartland, VT; Ernest Shute and Odessa Dow
Victoria, d. 9/7/1949 at 79 in Concord; married; b. NH; Asa Wallace and Carolly Taffen

SAWYER,
Charles, d. 6/22/1900 at 0/14/26 in Sandwich; b. Sandwich; George Sawyer (Campton) and Emma Clark (PEI)
Raymond C., d. 5/22/1901 at 0/7/13 in Sandwich; b. Sandwich; George S. Sawyer (Campton) and Emma G. Clark (PEI)

SCHMIDT,
Karl N., d. 8/27/1961 at 87 in Laconia; widower; b. Frankfurt, Germany; Carl Schmidt and Caterina Mueller

SCHNEIDER,

Suzita C. M., d. 11/2/1995 in Sandwich; b. Phillipines; Robert E. Cecil and Susan Jurika

SCHRADER,

Norma R. W., d. 1/6/1996 in N. Sandwich; b. Kingston, PA; Benjamin F. Rogers and Olive N. Johnson

SCRIGGINS,

Arthur, d. 5/31/1932 at 60/1/27; needle maker; married; b. Sandwich; Charles Scriggins (Sandwich) and Julia A. Mason

Augusta A., d. 9/21/1889 at 47; housewife; married; b. Sandwich; David S. Mason (Sandwich) and Roxana Hatch (Tamworth)

Charles B., d. 7/30/1927 at 79/10/10; laborer; widower; Bradbury Scriggins (Barnstead)

Emily J., d. 1/19/1912 at 68/1/25; housewife; married; b. Sandwich; Jesse Mudgett (Sandwich) and Jane Burnham (Sandwich)

Flora B., d. 8/25/1898 at 32/8/22 in Sandwich; housewife; married; Jeremiah Blackey (Moultonboro) and Abbie Wallace

George H., d. 11/1/1940 at 73/11/30; laborer; single; b. Sandwich; William Scriggins (Sandwich)

John A., d. 12/13/1915 at 75/8/18; farmer; married; b. Barnstead; B. Scriggins (Barnstead) and Hannah Davis (Barnstead)

Julia A., d. 6/2/1926 at 75/0/8; housewife; married; b. Sandwich; David T. Mason and Roxanah Hatch

Mary A., d. 3/19/1934 at 105/11/15; at home; widow; b. Stafford; ----- Avery and ----- Holmes

Mildred E., d. 4/9/1891 at 0/3/11 in Sandwich; b. Sandwich; Arthur Scriggins (Sandwich) and Flora Blacke (Moultonboro)

William H., d. 5/21/1925 at 86/11/16; farmer; married; b. Barnstead; Bradbury Scriggins (Barnstead) and Hannah Davis (Barnstead)

SEARS,
Christie M., d. 5/8/1985 in Laconia; Hubbard Webber and Grace -----
Mildred L., d. 7/25/1956 at 64 in Sandwich; married; b. Hudson, MA; Ellsworth Locke and Mary Ross
Winthrop M., d. 9/27/1986 in Meredith; Eben W. Sears and Carolyn Roos

SEELEY,
Blanche M., d. 1/5/1953 at 47 in Concord; married; b. NH; Fred George and Alice B. Batchelder
Malcolm A., d. 7/25/2003 in Laconia; Lewis Seeley and Edith Webster

SEVERANCE,
son, d. 1/16/1891 at 0/0/21 in Sandwich; b. Sandwich; John Severance (Sandwich) and Helen Mills (Boscawen)
Alice M., d. 9/29/1894 at 23/8/4 in Sandwich; teacher; single; b. Sandwich; Asa Severance (Sandwich) and Hannah Webster (Sandwich)
Alonzo, d. 1/24/1924 at 81/3/11; farmer; widower; b. Sandwich; James M. Severance (Sandwich) and Adeline Randall (ME)
Asa, d. 4/1/1901 at 73/1/29 in Sandwich; farmer; widower; b. Sandwich; Asa Severance (Sandwich) and Rhoda Webster (Sandwich)
Ephraim, d. 9/18/1888 at 84/1/27; farmer; widower; b. Sandwich; Ephraim Severance (Sandwich) and Sally Leavitt (Tuftonboro)

Eva G., d. 8/26/1917 at 35/0/26; mill operator; single; b. Sandwich; John W. Severance (Sandwich) and Helen M. Mills (Boscawen)

John W., d. 10/20/1891 at 39/4 in Sandwich; farmer; married; b. Sandwich; Asa Severance (Sandwich) and Hannah Webster (Sandwich)

Laura, d. 9/30/1923 at 42/2/10; mach. stitcher; single; b. Sandwich; John W. Severance (Sandwich) and Helen Mills (Boscawen)

Louisa E., d. 11/1/1894 at 41/0/1 in Sandwich; housewife; married; b. Sandwich; Stephen Vittum (Sandwich) and Ruth Tappan (Sandwich)

Lucy B., d. 11/5/1889 at 75/6; housewife; widow; b. Sandwich; ----- Severance (Sandwich) and Lydia Thurston (Sandwich)

Sarah A., d. 8/7/1890 at 65/3/22 in Sandwich; widow; b. Sandwich; John Donovan (Sandwich) and Jane M. Brown (Sandwich)

Sargent F., d. 12/6/1895 at 73/4/11 in Sandwich; farmer; married; b. Sandwich; John Severance (Sandwich) and Dorothy French (Sandwich)

SHACKFORD,

Charles, d. 11/30/1939 at 49/6/8; carpenter; divorced; b. Conway; J. Fred Shackford (Conway) and Edith Beecham (Waterville)

SHANKLAND,

George W., d. 11/13/1920 at 67/5/14; rancher; married; b. Marshfield, IN; ----- Kendall (W. Lebanon, IN) and Amanda Harris (Lebanon, IN)

SHERMAN,

Cordelia R., d. 8/3/1925 at 76/10/21; retired; widow; b. Honeoye Falls, NT; Rufus Robbins and Hannah Crocker

Daniel H., d. 3/11/1910 at 69/26/1 (sic); civil engineer; married; b. Sandwich; Enoch Sherman (Gilmanton) and Julia M. Hoitt

Mary B., d. 8/6/1986 in Laconia; Clark Burdick and Elizabeth Peckham

SHORTH,

Thomas H., d. 10/16/1909 at 59/4/2; stone cutter; widower; b. MA; ----- (Ireland)

SHOUP,

Carl S., d. 3/23/2000 in Laconia; Paul Shoup and Rose Wilson

Ruth Snedden, d. 6/25/1998 in Laconia; b. Oakland, CA; David Snedden and Genevra Sisson

SIMMONS,

Philip E., d. 7/27/2002 in Sandwich; Alan J. Simmons and Mary M. Bachhuber

SKINNER,

Charles E., d. /53/1937 at 83/0/19; farmer; widower; b. Sandwich; Richard Skinner (Sandwich) and Caroline Moulton (Sandwich)

Cyrus E., d. 1/5/1933 at 82/10/11; farmer; widower; b. Sandwich; Daniel Skinner (Conway) and Sarah Shaton (Conway)

Daniel M., d. 4/30/1898 at 73 in Sandwich; inventor; widower; b. Sandwich; Elijah Skinner (Lyme Corner) and Abigail Moulton (Sandwich)

Flora E., d. 5/20/1962 at 79 in Concord; single; b. Holderness; Cyrus Skinner and Emma Lee

Hattie Emma, d. 2/16/1951 at 89 in Laconia; widow; b. Sandwich; John Horn and Martha Wellman

Jennie T., d. 7/26/1927 at 70/2/9; housewife; married; b. Patten, ME; Frank Torry (Dickfield, ME) and Sarah Mack (Albany)

Lizzie M., d. 11/22/1911 at 43/9/15; housewife; married; b. Bethlehem; A. W. Streeter (Lisbon) and Lidia A. Phillips (Bethlehem)

Lucien C., d. 3/21/1925 at 58/11/23; farmer; married; b. Sandwich; Daniel Skinner (Lime Corner) and Sarah Straten (Conway)

Sarah P., d. 10/17/1896 at 68/0/15 in Sandwich; housewife; widow; b. Conway; Samuel ----- (Andover, MA) and Lois Dinsmore (Ossipee)

SLAKER,

Harrison J., d. 5/23/1954 at 79 in Concord; married; b. Aurora, IL; Valentine Slaker and Anna L. Sedgewick

SMITH,

daughter, d. 3/18/1914 at 0/0/¼; b. Sandwich; Leon A. Smith (Sandwich) and Maude L. Tilton (Sandwich)

son, d. 10/13/1920 at 0/0/0; b. Sandwich; Julius H. Smith (Sandwich) and Isabel E. Smith (Holderness)

Abigail M., d. 1/8/1895 at 85/5/16 in Sandwich; housewife; single; b. Sandwich; Daniel Smith (Sandwich) and Betsey Moulton (Sandwich)

Albert, d. 2/20/1957 at 79 in Laconia; widower; b. Grafton; Alfred Smith and Sarah J. Woodman

Alice D., d. 1/25/1966 at 70 in Wolfeboro; married; b. Sandwich; George Davey and Jennie Vittum

Alice H., d. 10/30/1936 at 80/7/17; at home; widow; b. Burke, VT; Asiah Umphrey (Burke, VT) and Lacy Evans (Ashland)

Angelia A., d. 10/19/1937 at 86/6/3; at home; single; b. Sandwich; James M. Smith (Sandwich) and Lydia P. Skinner (Sandwich)

Annie A., d. 7/7/1918 at 60; widow; Levi W. Smith

Bartlett, d. 6/26/1908 at 83/0/23; laborer; married; b. Holderness; Nathan Smith (Holderness) and Mary Carter

Benjamin J., d. 8/12/1916 at 85/9/7; wheelwright; widower; b. Sandwich; Samuel Smith (Sandwich) and Mercy Burleigh (Sandwich)

Bessie B., d. 5/29/1935 at 52/11/10; housewife; married; b. Sandwich; Arven Blanchard (Hopkinton) and Helen S. Creighton (Sandwich)

Betsey, d. 1/2/1901 at 89/8/26 in Sandwich; housewife; widow; b. Sandwich; Daniel Smith (Sandwich) and Betsey Moulton (Sandwich)

Beverly L., d. 10/10/2007 in Sandwich; George Moulton and Hazel Nickles

Carrie Willey, d. 2/17/1945 at 79/4/22 in Boston, MA; widow; b. Sandwich

Charles A., d. 3/17/1890 at 34/2 in Sandwich; farmer; married; Levi H. Smith (Sandwich) and Samantha Miller (Stansted, PQ)

Charles Omar, d. 7/8/1933 at 75/9/2; tinsmith; married; b. Sandwich; James M. Smith (Sandwich) and Lydia P. Skinner (Sandwich)

Clyde R., d. 2/28/1923 at 3/3/14; b. Sandwich; George R. Smith (Sandwich) and Alice P. Davey (Sandwich)

Cynthia Y., d. 1/16/1891 at 88/7/2 in Sandwich; housewife; widow; b. Gilmanton; David Young and Susan Mudett

Demerit E., d. 10/27/1935 at 66/7/24; farmer; married; b. Sandwich; L. Q. Smith (Sandwich) and Mary E. Paine (Sandwich)

Dorothy E., d. 9/30/1918 at 15/10/5; student; single; Clarence L. Smith (Gloucester) and Lulu B. Sanborn (Campton)

Eliza, d. 10/24/1896 at 84/6/10 in Sandwich; housewife; widow; b. Holderness; David Merrill (Plymouth) and Sarah Lee (Salem, MA)

Ella M., d. 8/6/1888 at 26/7/5; married; b. Thornton; Joseph Fadden (Thornton) and Harriet Fadden (Thornton)

Elmer A., d. 3/9/1965 at 65 in Sandwich; b. Bethel, ME; Alfred Smith and Emma Robinson

Elsie E., d. 10/10/1929 at 75/4/26; married; Benjamin B. Locke (Epsom, MA) and Julia M. Currier (Sandwich)

Emma A., d. 11/24/1935 at 79/5/5; at home; married; b. Holderness; Stephen Etheridge (Sandwich) and Nancy Wallace (Sandwich)

Erle H., d. 7/25/1975 at 81 in Gardiner, ME; chauffeur; single; b. NH; Charles O. Smith and Mary Pierce

Eva G., d. 7/20/1953 at 81 in Moultonboro; widow; b. Sandwich; Nathaniel Burrows and Sarah D. Thompson

Evelyn N., d. 9/21/1983 in Sandwich; Thomas Nelson and Henrietta Brown

Frank M., d. 8/5/1924 at 75/4/25; merchant; married; b. Sandwich; James M. Smith (Sandwich) and Lydia P. Skinner (Sandwich)

Fred P., d. 6/21/1923 at 76/4/7; shoemaker; single; b. Sandwich; James M. Smith (Sandwich) and Lydia P. Skinner (Sandwich)

Frederick E., d. 7/7/1936 at 63/4/28; laborer; single; b. Holderness; Bartlett Smith (Sanbornton) and Rosina George (Holderness)

George H., d. 4/22/1928 at 87/2/28; farmer; single; b. Sandwich; Joseph Smith (Sandwich) and Eliza Merrill

George N., d. 9/24/1887 at 37; laborer; widower; Bartlett Smith (Tilton) and Rose George (Sandwich)

George R., d. 7/12/1970 at 75 in Portsmouth; widower; b. NH; Samuel Smith and Nellie Taylor

Glenn, d. 9/23/1974 at 69 in Laconia; store owner; married; b. NH; Charles O. Smith and Mary Pierce

Harry H., d. 3/11/1964 at 87 in Concord; b. Sandwich; Charles Smith and Margaret Hale

Hebsibeth Ann, d. 1/27/1954 at 93 in Ctr. Harbor; widow; b. Sandwich; Lewis S. Smith and Mary -----

Hollis B., d. 10/31/1895 at 37/10/7 in Sandwich; laborer; married; b. Holderness; Bartlett Smith (Holderness) and Rosina George

I.Hartwell, d. 1/29/1908 at 55/4/12; farmer; married; b. Sandwich; Thomas Smith (Sandwich) and Betsy Smith (Sandwich)

Isabel E., d. 4/1/1979 at 86 in Laconia; teacher-retired; married; b. NH; Henry Smith and Flora Pulsifer

James M., d. 12/3/1896 at 79/3 in Sandwich; tinsmith; married; b. Sandwich; Jeremiah Smith and Dorothy Ethridge (Sandwich)

Jennie J., d. 12/28/1979 at 80 in Sandwich; housewife; widow; b. NH; Paul Jaques and Melina Nouri

John M., d. 4/27/1891 at 72/1/17 in Sandwich; farmer; widower; b. Sandwich; Jeremiah Smith (Sandwich) and Dolly Ethrige (Sandwich)

Joseph, d. 12/10/1887 at 80/5/26; farmer; married; b. Sandwich; Gilman Smith (Brentwood) and Anna Mooney

Julia S., d. 3/26/1946 at 71/10/6 in Manchester; home; widow; b. Buffalo, NY; Daniel H. Sherman (Sandwich) and Cordelia E. Robbins (Monroe)

Julian A., d. 8/5/1943 at 87/10/14 in Sandwich; retired; married; b. Sandwich; James M. Smith (Sandwich) and Lydia P. Smith (Sandwich)

Julius H., d. 12/6/1987 in Laconia; Willis Smith and Clara E. -----

Leland L., d. 1/16/1956 at 77 in Waterbury, CT; married; Frederick L. Smith

Leon A., d. 12/11/1939 at 65/0/22; farmer; married; b. Sandwich; I. Hartwell Smith (Sandwich) and Mary Alice Nute (Sandwich)

Leonard A., d. 1/21/1941 at 68/9/30; retired; single; b. Sandwich; Lewis Q. Smith (Sandwich) and Mary E. Paine (Moultonboro)

Levi H., d. 3/27/1911 at 80/2/27; farmer; married; b. Sandwich; Levi Smith (Sandwich) and Betsey Moulton (Sandwich)

Lewis E., d. 12/24/1939 at 76; meat packer; married; b. Sandwich; Lewis I. Smith (Sandwich) and Mary Paine (Sandwich)

Lewis Q., d. 12/14/1913 at 81/10/24; farmer; married; b. Sandwich; John Smith (Sandwich) and Eliza Webster (Fulton, VT)

Lucy Ann, d. 2/19/1890 at 56/10 in Sandwich; housewife; married; b. Stansta, Canada; Loomis Miller (VT)

Lydia, d. 3/21/1897 at 76/1/9 in Sandwich; housewife; widow; b. Sandwich; Elijah Skinner (Sandwich) and Abigail Moulton (Sandwich)

Margaret H., d. 8/1/1921 at 80/11/9; housewife; widow; b. Bethlehem; Jacob Hale (Bethlehem) and Esther Horne (Sandwich)

Mary E., d. 12/23/1915 at 84/1/2; housewife; widow; b. Moultonboro; Amos Paine and Hepsis Lee

Mary Emaline, d. 2/14/1934 at 68/11/14; at home; widow; b. Sandwich; Leander Pierce (Thornton) and Caroline Burleigh (Sandwich)

Mary Emma, d. 2/10/1939 at 85/1/20; housekeeper; widow; b. Exeter; Andrew J. Brown (Exeter) and Mary S. Dudley (Exeter)

Maude T., d. 1221/1944 at 60/8/15 in Sandwich; housewife; widow; b. Sandwich; Elijah S. Blackey (Sandwich) and Caroline Blanchard (Sandwich)

Mercy, d. 11/8/1892 at 80/7 in Sandwich; housewife; widow; b. Sandwich; Simon Burleigh (Sandwich) and Ruth Prescott (Sandwich)

Rosina, d. 3/2/1924 at 93/6/15; housekeeper; widow; b. Holderness; Levi George (Holderness) and Rosina ----- (Wheelock, VT)

Ruth M., d. 7/16/1891 at 92/2 in Sandwich; housewife; widow; b. Sandwich; Daniel Smith (Raymond) and Betsy Moulton (Rye)

Samantha M., d. 1/23/1921 at 83/10; housewife; widow; b. VT

Samuel B., d. 11/2/1929 at 67/11/25; farmer; married; b. Sandwich; George W. Smith (Sandwich) and Mary A. Clifford (Laconia)

Samuel Maurice, d. 1/4/1996 in Concord; b. Sandwich; George R. Smith and Alice P. Davie

Willis H., d. 1/12/1948 at 70/10/8 in Sandwich; widower; b. Sandwich; Levi H. Smith (Sandwich) and Samantha Miller (Canada)

SNOW,

James, d. 12/17/1890 at 70 in Sandwich; blacksmith; married; Stephen Snow (Strafford) and Betty ----- (Strafford)

Lucy M., d. 2/16/1923 at 67/8/20; housework; widow; b. Sandwich; John R. Clark (Sandwich) and Grace E. Vittum (Sandwich)

SNYDER,

Theodore C., d. 12/12/2001 in Lebanon; Clark Snyder and Adelide Gardner

SORELL,

Ames O., Sr., d. 1/21/1974 at 61 in Ctr. Sandwich; laborer; married; b. VT; Napoleon Sorell and Sarah Dupre

SPAULDING,

daughter, d. 5/11/1905 at 0/1/1; Ralph Spaulding (Tamworth) and Essie I. Hanson (Winchester, MA)

Essie Isabelle, d. 11/5/1953 at 77 in Moultonboro; widow; b. Sandwich; Ruel Hanson and Vandelia Bean

Ralph, d. 6/8/1907 at 46/6; farmer; married; b. Tamworth; A. Spaulding (Tamworth) and Ida Felch (Compton, PI)

SPEARS,

Rev. T. Guthrie, d. 5/9/1984 in Baltimore, MD

SPENCER,

Henry Heath, d. 3/15/1995 in Sandwich; b. Plymouth; Louis Spencer and Mabel McQuesten

Margaret Elizabeth, d. 12/30/1986 in Sandwich; George H. Greeley and Donna Palkey

SPRAGUE,
Lucy A., d. 5/25/1888 at 59; widow; H. Allenwood (Hillsboro) and Betsey Mosier (Hillsboro)

SPRENGLING,
Dora, d. 9/13/1951 at 91 in Sandwich; single; b. Newton, WI; Phillip Sprengling and ----- Eichhorst

STACKPOLE,
Eliza A., d. 7/29/1906 at 63/2/29; married; b. Lynn, MA; Samuel F. Heath and Eliza Townsend

STANTON,
Levi W., d. 9/8/1903 at 76/7/20 in Sandwich; teacher; married; b. Lebanon, ME; James Stanton (Lebanon, ME) and Sabra Wentworth (Lebanon, ME)

STAPLES,
Florence E., d. 8/9/1983 in Manchester; Ernest Townsend and Florence Rowley
Laurence E., d. 6/19/2005 in Laconia; Frank Staples and Hazel Moulton

STEELE,
Frederic L., d. 5/14/1999 in Wolfeboro; Frederic Steele and Margaret Twitchell

STEVENS,
Evelyn D., d. 11/9/2002 in Meredith
Richard R., d. 6/1/1973 at 65 in Sandwich; caretaker; married; b. ME; Frank Stevens and Myrtle -----

STEVENSON,

Charles, d. 8/23/1936 at 82/5/17; lumber widower; b. S. Tamworth; Lorenzo Stevenson and Lucy Mears

Edwin A., d. 11/8/1903 at 25/9/6 in Sandwich; electrician; single; b. Jersey City; James M. Stevenson (Sandwich) and Susan Cantwell (Dublin, Ireland)

Hannah H., d. 8/9/1935 at 76/8; housewife; widow; b. Rockland Lake, NY; John J. Allspeck (Alsace, Germany) and Helena Froelick (Bavaria, Germany)

Ida Lillian, d. 10/13/1966 at 85 in Sandwich; married; b. Cambridge, MA; Frank Collins and Ida Lovejoy

Susie M., d. 4/14/1948 at 61/2/17 in No. Sandwich; single; b. Jersey City, NJ; James M. Stevenson (Tamworth) and Hannah Allsfach (Rockland Lake, NY)

STILES,

Emeline B., d. 2/25/1903 at 60/10/12 in Sandwich; housewife; widow; b. Albany, VT; Benjamin Smalley and Polly Abbott

STOCKTON,

Lloyd G., d. 12/10/1982 in Hanover; Samuel S. Stockton, Sr. and Ida Smith

STOKES,

Janice A., d. 2/25/2005 in Ossipee; Roscoe Peaslee and Dorothy Robinson

Reginald E., d. 12/19/1992 in Laconia; Arthur P. Stokes and Harriet M. Hutchins

STONE,

Florentine L., d. 7/4/1959 at 93 in Belmont; widow; b. Strafford; George Stevens and Jane Styles

Louise C., d. 2/27/2002 in Sandwich; James Bennett and Anna C. Robertson

Wilfred, d. 12/4/1963 at 59 in Sandwich; married; b. Strafford; William Stone and Lillian Stone
William J., d. 5/26/1944 at 67/4/4 in Ossipee; laborer; married; b. Strafford

STUNTZ,
Hilda E., d. 1/20/1999 in Sandwich; William Phillips and Bertha Pugh

STURGEON,
Wilfred J., d. 9/24/1967 at 54 in Sandwich; b. Van Buren, ME; Edward Sturgeon and Ida -----

STURGIS,
Philip, d. 2/27/1927 at 80/9/10; woodman; widower; b. Canada; John Sturgis (Canada) and Julia Martin (Canada)

SULLIVAN,
Ada H., 7/10/1938 at 79/11/11; housekeeper; married; b. Madison; John A. Forrest (Madison) and Eliza Richardson (Fryeburg, ME)
James E., d. 11/18/1948 at 75/5/16 in Sandwich; widower; b. Arlington, MA; James Sullivan (Lexington, MA) and Annie Kelleher (Arlington, MA)
John, d. 1/13/1909 at --; mason

SWAN,
Bernard E., d. 9/11/2006 in N. Sandwich; Bernard Swan and Helen Emery

SWEATT,
Mary E., d. 1/20/1918 at 68/3/24; preceptress; single; b. Sandwich; Thomas S. Sweatt (Gilmanton) and Emeline Foss (Sandwich)

TALBOT,

Hazel P., d. 1/6/1990 in ME

TAPPAN,

Abbie E., d. 3/12/1926 at 49/5/8; housewife; married; b. Melbourne, Canada; Henry R. Wakefield (Melbourne, Canada) and Elvira O. Horne (Moultonboro)

Abram E., d. 2/22/1909 at 66/1/29; farmer; married; b. Moultonboro; A. Tappan (Exeter) and Dorothy A. Tilton (Exeter)

Beryl V., d. 7/11/1972 at 97 in Meredith; housewife; widow; b. NH; George Grant and Clara Hettle

Daniel, d. 8/13/1887 at 76/9/4; farmer; married; b. Sandwich

Dorothy, d. 7/28/1905 at 82; housewife; widow; b. Exeter; John F. Tilton (Exeter) and Sarah Fogg (Sandwich)

Fannie, d. 6/8/1919 at 66/11/22; housekeeper; single; b. Sandwich; Daniel Tappan (Sandwich) and Rhoda S. Hadley (Sandwich)

Frank H., d. 7/2/1929 at 66/11/16; farmer; married; b. Sandwich; John Tappan (Sandwich) and Sarah L. Bennett (Moultonboro)

Fred, d. 5/2/1956 at 86 in Tamworth; b. Sandwich; Abram Tappan and Abbie A.

George H., d. 5/31/1944 at 84/8/22 in Newfield, ME; single; b. Sandwich; Daniel Tappan (Sandwich) and Rhoda S. Hadley (Sandwich)

Ina V., d. 8/13/1957 at 76 in Laconia; widow; b. Sandwich; Jacob F. Vittum and Mary O. Vittum

John, d. 9/23/1894 at 87/8 in Sandwich; farmer; widower; b. Sandwich; Abraham Tappan (Sandwich) and Annie Blanchard (Sandwich)

Jonathan, d. 12/14/1918 at 80/5/6; farmer; married; b. Sandwich; Jonathan Tappan (Sandwich) and Dorothy Hurd (Sandwich)

Rhoda S., d. 5/14/1895 at 76/0/21 in Sandwich; housewife; widow; b. Sandwich; Wentworth Hadley (Sandwich) and S. Worthing (Sandwich)
Walter S., d. 12/5/1939 at 77/5/7; lumber; married; b. Sandwich; Daniel Tappan (Sandwich) and Rhoda Hadley (Sandwich)

TARBOX,
Sophronia, d. 3/3/1936 at 85/5/24; at home; single; b. Biddeford, ME; Jastham Tarbox (Biddeford, ME) and Diana Fletcher (Biddeford, ME)

TASKER,
A.Birnay, d. 11/13/1898 at 54/8/10 in Sandwich; lawyer; single; b. Northwood; Levi B. Tasker (Northwood) and Hannah Caswell (Northwood)
Hannah P., d. 8/7/1895 at 78/11/5 in Sandwich; housewife; widow; b. Northwood; William S. Caswell (Northwood) and Betsey Tasker (Strafford)

TAYLOR,
Agnes W., d. 10/12/1966 at 80 in Laconia; widow; b. Tamworth; Henry Wallace and Frances Glidden
Agustus F., d. 5/27/1908 at 72/4/19; farmer; married; b. Sandwich; William Taylor (Sandwich) and Hannah Seavy (Brentwood)
Aldrich, d. 7/1/1968 at 75 in Sandwich; married; b. MA; Bertrand Taylor and Helen C. Payne
Ann P., d. 8/6/1893 at 68/5/15 in Sandwich; housewife; b. Sandwich; William Freese
Charles E., d. 9/4/1972 at 61 in Sandwich; carpenter; divorced; b. MA; Walter L. Taylor and Agnes Wallace
Charles G., d. 1/4/1893 at 38/0/11 in Sandwich; blacksmith; married; b. Sandwich; N. H. Taylor (Tamworth) and Ann Freese (Moultonboro)

Eldora F., d. 1/19/1927 at 75/3/24; at home; widow; b. Center Harbor; Lyman Thompson (Sandwich) and Filen Dow (Center Harbor)

Frederick F., d. 7/22/1986 in Wolfeboro; William Denton Taylor and Florence Wiss

Harold E., d. 3/14/1999 in Laconia; Walter Taylor and Agnes Wallace

Hortense Weed, d. 1/7/1941 at 52/7/1; housework; married; b. N. Sandwich; Larkin D. Weed (N. Sandwich) and Elsie Peaslee (N. Sandwich)

James G., d. 1/10/1992 in Sandwich; James G. Taylor and Mary Richards

John R., d. 4/27/2001 in Sun City Ctr., FL; Aldrich Taylor and Marion Lord

Lawrence E., d. 9/29/1969 at 63 in Laconia; divorced; b. MA; Fred D. Taylor and Carrie Greene

Marion L., d. 12/1/1979 at 87 in Wolfeboro; housewife; widow; b. MA; Charles E. Lord and Effie Rogers

Mary A., d. 10/1/1899 at 77/2/11 in Sandwich; housekeeper; widow; b. Effingham; William Sandon (Effingham) and Betsy Taylor (Effingham)

Paul Augustus, d. 3/9/1955 at 45 in Laconia; married; b. NH; William Taylor and Christine Skinner

Ralph W., d. 5/15/1973 at 86 in Laconia; dean retired; married; b. MA; Albert J. Taylor and Emma Nason

Renee Brebion, d. 4/7/1985 in Meredith; Edouard Brebion and Margueirte Brebion

Robert E., d. 10/26/1925 at 0/1/13; b. Sandwich; Walter Taylor (Sandwich) and Agnes Wallace (Tamworth)

Sarah J., d. 3/16/1887 at 36/8/23; single; b. Sandwich; N. H. Taylor (Tamworth) and Ann Freese (Sandwich)

Walter Ludlow, d. 7/24/1953 at 71 in Sandwich; married; b. Sandwich; Charles Taylor and Eliza Henderson

William, d. 12/26/1910 at 50/9/17; farmer; single; b. Sandwich; William C. Taylor (Effingham) and Mary A. Sanborn (Effingham)

William H., d. 10/26/1929 at 43/11/18; farmer; married; b. Sandwich; Augustus Taylor (Sandwich) and Eldora Thompson (Ctr. Harbor)

Wilmot J., d. 3/12/1914 at 53/11/27; farmer; single; b. Sandwich; William C. Taylor (Effingham) and Mary A. Sanborn (Effingham)

TELFER,

Claud E., d. 9/7/1926 at 30/8/8; laborer; widower; b. NB; John Telfer (NB) and Annie Clark

TERRELL,

Lillian, d. 11/11/1896 at 4/11/17 in Sandwich; b. Sandwich; Charles Terrell (Nashua) and Nellie E. Smith (Sandwich)

TEWKSBURY,

Carrie, d. 12/8/1923 at 18/11/20; at home; single; b. Conway; Isaac Tewksbury (Tamworth) and Eva M. Swain (Meredith)

James H., d. 1/18/1903 at 52/10/16 in Sandwich; farmer; married; b. Sandwich; William Tewksbury (Sandwich) and Nancy Neally (Tamworth)

Willie Wesley, d. 1/27/1949 at 70 in Sandwich; married; b. Albany; James H. Tewksbury and Sarah L. Hurley

THOMAS,

Millie M., d. 8/17/2005 in Sebago, ME; Frank DeWitt and Julia Stewart

THOMPSON,

son, d. 7/15/1892 at 0/1 in Sandwich; b. Sandwich; Elmer Thompson (Sandwich) and Eva Smith (Sandwich)

Arthur G., d. 9/27/1963 at 80 in Sandwich; married; b. Sandwich; George Thompson and Lydia Smith
Carl E., d. 4/27/1974 at 78 in Laconia; laborer; single; b. MA; Elmer S. Thompson and Eva Smith
Elmer S., d. 1/7/1944 at 76/5/22 in Laconia; retired mail carrier; widower; b. Sandwich; George W. Thompson (Sandwich) and Lydia Smith (Sandwich)
Eva A., d. 3/14/1941 at 75/2/23; housewife; married; b. Sandwich; Benjamin J. Smith (Sandwich) and Lucy Miller (Canada)
Forrest H., d. 11/16/1976 at 84 in Epsom; insurance executive; married; b. ME; William H. Thompson and Mabel A. Thompson
George W., d. 5/3/1924 at 83/1/21; farmer; widower; b. Sandwich; Samuel Thompson (Farmington) and Betsy Seavey (Sandwich)
Guy B., d. 9/26/1957 at 67 in Hartford, VT; single; b. Sandwich; Elmer S. Thompson and Eva Smith
Helen M., d. 5/7/1940 at 67/11/15; housewife; married; b. Ireland; ----- Stewart (Ireland)
Henry W., d. 11/29/1948 at 77/4/20 in Concord; widower; b. Sandwich; George W. Thompson (Sandwich) and Lydia V. Smith (Sandwich)
Jeanette S., d. 1/31/1973 at 73 in Wolfeboro; at home; widow; b. IL; Frederick L. Sperry and Grace Draper
Lulu B., d. 3/6/1954 at 74 in Plymouth; married; b. Campton; Smith Sanborn and Ida Plaisted
Lydia, d. 9/18/1917 at 75/10/11; housewife; married; b. Sandwich; John Smith and Eliza J. Beede (Sandwich)
Richard H., d. 4/4/1948 at 80/2/9 in Laconia; widower; b. Worcester, MA; William Thompson (Burlington, VT) and Eliza Jennie Slye (St. Johns, PQ)
Susan S., d. 1/5/1940 at 64/0/21; housewife; married; b. Woodstock, VT; Mark Slayton (Woodstock, VT) and Mary J. Parkhurst (Woodstock, VT)

TIBBETTS,
Elmer Haven, d. 12/12/1985 in Meredith; Henry T. Tibbetts and Blanche Scriggins
Henry T., d. 6/21/1948 at 63/9/22 in Laconia; divorced; b. Benton; William Tibbetts (England) and Catherine King (Stanstead Plain, PQ)
Katherine, d. 9/21/1924 at 75/6/8; housewife; widow; b. Canada; James King (England) and Jane Crowley (Ireland)
Maude W., d. 2/20/1979 at 66 in Hanover; housewife; married; b. NH; Herbert P. Whitehouse and Bernice Campbell
Paul William, d. 5/2/1952 at 45 in Sandwich; widower; b. Sandwich; Henry T. Tibbetts and Blanch Scriggins
Willard R., d. 2/15/1941 at 46/5/13; retired; married; b. Sandwich; Mildred M. Tibbetts (Haverhill)
William, d. 12/28/1910 at 90/8/26; farmer; married; b. England; Walter Tibbets (England)

TIEDMAN,
Maude, d. 1/26/1966 at 90 in Laconia; widow; b. Cassville, PQ; Henry Quimby and Clara Lee

TILTON,
son, d. 1/18/1923 at 0/0/0; b. Sandwich; John F. Tilton (Sandwich) and Sadie M. Dow (Sandwich)
Albert H., d. 1/10/1913 at 49/8/2; farmer; divorced; b. Sandwich; Albert H. Tilton (Sandwich) and Sarah Hoyt (Tuftonboro)
Alice E., d. 3/17/1919 at 0/0/1; b. Sandwich; John F. Tilton (Sandwich) and Sadie M. Dow (Sandwich)
Alvin, d. 7/13/1915 at 73/9/25; farmer; widower; b. Sandwich; Ebenezer Tilton (Exeter) and Lucy Tappan (Sandwich)
Bessie H., d. 5/2/1940 at 67/2/7; housewife; married; b. Bridgeton, ME; Elijah S. Haley and Fannie E. Dore (Somersworth)

Charles E., d. 11/18/1919 at 81/4/9; farmer; married; b. Sandwich; John F. Tilton (Exeter) and Sarah Fogg (Salem, MA)

Charles P., d. 10/24/1892 at 22/7/11 in Sandwich; laborer; single; b. Sandwich; Charles E. Tilton (Sandwich) and Fannie E. Ward (Freedom)

Edith May, d. 8/23/1888 at 18/5/3; single; b. Moultonboro; Alvin Tilton (Sandwich) and Mary A. Clement (Sandwich)

Frances E., d. 12/1/1923 at 81/8/3; at home; widow; b. Freedom; Sewell Ward (Freedom) and Betsy Parker (Effingham)

Frank Edward, d. 9/21/1934 at 66/3/13; farmer; widower; b. Moultonboro; Albert Tilton (Exeter) and Sarah Hoyt (Tuftonboro)

Frank P., d. 1/16/1920 at 67/1/4; mail carrier; single; b. Sandwich; David Tilton (Sandwich) and Susan W. Hill (Sanford, ME)

Gertrude A., d. 12/9/1964 at 68 in Sandwich; b. Brockton, MA; Forrest Martin and Annie Cox

Howard Forest, d. 4/8/1996 in Ctr. Sandwich; b. Sandwich; Herman Tilton and Gertrude Martin

John Folsom, d. 8/19/1950 at 74 in Laconia; widower; b. Sandwich; Charles Tilton and Frances E. Ward

Lucy, d. 4/8/1887 at 81; widow; b. Sandwich; Abraham Tappan

Mary A., d. 6/6/1915 at 74/0/6; housewife; married; b. Sandwich; Benjamin Clement (Moultonboro) and Mary G. Smith (Newmarket)

Orrin H., d. 12/29/1975 at 68 in Sandwich; carpenter; single; b. NH; Charles O. Tilton and Bessie F. Haley

Sandria D., d. 9/2/1937 at 1/1/6; b. Laconia; Herbert Tilton (Sandwich) and Eleanor Davis (Moultonboro)

Sarah, d. 9/19/1909 at 81/4/21; housewife; widow; b. Tuftonboro; Jesse Hoyt (Tuftonboro) and Sarah Comson (New Durham)

Susan W., d. 9/10/1899 at 75/4/11 in Sandwich; housewife; widow; b. Sanford, ME; Abner Hill and Mercy Nowell (York, ME)

TIVEY,
Lilla M., d. 7/14/1970 at 62 in Plymouth; married; b. NH; Eugene Mudgett and Eva Davis

TOBIN,
James Frederick, Jr., d. 5/29/1986 in Framingham, MA; James F. Tobin and Mary E. Hughes

TORSEY,
Amy Burrows, d. 1/11/1949 at 71 in Laconia; widow; b. NH; John Cotton Gilman and Maria E. Beede
Guy B., d. 11/20/1946 at 76/11/29 in Sandwich; carpenter; married; b. Meredith; Winthrop G. Torsey (No. Haverhill) and Lavinia J. Cotton (Holderness)

TOWLE,
Irving R., d. 7/30/1889 at 26; farmer; single; b. Porter, ME; James F. Towle (Porter, ME) and Emma Moulton (Gilmanton)

TOZZER,
Caroline M., d. 7/20/1926 at 78/10/21; at home; widow; b. Sandwich; Moulton H. Marston (Moultonboro) and Ann Ambrose (Moultonboro)

TRASK,
Charles, d. 1/11/1914 at 67/11/2; laborer; married; b. Danvers, MA; Alfred Trask and Mary Blackey
Dora W., d. 12/4/1918 at 84/10/24; housekeeper; widow; b. Sandwich; Jacob Webster (Sandwich) and Nancy Dinsmore (Sandwich)

TURNER,
daughter, d. 7/1/1912 at --; b. Sandwich; C. Turner (Bangor, ME) and Bertha Canney (Sandwich)
Carrie J., d. 11/1/1891 at 31/0/25 in Sandwich; housewife; married; b. Oskaloosa, IA; Amos V. Hurd (Gilmanton) and Gulielma Hoag (Sandwich)
Cheryl, d. 1/15/1992 in Sandwich; Robert Turner and Norma Mastin
Olive E., d. 5/31/1938 at 79/0/16; widow; b. Waterboro, ME; David M. Brock (Lebanon, ME) and Emmeline Ricker (Waterboro, ME)

TUTTLE,
Arthur J., d. 6/7/1965 at 85 in Ctr. Harbor; b. Plaistow; Ivory Tuttle and Eva Dinsmore
Bessie M., d. 8/20/1934 at 59/8/20; housewife; married; b. Haverhill, MA; Orren T. Batchelder (Northwood) and Ada M. Ayer (Manchester)

UHLE,
Janet P., d. 7/2/2006 in Hockessin, DE; Charles Adams and Carolyn Patterson

ULMAN,
Kenneth W., d. 7/26/1976 at 67 in Sandwich; real estate rep., Mobil Oil Co.; married; b. MA; Julius A. Ulman and Florence Willis

VINCENT,
John H., d. 12/26/1982 in Sandwich; George E. Vincent and Louise Palmer

VISSER,

Sheila N., d. 12/20/2003 in Laconia; George Ross and Marjorie Grant

William Warren, d. 11/29/1998 in Laconia; b. Hingham, MA; J. Frederick Visser and Hilda Van Der Zee

VITTUM,

daughter, d. 6/2/1898 at – in Sandwich; b. Sandwich; Otis Vittum (Sandwich) and Alberta Danforth (Lynn, MA)

Abbie V., d. 8/11/1895 at 75 in Sandwich; housewife; married; b. Gilford

Albertha D., d. 12/17/1945 at 73/10/1 in Laconia; housewife; married; b. Lynn, MA; Allen R. Danforth (Lynn, MA) and Mary A. Courtney (Lynn, MA)

Allen L., d. 4/20/1930 at 73/3/17; farmer; married; b. Sandwich; Lemuel F. Vittum (Sandwich) and Clemina Wallace (Sandwich)

Almon E., d. 3/19/1887 at 24/10/12; carpenter; single; b. Sandwich; Charles Vittum (Sandwich) and Mahala Watson (Sandwich)

Annie A., d. 3/1/1927 at 72/11/23; at home; widow; b. Sandwich; Ezra D. Palmer (Sandwich) and Sophia A. Chase (Sandwich)

Aubrey M., d. 4/11/1938 at 64/3/29; farmer; married; b. Sandwich; Lemuel Vittum (Sandwich) and Climia Wallace (Sandwich)

Bernard A., d. 9/22/1935 at 0/0/0; b. Laconia; Alfred Vittum (Lynn, MA) and Mildred Brown (VT)

Charles, d. 3/31/1902 at 85/8/1 in Sandwich; carpenter; married; b. Moultonboro; Jonathan Vittum (Moultonboro) and Mary Weed (Sandwich)

Charles Horace, d. 8/12/1901 at 50/8/17 in Sandwich; farmer; married; b. Sandwich; Alpheus Vittum (Sandwich) and Elmira Hamlin (Sandwich)

Charles W., d. 6/4/1916 at 62/2/4; farmer; married; b. Sandwich; George S. Vittum (Sandwich) and Margaret Osgood (Gardiner, ME)

Climena H., d. 7/12/1899 at 67/4/21 in Sandwich; housewife; married; b. Sandwich; Mary Palmer

Cyrus B., d. 6/10/1895 at 63/1 in Sandwich; farmer; married; b. Sandwich; Tufton Vittum (Sandwich) and Phoebe Bradbury (Wentworth)

Edmund, d. 7/25/1930 at 79/3/3; farmer; married; b. Sandwich; Charles Vittum and Mahala Watson

Elmired, d. 9/18/1892 at 72/3/2 in Sandwich; housewife; widow; b. Sandwich; Levi Wallace (Sandwich) and Sally Hamblin

Hiram A., d. 1/28/1927 at 72; laborer; single; b. Sandwich; Alpheus Vittum (Sandwich) and Almira Wallace (Sandwich)

Isabel M., d. 1/22/1892 at 42/2/4 in Sandwich; housewife; married; b. Hampstead; Caleb Moulton (Hampstead) and Abbie A. Morse (Hampstead)

Jennie A., d. 2/25/1938 at 87/5/17; housewife; widow; b. Salem; Aaron Wilson and Abbie Bailey

John B., d. 8/25/1898 at 77/9 in Sandwich; farmer; widower; b. Sandwich; Tufton Vittum (Tamworth) and Phoebe Bradbury (Gilford)

Lewis M., d. 6/29/1942 at 32/2/25 in Laconia; painter; married; b. Sandwich; Marshall Vittum (Sandwich) and Emma L. Campbell (Sandwich)

Lucy, d. 10/--/1891 at 76/11/1 in Sandwich; housewife; widow; b. Sandwich; Thomas Vittum (Sandwich) and Sally Weed (Sandwich)

Lucy G., d. 1/20/1892 at 40 in Sandwich; single; Nathaniel Vittum (Sandwich) and Lucy A. Vittum (Sandwich)

Mahala, d. 1/24/1904 at 81/1/25; housewife; widow; b. Sandwich; John Watson and ----- Brown

Martha, d. 3/25/1932 at 75/3/8; housewife; widow; b. Sandwich; Benjamin Corliss (Sandwich) and Mary Hubbard (Acton, ME)

May Belle K., d. 12/31/1961 at 90 in Wolfeboro; widow; b. Providence, RI; William Knight and Belle -----

Nathaniel, d. 5/28/1889 at 73/6; farmer; married; b. Sandwich; Thomas Vittum and Jane Kenshaw

Orrin E., d. 1/24/1914 at 70/9/28; laborer; married; b. Sandwich; Charles S. Vittum (Sandwich) and Mahala Watson (Sandwich)

Oscar T., d. 5/9/1918 at 79/7/7; farmer; married; b. Sandwich; Nathaniel Vittum and Lucy Vittum (Sandwich)

Ruth, d. 7/19/1895 at 76 in Sandwich; housewife; widow; b. Sandwich; Jerry Vittum (Moultonboro) and ----- (Sandwich)

Ruth A., d. 2/24/1898 at 71/10/25 in Sandwich; housewife; married; b. Sandwich; Jonathan Tappan (Sandwich) and Dorothy Heard (Sandwich)

Samuel F., d. 3/20/1890 at 64/3 in Sandwich; farmer; widower; b. Sandwich; John Vittum (Sandwich) and Polly Flanders (Sandwich)

Sargent N., d. 5/19/1888 at 32; farmer; single; b. Sandwich; Nathaniel Vittum (Sandwich) and Lucy ----- (Sandwich)

Stephen, d. 5/14/1902 at 84/8/4 in Sandwich; farmer; widower; b. Sandwich; Stephen Vittum (Sandwich) and Abigail Jewett (Tamworth)

William, d. 8/8/1934 at 63/8/13; marmer; b. Sandwich; Cyrus B. Vittum (Sandwich) and Lizzie B. Dodge (Beverly, MA)

WADE,

son, d. 3/8/1893 at 0/0/1 in Sandwich; b. Sandwich; Edwin D. Wade (Moultonboro) and Ida M. Martin

Frank M., d. 12/1/1910 at 36/4/27; engineer; married; b. Moultonboro; Lyman M. Wade (Moultonboro) and Martha A. Blackey (Moultonboro)

Lyman M., d. 12/25/1907 at 73; laborer; married; b. MA; Melvin Wade (Moultonboro) and ----- Garland (Moultonboro)
Maurice, d. 8/22/1942 at 39/0/9 in Dover; shoe worker; b. Ashland; Frank Wade (Moultonboro) and Mary Wentworth (Tamworth)

WADLEY,
William, d. 11/20/1919 at 0/0/6; b. Laconia; Everett J. Wadley (Gilford) and Geraldine Garland (Sandwich)

WAKEFIELD,
Albert B., d. 12/21/1943 at 75/10/10 in Wolfeboro; farmer; widower; b. Moultonboro; Henry Wakefield (Canada) and Elvira Horne (Canada)

WALLACE,
daughter, d. 2/3/1895 at 0/0/1 in Sandwich; b. Sandwich; Harry Wallace (Sandwich) and Effie Hatch (Groveton)
Adaline, d. 4/18/1907 at 64/3/20; housekeeper; single; b. Sandwich; William Wallace and Susan Jewell
Alfred, d. 5/30/1889 at 61/2/10; farmer; married; b. Sandwich; William Wallace (Sandwich) and Sarah Bryant
Alonzo M., d. 8/7/1935 at 57/7/2; retired; single; b. Sandwich; Asahel Wallace (Sandwich) and Caroline Tappan (Sandwich)
Ann P., d. 12/6/1909 at 81/8/16; housewife; widow; b. Sandwich; J. Penniman (Moultonboro) and ----- Strong (Moultonboro)
Asahel, d. 3/24/1896 at 71/10/4 in Sandwich; farmer; married; b. Sandwich; Samuel Wallace
Beverly Ann, d. 2/23/1944 at 4/5/17 in Laconia; b. Gilford; Asahel Wallace (Sandwich) and Ethelyn Davis (Warren)
Bradley, d. 9/11/1928 at 28/2; laborer; married; b. Concord; M. C. Wallace (Thornton) and Harriet M. Smith (New Hampton)

Carl, d. 12/20/1908 at 11/4/6; b. Sandwich; Harry Wallace (Sandwich) and Effie M. Hatch (Groveton)

Caroline I., d. 10/17/1916 at 80/11/17; housewife; widow; b. Sandwich; Jonathan Tappan (Sandwich) and Dollie Heard (Sandwich)

Clyde Edwin, d. 11/16/1934 at 14/7/2; student; single; b. Sandwich; Harry Wallace (Sandwich) and Hattie Plummer (Sandwich)

David I., d. 11/23/1896 at 77/6/2 in Sandwich; farmer; married; b. Sandwich; William Wallace (Sandwich) and Abagail Bryant (Sandwich)

Edward F., d. 4/15/1917 at 60/11/1; farmer; married; b. Sandwich; Alfred Wallace (Sandwich) and Ann Penniman (Sandwich)

Effie, d. 3/15/1965 at 0/5 in Plymouth; b. Plymouth; Bruce Wallace and Joyce Pfeifer

Eugene P., d. 5/28/1945 at 82/2/13 in Sandwich; farmer; widower; b. Ctr. Harbor; Ira Wallace (Campton) and Martha Potter (Conway)

Frances J., d. 9/24/1926 at 75; housewife; widow; b. Sandwich; Jerry Glidden and Alma Quimby (Madison)

Harriet Langdon, d. 8/25/1953 at 82 in Laconia; widow; b. NH; Arthur Smith and ----- Langdon

Harry, d. 11/15/1941 at 72/4/5; farmer; married; b. Sandwich; Adline Wallace (Sandwich)

Harry E., d. 1/18/1929 at 38/5/24; farmer; single; b. Sandwich; Eugene P. Wallace (Ctr. Harbor) and Mary F. Estes (Moultonboro)

Hattie Mae, d. 4/28/1961 at 71 in Sandwich; widow; b. Sandwich; William Plummer and Elizabeth P. Webster

Henry J., d. 1/13/1909 at 60/6/15; farmer; married; b. Sacarappa, ME; James F. Wallace (Sandwich) and A. M. Wallace (Sandwich)

Iva May, d. 6/11/1936 at 25/0/19; housewife; married; b. Ashland; Enoch Archer (VT)

Jane B., d. 11/18/1902 at 85/4/13 in Sandwich; widow; b. Sandwich; Daniel Rowe and Jane Bean (Sandwich)
Levi, d. 6/30/1890 at 77 in wx; farmer; widower; b. Sandwich; Levi Wallace (Sandwich) and Sarah Hareblin (Saccarrappa)
Marcellus C., d. 9/7/1933 at 68/0/27; stone mason; married; b. Thornton; Asahel Wallace and Caroline I. Tappan
Martha L., d. 12/6/1894 at 71/8/28 in Sandwich; housewife; widow; b. Conway; Samuel Potter (Concord) and Martha Hazelton (Chatham)
Mary E., d. 8/1/1919 at 16/5/29; waitress; single; b. Sandwich; Marcellus Wallace (Thornton) and Harriet C. Smith (N. Hampton)
Mary E., d. 1/2/1942 at 76/2/27 in Sandwich; at home; married; b. Sandwich; Joseph Estes (Sandwich) and ----- Mason (Sandwich)
Moses V., d. 9/27/1898 at 80/2/27 in Sandwich; farmer; married; b. Sandwich; Tufton Wallace and Mary -----
Newell H., d. 2/17/1910 at --; laborer; single; b. Sandwich
Omar, d. 3/9/1905 at --; b. Sandwich; Ellen Wallace (Strafford)
Raymond, d. 11/15/1928 at 0/5/27; b. Sandwich; Bradley L. Wallace (Concord) and Gladys Lock
Scott Emerson, d. 9/28/1955 at 48 in Center Harbor; divorced; b. New Hampton; Marcellus Wallace and Harriet Smith
Theodore R., d. 9/4/1960 at 59 in Sandwich; widower; b. Sandwich; Marcellus Wallace and Harriet Smith
William, d. 5/9/1918 at 77/6/12; farmer; married; b. Sandwich

WALLINGFORD,
S. O., d. 6/--/1907 at 83; farmer; b. Alton; R. Wallingford (Alton) and R. Richards (Alton)

WALSH,
Frances V., d. 9/17/2005 in Newton, MA; John Vincent and Frances Ballard

Richard L., d. 8/7/2003 in Wolfeboro; James Walsh and Mary Leonard

WARD,

David W., d. 4/17/1912 at 24/2; lineman; single; b. NB; Charles W. Ward (NB) and Emily Waller (NB)

James G., d. 8/4/1913 at 29/1/8; lineman; single; b. Harcourt, NB; Charles W. Ward (Harcourt, NB) and Em. W. Waller (Rexton, NB)

Julia A., d. 2/1/1911 at 78/1/6; tailoress; single; b. Freedom; Sewell Ward (Freedom) and Betsy Parker (Effingham)

WATERMAN,

Robert R., d. 7/28/1927 at 32; woodwork; single; b. England; ----- (Russia) and ----- (Russia)

WATSON,

Amanda, d. 4/10/1919 at 83/2/22; housewife; widow; b. Searsmont, ME; John B. Wellman (Searsmont, ME) and Eliza Bennett (Searsmont, ME)

Ann H., d. 2/5/1890 at 77/3 in Sandwich; housewife; married; b. Ossipee; Elisha Beede (Sandwich) and Sally Flanders (Poplin)

Annie E., d. 7/22/1915 at 77/11/5; housewife; married; b. Sandwich; Ezekiel French (Sandwich) and Bethiah Paine (Moultonboro)

Calvin, d. 5/18/1894 at 77/6 in Sandwich; farmer; widower; b. Sandwich; Jonathan Watson (Sandwich) and Dorothy Vittum (Sandwich)

Daniel S., d. 3/7/1939 at 83/5/3; laborer; married; b. Tamworth; Thomas Watson (Tamworth) and Julia Marston (Tamworth)

Eva M., d. 7/17/1928 at 38/7/5; housework; single; b. Sandwich; Daniel S. Watson (Tamworth) and Fannie Pitman (Alexandria)

Fannie Mona, d. 7/3/1944 at 75/3/5 in Laconia; housewife; widow; b. Alexandria; Warren L. Pittman and Julia Tappen
Ferd J., d. 4/13/1889 at 34/2/22; teacher; married; b. Sandwich; Oliver Watson (Sandwich) and Susan Quimby (Sandwich)
Florence B., d. 1/25/1923 at 41/4/12; housewife; married; b. Sandwich; J. Page Brown (Sandwich) and Angeline Bennett (Gray, ME)
Frank B., d. 3/20/1921 at 79/9/17; farmer; widower; b. Sandwich; Daniel M. Watson (Sandwich) and Almira Webster (Sandwich)
George D., d. 8/13/1896 at – in Sandwich; farmer; married; b. Sandwich; James Watson (Sandwich) and Sarah Keezer (MA)
Julia L., d. 2/24/1924 at 83; none; widow; b. VT; William Ward
Maria L. W., d. 7/7/1924 at 80/3/26; dressmaker; married; b. Freedom; Sewell Ward and Betsey Parker
Olive, d. 2/28/1951 at 51 in Concord; single; b. Sandwich; Daniel S. Watson and Fanny Pitman
Oliver, d. 7/19/1912 at 86/3/4; married; b. Sandwich; J. Watson and Elmira Weed
Sophia A., d. 11/29/1907 at 63/11/29; housekeeper; single; b. Sandwich; Calvin Watson (Sandwich) and Ann ----- (Sandwich)
Wealthy, d. 2/26/1919 at 84/5/23; housewife; married; b. Weirs; George Hilliard

WATT,
son, d. 7/23/1920 at 0/0/0; b. Sandwich; George G. Watt (W. Roxbury, MA) and Elizabeth Eddy (Auburn, NY)

WATTS,
Carl A., d. 5/15/1988 in Hanover; John P. Watts and Arvilla Stevens

WAUGH,

Adelaide Smith, d. 10/19/1994 in Sandwich; b. Lawrence, MA; Daniel Clark Smith and Adelaide Bicknell

WEBB,

John L., d. 1/27/2005 in Laconia; John Webb and Elizabeth McGinnis

WEBBER,

Amy Selina, d. 11/7/1988 in Sandwich; Ernest C. Irish and Isabelle S. Williamson

WEBSTER,

Abigal M., d. 1/5/1904 at 92/10/2; housewife; widow; b. Sandwich; Philip Bean (Sandwich) and Betsy Morrill (Sandwich)

Charles K., d. 2/22/1990 in FL

Elizabeth, d. 8/12/1939 at 72/6/22; retired; widow; b. Sandwich; Abram Tappan (Sandwich) and Abbe Graves (Peabody, MA)

Frank, d. 2/11/1891 at 39 in Sandwich; single; b. Sandwich; William Webster (Sandwich) and Mary Clark (Sandwich)

Frank H., d. 11/3/1916 at 65/7/29; farmer; married; b. Sandwich; Samuel L. Webster (Sandwich) and Mary Cogan (Sandwich)

George N., d. 12/30/1889 at 59/2/25; farmer; married; b. Sandwich; Josiah T. Webster (Sandwich) and Rebecca Severance

Hannah L., d. 9/--/1893 at 73 in Sandwich; housewife; b. Sandwich; Ephraim Severance (Brentwood) and Sally Leavitt

J. Frank, d. 11/6/1890 at 25/2/12 in Sandwich; farmer; single; b. Farmington; George W. Webster (Sandwich) and Anna M. Hodgdon (Farmington)

James Y., d. 9/26/1904 at 68/4/29; carpenter; widower; b. Sandwich; Samuel Webster (Sandwich) and Ruth Y. Sawyer (Canada)

John, d. 7/28/1888 at 84; married; b. Sandwich; Jacob Webster (Sandwich)

William B., d. 12/1/1887 at 59/2; farmer; b. Sandwich; James Webster (Sandwich) and Abigail M. Bean (Sandwich)

Winslow M., d. 5/28/1910 at 39/2/5; laborer; single; b. Moultonboro; James Y. Webster (Sandwich) and Emma F. Swett (Sandwich)

WEED,

Charles, d. 10/19/1903 at 78/10/19 in Sandwich; machinist; married; b. Sandwich; Henry Weed (Sandwich) and Annie Foss (Sandwich)

Chester A., d. 2/18/1955 at 72 in Sandwich; married; b. Sandwich; Larkin Weed and Elsie Peaslee

Cleveland, d. 10/28/1973 at 83 in Conway; contractor; widower; b. NH; Larkin E. Weed and Elsie Peavey

Eliza N., d. 5/16/1891 at 73/2/22 in Sandwich; housewife; married; b. Sandwich; Elisha Hanson (Madbury) and Hulda Scribner (Sandwich)

Elise A., d. 1/19/1926 at 65/11/4; housewife; married; b. Sandwich; David Peaslee (Pittsfield) and Harriet W. Fogg (Sandwich)

Ella Cynthia, d. 3/15/1954 at 73 in Sandwich; married; b. Tamworth; Thomas W. Hoag and Martha Cartland

F. Herbert, d. 8/19/1940 at 80/4/4; retired broker; married; b. Sandwich; W. M. Weed (Sandwich) and Eliza N. Hanson (Sandwich)

John J., d. 6/14/1957 at 73 in Sandwich; married; b. Sandwich; Larkin D. Weed and Elsie A. Peaslee

Larkin D., d. 4/11/1937 at 81/11/7; contractor; widower; b. Sandwich; Henry Weed (Sandwich) and Clara Smith (Sandwich)

Martha E., d. 11/1/2003 in Norwood, MA; Chester Weed and Ella Hoag

Samuel S., d. 2/8/1890 at 75/8/14 in Sandwich; jeweler; single; Isaac Weed and ----- Smith

Sarah F., d. 6/13/1908 at 82/9/4; housewife; widow; b. Sandwich; Neal McCrillis (Sandwich) and Abigal B. Foss (Sandwich)

William M., d. 3/9/1892 at 77/7/10 in Sandwich; lawyer; widower; b. Sandwich; William Weed (Sandwich) and Rebecca Foss (Sandwich)

WEEKS,

stillborn son, d. 10/25/1970 at 0/0/0 in Laconia; George I. Weeks and Jill M. Morse

C. Colby, d. 12/7/1887 at 0/0/20; b. Sandwich; Calvin Weeks and Alida M. Hines

Daniel W., d. 6/7/1915 at 71/11/19; farmer; widower; b. Sandwich; Thomas B. Weeks (Gilmanton) and Philanda Way (Leominster, MA)

Elizabeth T., d. 3/3/1896 at 57/7/5 in Sandwich; housewife; married; b. Alna, ME; Benjamin Lane (Hampton) and I. Tucker (Bath, ME)

Ella F., d. 9/8/1930 at 59; single; b. Sandwich; Daniel Weeks and Elizabeth Lane

WEINER,

Margaret Hedwig, d. 11/28/1989 in Sandwich; Paul Engemann and Hedwig Beyer

WEINERT,

Gertrude B., d. 9/3/1991 in Sandwich; Henning N. Borgstedt and Jennie E. Klotz

WENTWORTH,

Fannie D., d. 11/22/1945 at 64/1/3 in Sandwich; housewife; divorced; b. Bermingham, England; Alfred Ford

(Bermingham, England) and Fanny Thompkinson (Bermingham, England)

Jessie L., d. 10/24/1967 at 84 in Ctr. Harbor; b. Hebron; Andrew Morgan and Fidelia -----

Louise C., d. 10/23/1893 at 20/1/23 in Sandwich; scholar; b. Sandwich; Paul Wentworth (Sandwich) and Ellen S. Dunklee (Concord)

Paul, d. 9/30/1915 at 68/11/2; lawyer; married; b. Sandwich; Joseph Wentworth (Sandwich) and Sarah P. Jones (Brookline, MA)

WHIPPLE,

Parker C., d. 5/7/1979 at 55 in Sandwich; forest consultant; married; b. MA; Melville C. Whipple and Dorothy Wakefield

WHITE,

Annie T., d. 10/18/1935 at 69; housework; widow; b. Sandwich; Jonathan Tappan (Sandwich) and Augusta Webster (Sandwich)

Catharine P., d. 2/10/1990 in Meredith; Frank Putnam and Minnie Davis

Charles H., d. 7/25/1914 at 75/8/6; naval surgeon; divorced; b. Sandwich; Charles White (Nelson) and Sarah D. French (Sandwich)

Earle, d. 10/6/1908 at 7/3/2; b. Sandwich; Charles M. White (Hallowell, ME) and Hattie M. Bryant (Sandwich)

Elmer L., d. 8/16/1888 at 0/4; b. Sandwich; Benjamin B. White (Sanbornton) and Abbie S. Bryer (Sandwich)

Emma A., d. 4/14/1893 at 31/11/14 in Sandwich; dressmaker; single; b. Sandwich; James E. White (Northfield) and Sophia Watson (Sandwich)

Erskine N., d. 6/14/1980 in Concord; Stanley White and Henrietta Kneass

Florence C., d. 10/26/1932 at 50/10/9; housewife; married; b. Sandwich; Charles S. Clark (Sandwich) and Nellie Brown (Exeter)
Fred L., d. 2/4/1915 at 57/11/17; farmer; married; b. Sandwich; James E. White (Sandwich) and Sophia Watson (Sandwich)
James H., d. 9/12/1925 at 70/3/10; retired; married; b. Bartlett; James White (Bartlett) and Mary White (Holderness)
Katharine Bryar, d. 8/11/1952 at 64 in Laconia; married; b. MA; George C. Flett and Margueritta Watson
Mary J., d. 1/2/1910 at 82/8/15; teacher; single; b. Sandwich; Charles White (Nelson) and Sarah D. French (Sandwich)
Sophia, d. 1/16/1901 at 72/3/27 in Sandwich; housewife; widow; b. Sandwich; Jedediah Watson and Elmira Weed (Sandwich)
Walter L., d. 9/4/1962 at 78 in Wolfeboro; widower; b. Phillipston, MA; Walter White and Clara Powers

WHITEHOUSE,
Bernice C., d. 11/7/1960 at 68 in Wolfeboro; widow; b. Sandwich; John N. Campbell and Bernice Bancroft

WHITING,
Annie H., d. 1/17/1941 at 85/4/3; housework; widow; b. Sandwich; Jonathan Choate (Sandwich) and Sarah Shannon (Sandwich)
Charles E., d. 10/3/1956 at 80 in Sandwich; widower; b. Moultonboro; Frank Whiting and Annie Choate
Elizabeth Reid, d. 2/4/1953 at 83 in Moultonboro; widow; b. Sandwich; Ambrose Palmer and Carolyn Moulton
Jennie, d. 6/20/1935 at 61/3/15; housewife; married; b. Moultonboro; Lyman Wade (Ctr. Harbor) and Martha Blackie
Lena M., d. 11/15/1963 at 59 in Laconia; single; b. Tamworth; Charles Whiting and Jenney M. Wade

Mary E., d. 9/13/1963 at 75 in Tamworth; divorced; b. Tamworth; William Davis and Mary Mooney

WHITMAN,
Annie J., d. 5/10/1922 at 59/7/12; housekeeper; widow; b. Meredith

WHITTEMORE,
Sarah L., d. 12/24/2006 in N. Sandwich; Herbert Prescott and Adelaide Turner

WHITTLE,
Herbert H., d. 10/31/1887 at 36/8; mail carrier; married; b. Henniker; William Whittle (Weare) and Eliza Beard (Weare)

WHITWELL,
F. A., d. 7/20/1912 at 92/4/10; widower; b. Boston, MA; S. Whitwell (Newton, MA) and Sophia Storey (Marblehead, MA)

WIGGIN,
Mehitable, d. 4/6/1903 at 84/6 in Sandwich; housewife; married; b. Thornton; Samuel Pierce and Mary Sargent
Samuel B., d. 5/12/1903 at 65/11/14 in Sandwich; dentist; widower; b. Sandwich; Richard Wiggin and Mehitable Wiggin (Sandwich)
Samuel D., d. 7/9/1906 at 84; farmer; widower; b. NH; Samuel Wiggin (NH) and Nancy Chase (NH)

WILCOX,
Josephine F., d. 8/2/1964 at 79 in Sandwich; b. E. Boston, MA; Joseph L. Fletcher and Eunice West

WILKINS,

Elizabeth Hilton, d. 2/23/1953 at 82 in Ctr. Harbor; widow; b. NE; Charles H. Kelley and Sarah E. Norris

Joseph W. G., d. 5/12/1944 at 79/2 in Sandwich; gardner; married; b. Middleton, MA; Samuel Wilkins (Middleton, MA) and Elizabeth Mason (E. Swanzey)

Walter W., d. 10/25/1929 at 78/11/16; farmer; widower; b. MA; Samuel Wilkins (Middleton, MA) and Elizabeth Moses (W. Swanzey)

WILLAND,

Marion E., d. 1/27/1973 at 71 in Sarasota, FL; at home; married; b. MA; Joseph Lee and Elizabeth Small

WILLEY,

Susan, d. 9/30/1903 at 73/2/6 in Sandwich; housewife; widow; b. Gray, ME; Philip Atwood (Sandwich) and Mary Elliott (Sandwich)

WILLIAMS,

Agnes, d. 4/25/1907 at 47/10/18; housewife; married; b. Kingsport, TN; N. P. Bowker (Harrisburg, PA) and Lucy Johnson (VA)

Margaret C., d. 1/9/1920 at 73/6/1; housewife; widow; b. Scotland; Mr. Slavin (Scotland)

WILLIS,

George S., d. 12/5/1909 at 62/4/10; mfg.; married; b. Pittsfield, MA; George S. Willis (Rochester, MA) and L. A. Packard (Boston, MA)

Lila T., d. 8/19/1911 at 53/1/19; music teacher; single; b. Pittsfield, MA; George S. Willis (Rochester, MA) and Louisa A. Packard (Boston, MA)

Sophia A., d. 2/6/1909 at 67/8/24; at home; single; b. Boston, MA; George S. Willis (Rochester, MA) and L. A. Packard (MA)

WILSON,
Randall P., d. 9/28/1987 in Sandwich; Stanley Wilson and Barbara Martin

WINDSOR,
James T., III, d. 10/26/2002 in Sandwich; James T. Windsor, Jr. and Betty Ferguson

WING,
Charles S., d. 9/25/1942 at 80/0/27 in Sandwich; dentist; married; b. Fayette, ME; Charles Wing (Fayette, ME) and Georgianna Knight (Portland, ME)
Dora P., d. 11/17/1943 at 73/5/21 in Sandwich; housewife; widow; b. Springfield, MA; Evender Preston (Auburn) and Eliza J. Stewart (Auburn)

WINKLEY,
Hobart W., d. 7/13/1944 at 84/3/7 in Sandwich; retired; widower; b. Boston, MA; Samuel Winkley (Portsmouth) and Martha W. Parker (Boston, MA)

WINSHIP,
Stephen, d. 3/11/2006 in Charlottesville, VA; George Winship and Claire Bliven

WOOD,
Margaret Levering, d. 2/28/1996 in Sandwich; b. Philadelphia, PA; Theodore Edmunson Brown and Margaretta -----

WOODALL,
Amy C., d. 7/28/1973 at 15 in Gilford; student; single; b. NY; Merle P. Woodall and Elaine Vavrinek

WOODBRIDGE,
Clara, d. 12/17/1924 at 80/8/17; housekeeper; married; b. Sandwich; George E. Perkins and Maria Blackey (Sandwich)

WORTHEN,
Walter E., d. 8/4/1963 at 84 in Tilton; widower; b. E. Hampstead; Walter Worthen and ----- Ordway

WRIGHT,
Barbara S., d. 12/29/1976 at 64 in Wolfeboro; housewife; married; b. CT; Leland L. Smith and Bertha Guild
Robert R., d. 12/9/1969 at 80 in Ctr. Harbor; widower; b. NY; Bardo Wright and Mary Walsh

WYMAN,
Edgar Pitkin, d. 7/13/2004 in Ossipee; Harry Wyman and Lucy Allen

YORK,
Carrie G., d. 10/31/1893 at 36/0/5 in Sandwich; housewife; b. Sandwich; Charles Vittum and Mahale Watson
George W., d. 4/11/1905 at 49/5/7; farmer; married; b. Sandwich; George T. York (Sandwich) and ------ Bragg (Moultonboro)
Helen M., d. 5/22/1922 at 71/4/22; housewife; widow; b. Boscawen; Jonathan Mills and Marian Davis

UNKNOWN,
male, d. --/--/1927 at about 45

Other Heritage Books by Richard P. Roberts:

Alton, New Hampshire Vital Records, 1890–1997

Barnstead, New Hampshire Vital Records, 1887–2000

Barrington, New Hampshire Vital Records

Dover, New Hampshire Death Records, 1887–1937

Gilmanton, New Hampshire Vital Records, 1887–2001

Marriage Records of Dover, New Hampshire, 1835–1909

Marriage Records of Dover, New Hampshire, 1910–1937

Milton, New Hampshire Vital Records, 1888–1999

Moultonborough, New Hampshire Vital Records

New Castle, New Hampshire Vital Records, 1891–1997

New Hampshire Name Changes, 1768–1923

New Hampshire Name Changes, 1923–1947

Ossipee, New Hampshire Vital Records, 1887–2001

Rochester, New Hampshire Death Records, 1887–1951

Vital Records of Durham, New Hampshire, 1887–2002

Vital Records of Effingham and Freedom, New Hampshire, 1888–2001

Vital Records of Farmington, New Hampshire, 1887–1938

Vital Records of Lyme and Dorchester, New Hampshire, 1887–2004

Vital Records of New Durham and Middleton, New Hampshire, 1887–1998

Vital Records of North Berwick, Maine, 1892–2002

Vital Records of Orford and Piermont, New Hampshire, 1887–2004

Vital Records of Pittsburg, New Hampshire, 1904–2008

Vital Records of Sandwich, New Hampshire, 1887-2007

Vital Records of Tamworth and Albany, New Hampshire, 1887–2003

Vital Records of Tuftonboro and Brookfield, New Hampshire, 1888–2005

Vital Records of Wakefield, New Hampshire, 1887–1998

Vital Records of Warren, New Hampshire, 1887–2005

Wolfeboro, New Hampshire Vital Records, 1887–1999

www.ingramcontent.com/pod-product-compliance
Lightning Source LLC
LaVergne TN
LVHW020517100826
845148LV00010B/1260

9780788450266